Park

"Vincent Orange has produced a long-awaited, very substantial biography . . . The author has succeeded in presenting the facts and well-deserved tributes to Sir Keith Park in a pleasant, easy-to-read style."

Aerospace

"The flow of books devoted to various aspects of air operations in World War II continues unabated. They include, from time to time, a work of particular importance . . . *Park* is an overdue biography . . . Vincent Orange, author of this excellent biography . . . has clearly taken a scholarly approach to the research necessary to produce such a definitive work."

Air International

"This fine biography of one of the war's greatest unsung heroes, researched in commendable depth, reveals how Park's career survived the "scheming and deceit" of envious senior officers after he was prematurely replaced by one of the principal culprits, Leigh-Mallory of No.12 Group, a less able commander, without Park's clear and detailed understanding of the defence system."

Daily Telegraph

"Park emerges from this very thorough and scholarly biography not as The Great Man, but as a human being with strengths and weaknesses like the rest of us: a man whose greatness is delineated alongside his more everyday qualities, and who seems all the more impressive for that . . . It is one of the many strengths of this biography, however, that the "warts and all" approach in no way detracts from the sense of Park's greatness . . . Vincent Orange never assumes that Park was right until he has proved it for himself, and as an historian, scrupulous about his sources, listed in detail in endnotes, he provided us with the basis for reaching decisions of our own."

Christchurch Press

"It is a magnificent record, well and clearly set out by Vincent Orange, and its telling establishes a proud heritage for New Zealanders."

Sunday Times, New Zealand

Park

The biography of
Air Chief Marshal
Sir Keith Park

GCB, KBE, MC, DFC, DCL

Vincent Orange
with an introduction by Christopher Shores

GRUB STREET · LONDON

This new edition published by Grub Street
4 Rainham Close, London SW11 6SS

Copyright © Grub Street 2001
Text Copyright © Vincent Orange 2001

Reprinted 2009, 2010, 2012, 2013, 2015, 2017

Originally published as *Sir Keith Park* by Methuen, 1984

British Library Cataloguing in Publication Data
  Orange, Vincent, 1935-
  Park: the biography of Air Chief Marshal Sir Keith Park GCB,KBE,MC,
  DFC, DCI.
  1. Park, Sir Keith, 1892-1975 2. Great Britain. Royal Air Force –
  Biography 3. Marshals – Great Britain – Biography
  I. Title
  358.4'331'092

  ISBN 978 1 902304 61 8

Printed and bound in Great Britain by 4edge Ltd

Grub Street only uses FSC (Forest Stewardship Council) paper for its books

All who know
Ann Margaret Orange
know also how much of this book is hers

Contents

Contents

Illustrations

Acknowledgements and thanks are due to Mr Neill B. Park for plates la and lb; to 48 Squadron for plate lc; to Mr F.C. Ransley for plate 2a; to Dr Stanley Rycroft for plate 2b; to the Department of Aviation Records, Hendon, for plate 2c; to Mr I.K.W. Park for plates 3a, 5a and 8b; to Mrs Noel Wells for plates 3b, 4d and 8c; to the Museum of Transport and Technology, Auckland, NZ for plate 3c; to the Imperial War Museum for plates 4a, 6a, 6b and 7a; to the BBC Hulton Picture Library for plates 4b and 4c; to the SAAF Museum, Valhalla, South Africa for plate 5b; to Miss Betty Neill for plate 7b; and to Mrs Keithia Harasimick for plate 8a.

The maps were redrawn from the author's roughs by Neil Hyslop.

Acknowledgements

I am glad to have this long-awaited opportunity to thank all those who have helped me to complete this book. Pride of place, after my wife, must go to Ian Park, Sir Keith's son, who freely permitted me to use his father's papers. I have also benefited from many conversations with Ian and his wife Dorothy. All other members of the Park family have cooperated fully, offering me their memories, papers, photographs and, not least, their generous hospitality: Miss Betty Neill and her brother Bill; Dr Keith Park, his brother Neill and their families; Mrs Marie Stevenson and her daughter Mrs Keithia Harasimick; and Mrs Noel Wells. No member of the family has attempted to restrict or influence in any way the use I have made of the material they have provided.

Many men and women who served with Sir Keith have helped me – more than I can thank individually, but I must single out (in alphabetical order) Group Captain Sir Douglas Bader, Air Marshal Sir Edward Chilton, Flight Lieutenant Michael Crossley, Air Commodore Alan Deere, Derek, Lord Dowding, Sergeant Norman Davis, Flight Lieutenant Peter Ewing, Captain Edward Griffith, Group Captain Tom Gleave, Air Marshal Sir Gerald Gibbs, Marshal of the Royal Air Force Sir John Grandy, Group Captain Colin Gray, Squadron Leader Sir Archibald Hope, Air Vice-Marshal J.E. Johnson, Air Vice-Marshal A.V.R. Johnstone, Captain Alan Light, Group Captain P.B. Lucas, Wing Commander Michael Constable Maxwell, Air Marshal Sir Kenneth Porter, Lieutenant John Pugh, Captain Coralie Pincott (née Hyam) Lieutenant Stanley Rycroft, Squadron Leader Joseph Rank, Group Captain W.G.G. Duncan Smith, Flight Sergeant Tet Walston, Colonel Stanley Walters, Group Captain George Westlake, Group Captain Donald Wiseman, Wing Commander Robert Wright and Air Marshal Sir Peter Wykeham.

Others who deserve my grateful thanks include my colleagues Sam Adshead, David Gunby and David MacIntyre for reading drafts of the manuscript, and two graduate students in the History Department of the

Acknowledgements

University of Canterbury, Wilma Falconer and Christina Goulter, for helping to gather and sort my material. I am also grateful for information and advice to Christopher Barnes, Trevor Boughton, Ernest Edwards, Marjorie Jones, Paul Leaman, Peter Liddle, Ronald Lewin, Timothy Lovell-Smith, Errol Martyn, Colonel Neil Orpen, Phillip O'Shea, Arthur Parrish, Edward Rubython, James Sanders, John Seabrook, Christopher Shores and Elaine White. My particular thanks go to Christopher Falkus, Chairman of Methuen London, for offering me a contract to write this book, to Liz Hornby, my editor, for helpful suggestions and to Nigel Nicolson for his thoughtful introduction. Without the prolonged hospitality of my brother-in-law, David Jeffery, who lives in London, the collection of material would have been far more expensive than it was. I have left until last, traditionally a position of great honour, two friends without whose generosity, advice and encouragement this book could hardly have been begun, let alone completed: John and Fenella Barton of Auckland.

As for the institutions which have helped me, I gladly record my debt to the Air Historical Branch, Ministry of Defence, London; the Auckland Institute and Museum; the RAF Museum, Hendon; the House of Lords Record Office, London; the Imperial War Museum, London; the National War Museum, Malta, G.C.; the Museum of Transport and Technology, Auckland; the Public Record Office, London, and the National Archives and Defence Library, Wellington. I owe a special debt to the New Zealand branches of the Royal Aeronautical Society, which have for years invited me to address their meetings up and down the country. This book grew out of one such address. Numerous individuals in these institutions helped to make my work a pleasure. All the men and women mentioned above are collectively responsible for whatever merit this book has; I made all the mistakes and misjudgements myself. Finally I must also record my sincere gratitude to the University of Canterbury for granting me financial assistance and leave to visit England for seven months in 1981.

Vincent Orange

Introduction

I am delighted to be invited to write the Introduction to this new edition of Vincent Orange's biography of Sir Keith Park. Here was a man and a pilot whose career has repeatedly intertwined with many of the aspects of British military aviation history towards which my own interests have led me to research.

Following his early war service with the Artillery, both New Zealand and British, he followed the route of numerous servicemen, wounded or too sick to continue to serve on the ground, but who discovered during those early days of aerial warfare that they were still acceptable to the fledgling air forces. His service was without doubt both meritorious and gallant, and he ended the war amongst the 80 pilots of the British Empire air forces considered to have amassed the greatest totals of successes against hostile aircraft.

Here unfortunately, on behalf of the 'purists' I have to depart a little from the author on matters of detail. Recent research undertaken by my colleague Norman Franks and myself indicate firstly that Vincent Orange appears on occasion to have missed the fact that the RFC/RAF Communiques recorded events from 4 o'clock in the afternoon of one day until the same hour on the next; this led to activities occurring during the early evening of the preceding day frequently being depicted as occurring a day later. This seems to have led him to the conclusion that Captain Park and his gunner were responsible for shooting down the German 'ace' and commander of Jasta 28, Hauptmann Otto Hartmann on 3 September 1917. In fact Park had made two claims on the previous day, but did not on the 3rd, so it is likely that Hartmann fell to Lts R.E.Dodds and T.C.S. Tuffield, also of 48 Squadron.

Further, Park's combat reports indicated that between 12 August and 14 September 1917 he made 15 claims to add to his first, recorded in July. Subsequently he was to claim four more – not three. This total of 20 appears to have been made up of five destroyed plus 15 'out of control' –

one of the latter shared with another pilot.

Nonetheless, the book adequately reflects Park's outstanding leadership qualities, and the respect in which he was held by those who served with, or under him.

The interwar years, initially plagued by problems in resolving a clear medical category, subsequently brought remarkably rapid promotion during a period of economic stringency, and to have become Group Captain by 1929 was no small achievement. It certainly offered promise of a career reaching the highest levels.

Whilst undertaking a range of duties as did most career officers at that time, his command of 111 Squadron marked him very much as a 'fighter man'. His appointment to command Tangmere, one of the premier fighter airfields, in 1936 cemented this further into place. Consequently his posting to Fighter Command as a newly-promoted Air Commodore and Senior Air Staff Officer, although not the move intended for him, proved in practice to be a wholly logical progression.

His relationship with his AOC, Sir Hugh Dowding; and his elevation to command 11 Group just in time for the start of the real air war, are well documented herein, and require little expansion by me. Park's brilliant conduct of the defensive battle is now generally agreed to have been correct in the circumstances which events dictated and with the resources available to him and the author highlights this part of his career magnificently.

Subsequently there has been much controversy at the manner in which he and Dowding were replaced in their roles at the end of 1940, apparently without due immediate recognition and reward. There are however certain factors to be considered here which upon mature reflection may ameliorate these understandable and rather emotional reactions. Firstly, Dowding had already passed his age for retirement, and had been retained specifically to see the crisis through. Indeed, he had been in command for more than four years – a far longer period than any of his successors were to enjoy – two to two and a half years were the normal span for any such position of command in the RAF.

Whilst Park had been with 11 Group less than a year, his time with Fighter Command had already lasted such a normal span. Further, he had indeed just been through a period of massive stress, and was known from his past record not to be a man of the most robust health. The situation was also changing, and the need for a different style of leadership as the Command moved from mainly defensive to increasingly offensive tactics, may well have intruded – particularly when pressed at high level by self-publicists well able to play the political card, such as Sholto Douglas and Leigh-Mallory undoubtedly were.

Park's skills had however, been appreciated by others, and his example was to be put to telling effect in a totally different environment. I well recall a conversation with the veteran Finnish fighter leader, Colonel Gustav Erik Magnusson, who recounted that during 1940, after the conclusion of his country's 'Winter War' with the Soviet Union, he had visited England to study the defensive techniques employed by 11 Group. These he was to adopt in the defence of the Karelian Isthmus in early summer 1944, when the Soviets attacked in overwhelming strength. He too found them to be appropriate, and his pilots were enabled to achieve some outstanding successes.

After his spell with Training Command, and the renewal of his experience in organising the air defence of Egypt, his arrival on Malta in July 1942 was again timely. Many of the fighter pilots there were not particularly enamoured of their then AOC, a bomber man who had been sent to the island in 1941 to develop its offensive capability. Park was then to see the island through the period of its most successful defence, employing his specific skills. That he stayed on for another year during which the Sicily offensive was launched, proved fortuitous in providing him with valuable experience of attacking operations which would increasingly become the role of the RAF during the years ahead.

His promotion to Air Marshal and AOC-in-C, Middle East, seem hardly to have been a denigration of his skills, despite Slessor's concerns regarding his lack of political acumen, whilst his final appointment as Air-in-C, South East Asia Command, looks to have been a fitting recognition of a very able tactical commander. That considerable efforts were necessary to ensure that his acting rank as Air Chief Marshal be confirmed before retirement, were perhaps no more than any other officers have experienced when faced with the legendary parsimony of the British establishment – usually it must be said, at the behest of the Treasury.

So was Keith Park justified in feeling slighted, as he obviously did, that no further position was offered to him and that he was required to retire at the end of 1946? Was he denied honours that he might fairly have anticipated receiving?

To answer the first of these questions, it is appropriate to consider the normal policy for the retirement of officers of Air Rank. For the majority, certainly in the 1940s, 50 was the age at which they went. Very few have ever gone beyond 55. In 1946 Park was 54; unless his services were to be extended, there was no time remaining for him to undertake a further full appointment.

What then had happened to his contemporaries, which might give guidance to the answers to either question? Aside from Sholto Douglas, who had been a unit commander on the Western Front as early as 1916, at least nine fighter pilots of note during the First War were to become officers of Air Rank. Perhaps the most directly comparable was Air Vice-Marshal Sir Christopher Quintin-Brand, KBE, who in 1940 commanded 10 Group, providing the back-up to Park's 11 Group in the South-West.

Born a year later than Park, Sir Christopher retired in 1943, aged 50.

Park's fellow New Zealander, Air Marshal Sir Arthur Coningham, KCB, KBE, born three years after Park, commanded the Western Desert Air Force and the 2nd Tactical Air Force in North-West Europe, both with great distinction. He was required to retire in 1947 at the conclusion of 30 years' service. Air Marshal Sir James Robb, KBE, GCB, born like Coningham in 1895, commanded Fighter Command after the end of the war, and retired in 1951 – he managed two more years of service, but did not make Air Chief Marshal.

The great Canadian pilot, Air Vice-Marshal Raymond Collishaw, who commanded the air force in the Western Desert during the opening years of the war, retired in 1943, aged 50. Stanley Vincent, who served with Park in SEAC, already an Air Vice-Marshal in 1945, retired in that rank after being AOC, 11 Group, in 1950, aged 53. And so on.

Only one, Sir Arthur 'Bert' Harris, GCB, OBE, reached the exalted rank of Marshal of the RAF, and that after his role as AOC, Bomber Command – possibly the most important post in the air force during the war.

By 1946 the war years had brought forward many brilliant young leaders such as Basil Embry, Harry Broadhurst, Tom Pike, Fred Rosier and Dermot Boyle, for whom a path to the top was vital. On the balance of the evidence, it does not appear that Keith Park was under promoted, under rewarded or pensioned off early.

Could he have done better? Certainly Park does not seem to have been either politically aware or a notable self-publicist. His health had on occasion let him down, and he was frequently considered to be "difficult". What he did achieve needs to be considered against that background. He does not appear to have manoeuvred or intrigued for personal advancement, which may perhaps have held him back a little, the world being what it is – but he was probably the better man for that! In conclusion, I'd like to say that I enjoyed revisiting this book immensely and I commend it to the reader.

Christopher Shores
Sherborne, Dorset, February 2001

'If ever any one man won the Battle of Britain,
he did. I don't believe it is realized
how much that one man, with his leadership,
his calm judgment and his skill,
did to save not only this country,
but the world.'

Marshal of the Royal Air Force
LORD TEDDER, GCB, KCB, CB
February 1947

PART ONE

1892 - 1936

An Undistinguished Young Man

1892–1914

Keith Rodney Park was born in Thames, a small town south-east of Auckland, on 15 June 1892. His father, James Livingstone Park, was a Scotsman, born near Aberdeen in July 1857. He was the second son of another James Park and of Mary Elphinstone, a niece of Mountstuart Elphinstone, Governor of Bombay from 1819 to 1827. In 1874, having already travelled down from Aberdeen to study at the Royal School of Mines in London's South Kensington, James made a far longer journey to Wellington, New Zealand. He spent nearly four years as a sheep farmer before turning to geology and a career that would earn him an international reputation. In May 1880 he married Frances, daughter of a Captain William Rogers, in Wellington. They had seven daughters and three sons, of whom Keith was the ninth child and third son.

By the time of Keith's birth, James had made a name as a mountaineer and explorer as well as a geologist. Since 1889 he had been Director of the Thames School of Mines and Keith retained several sharp memories of Thames even though he was only six when the family moved to Birkenhead, on Auckland's North Shore. He remembered his father bringing home an amazingly heavy gold ingot from the Maunahie mine; but the 'stampers' or quartz crushers made the nights hideous when the Parks lived down by the mine and Keith was greatly relieved when they moved to the hill above the Maori village at Totara Point. He also remembered being told about famous men who had done poorly at school. This information encouraged him in later years because his own school record was, as he admitted, 'undistinguished'.

In March 1901, when Keith was eight, James Park was appointed Professor of Mining at Otago University in Dunedin in the South Island. The family therefore moved again, to the other end of New Zealand, but Keith remained in Auckland, as a boarder at King's College, until 1906. Strangely, for a man destined to earn fame as an airman, Keith loved the sea from his earliest days. He was much too keen on playing about among the ferry boats at Birkenhead to concentrate on school work. As a very small boy he would sail his father's dinghy in the Waitemata harbour, using a stick and a holland blind for a sail. He would also swim out to ships anchored in the harbour, climb aboard and talk to sailors from many lands. That self-reliance and self-confidence remained with him all his life; so, too, did his love of the sea. His ability to swim was put to excellent use one day to save his sister Lily from drowning in a large pond. No details of this dramatic incident survive and Keith characteristically made light of it, but Lily never did.

The Park children were evidently a boisterous lot and on one occasion they prevailed upon Keith to go up a bank near their home dressed in a white sheet and wander about, moaning and groaning. Screaming with fear, the children called their father, telling him they had seen a ghost. James grabbed a gun and charged up the bank. Keith scuttled for cover when he saw his father coming, knowing him to be an accurate shot, and took some persuading home again. Thus ended ghost games in the Park household. However, on another occasion – when James was away – Keith helped to 'lay out' his sister Maud in a winding sheet, ringed by lighted candles and with her face chalked. The children then called their mother, lamenting poor Maud's untimely demise. Her views on such games are not known. What is known is that she left James some time after his move to Dunedin and went to live in Australia, where she died in March 1916.

Keith, meanwhile, completed his education at Otago Boys' High School. According to the school's historian, there was in those years 'an intense patriotism and enthusiasm for things military' and Keith enrolled in the cadet force in February 1909, at the age of sixteen. Exactly a year later, Lord Kitchener of Khartoum visited the school and was practically mobbed by excited boys – and their parents. Although Keith enjoyed his first taste of military life, he did not then intend to become a professional soldier. He loved guns and horses now, as well as the sea, but he did not yet know what he wanted to do with his life.

'I investigated the origins of Dunedin wealth,' Keith recalled many years later, 'and quickly learned that few men who work for anybody else accumulate much capital.' Nevertheless, even the greatest tycoons have usually started out on someone's payroll and so, on 1 June 1911, a fortnight before his nineteenth birthday, he joined the Union Steam Ship Company in Dunedin as a Cadet Purser. By the following April, he was a Purser (Class IV) earning £6 per month. He was employed on colliers and other coastal vessels until he graduated to the inter-colonial ships, visiting Australia and several Pacific islands. To become a purser aboard a passenger vessel naturally required a talent for discretion and at least the appearance of wide experience. Men occupying such positions were usually over twenty-five, but Park served as purser aboard three passenger vessels in 1914 when he was only twenty-two.

4

In December 1914 he was granted war leave and although his ambitions were to be transformed during the next four years, Park cannily withheld his resignation from the company until December 1918. Unfortunately, from a biographer's viewpoint, he kept out of trouble throughout his three and a half years as a purser and consequently little is known about his life at that time. With his experience, he could have become an Assistant Paymaster in the New Zealand Division of the Royal Navy when war broke out, but his friends were joining the Army in the ranks and so he did too. This is Park's own explanation, recorded many years later, but we shall see that within a year of joining up Park had chosen to cut himself off permanently from those friends and transfer to the British Army. He had already served in Dunedin as a Territorial. After the cadets at school, he had enrolled in 'B' Battery, New Zealand Field Artillery, in March 1911 and had remained with that battery on a part-time basis until his discharge in November 1913.

As a father of fighting-age sons, James Park had better luck than many in the First World War. All three served and all three survived. The two eldest came home, but James would not meet Keith again until 1923. In 1918 James married again. Keith also married in 1918 and so father and son performed the rare feat of taking wives in the same year – a matter which afforded all concerned wry amusement for the rest of their lives. James and Keith had much in common. James was a handsome, upright man, friendly but firm with colleagues and students. He kept himself physically fit and believed in hard work. He was resilient and abstemious. Ambitious, conscientious, unwilling to countenance foolishness, particular about his rights as well as his duties, he was more widely respected than loved. James was often referred to, by friends and family alike, as 'Captain'; Keith was known to his family as 'Skipper'. James retained his vigour into advanced old age, dying in Oamaru on 29 July 1946, aged eighty-nine, at a time when his now-famous son was in New Zealand for the first time in over thirty years, enjoying a triumphant tour of his native land.[1]

CHAPTER ONE

Artilleryman: Gallipoli and the Western Front

1915 - 1916

In January 1915 the British War Council resolved that the Admiralty 'should prepare for a naval expedition to bombard and take the Gallipoli Peninsula, with Constantinople as its objective.' British, French, Australian and New Zealand troops were required to support this enterprise, under the command of Sir Ian Hamilton. It was supposed that the fall of Constantinople would open a line of supply to Russia, force Turkey out of the war, secure allies in the Balkans and contribute significantly to the defeat of Germany.

Purser Park and the *Maunganui* had returned to New Zealand from Vancouver in 1914, ending their peacetime careers. Early in the new year they set sail once more, bound this time for Egypt, as part of the Third Reinforcements for the New Zealand contribution to the Gallipoli campaign. Both were now in military guise: Park as a Lance-Bombardier, the *Maunganui* as HMNZ Troopship No. 17. Park was promoted to Corporal on 1 February and transferred to the main body on arrival in Egypt. There he served with the 4th (Howitzer) Battery, commanded by Major N.S. Falla. Falla, like Park, was an employee of the Union Steam Ship Company. During 1915 he lent him books and encouraged his growing ambition to get on. It was in Egypt that Park saw his first aircraft. Although he and his friends were keenly interested in them, they learned only later that these aircraft were serving a useful purpose: locating and reporting a Turkish advance several days before an attack was launched.

Early on 25 April 1915, British troops landed at Cape Helles on the southern tip of the Gallipoli Peninsula, French troops at Kum Kale on the Asiatic mainland and Australian and New Zealand troops on the west coast of the peninsula. The landings were fiercely opposed by Turkish forces and narrowly saved from complete disaster by the astounding bravery and resolution of the invaders. The Australians and New Zealanders scrambled ashore at what became known as Anzac Cove. Owing to the accuracy of

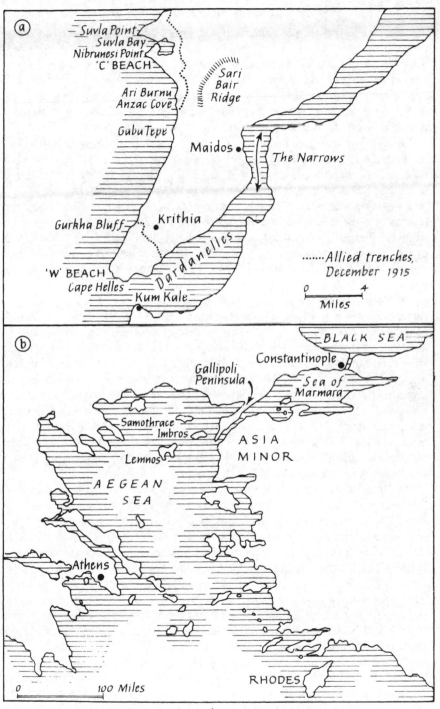

1a: Gallipoli Peninsula   **b:** Surrounding area

Turkish artillery fire, the transports carrying the field guns and howitzers were forced to stand out of range. Support from the fleet's guns was inadequate because of difficulties in communicating with the shore to direct fire to where it was most needed. Consequently, the foothold was so precarious that it would have been abandoned had it not been thought that a withdrawal would cost even heavier casualties. Thus Park spent the first Anzac Day afloat, unable to help his comrades on the shore.

Throughout that dreadful day and night, the infantry hung on in the face of ceaseless rifle and machine-gun fire. Six guns were landed at about 5.30 p.m. and their crews performed bravely until the guns were silenced. Clearly, more guns had to be got ashore somehow before dawn if the positions so courageously won were to be retained. By 6 a.m. a section of Park's howitzer battery had been landed and set up in a gully running up to the foot of Plugge's Plateau. It went into action as soon as possible, lifting the spirits of every surviving infantryman. 'We had never fired the guns before,' remembered Park fifty years later. 'We were so short of ammunition that we had not been allowed to expend any in training.'

Once the first frenzied charges and counter-charges were spent, both sides dug in and their lines were often no more than a few yards apart. Densely packed trenches, virtually unroofed, made ideal targets for attack by howitzers, which aim to lob shells over vertical defences, unlike field guns, which try to knock them down. But Park's battery, consisting of four 4.5-inch pieces, was the only howitzer battery at Anzac and ammunition was so scarce that it was frequently restricted to two shells per gun per day. Park's exasperation was tempered by relief that the Turks appeared to have no howitzers at all. He was not, of course, permitted to sit idly by his silent guns. He was sent forward to pass messages down from observation officers and carried out all manner of jobs: telephonist, battery runner and general scrounger (of food and clothing).

By June, it was clear that the Allied forces were pinned down to small bridgeheads at Helles and Anzac and that a new trench warfare had begun, as fierce and sterile as that on the Western Front. Early in August an attempt was made to end the deadlock. Strong reinforcements were smuggled into the Anzac bridgehead to permit a sudden and powerful breakout, aided by a new landing a little farther north at Suvla Bay. The object was to gain the Sari Bair Ridge: that ridge, dominating the battle area, was the key to the campaign. The offensive surprised the Turks, but hesitation and incompetence among the local commanders nullified the initial advantage and led to heavy losses.

Park had been commissioned as a Second Lieutenant in July and the Suvla landings gave him his first chance to distinguish himself. His battery was on the left of the Anzac position, covering the landing of eighteen-pounders on 'C' Beach, south of Nibrunesi Point. The guns were put ashore without carriages, adequate supplies of ammunition or horses, and volunteers were asked to go down and impose some sort of order on the chaos. Park had never seen eighteen-pounders in action, but he agreed to go. He and his men ran along the beach to where the guns lay and man-handled them into position. They had no means of judging range, he recalled, 'except to see that we weren't going to blow the head off the nearest battalion commander' and that they could clear the crest. The Turks were above them and Park's men fired only a few rounds before they were swept by machine-gun fire. Park spent the rest of the day flat on his face in the sand.

During that month of August 1915, while taking part in a grossly mismanaged campaign in conditions of squalor such as he cannot have imagined even in nightmares, Park decided to become a regular officer in the British Army. He never subsequently commented on this momentous decision which separated him from his own countrymen and led to his shaping a career outside New Zealand. He transferred to the Royal Horse and Field Artillery as a Temporary Second Lieutenant on 1 September and was attached to the 29th Division. That division, having fought at Cape Helles since April, had been brought round to Suvla Bay to take part in the August offensive. After that offensive failed, Park returned with the 29th to Helles where he served until the evacuation.

On 24 September he was posted to No. 10 Battery, 147th Brigade, Royal Field Artillery. The gun line lay on the west of the peninsula, facing Turkish trenches in front of Krithia. The forward observation post was in the front line near Gurkha Bluff, where the trenches were only twenty-five yards from those of the enemy. The battery's horse lines, in which Park took a particular interest, were at the bottom of Krithia Gully, well protected from enemy fire. Most of the men were reasonably fit by Gallipoli standards, although the effects of hard fighting, constant tension, bad food, worse cooking and lack of exercise were wearing them down. Nothing was done, as far as Park could remember, to provide books, papers or games to help them forget, even for a few minutes, their fear and misery.

He remembered Little Kate more happily. She was a naval twelve-pounder, well supplied with ammunition by the Navy, and despite her small size she did more damage than the rest of the battery put together. A covered emplacement was built for her on Gurkha Bluff and she did such splendid service, scattering Turkish ration parties and making their trenches dangerous, that they brought up a couple of field guns in an attempt to silence her. Although Little Kate's position was often hit, repairs were made with sandbags each night to enable her to fire the next day.

A surviving letter written by Second Lieutenant A. Jennings, RFA, on 9 November 1915, describes his arrival at Helles in October and his early experiences in No. 10 Battery:

> Park [he wrote] had landed at Anzac with the first lot and so has seen plenty of service, mostly in the ranks. He has only had his commission a few weeks. He is about my age but has seen more life than I have. When I

9

arrived, he was 'up forward' in the trenches. There was no dugout for me, so I slept in Park's. It was tiny and quite cold, but he didn't seem to mind so I couldn't.

Another glimpse of Park appears in his battery's War Diary, which recorded in December that it became rather unpopular 'because 2nd Lt. Park exercised the horses on the sky line near to Corps Headquarters resulting in the enemy shelling the sacred area.'

The evacuation from Cape Helles began for Park's battery on 2 January 1916. Sixty rounds were fired during the afternoon and Little Kate was then removed from her position and taken to 'W' Beach. There she was embarked at night under the command of Park and nine men. Not long before he died, Park recalled this dangerous exercise. He felt 'most frightened' when ordered to take Little Kate and other guns off on flat-bottomed 'lighters' and sail them to Mudros harbour, on the island of Lemnos. These unseaworthy craft had little freeboard and under shelling from the Turks, 'I was bloody scared and so were my men.' Even when they passed beyond the range of Turkish fire, Park and his men merely exchanged one fear for another: Mudros lay some fifty miles from Cape Helles, the night was black and a heavy sea was running. As with so many other dramatic incidents in his long life, Park rarely mentioned it in later years and never in detail. By the early hours of 9 January, the battery, in the words of its War Diary, was 'in abeyance': scattered about ashore and afloat in the eastern Mediterranean.

Park looked back in 1946 on his Gallipoli service with a nostalgia unusual for him. He remembered the Anzac commander, Sir William Birdwood, prancing naked across the beach for his daily swim. Known as 'Birdie' to the troops and 'the Soul of Anzac' in the history books, he earned both styles, showing Park how a leader can relax without cheapening his authority. Park tried to follow many of Birdwood's precepts: attention to detail, regular tours of inspection, indifference to personal danger and, not least, Birdwood's recognition that the uniformed civilians of a wartime army should not be treated 'with barrack-square discipline'. Sir Aylmer Hunter-Weston, commander of the 29th Division, taught Park equally valuable lessons. 'Hunter-Bunter', in Park's opinion, was 'a great hot air merchant'. One day he began an inspection of Park's battery shortly after a two-man ration party had had an 'accident' with a jar of rum. Both men were incapable by the time the General arrived and had been hastily laid out on stretchers and covered with blankets. Hunter-Weston gazed solemnly down at the stretchers, drew himself upright and said in his best graveyard voice: 'I salute the dead.' As he moved away, a muffled voice rose from one of the stretchers: 'What was the old basket saying?' Park learned that a pompous manner earns contempt rather than respect.

He had survived a prolonged test under fire and chosen a new career. Gallipoli marked him both physically and mentally, for he was there in the ranks, seeing and sharing the exceptional squalor of that campaign, observing and suffering from the exceptional bungling of those responsible for conducting it. He had shown himself resourceful as well as brave under fire. No less important, he had also shown that he had the mental and physical toughness to function efficiently in conditions of acute, prolonged discomfort. Gallipoli has a unique place in the history of warfare: 'for the first time,' wrote H.A. Jones in the official history of the war in the air, 'a campaign was conducted by combined forces on, under, and over the sea, and on and over the land.' In the next war, Park would be among the commanders of similar combined operations in the Mediterranean and in the Indian Ocean, where many of the mistakes made at Gallipoli were avoided. But Gallipoli remains one of the greatest disasters in British history: ten thousand Anzacs left their bones there and the losses suffered by the British and French were much heavier, and all to no purpose.[1]

Six months after the evacuation, Park was thrust into a disaster of even greater magnitude: the Somme Offensive. Early on 16 January 1916, No. 10 Battery's headquarters staff arrived in the 29th Division's camp near Suez. Most of the men caught up during the next few days and strict training began because it soon became known that a transfer to the Western Front was likely. Training at Suez, Park recalled, included no work with aircraft. Not the slightest account was taken of the certainty that when they reached France, German aircraft would try both to observe and to attack their positions. He and another subaltern asked permission to be flown over the brigade, when it was in position under cover, to see what could be seen from above. The request was curtly rejected. Observation from the air, they were told, was all stuff and nonsense. Park found this attitude only too common among senior officers.

On 21 February the division was ordered to get ready to go to France. These orders were a great relief to all because living conditions were primitive, the flies a great nuisance (even to veterans of Gallipoli) and few officers or men had any tropical kit. The battery entrained for Alexandria on 10 March. It was a rough journey but at least they were away from the heat and sand of Suez. They arrived early next morning and, naturally, found Alexandria wet and cold. During that day, the brigade embarked on Horse Transport *Elele*, bound for Marseille. After a miserable week at sea, the *Elele* docked at Marseille late on the 17th.

Next day the battery set off for Pont Rémy on the Somme front in open cattle trucks, arriving at 3 a.m. on 21 March – frozen, hungry and filthy. There had been no opportunity to cook or wash throughout the fifty-five hours that the journey lasted; nor was there any at Pont Rémy. After a few more dispiriting hours spent assembling gear, the battery trudged off to Vauchelles, some ten miles away, in driving rain. Horses and men were soon slithering in thick mud. Park was thrown from his horse, which then fell on

11

him, and he was dragged away to hospital on a stretcher. Four days later he rejoined the battery, although still unable to walk unaided. On 25 April 1916, the first anniversary of the Gallipoli landings, Park's battery (equipped with eighteen-pounders) fired 120 rounds of shrapnel 'in registering a piece of wire at Hawthorn Redoubt' from a position east of Englebelmer.

Life settled into a routine for the battery. It registered positions, cut wire, retaliated, supported small raids and tested guns for calibration. The battery's command post was a deep pit connected by a trench to the signallers' pit. It contained a small table, a telephone and message pad, and an empty ammunition box to use as a bench. There were two bunks, one above the other, for the officer on duty and the signaller at rest. The officer climbed up a ladder to shout his orders (using a megaphone) through an opening in the rear wall of the pit to the gun crews. During this quiet time, Park learned that on 23 May he would be promoted from Temporary to Substantive Second Lieutenant.

The brigade commander, wrote Park after the war, was urgently advised by experienced troops that concealment **from** the air was necessary, but ignored the advice until a battery on his flank was accurately shelled following enemy aerial reconnaissance. Park was then permitted to accompany a pilot of 8 Squadron in a flight over all the brigade's gun positions. Every position, Park reported, was plainly visible because of the huge areas of newly-turned earth, new tracks and shadows cast by high emplacements. In fact, the guns would have been less obvious standing in the open. Perfunctory attempts were made to remedy the situation.

The British trenches ran for twenty miles from the village of Hébuterne south across the river Ancre to Maricourt Wood, held jointly by British and French troops. Two miles farther south lay the Somme. For such an extended front the artillery available was inadequate, but the offensive depended on the artillery destroying the Germans in their trenches. Many shells would fail to explode and the German fortifications proved immensely strong – which was hardly surprising on a front undisturbed for nearly two years. The bombardment began on 24 June. The task of Park's battery was to destroy the broad, dense tangle of barbed wire protecting German trenches in front of the fortress of Beaumont Hamel. Throughout the week-long bombardment, No. 10 Battery was allotted 160 rounds per gun per day and half the battery was at work each night, attacking communication trenches in the hope of delaying the movement of reinforcements and ammunition. During these hectic days, Park was all over the place. On the evening of 30 June he was observing for a 9.2 howitzer battery as well as attempting to cut wire with his own guns. Park thought them useless: 'little pipsqueaks' with a flat trajectory which caused little damage even when they did hit the wire.

The infantry assault was timed for 7.30 a.m. on 1 July, to be preceded by an intense bombardment lasting sixty-five minutes. At 7.20 a.m. a colossal mine was exploded under Hawthorn Redoubt. This proved to be a disastrous

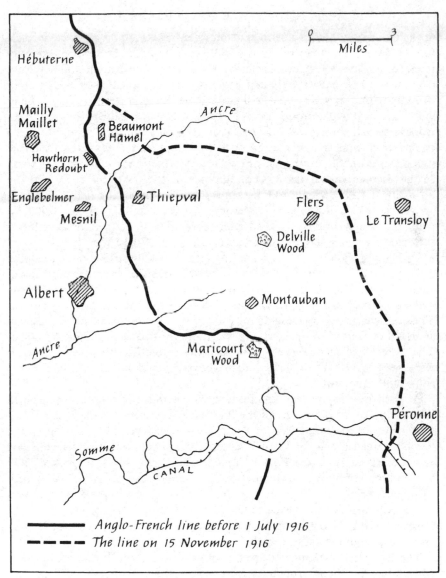

Hébuterne

Mailly
Maillet

Beaumont
Hamel

Hawthorn
Redoubt

Englebelmer

Mesnil

Thiepval

Ancre

Flers

Delville
Wood

Le Transloy

Albert

Montauban

Ancre

Maricourt
Wood

Péronne

Somme

CANAL

0   3
Miles

—— Anglo-French line before 1 July 1916
--- The line on 15 November 1916

2: The Somme

error, indicating that an assault was imminent and making an extra obstacle for the advancing infantry. Worse still, the crater's edges were promptly manned by numerous German machine-gunners. The British infantry went over the top in broad daylight at a slow walk, carrying half their body weight in equipment. They advanced in dense masses across a wide No Man's Land with their bayonets upward, catching the sun. As for the British guns, they worked to a timetable, lifting by increments of a hundred yards from the enemy front-line trenches as the infantry supposedly advanced. But the infantry was unable to advance in the face of withering machine-gun fire and so the barrage ahead was wasted. Because of the dust, the noise and the difficulty of telling friend from foe, it was impossible to stop firing as soon as an attack failed. By evening, infantry casualties amounted to 57,000, of whom 19,000 were dead or died later of their wounds: the heaviest losses suffered in a single day by any army in the First World War.

By 5 July it was already clear that no breakthrough was likely. On that day, consequently, Park's battery was moved back to positions on the outskirts of Englebelmer. The positions were French-built and in poor condition, filthy and wet. Heavy rain set in until the 20th, when the sun at last reappeared. This rare warm day was wasted on Park, who was sent to hospital suffering from a severe attack of malaria. He was there for two weeks, until 4 August. The battery had just moved to new positions in the Mesnil valley. The days were again cold, wet or windy; many horses fell sick and enemy fire was heavy and accurate.

At last, on 6 September, the brigade was withdrawn and marched north into a supposedly quiet part of the line for a rest. Park's battery spent four weeks near the Menin Gate in the Ypres salient before returning to the Somme front, arriving at Montauban on 13 October. Its positions were new and inadequately camouflaged, the terrain was so shell-pocked that ammunition supply was difficult, and the battery had many problems with weak gun springs as a result of the excessive use to which the guns had been subjected. Park was interested to hear the infantry praising the Royal Flying Corps and the heavy-gunners now admitted that aerial observation was essential to counter-battery work.

The 29th Division launched an attack towards Le Transloy before dawn on 18 October. By the afternoon, however, two of No. 10 Battery's three guns were out of action. Nothing could be done to repair them the next day and on the 20th the last serviceable gun was destroyed by a direct hit. On 21 October, while Park was trying to withdraw his guns for repair, a shell exploded under his horse, killing it and wounding him. After lying for hours in the gun line on a muddy stretcher, he was loaded into a horse-drawn ambulance with steel tyres and no springs and carted for miles over a shell-holed road to the nearest casualty clearing station. After a day or two there, he was taken by ambulance and train to the coast and thence by ship to England.

Park later regarded this wound as a great stroke of good fortune because for several months he had been seeking a transfer to the Royal Flying Corps. Despite orders from the highest level encouraging such transfers, the 29th Division strictly forbade officers or men to transfer while on active service in France. He was openly ridiculed for wanting to join a 'Ragtime Show' and asked if he was tired of the war. This attitude, wrote Park, was 'uncommonly annoying' to those who had friends in the RFC and knew what good work was being done. Back in England, after a short spell of instructing at the Artillery Depot at Woolwich, Park 'managed to effect' (by means which he never revealed) a transfer to the RFC. All told, he had served nearly two years as an artilleryman. Ahead of him lay thirty years of active service as an airman.[2]

CHAPTER TWO

Fighter Pilot

1917

At Woolwich, Park had been graded permanently unfit for active service. Specifically, he was 'unfit to ride a horse'. More than half a century later, he explained this grading: 'It may seem strange that I was considered unfit to ride a horse but fit to fly an aeroplane. But tradition was still strong in those days of horse-drawn artillery – and an officer and gentleman was expected to ride into battle on a charger.' On 9 December 1916, just as Park arrived in the RFC, it was decreed that as from the 15th prospective pilots must pass a course of instruction at one of the Schools of Military Aeronautics, at Reading or Oxford. Park was sent to Reading. Old campaigners were taught alongside cadets and all had to 'pass out' in elementary infantry drill. They were taught a smattering of rigging, including wire splicing, Morse code and so on, but there were no aeroplanes.

From Reading, Park went to Netheravon, on Salisbury Plain, where he learned to fly. He had two and a half hours' dual instruction in an Avro 504K and made his first solo flight in a Maurice Farman: the throttle froze and he was obliged to land without his engine. Park benefited from a more rigorous course at Netheravon than his predecessors had undergone. He was required to complete at least twenty hours' solo, to carry out a cross-country flight of at least sixty miles (landing at two designated places en route) and he must have climbed to 8,000 feet, remaining there for at least fifteen minutes, after which he must make his landing within a circle fifty yards in diameter. There had been no standard method of flying training in 1916 and few instructors were both interested and competent. Although new tests were introduced at the end of that year, pilots going to France early in 1917 were barely able to take off and land successfully. Methodical reconnaissance and aerial combat were quite beyond them.

Park was therefore very lucky to be posted in March 1917 to Rendcomb, near Cirencester, as an instructor. But the fact that a man of his brief experience could officially be considered capable of instructing others is a revealing comment on the dire standard of flying training. Park spent nearly four months at Rendcomb, adding one hundred hours as an instructor on four types of aircraft to the thirty-five hours he managed under tuition at Netheravon. With 135 hours in the air he was far better prepared for combat duty on the Western Front than most of his predecessors – or successors: the average flying time of a pilot going overseas in September 1917 was less than fifty hours.

Another stroke of good fortune for Park was contained in a secret letter received by all five brigades from Major-General Trenchard, commanding the RFC in the field, on 10 June 1917. He asked his Brigadier-Generals to point out to their respective army commanders 'that it is of the utmost importance that the Flying Corps should avoid wastage in both pilots and machines for some little time.' Reserves were dangerously low, reinforcements from England were not coming forward in sufficient numbers and low flying should therefore be stopped except when absolutely necessary and bombing raids should be severely curtailed. To complete Park's good fortune, when he reported to the Air Board before his departure for France at the end of June, he was told that he would be posted to the first operational Bristol Fighter squadron, the type on which he had specialized at Rendcomb. The two-seater Bristol Fighter proved to be one of the finest aircraft of the First World War.

When he arrived at Boulogne, however, Park was handed a slip of paper telling him that he was to be a day-bomber pilot, even though he had specialized as a fighting pilot. He was sent to the Pilots' Pool at St Omer, where he found many pilots hanging about who had left England weeks before. None of them had been up in an aeroplane since arriving in France, most of them had seen no active service and all of them were becoming demoralized by having nothing to do except listen to rumours of heavy casualties. But Park was now twenty-five and had more than two and a half years of wartime service behind him, much of it in areas of bitter conflict. Even as a pilot he was already experienced by the standards of those days. He was not prepared to rot in St Omer nor to allow an unwelcome slip of paper to determine his fate. On his second day there, he got in touch with 48 Squadron (the only Bristol Fighter unit then in France) and before a week had passed was posted to that squadron. Characteristically, Park made full use of his few days at St Omer. Others might be content to hang about, listening to idle gossip, but Park set himself to learn what he could about aeroplanes and engines that he had not seen before.

Forty-eight Squadron was then at La Bellevue, between Doullens and Arras. It had begun war flying on 5 April and at first followed the accepted two-seater tactic of manoeuvring so as to permit the observer to fire. Fearful casualties resulted until some pilots began to use the aircraft as if it were a single-seater, regarding the forward-firing front gun as the main weapon and the observer's rearward-firing gun as an auxiliary. Not only did they live

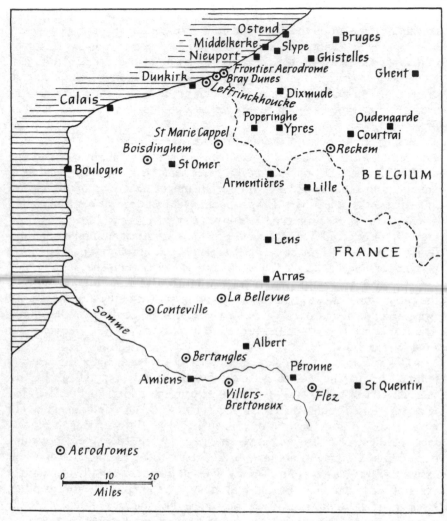

3: Aerodromes on the Western Front, 1917–18

longer, but they also began to inflict losses on the enemy. Park, joining the squadron on 7 July, was lucky enough to avoid the initial disasters and experienced enough to share the later triumphs.

Unlike so many pilots coming fresh to aerial combat, he was a man of comparatively mature years who understood what was happening on the ground and what was expected of him in the air. Until he was tested, however, neither he nor anyone else could know whether he had certain qualities essential to the successful fighting pilot: a cool head in a crisis and skill as a shot. Valuable, too, was a willingness to take personal care of guns and sights, indeed of the whole aircraft. Alan Light (an observer with 48 Squadron in 1917) recalled that Park was in the habit of spending long hours in the hangars, taking a much more direct interest in his machine and its equipment than was usual among pilots. On the other hand, unlike some other aces of his generation, Park was never a man who shot for sport. Even rabbits were safe from him. He would not even follow the military expedient of shooting horses.

Within a week of his arrival at La Bellevue, the squadron moved to Frontier Aerodrome, on the Channel coast a few miles east of Dunkirk. Park was sent up in the oldest and poorest machine to show what he could do. Even though he survived this test, more than a week passed before he was taken on patrol and during that time no flying practice was possible because the squadron was so short of machines. He therefore went on his first patrol with no experience in formation flying or in handling an aircraft at high altitude, let alone in fighting tactics. Although he had known two of the flight commanders in England, these experienced pilots gave Park little help. He was told no more than his position in the formation, the area to be patrolled, the height at which the patrol should begin and the time of departure. No plans were made on the ground regarding what should be done if enemy aircraft were met above, below, to the east, on the same level, in larger, similar or smaller numbers. Everything was decided in the air, on the spur of the moment. The result was that the squadron seldom fought in any formation, but immediately split up and engaged in a free-for-all. This 'method' worked well enough for pilots who could handle their machines and guns competently. As a rule, new pilots went down first followed by old hands who in turn were followed by even older hands. Novices, Park found, served as 'good bait' for the rest. Such tactics were, of course, most dangerous to single-seaters; Bristol Fighters were often saved by their observers.

Park's first year as an airman was, in some respects, his best. Despite his regrets about the reluctance to share experience and to discuss tactics, he immediately felt at home in 48 Squadron. He was greatly impressed by the cheerful spirit of air crews and the uncomplaining efforts of mechanics who regularly worked a fourteen-hour day. Enthusiasm was high and discipline good – though 'of the unconventional type'. His experiences in 1917 set for

Park a standard of achievement and team spirit that he would seek to recapture throughout his career.

The squadron's morale owed much to the Bristol Fighter. Its performance marked a distinct advance over earlier two-seaters, there were few blind spots that could not be quickly covered by pilot or observer and the back-to-back seating of the crew – 'classic position of those fighting against odds' – made possible instant changes from offence to defence and back again. The Rolls-Royce Falcon engine was reliable at any height or speed and the airframe was very strong. For its size and weight, the Bristol was an agile machine and would remain in service for fourteen years after the war.

Good as it was, it could easily have been better. It could have been provided with twin forward-firing machine-guns, armoured cockpits, rubber casing of the thin-gauge fuel tanks and padding of the steel butt of the machine-gun in front of the pilot's head; simple toggles fixed to the rudder wires passing through the rear cockpit could, with an emergency stick, have enabled observers to put the aircraft down safely when the pilot was incapacitated. 'But it was not the habit of senior officers in those days to discuss the points of their aircraft with those who flew them in action,' wrote Major W.F.J. Harvey, a Bristol pilot. Park, when a senior officer in the Second World War, would do precisely that.[1]

By July, the focal point of aerial activity on the British–German front had moved north from Arras to Flanders and a desperate struggle took place between Armentières and the Channel. Forty-eight Squadron was constantly engaged either in air fighting, long-range reconnaissance or the escort of day-bombers in raids upon German aerodromes in Belgium – all in preparation for and then support of a major offensive which began on 31 July. The opposing fighter squadrons largely cancelled out each other's effect during the rest of 1917 and so permitted their respective infantry and artillery cooperation squadrons to work effectively.

Alan Light recalled flying with Park on one patrol when their Bristol suffered engine trouble and Park was obliged to leave the formation. On the way home, however, the engine recovered and Park therefore decided to try to rejoin the formation. Flying alone, with no sign of another aircraft in the sky and feeling cold and bored, Light suddenly loosed off a drum of ammunition into Ostend without a word to his pilot. Every gun in the town, so it seemed, opened up on the lone Bristol and Park fled out to sea before turning for home. 'He never said anything,' Light remembered, 'but he looked at me – and I didn't do it again.'

On 24 July, after several strenuous patrols, monitoring the movement of trains and barges despite poor weather and smoke-screens, Park made his first appearance in an official combat report. He and Second Lieutenant A.W. Merchant were attacked by three Albatros scouts from the north-east while crossing the coast near Middelkerke. Merchant fired at one when it was about two hundred yards away. It spun, partly recovered, and then went into a steep nose-dive. The other two were fired on as they fled eastwards. Eleven enemy aircraft were seen during this patrol and Park's machine was attacked by six of them. Anti-aircraft batteries on the Belgian coast were notoriously accurate and wise pilots plotted their positions carefully. At dawn on 26 July, Park and Merchant cleverly evaded the screen around Middelkerke and caught a column of twelve lorries standing in the main street. Merchant fired a drum of ammunition into the column from 1,000 feet, but Park's machine-gun jammed. A simple mechanical failure, common to the guns used on both sides, thwarted a well-planned attack and left Park and Merchant more than usually vulnerable – as well as exasperated.

Raids by large German bombers – Gothas – were carried out on England in daylight during the summer of 1917. To counter them, it was decided to send up patrols from the Dunkirk coast whenever warning was received of a raid in progress. These patrols would climb out to sea with the intention of intercepting the Gothas on their return journey. All crews and machines not actually on patrol were kept standing by to take to the air at immediate notice on days favourable for Gotha raids. For all his hours of standing by and patrolling over the Channel, Park was not rewarded with even the sight of a Gotha. As the daylight raids decreased, so German night-bombing of Dunkirk increased. Late in August, Park's squadron was ordered to begin night-flying with a view to intercepting the bombers which came over every clear night. Intensive training began at dusk each evening, but the daily routine of offensive patrols was not changed to allow time off for those practising at night. To Park's relief, these night operations were quickly abandoned. Frontier Aerodrome was very small, bounded on the west by low sandhills and a thick belt of wire; on the north and south were small, deep canals and on the east an unbroken row of tall trees. It was not at all uncommon, he recalled, to see Bristols standing on their noses in the canals on the morning after night practice.

On 12 August Park earned his second appearance in a combat report. In the morning he was assigned bombing escort duty, with an observer called Arthur Noss. As the patrol was flying home, two Albatros scouts attacked the Bristols from below and behind. Noss fired two drums at one, which made 'steep wobbling dives' towards the ground. Its fall was observed by their companions. Park had not fired because he was holding position in the formation. Having been airborne for ninety-five minutes and with fuel running low, he preferred not to go dog-fighting on the wrong side of the lines. That evening Park and Noss were in action again, patrolling south of Nieuport. A dozen enemy aircraft were seen approaching from Ostend. Two came close and fired a few rounds; Noss replied, without effect. Both enemy machines kept their distance and patrolled with the Bristols for about half an hour. One of the Germans then fired a white light and both cleared off.

Five days later, on 17 August, Park experienced the greatest day of his career as a fighting pilot. He and Noss took off early that morning with two other

21

Bristols on a Special High Patrol. Several enemy aircraft were encountered and a general engagement began at 15,000 feet, three miles west of Slype, and went on till they were only 3,000 feet over Ghistelles. Park's two companions were soon put out of the fight, but he was undaunted. He saw three enemy aircraft diving on a lone Sopwith Camel and attacked so fiercely that he drove them off. Two enemy machines then dived on his tail. Noss fired half a drum into one, which fell out of control. Park followed it down, firing hard at a close range of no more than twenty-five yards. Two more aircraft dived at him and, as they overshot, both Park and Noss were able to fire, and watch one of them crash into the sea. Another enemy formation now attacked from above and Noss damaged one machine. It began to spin slowly, wobbling from side to side. Park followed it down, firing at close range until his gun jammed and he decided to make for home, with Noss vigorously engaging three pursuers. Park cleared his gun, throttled back, and fired at them as they shot past. He caught sight of another Camel, at 5,000 feet over Slype, diving under control with two enemy aircraft following. Park fired hard into the second machine, sending it down out of control. He and Noss fought on until they were both out of ammunition and then made good their escape. Despite their exertions, they were both out again in the afternoon, escorting other Bristols on photographic duty.

'We had six separate combats in quick succession,' wrote Park in his combat report, to which his commanding officer, Major A.V. Bettington, added: 'A magnificent series of fights carried out with considerable dash and determination against superior odds. The front gun fired over 600 rounds and the rear gun over 400.' He assessed their score as one crashed and two completely out of control at low altitude, although in fact they also at least damaged a fourth. Two days later, on 19 August, Brigadier-General J.H.W. Becke (Commanding Officer, 4th Brigade) successfully recommended them both for the immediate award of the Military Cross. 'Lt. Park has performed several other fine feats,' the citation concluded, 'and has at all times set a most inspiriting example by his dash and tenacity.'

Noss had a deserved rest on 21 August and Second Lieutenant W. O'Toole accompanied Park on a morning patrol. Six Albatros scouts were seen approaching below from east of Westende. Following his leader, Park dived and fired at one from close range. It fell away, apparently under control, as he zoomed to allow O'Toole to fire at a second scout. Another formation of eight machines came at Park while he was climbing back to rejoin his own formation. He turned under them and both he and O'Toole fired to good effect. O'Toole saw his opponent go down and Park got his to fall, firing at fifty yards 'to make certain of it'.

According to the 4th Brigade's Intelligence Summary, an outstanding feature of the fighting in August was the success of 48 Squadron, although its casualties were severe: eight pilots lost out of an effective strength of around sixteen. Aerial combat, however, was only the spectacular aspect of air work.

More directly useful to the Allied offensive was the number of enemy batteries located by air observation for attack. Information about the movement of trains, barges and ground forces was potentially even more useful. Most patrols operated between 15,000 and 18,000 feet and at that height the wind was almost always strong – and almost always from the west. The Germans therefore tried to entice British aircraft as far east as possible. In countering this tactic the Bristol Fighter, with its rear gunner, had a great advantage over single-seaters which could not afford to venture too far over 'Hunland' because they were unable to protect themselves from a rearward attack when heading home west, short of fuel and battling against the wind. By operating so far over enemy lines, the Bristol performed more detailed and extensive observation work on its own account and afforded the best available protection to British artillery observation aircraft. Army headquarters gradually became aware of the Bristol's exceptional value and, as Park would complain, found it too many jobs to do; jobs which restricted more and more its opportunities to engage in aerial combat.

On 2 September, Park and Alan Light were on patrol at about 9.15 a.m. when Park spotted a Bristol Fighter far below, east of Dixmude, losing height with an Albatros on its tail. He left his formation, diving steeply, and got in a long burst at close range. The Albatros dived under the Bristol it had been attacking, but Park followed and fired again until the enemy machine disappeared into cloud, apparently out of control. Since the rest of Park's formation had now also disappeared, he made his way north-west to Dixmude where he engaged in further skirmishes. (Park and Light never flew together again. Light was injured on 10 September in a night landing and invalided home. They next met half a century later in Auckland. Park told Mrs Light that he would not have survived but for her husband, to which she replied that he always said the same about Park. 'In my long life,' wrote Light in December 1980, 'I have met several men of great character and integrity. Park was not excelled by any of them.')

On 3 September, Leutnant Josef Peter Jacobs, commanding officer of *Jasta 7*, an important German unit in the Flanders area, was circling over the front at about 7.40 in the morning when he noticed an Albatros in difficulty with a Bristol Fighter. Jacobs raced to assist but before he came within range the German aircraft exploded. Park and his rear-gunner – Air Mechanic Lindfield – had killed Hauptmann Otto Hartmann, commanding officer of *Jasta 28*, a well-known pilot with seven victories to his credit. They killed another known pilot on 5 September: Franz Pernet, the stepson of General Ludendorff and a member of a famous unit, *Jasta Boelcke*, based at Jabbeke, near Bruges. Their formation of six Bristols had been on escort duty that morning and as they returned along the coast about noon, six Albatros scouts attacked them north of Ostend. Park, the rear-most man, was singled out but managed to put several bursts into Pernet's machine at very close range. It crashed into the sea and the pilot's body was washed ashore some weeks later.

23

Shortly after that engagement, Park and Lindfield sent a two-seater DFW reconnaissance aircraft into the sea.

Park was promoted to Temporary Captain on 11 September 1917, while serving as a flight commander. On the 15th, the new captain celebrated his elevation by shooting down an Albatros behind British lines in the region of St Jean Capelle. The pilot, Leutnant Max von Chelius of *Jasta Boelcke*, appears to have become separated from his comrades while on patrol and then compounded the error by joining a flight of Bristols. The result, as one of those comrades later wrote, was that 'the many hounds caused the rabbit's death'. For good measure, Park and his observer destroyed another German aircraft in the evening.

Park's victories that 15 September 1917 ended a remarkable run of success lasting twenty-six days, during which time he and his observers certainly destroyed seven enemy aircraft and at least damaged five others. He would claim only three more victories in the rest of the war. Brigadier-General Becke recommended him for the Distinguished Service Order, but Trenchard decided that the immediate award of a Bar to his Military Cross would be sufficient recognition. For the rest of his life, 15 September would be a date of special significance to Park. On that same evening in 1917, Arthur Noss – with whom he had earned his first Military Cross – was killed in a forced landing. It was the birthday of Park's future wife, Dol, whom he was to meet a few weeks later. And finally, from 1940, 15 September had even more importance for him as Battle of Britain Day.[2]

It was also on that day in 1917 that 48 Squadron moved to Leffrinckhoucke, a little closer to Dunkirk. Until August, Park recalled, the squadron had been employed almost exclusively on offensive patrols, but in that month photographic work and long reconnaissance patrols had begun. These new – and additional – duties caused much frustration among 'the more offensive element' in the squadron; the 'spirited' pilot did not bring back such good pictures and reports as the 'duller' man and was censured if his failure was caused by chasing after enemy aircraft.

Only three men were lost in October, but one of them was the highly-regarded Captain John Theobald Milne, killed on the 24th. He and Park had become friends and Milne had given him his wife's address in London for when his leave fell due because Park knew no one there. Park now had the task of delivering Milne's personal belongings to his widow. Janie Milne introduced him to her cousin, Dorothy Parish. Dorothy (always known as 'Dol') was then just twenty-four and working as a nurse in a London hospital. Her family was wealthy and had close connections with Argentina, although she herself had never been there and was very much a London girl; a genuine Cockney, in fact, born within the sound of Bow Bells. Dol was a beautiful woman. Better still, she had a lively sense of humour, a most attractive personality and enjoyed a prominent position in London society. Perhaps it is not surprising that she and Keith should promptly fall in love, for each found the other not only physically attractive, but also quite unlike anyone else they had ever met. Then twenty-five, he was very tall (at least a foot taller than Dol) and strikingly handsome. Three years of active service in notoriously dangerous campaigns had given an edge to a naturally masterful character. He was grave and serious, she was light-hearted and cheerful; they seem to have responded instantly to each other and there was an 'understanding' between them even before Park returned to France a few days later. She had had many admirers, but none of Park's distinction, and he had never met anyone like her. He would give a sense of purpose to her life and she would bring humanity to his.

On 4 November Temporary Captain Park received his first substantive promotion, to full Lieutenant. As a flight commander, he had inspired confidence in his followers, keeping the flight together and not allowing straggling. He had learned to see everything there was to be seen in the sky and to judge when to attack and when to keep away, avoiding traps. After a fight, he did what he could to reassemble his forces for the journey home. In return for his responsibilities, he had almost the pick of the squadron's aircraft and ground crews, his tail was well protected and he got the first and often the only shot at the enemy. On 27 November he was decorated for the third time in four months: this time he was awarded the Croix de Guerre by the General Officer Commanding of the 1st French Army. According to the citation, he had performed 'conspicuous services' to that army in Flanders during 1917.

The squadron's 'Schedule of Work for Winter Training' had been published on 19 November. As well as an emphasis on games and drill, specialist training was prescribed: photography, aerial gunnery, signalling (wireless and lamps), bomb dropping, compass use without the aid of maps (to give practice in cross-country flying, 'the course being so arranged that there is no danger of the pilot going over the enemy's lines'), formation flying and liaison with other squadrons and wings. There were to be machine-gun competitions and tests in assembly, stoppage clearance and accurate shooting. In the interests of realistic practice, flying coats, goggles and gloves were to be worn when firing. Concerts were to be arranged for off-duty hours and good concert-parties exchanged between squadrons.

The winter of 1917–18 proved bitterly cold. Unfortunately for its pilots, the Bristol Fighter performed at its best where it was coldest: above 15,000 feet. A long reconnaissance meant two or three freezing hours with no oxygen supply and a face thickly smeared with whale-oil to avoid frostbite. Park and his men got airborne well before dawn, without the help of a lighted path, trying to get forty miles over the lines in near-darkness and come home with the sun behind, noting ground movements and hoping to catch an early German artillery-spotter napping. But the westerly wind usually drove the aircraft father east than the crews realized in the darkness of the outward

25

journey, and grinding westward at a ground speed of no more than 80 m.p.h. was a tedious, dangerous business. Park much preferred photographic duty: the observer did the work and they rarely went so far over the lines.

In December, 48 Squadron transferred to Flez, west of St Quentin. On 3 January 1918 Park and Lieutenant J.H. Robertson were out alone about midday, taking photographs of a railway line, when a DFW two-seater attacked. They drove it off, but a few minutes later a loose formation of six Albatros fighters attacked from the west, the Allied quarter. The two highest were driven off, but the other four continued climbing and attacked vigorously. It was at this desperate moment that Robertson's rear gun jammed and Park had to work very hard to maintain his height advantage and fend off the German scouts at the same time. One came level with him and attacked head-on. Park replied and the two machines were only yards apart when the German suddenly fell into a side-slip and rolled over into a vertical dive. Although the remaining scouts maintained the attack, their fire was wild. When they were all above Ramicourt, one of the scouts got an effective burst into Park's engine, and it began to smoke and vibrate noisily. Waiting his chance, Park put the Bristol into a steep, side-slipping dive towards St Quentin. He out-distanced his opponents, glided over the lines and managed to land safely with his engine seized solid.

Shortly after that narrow escape, Park was sent home to England for a necessary break from front-line flying. While he was enjoying a so-called 'rest', the authorities arranged for him to work harder than ever, passing on his experience to others. By the end of January he was training Canadian airmen at Hooton Park, Liverpool. He also attended the Course of Special Flying devised by Lieutenant-Colonel R.R. Smith-Barry at Gosport and was amazed at the progress in training methods. Had it not been for the massive German offensive launched on 21 March, he might well have spent longer out of the front line. Fortunately for his peace of mind, however, he was able to rejoin the fight early in April. Better still, he went back to France as Major Park, in command of the squadron he had joined only nine months before as a Second Lieutenant.[3]

CHAPTER THREE

'Major Sparks'

1918

It was unusual for a man to command a squadron in which he had served as a junior pilot and unusual for a man to serve all his time in France, as Park did, with a single squadron. Forty-Eight Squadron had only three wartime commanders: A.V. Bettington (7 March to August 1917), H.S. Shield (18 August 1917 to April 1918) and Park from 10 April 1918 onwards. In those twenty months it was credited with 148 aircraft destroyed, 150 driven down out of control and 103 driven down. Its pilots and observers thus enjoyed, or at least claimed, some kind of success on 401 occasions: an average of two every three days. Thirty-seven medals were awarded to members of the squadron, nearly two a month. Three went to Park for his actions in the summer and autumn of 1917.

He had proved himself a brave, skilful pilot and an able flight commander. Now, with his first independent command, he came to a turning-point in his career. It was a clear opportunity to make or break his reputation, especially since at the moment of his taking command, the squadron (and, it seemed, the entire British Army) was in imminent danger of being overwhelmed by a fierce German offensive. When that offensive began on 21 March 1918, 48 Squadron was forced to retreat over thirty miles westward, from Flez to Bertangles (north of Amiens) and then a further fifteen miles north-west to Conteville. There the retreat ended and after ten days, when the new front line stabilized east of Amiens, the squadron returned to Bertangles. The worst of the crisis was over by 10 April, when Park assumed command, although that was not immediately obvious.

The daily routine, Park remembered, was to make continuous reconnaissance of back areas, attack ground targets with bombs and machine-guns and knock down low-flying enemy aircraft which had been strafing Allied troops. Although the weather was generally bad, the squadron worked hard and kept Army Headquarters thoroughly informed about movements in the German rear. Casualties had been heavy since 21 March and the counter-offensive began, Park wrote, with not a single pilot other than himself who had had the benefit of fighting on the coast in the summer and autumn of 1917.

As for his personal contribution to all this work, squadron commanders were only to fly over the lines by permission of their wing commanders, and that permission was granted sparingly. Consequently, he was not in the air on the morning of 21 April 1918 when the most celebrated German pilot of the war, Rittmeister Manfred Freiherr von Richthofen, crashed near Bertangles. As the legend of the Red Baron flourished in later years, Park would sometimes say that he was the only Allied airman or soldier on the Somme front who neither killed Richthofen nor saw him killed. It must have been dangerous up there, he would muse gravely, with all those aeroplanes milling about, not to mention 40,000 Australian soldiers firing away. Richthofen's body was brought to Poulainville, adjoining Bertangles, and laid 'in state' in one of the hangars of 3 Squadron, Australian Flying Corps. Park was among those who went to look at the body and attended his funeral next day in the village cemetery. He asked everyone not on duty to attend. It was not an order, said Captain Frank Ransley, one of his flight commanders, but one always did as Park asked.[1]

According to Vivian Voss, a South African pilot serving with 48 Squadron in April 1918, 'Major Field' returned to England and was replaced by 'Major Sparks'. Voss first published *Flying Minnows* in 1935, an account of his wartime experiences, changing many names – including his own – and it was not until 1977 that their identities were revealed. Field was Shield and Sparks was Park. The new commanding officer, wrote Voss, 'took a more active part in the life of the squadron than Major Field had done, and on several occasions he led the patrols himself.' Consequently, he 'was soon voted a jolly good fellow by Officers and Ack Emmas [Air Mechanics] alike.' Park had 200 officers and men under his command, to keep eighteen aircraft in service as well as numerous ground vehicles – lorries, trailers, motorcycles, a motorcar and a water-cart. Most of his men were tradesmen in civilian life, intelligent and skilled, easier to lead than drive. Many of them had served with the squadron since its arrival in France and would go on doing so until long after the Armistice. They were its backbone and their opinions on technical matters indispensable. Unlike the air crews, who rarely lasted more than a few months in any particular squadron before they were killed, injured, captured or simply posted away to fill gaps elsewhere, many of the ground personnel who greeted Major Park in April 1918 well remembered Second Lieutenant Park of the previous summer.

In fact, Park was responsible for far more than 200 men. A dozen soldiers were attached to the squadron for ground defence, considerable numbers of photographic staff were attached from time to time, there were medical personnel and intelligence officers, tent-erecting detachments, maintenance sections and construction parties – all formally under orders from aircraft depots or Air Construction Corps, but in practice under local control. Among these were the Chinese labourers. Many of them had tame sparrows, recalled John Pugh, an observer, which they kept in cages. The Chinese were in charge of the bath hut. The baths, made of tin, were just long enough to squat in and the Chinese would fill them with boiling water and watch the airmen's antics through the hut windows, laughing loudly and chattering to each other. But they were terrified by bombing or shelling and for a while after a nearby explosion would only work if the interpreter stood over them with a revolver in his hand.

Park redesigned the squadron's Reconnaissance Report Form to permit information to be recorded and read more easily. The new form had provision for time, height, visibility, course taken, movement observed (railways and roads), enemy aircraft, general remarks and the observer's name and signature. A typical report – of a reconnaissance by five aircraft, signed by the senior observer – contained detailed information about road and rail movements, rolling stock (recording the number of trucks), locomotives with or without steam up, hospitals, aircraft up or on the ground, anti-aircraft fire (location, intensity) and fires seen. All this at various times of the day and as seen from a variety of heights. Second Lieutenant J.W. Whitmarsh provided a good example of the squadron's alertness on 5 June when he reported that he had seen fake stationary trains at Chaulnes and Nesle using smoke-bombs to simulate steam up.

On 22 May, five certain victories in air combat were claimed, the most since Park had assumed command. He himself was leading a patrol of ten Bristols that evening, with Second Lieutenant G.J. Maynard as his observer, when he caught sight of thirteen triplanes and Pfalz scouts approaching overhead from the north. Firing a red light to alert his patrol, he climbed to meet the enemy formation. It swerved away to the east, allowing the Bristols to reach the same altitude. A Pfalz scout attacked from the front, but both Park and Maynard managed to reply: 'he gave way, turned across my sights and tried to dive away,' wrote Park later. 'I kept him in my sights and continued firing until the enemy aircraft fell into a side-slip, stalled, still straight in front of me, and fell into a very slow spin.' As often happened in the hurly-burly of combat, Park had no opportunity to follow the Pfalz down and make certain of it.

He recommended Captain Ransley for the immediate award of the Distinguished Flying Cross on 24 June. Ransley, he wrote, had joined the squadron the previous November and carried out several unescorted long-distance photo-reconnaissance missions. Throughout the 'retirement' (as Park delicately described the wholesale retreat beginning on 21 March), Ransley had performed a great deal of low-level work and also brought down six enemy aircraft. Ransley got his medal and on 13 July was also awarded the Croix de Guerre. He returned home later that month. Park wrote to him on the 17th to tell him about the Croix de Guerre and enclosed a letter from the

French Army Commander commending his 'offensive and daring spirit'. Park was a fine, upstanding man, in Ransley's opinion: very pleasant to talk to, but not at all gregarious. He was an excellent leader, both of a flight and later of the whole squadron. 'Major Keith Park inspired us all with his calm certainty that we should win through, although he hated sending us out on those near-suicide missions,' reported Ransley, referring to the trench-strafing in April.

Park gained his last aerial victories on 25 June, neatly picking off two Rumpler two-seaters within the space of a few minutes. It was a brilliantly successful patrol for him, but celebration was muted by the fact that in only four days (25–28 June) ten of his airmen went missing and two others were wounded. During the long summer evenings, he often flew alone to observe the tactics employed by both sides. German tactics, he thought, were better than they had been in 1917 – high and low formations cooperated effectively and rarely left reconnaissance machines unprotected – whereas cooperation between British formations was poor. Two or even three squadrons frequently patrolled a line parallel to an equivalent number of enemy aircraft, but the squadrons hesitated to attack, presumably because each leader was uncertain whether the others would follow. British pilots in 1918 were better trained than they had been in 1917, but were not, in Park's opinion, 'as good a type': he had occasion to get rid of several pilots and observers who were too lazy to learn from their experienced ground crews how to get maximum performance from their aircraft, weapons or cameras and were too easily discouraged even by poor weather, let alone by enemy fighters and anti-aircraft fire. Those who had transferred from army units at the front were the best, although they needed special training – in formation and high flying, aerial firing, map reading, photography and aircraft recognition – before they could pull their weight. To help teach aircraft recognition, Park had a set of scale-models made of the most common British, French and German types.

John Pugh, an observer, who joined the squadron in July, recalled that Park expected a very high standard of performance and appearance from everyone under his command. On one occasion, all air crew were summoned to a hangar where Park pointed out how fortunate they were to be flying Bristols and that if they did not wish to continue doing so, this could be swiftly arranged. He was not, however, a hard or unreasonable man. On the contrary, everyone respected him for his strictness, tempered as it was by kindness. Pugh 'had the honour' (as he put it) to be chosen by Park as his observer on a special mission to attack some enemy observation balloons. They approached at low level while the rest of the formation flew high above. The Bristols were to dive and join the attack on Park's signal. Unfortunately, they failed to see it the first time and when he signalled again, the balloons were already being pulled down. Park's response was typical. When the patrol returned to base, he commented calmly and briefly on the need to stay awake while in the air and ordered every machine refuelled and sent off immediately on an offensive patrol. In 1981 Pugh still had a photograph of Park taken in 1919 and had always kept an eye on his career.[2]

An American pilot called Sydney Whipple arrived at Bertangles on 7 August 1918 to join 48 Squadron after an exhausting journey along roads crammed with troops, horses, guns and supply waggons. He found an atmosphere of intense excitement in the mess. That night Park called everyone together 'for a little talk'. A major offensive – the Battle of Amiens – was to begin at dawn, he said. The squadron would be in the thick of it and he went on to explain what was expected of them. Whipple's most vivid memory of his arrival at Bertangles, however, was the sight of tanks: field after field was covered with them. Over 300 tanks rolled forward, concealed by a dense mist, at dawn on 8 August. There had been no preliminary bombardment and the offensive came as a complete surprise to the enemy. Whipple had nothing to do on the first day, but casualties were so heavy that he was employed every day from then on.

In 1936, Jack Slessor (an officer who had an important influence on Park's career during the Second World War) published an analysis of this battle. The Officer Commanding 48 Squadron, whom Slessor did not name, was ordered to reconnoitre the battle area at close intervals during the critical early days, but not enough aircraft were employed nor were enough reports obtained from a distance about German movements into that area. Although Slessor's strictures were aimed chiefly at the overall direction of air power available, he clearly implied that Park had failed to make the best use of his (admittedly meagre) resources. No other criticism, then or later, is recorded of 48 Squadron's performance in the Battle of Amiens and Park, having put his case to Slessor, asked him to amend his criticism. Slessor refused and Park never forgave him.

During the first half of August, German night-bombers twice attacked the aerodrome at Bertangles without causing any damage. Then, on 24 August, a raid by five Gotha bombers put Park's squadron out of action. The first Gotha flew low over the aerodrome in brilliant moonlight, dropping three bombs. Two landed in open country, but the third exploded in a hangar containing six Bristols, fully loaded with petrol, ammunition and bombs. The aircraft burst into flames, one after another, illuminating the entire station perfectly. A few minutes later, a second hangar was hit and also the living quarters and transport lines.

Between these two hangars stood one which Park had set aside as the station cinema and concert hall. A group of entertainers from other squadrons had come to put on a variety show and at least 200 men were packed into the middle hangar that evening, among them men from other squadrons based at Bertangles and some Australian troops. The first item on the programme, recalled Stanley Rycroft (then a new pilot in 48 Squadron) was Rachmaninov's Prelude in C sharp Minor. At the third bar, there came a loud explosion, quickly followed by others. For a moment, everyone sat in shocked silence. John Pugh remembered the compère shouting: 'Keep calm, there's no need to worry.' Then came more explosions, the hangar was plunged into darkness and a wild scramble to get clear began. Rycroft had been sitting at the front, near an exit. He followed some other officers out of the hangar, across an open field and into the trenches. The Gothas were clearly visible, circling overhead, and all around there were explosions and screams from wounded and terrified men. Pugh was one of the last to get clear and ran to a slit trench, scrambling over bodies in the dark. Other men milled about aimlessly, in a blind panic, and were caught by bombs falling clear of the buildings.

Park himself started to run as he emerged from the hangar – until he realized that he had work to do. He gathered a few men and helped to drag seven aircraft clear of the burning hangars. Nearly fifty-six years later, when Park was asked to recall the events of that fearful night, he thought he had been decorated for his efforts. In fact he was not, although his bravery certainly deserved official recognition. Vivian Voss had left the squadron by that time, but the next day he was given a graphic account of the raid by Captain Edward Griffith, one of Park's flight commanders. Park behaved magnificently, wrote Voss: 'He was badly cut about but he at once began organizing the rescue work. He himself carried several fellows out from the blazing huts.'

Three members of his squadron were decorated for their deeds that night. Private Kenneth Paterson received the Military Medal. For about fifteen minutes, 'while chaos reigned' (in the words of the citation), it was partly due to his coolness and disregard of danger that small parties were organized to remove machines from burning hangars. Second Lieutenant Frank Palmer (Park's Equipment Officer) received the Distinguished Flying Cross for helping to carry several wounded men to safety, even though he had himself been blown over by the explosions and was badly shaken. He organized a party, under Sergeant George Ridler, to continue that work. After the Gothas had departed, someone pointed out six boxes of bombs smouldering behind a small hut next to the Armoury. Ridler, with the help of Paterson, removed the boxes and extinguished burning embers. He, too, received the Military Medal.

Among the wounded was a young Russian, Second Lieutenant A. Urinowski, an observer. He had been going to play the part of a girl later in the concert and was wearing a long dress and flaxen wig. Captain Griffith last saw him being carried away, screaming with pain from splinter wounds. Sydney Whipple, who had been with the squadron less than three weeks, was hit in the neck by shrapnel and taken to a hospital in Amiens where he was put into a bed opposite Urinowski. Whipple recovered, but Urinowski died. Another American, J.E. Boudwin of 84 Squadron, had a friend killed by his side. It was a terrible experience, he wrote later, 'more terrible than any air battle.'

Sholto Douglas (then commanding officer of 84 Squadron and, like Slessor, destined to play a vital part in Park's later career) was another who never forgot that night. From his seat in the front row, he was able to dive under the piano when the first bombs exploded and then to sprint for the greater safety of a nearby trench before the next load came down. Twenty-five years later, while dining near Tripoli in 1943, Douglas heard German bombers droning overhead, 'apparently looking for a chink of light on which to lob some bombs' and was reminded of that night at Bertangles when they had found such a light. In fact, the night of 24 August 1918 had been a clear moonlit night and the Germans were well aware of the location of the several squadrons at Bertangles.

The next morning, Park led a flight of five Bristols (now the full fighting strength of his squadron) fifty miles north to Boisdinghem, west of St Omer. First-class staff work not only saw his squadron promptly restored to full strength but also provided a replacement squadron at Bertangles so that, by flying strong patrols over the area normally covered by 48 Squadron, they could conceal the heavy blow suffered. When Park and his four companions landed, they found new Bristol Fighters waiting for them. Slessor later wrote that 48 Squadron was 'taken out of the line for several weeks to refit' after the raid. In fact, the squadron was at work again within two days, Park and his air crews having already made themselves familiar with their new locale. Nevertheless, the squadron had been badly hurt. The effect of the raid on everyone's nerves was very marked, Park wrote, 'and the month of September was full of uphill work.'

Nine Bristols had been destroyed and two badly damaged. Most of the heavy transport, five hangars, the squadron office and several huts were also destroyed. Fifteen pilots and observers were so badly wounded that they were lost to the squadron (although only two died) and four more were slightly injured. Many ground personnel were struck off strength at this time, but it is impossible to tell whether these were lost because of the raid or because of the move north, nor is it known how many men were killed or injured who did not belong to the squadron. Luckily, the bombs dropped were small and, as Charles Steel (one of the wounded pilots) later wrote, many casualties were saved because Park had had all huts and hangars sandbagged to a height of four feet from the ground. As for the five Gothas, four returned home safely, but the fifth was forced to land on the British side of the lines.[3]

Park now had an almost new squadron under his command. For example, during the five days 9 to 13 September, seventeen new air crew were posted in; he also received a new Armament Officer with eleven men, and a photographic section of thirty-three men was attached to the squadron.

These imports restored his paper strength, but building up team spirit with so many new men was certainly 'uphill work'.

Early in September he had lost Edward Griffith, his senior flight commander. Griffith was injured in a collision with another Bristol and invalided home to England. Park drove him in the squadron car to Boulogne, where they sat on the beach for a while, talking about the year that was passing. After the war, when Park returned to England, he asked Griffith to accompany him in an attempt to fly to Australia. Nothing came of this talk, however, and Griffith did not see Park again until the early thirties. He admired Park, although he thought him too serious: dry as a stick, in fact, and quite without a sense of humour. In Griffith's opinion, Park was a tough commander, well respected and promptly obeyed, but too remote and stern to be popular.

Stanley Rycroft remembered Park's strong personality, his impressive appearance and his insistence on things being done properly, even to formal greetings at the breakfast table. And yet he did not find him 'remote and stern'. The officers' lavatory at Buisdinghem, for example, was a small, wooden 'two-seater' – almost as intimate as the cockpit of a Bristol Fighter, and not the place to share with a formidable commanding officer. One morning, as Rycroft pushed open the door, he saw Park already enthroned. He turned to leave, but Park smiled and called him back: 'No, no, Rycroft. Come in and make yourself at home.'

A few days later, on 28 September, an Australian pilot – Lieutenant Cowan – told Rycroft that Park wanted him and two other pilots to provide cover at dawn next day for some artillery spotters. Cowan asked Rycroft to accompany him and he agreed at once. Early next morning, anti-aircraft fire in the Lille–Ypres area was alarmingly accurate and the Bristols were badly buffeted. The wheels of Cowan's machine struck Rycroft's tail and he lost control. Rycroft's observer, Henry Wood, scrambled out of the cockpit and after some terrifying moments when the slipstream almost whipped him away from the Bristol, managed to sprawl full-length along the fuselage, gripping the gun-mounting with both hands. In this way he brought the tail down and Rycroft was able to make a heavy landing. Both men were badly injured but Rycroft managed to write to Park from hospital, telling him of Wood's bravery and quick thinking. Park at once forwarded the letter to Wing Headquarters and in 1919 Wood was awarded the Distinguished Flying Cross and the Belgian Croix de Guerre. Wood wrote to Rycroft in October from a hospital in Surrey to say that he had just received a friendly letter from Park, who was pleased with Rycroft's performance in getting the Bristol down safely and had so informed Wing Headquarters.

Another Allied offensive had begun on 28 September with a successful surprise attack along a broad front in the general direction of Ghent, in north-east Belgium. As in 1917, the intention was to clear the Belgian coast and turn the German flank. Park's squadron advanced twenty miles eastward to St Marie Cappel near Poperinghe on 30 September and three weeks later a further twenty-five miles to Reckem, near Courtrai, where it remained until the Armistice. Despite persistent rain and low cloud, 48 Squadron was constantly employed on every available task – photo-reconnaissance and bombing escort as well as strafing railway traffic, road transport and German troops. Park often sent out three or four groups of three aircraft under the most experienced leaders and would himself follow alone. On several occasions he sighted enemy aircraft at low level and fired signals, but these were never spotted quickly enough. By November, however, his new patrol leaders were mastering their duties and the squadron's offensive spirit was reviving.

John Pugh's war ended prematurely on 4 November when he and his pilot, Lieutenant J.F. McNamara, were forced down and captured. Park wrote to Pugh's mother on the 8th, describing the last mission of 'your brave son' who was now missing. He enclosed the address of McNamara's mother in case Mrs Pugh wished to write to her. This detailed, handwritten letter indicates Park's personal concern for members of his squadron. It was but one of six letters facing him after the combats on 4 November.

Park himself came close to becoming a casualty just before the Armistice. By this time, the constant strain of managing a considerable force of men and machines had practically exhausted his limited strength. Never a robust man, for all his efforts to keep fit, he was now so tired that – with hindsight – one can see that he was likely to kill himself in a simple accident. On 9 November, he chose to test a new Bristol. It was a routine task, one which he had no need to take upon himself. He made a careless take-off, allowing his right wing to strike telephone wires strung between two hangars. By some merciful combination of luck and skill, his career did not end there and then. He avoided the hangars and the buildings near them and managed to put the Bristol down on an open space. It was severely damaged and he was thoroughly shaken, but not otherwise injured. Two days later, the war was over.[4]

Park survived several forced landings. He was never badly hurt and must therefore have been skilful as well as lucky. At least twice he was hit over enemy lines, but managed to glide back to safety. On one occasion, artillery fire hit his radiator and he was saved only by having good men with him who kept enemy scouts away while he nursed his Bristol home. He came down near Dunkirk, where the fields were tiny and surrounded by deep dykes full of water: not a region favourable to forced landings. On another occasion, he was manoeuvring to attack some scouts when a 'wily little Hun' came at him head-on, firing into his radiator. In 1940 Park often remembered this frightening moment and encouraged his pilots to do the same: 'squirt in the front window, quite painless.'

When pressed about his victories, Park thought he might have scored 'about eleven or twelve'. Most reference books, admittedly repeating each other, credit him with twenty. He certainly did not *personally* shoot down so many German aircraft. In November 1918, an official report on his conduct of 48 Squadron credited him with nine personally destroyed and eleven sent down out of control. There is an Air Ministry list (dated 23 January 1920) which credits him with fourteen victories, a figure placing him fifty-ninth in a list of 130. Most of those ahead of him achieved their victories in single-seat scouts and Park had few opportunities for aerial combat in 1918. Pilot and observer in a two-seater obviously depended on each other: each fired as and when he could and it therefore seems unrealistic – as well as unfair – to attempt to separate their victories. The most one can say is that Bristol Fighters flown by Park certainly destroyed eleven enemy aircraft and damaged at least thirteen others to a greater or lesser degree.

Park thought the average German pilot in the First World War was more experienced than his British opponent. This was because German aircraft rarely came over the lines and therefore suffered fewer casualties. British losses were heavy and air crews were placed under constant strain. And yet they were better off, Park emphasized, than the soldiers. Off duty, airmen had many comforts and could relax completely. They lived in tents, much cleaner than the billets they were offered. Park had endured many verminous, damp or dusty billets in the artillery and was glad to have escaped them.

He was a horseman before he was a pilot and it is said that horsemen made the best pilots: both had to learn to handle sensitive, unpredictable beasts, calmly but firmly. Perhaps also it was necessary to love them. Shooting German horses disrupted the movement of guns, supply and transport waggons. It was a sensible thing to do but Park never did it. As a squadron commander, he never drew attention to specific orders to shoot horses. Other orders were carried out to the letter but this one was silently left to the decision of individual crews.

Park was also a soldier and an officer before he became an airman. He knew what it was to be in the ranks and had been taught what an officer should do. He had himself marched across the country he later flew over: he knew what it was like down there, he knew what information or help soldiers needed from him and he knew how to win the cooperation of his men in providing that information or help. After the First World War, officers at the RAF Staff College often remarked on the poor relations between officers and men in the Air Service during the later stages of the war. One wrote that in 1916 it was the custom for a pilot, no matter how tired, to visit his fitter or rigger before going to bed if work was being done on his aircraft during the night. This custom was weakening in 1917 and rare in 1918. Park, however, upheld it.

Lieutenant Stanley Walters, of 20 Squadron, was once ordered to deliver a Bristol Fighter to 48 Squadron. His commanding officer having urged him to show Park's men how to handle that machine, Walters performed a spectacular display over Bertangles, but as he landed his engine cut. He sat there in a dead aircraft, in the middle of the aerodrome, waiting for help. None came and Walters began to seethe. Eventually, a very tall mechanic appeared, who grasped the Bristol's wing tip and rocked the aircraft vigorously. 'What the hell do you think you are doing?' yelled Walters. 'Ah, the thing is alive,' replied the mechanic, who then walked round to the propeller, tapped it with a stick, and asked if it were not supposed to go round and round. Walters expressed his feelings forcefully until the mechanic came up to the cockpit and revealed his identity. It was, of course, Park himself. Very quietly, he reprimanded Walters, making him feel small and foolish. Walters served in the South African Air Force after the war and was posted to Egypt in 1942. There he met Park again, for the first time in twenty-four years, and yet Park knew him at once. 'It was not such a bad exhibition of flying in a Bristol Fighter really,' he said, smiling. 'He was a great man', Walters thought. 'His direction of 11 Group during the Battle of Britain will go down in history as magnificent handling and judgment.'

By the end of 1918, Park had already shown, on the ground and in the air, clear evidence of the character, energy and skill which would one day justify such a tribute. Reflecting in 1922 on the lessons he had learned during the war, Park made four points. Firstly, in a future war, squadrons should be more widely dispersed on the ground, but even if they were, continuous bombing – night and day – should be necessary to put an aerodrome out of action. Secondly, ground-strafing would best be carried out by small, fast, agile scouts with two or more forward-firing guns. Thirdly, he believed that 'close escorts are not as effective as offensive patrols over selected areas where opposition is likely to be encountered.' And fourthly, Park believed that 'against an enemy of equally high morale, we shall be forced to study tactics on the ground, instead of leaving decisions and methods to be devised on the spot.' Clearly, Park already had a sound grasp of some important problems in military aviation. Given his forceful personality and powers of application, a successful career for him in the postwar RAF could have been predicted. Yet, in the event, he needed all his determination merely to stay in the service. For some years, reflections on the principles and employment of air power were luxuries which he could not afford.[5]

CHAPTER FOUR

The Hardest Time

1918 - 1926

On 20 November 1918, Brigadier-General B.C. Fellows reported on Major Park to the Air Ministry. 'His work has been of a very high order,' he wrote, 'and he is now recommended for a rest. He is also anxious, if possible, to obtain leave to New Zealand.' It was then nearly four years since Park had left home, but another twenty-eight would pass before he saw New Zealand again. As for special qualifications, Fellows continued, he had a thorough knowledge of the duties of the commander of a squadron in the field. He was to leave France on 25 November and report to the Air Ministry on arrival in England.

For once in his life, Park disobeyed orders. By 25 November he was already in England and instead of reporting to the Air Ministry, married the girl he had met in London late in 1917 when returning John Milne's effects to his widow. He and Dol were married at Christ Church, Lancaster Gate, by the Bishop of Hull, two weeks after the Armistice and only twenty hours after Park's arrival in England. At home, Dol had been used to servants and chauffeurs; now, while Park was anxiously trying to make his way in the world, she had to settle for furnished rooms and travel by motorcycle and sidecar. Keith, always more concerned about appearances than Dol, found the situation embarrassing, but Dol took it in her stride. She relished change for its own sake and was therefore very happy as an officer's wife. She positively enjoyed the upheavals caused by frequent and unpredictable postings from one place to another. As long as she and Keith were together, she never minded where or how they lived.

Park had applied for a permanent commission in the RAF in June 1918. He was 'very strongly' recommended by his wing commander, but nothing came of it and in February 1919 he applied again. He was then at a training depot in London Colney, Hertfordshire, and named five officers not below the rank of Lieutenant-Colonel to whom reference could be made: Lieutenant-Colonels A.V. Bettington and H.A. van Ryneveld, and

Brigadier-Generals A.V. Holt, T.I. Webb-Bowen and L.E.O. Charlton. A medical officer noted on his application that he was temporarily unfit for full flying duties, but fit for light flying and general ground duties. Van Ryneveld, who was Chief of the South African General Staff during the Second World War, described him on 5 February as:

> A keen and highly capable officer of strong personality whom it is most desirable to retain in the RAF. Besides being a keen and skilled flying officer he is excellent at administrative work, looks after his men and every detail of his station and takes a full part in the life of the station. He is well educated and fond of games.

Park was also exploring the prospects of returning to New Zealand. On 14 February his father wrote to the Minister of Defence in Wellington, applying on his behalf for an appointment in the Air Service then being considered in New Zealand. James Park outlined his son's admirable war record with a no less admirable restraint, concluding that he 'has spared no pains by study and service to qualify himself as an efficient airman.' James asked only that his son, 'as a young New Zealander', be given a chance, 'all other things being equal'. Keith Park's name had been noted, replied the Minister, and as soon as Lieutenant-Colonel Bettington arrived in New Zealand (to advise the Government on aviation matters), all applicants would be considered.

Meanwhile, Park sought an appointment as instructor for the Canterbury Aviation Company in New Zealand. In March 1919 he asked for a two-year contract at £1,000 per annum and first-class passages to New Zealand for himself and his wife, who was now pregnant: their first son – Ian – would be born in October. The High Commissioner in London reported that Park had had charge of aerodromes in France and command of two training depots in England; he also had experience of no fewer than fifteen types of aircraft and 'possesses executive ability of high standard'. The Canterbury Aviation Company had been established by Henry Wigram near Christchurch in 1916 to provide initial training for prospective pilots in the Royal Flying Corps. Now that war work had ended, Wigram sought a competent pilot who understood aircraft construction and was capable of recognizing and exploiting prospects in commercial aviation. Bettington, who arrived in Christchurch on 25 March 1919, told Wigram that the only candidate with whom he was personally acquainted was Park, who had served under him in France, but that he was unable to judge his fitness for the position in question. He thought the salaries being asked were too high and advised Wigram not to offer more than £800 per annum. The job went to Captain Euan Dickson, a graduate in mechanical engineering from Sheffield University, who had lived in New Zealand from 1912 to 1916 before returning to England to join the Royal Naval Air Service. He had a distinguished war record, taking part in no fewer than 186 bombing raids, and had been decorated four times. On the face of it, he was a better choice than Park would have been.

Park's hopes of a position with the proposed Government Air Service were also dashed. In June 1919 he was informed that no decision had yet been taken to form an air service and there the matter ended.

> New Zealanders [said Bettington in a speech on 31 July 1919] made splendid fighters in the air and did marvellously good work. I mention the names Park and Brandon, amongst many others. The New Zealander is left a good deal to his own resources when he is young and he generally is a much better man in the air than the average Londoner. He learns to think and act quickly in his ordinary life.

Park may have been disappointed that his old Commanding Officer had not urged his case more strongly to Wigram, but at least he had the consolation of this public recognition in his native land.[1]

Park's first job after returning from France was to command No.54 Training Depot Station at Fairlop, near Ilford. He was there only four weeks, but during that time he had to deal with a nasty incident. Two of his three flight commanders were Stanley Lee and Cecil Bouchier, men who would enjoy successful careers and play significant parts in his life. There was little to do at Fairlop because scheduled instruction had ended and most of the cadets were waiting to be released. Lee arrived one morning to find that the cadets had gone on strike, following the example set at some army depots and RAF stations, in a bid to hasten their release. He and Bouchier were baffled and nothing was done until Park arrived. The Sergeant-Major told him that the men were in an angry mood, but Park merely asked him to assemble everyone in a hangar, where he would attend to their complaints. Park, standing on a box so that he could be easily seen, looked and sounded completely at ease as he spoke about the problems of dismantling a huge war machine quickly. There were no interruptions and when he finished, everyone went back to work. Park had no trouble communicating with men under his command at any time in his career. His method never changed: he simply explained what was going on in plain terms, making it clear that he knew his job and taking it for granted that his men would back him up. He had the personality, self-confidence, professional knowledge and clarity of thought and expression without which effective command is impossible, but in addition he had an uncommon concern to see that everyone understood his own place in the system – and, indeed, that there *was* a system.

From Fairlop, Park went to command the training depot at London Colney and applied for Lee and Bouchier to join him, which they were happy to do. Lee found London Colney even more 'dehydrated' than Fairlop, since there was not even a strike to liven things up. He and Bouchier did some 'fun flying': one would pilot a biplane, properly seated in the cockpit, while the other (without a parachute) clambered out and sat on the upper wing, presumably to enjoy a superior view and test his courage. That courage would, as Lee realized, have been subjected to an extra test if Park had caught them at it, 'for larks of this kind were not his idea of humour.'

Park escaped from London Colney to Andover in Hampshire at the end of February to undertake a course at No.2 School of Navigation and Bomb Dropping. As the school did no official training at the weekends, the commanding officer arranged voluntary long-distance flights. Between 19 and 22 April, Captains Stewart and Snook carried out the longest flight yet attempted – an eastward circuit of the British Isles – in two Handley Page 0/400 twin-engined bombers, then among the largest and most powerful aircraft in the world. At that time, such flights attracted great popular interest and the newly founded RAF needed all the publicity it could get. During that same month of April, competitors were assembling in Newfoundland to attempt the first non-stop crossing of the Atlantic (a feat successfully accomplished in June by two former RAF officers, Captain John Alcock and Lieutenant Arthur Whitten-Brown).

At the end of April, Park played his part in keeping the RAF in the public eye. He and Captain Stewart (who had just returned from his round Britain flight) completed a similar course in better time. They flew in a single 0/400 (Serial No.F3750) named *Last Days* with a double crew: two pilots, two navigators, two wireless operators and three engineer-fitters. In 28 hours and 30 minutes of flying time, they completed a circuit of 1,880 miles at an average speed of 66 m.p.h. Other, shorter, circuits of Britain had been flown before. In July 1911, a Frenchman had completed a circuit of 1,010 miles at 45 m.p.h.; an attempt on a much longer circuit (1,540 miles) in August 1913 had failed and a second attempt, planned for August 1914, had been thwarted by the outbreak of war. The flight of Captains Stewart and Snook was, however, the first to complete a circuit of most of Britain and that of Park and Stewart the second.

They took off from Andover in darkness one morning at 2.15 a.m., flew south to Portsmouth and then round the south and east coasts in poor visibility to Waddington (near Lincoln) arriving at 9 a.m., frozen and deafened by thundering engines after nearly seven hours in the air, more than ready for hot breakfasts and hot baths, hoping for better weather. They did not get it. Some work had to be done on the engines and it was not until 1.30 p.m. that they took off again, flying northward along the east coast to Alnwick in Northumberland, where driving rain and low cloud forced them to descend dangerously low – to no more than 350 feet – peering anxiously ahead for a sight of Abb's Head (north of Berwick), their cue to turn west for Edinburgh and a night's rest.

Next morning, they flew via Aberdeen to Inverness, then down the Great Glen and over Mull of Kintyre toward Aldergrove, Belfast. Here they came to the most perilous moment of the entire flight. The visibility was too poor, in Park's opinion, for a landing at the airfield, but his fuel was almost spent so he decided to land on a wharf at the Harland & Wolff shipyard. Although the light was better there, the wharf was only 400 yards long and 50 yards wide; there was also a stiff cross wind. It was a very difficult landing, but Park managed it. He knew that he could not take off again with any load, so next day he sent his crew by road to Aldergrove and took off solo with just enough fuel to get the aircraft there. The journey resumed that afternoon via Dublin to Bardsey Sound (an alarmingly long over-sea passage of sixty-eight miles in poor weather) and thence to Pembroke for a third overnight stop. The weather the next day was the best of the whole journey and Park flew to Barry, near Cardiff, before turning sharply south-west to Boscastle in Cornwall. He then flew to Plymouth and along the south coast to Bournemouth before heading inland to Andover.

Such are the bare bones of a splendid performance that many men would have talked about, with good reason, for the rest of their lives. It was, in the opinion of *Flight*, the leading aviation journal of the day, a 'remarkable and record flight'; Park's landing on the Belfast wharf 'constitutes a record in itself'. When Christopher Barnes was writing a history of Handley Page aircraft in the early seventies, he wrote to Park to ask if he cared to add anything to the brief press reports of his achievement which only hint at the fears and exhilaration of such a pioneer flight. Characteristically, Park merely replied that Barnes 'had got it more or less right'. Men and women who knew Park well in later years – or thought they did – were quite unaware of the fact that he had even flown such a large aircraft.[2]

In June 1919, a few weeks after this flight, Park was awarded the Distinguished Flying Cross. As a rule, Park took the greatest pleasure in the many honours and awards that were granted him during his long career, but not in this instance. It was, he knew, awarded purely to console him for a chapter of bureaucratic accidents which deprived him of a hard-earned promotion. The bungling began in September 1918 when he was shown in the Air Force List as *Lieutenant*, Temporary Major, when he should have been shown as *Captain*, Temporary Major. He had been made a Temporary Captain as long ago as September 1917 and believed that he had been made a substantive Captain, Acting Major from 10 April 1918, when he took command of 48 Squadron. The Director of Air Personal Services at the Air Ministry agreed, but when the New Year's Honours List for 1919 appeared, it announced that *Lieutenant*, Acting Major Park was now promoted to the substantive rank of Captain. Park visited the Air Ministry, pointing out that since he had already held that rank for eight months, no promotion had been conferred. The officials admitted that the intention had been to raise Park's substantive rank one step and were most sympathetic, but the mistake could not be rectified. For some reason which he could never discover, Major Park would have to remain Captain Park. All that could be done was to give him a medal. The whole episode infuriated Park and left him with a lasting dislike for the Air Ministry and the type of officer who was at home there. He was also left well behind many contemporaries in the race to the top, and making up the lost ground took years of exceptional effort.

In fact, during the middle months of 1919, Park came desperately close to being struck out of the race altogether. He was medically examined at Leamington early in May and found to be 'permanently unfit for further service' as a result of war flying, wounds and sickness. He was suffering from 'neurasthenia and general debility'. He had contracted malaria and dysentery and suffered gunshot wounds in the chest (some metal fragments remained there) and in the right foot. There was also marked evidence of nervous instability and the doctors thought it would be a long time before he was fit for any form of duty. Such was their verdict on a man who had within the last month shown the stamina to fly round the British Isles. No treatment was prescribed other than prolonged rest.

Park wrote to the Air Ministry on 7 July. 'Since May I have been on leave,' he said, 'and now feel so much better that I consider my state of health does not justify a Medical Board passing me *permanently* unfit for further service.' He asked for a re-examination. Two days later, the Air Ministry advised its bankers that Park would soon cease to be entitled to pay from Air Ministry funds. By this time, he knew that there was no opening for him in aviation in New Zealand and he had resigned from the Union Steam Ship Company there. He was twenty-seven years old, newly married, about to become a father, his health was officially considered impaired, he was about to be dismissed from his profession and he was 12,000 miles from home. Then, on 14 July 1919, an Air Ministry Medical Board found his condition much improved. Signs of nervous and cardiovascular debility were still evident, however, and he was therefore considered totally disabled for flying though fit for ground service.

The bankers were advised on 11 September that Park had been granted a permanent commission with effect from 1 August 1919. From that date he was a Flight Lieutenant (equivalent to Captain) in command of a store of Handley Page aircraft at Hawkinge in Kent. Stanley Lee found him there, 'not over pleased with his job as commanding officer of a dump for surplus aircraft.' Nor was Lee much better pleased with his own job, ferrying some of these aircraft, unwanted now that the war was over, to Hawkinge where the engines were dumped in the sea and the airframes burned. Early in 1920 Park's situation improved when 25 Squadron re-formed at Hawkinge under Wing Commander Sir Norman Leslie. For some months there was no other fighter squadron in the kingdom and Park therefore had his first experience as deputy commander of what passed at that time for Britain's entire air defence. Fortunately, neither he nor the system were then put to the test.

In 1920 it was decided to present a 'tournament' at Hendon, a display of flying by the RAF. Sholto Douglas suggested a flypast by three four-engined

Handley Page V/1500 bombers. There were some in store at Hawkinge and Douglas arranged with Park to make three serviceable. They flew one each and a man named MacFarlane the third. According to the editor of the *Aeroplane*, the display by the three bombers on 3 July was the tournament's highlight. 'It was truly a terrifying sensation,' he wrote, 'as the twelve Rolls-Royce Eagles roared towards the railings. Even Air Commodores in the cattle pens called boxes, and war-stained Squadron Leaders in the enclosures behind them, turned pale.' The editor was mightily relieved to see the tail skids pass fifteen feet overhead. So too was Trenchard, now Chief of the Air Staff. He was also mightily angry and delivered a stinging rebuke to Douglas. Trenchard's displeasure filtered down to Park, who was more than usually anxious about his career at this time. He and Douglas were never on close terms after this incident and it may help to explain why, twenty years later, Douglas got rid of Park as commander of 11 Group when he became head of Fighter Command at the end of 1940. The incident made a lasting impression in high places: on 8 April 1921 Trenchard announced that a second tournament would be held in July, but big machines were not to fly off 'as they did last year straight over the heads of enormous crowds.'

In August 1920 Park was sent to command a School of Technical Training at Manston, on the Kent coast, and there he remained for eighteen months. Apart from its lack of flying opportunities, Manston was an attractive posting. It was here that the marriage of Keith and Dol took on a pattern which lasted for the rest of their lives. Dol, very much an extrovert, loved plenty of lively company, but she also realized that her husband's natural reserve made such occasions difficult for him. Although proud of his integrity and courage, she made it clear to him that his ambition to get on in the service required him to master social graces. She encouraged him to play tennis, to attend dinner parties and dances and, best of all, to revive his old love of messing about in boats. Park's physical condition improved rapidly and on 1 January 1921 he was promoted to Squadron Leader – the rank (equivalent to Major) that he should have had two years previously. In May and June, however, he was given an unpleasant reminder of his war service: an attack of the tropical fever dengue, a notifiable disease, which he had contracted in Egypt in March 1915. He had suffered its recurrence in Gallipoli, on the Somme and once in Liverpool, but this attack at Manston proved to be its last appearance.[3]

Since the Armistice, Park had marked time while the RAF was transformed from a massive wartime to a small peacetime force. Conscious that ill-health threatened to end his own career, Park was also well aware that the force's very existence hung by a thread at this time. In 1921, however, even though that existence remained uncertain, it was decided to establish a Staff College. The first Commandant was Air Commodore H.R.M. Brooke-Popham, a pre-war graduate of the Army Staff College at Camberley and one of the first army officers to transfer to the RFC. He was an outstanding officer and among his assistants was Wing Commander Wilfrid Freeman, who would become one of the RAF's greatest officers. Brooke-Popham thought the first intake should be limited to twenty officers, who should be nominated, although an examination system could be instituted to select students in subsequent years. Park was among those nominated and thereby given a clear indication that he was marked out for an important career if he took his chances.

In April 1922 they presented themselves at Andover for the opening of the world's first air force Staff College. Among that first intake were at least seven officers who occupied vital posts during the Second World War, but even in that august company three stood out: Portal, Chief of the Air Staff for five years, Douglas and Park. Sadly, the rift which had opened between Douglas and Park at Hendon was not healed at Andover. Portal and Park, however, established a mutual respect which worked very much to Park's advantage in later years. At several critical moments during the war, Portal would show how highly he regarded Park.

'Our primary needs,' wrote Brooke-Popham, 'are the creation of a school of thought and the training of officers in the elements of staff work.' But the course would last only twelve months – too short to create 'a school of thought', though long enough to make reasonable staff officers. The list of subjects set down for study was formidable: the nature of war and its principles, imperial strategy, the tactics and organization of air, ground and naval forces, supply and communications, the relationship of economics, commerce and science to RAF affairs, intelligence, domestic and foreign policy. Basic staff duties – writing letters, reports and signals – were also to be mastered.

The year at Andover was active as well as studious. The college had its own flight of two Bristol Fighters and two De Havilland 9As, on which staff and students could keep in flying practice and put their tactical theories to the test. Brooke-Popham had hoped that horses would be provided as well. Instead, he got twenty-six bicycles. Park therefore found himself pedalling over Salisbury Plain, in the company of other aspiring Air Marshals, surveying sites for airfields. They also visited railway yards in London and sailed with the fleet in the Channel. They attended formal receptions because Brooke-Popham believed that the college should set a standard for the whole air force in social duties as well as in quality of work. To a great extent the manner in which the RAF would develop depended on the work done at Andover. Newly founded, the college was unhindered by precedent and everyone there in 1922 realized that he had a special opportunity – and responsibility.[4]

At the end of the course, in January 1923, Park was marked for posting to Egypt. During that month, his father and stepmother, Janey, visited Europe and enjoyed a holiday there with Keith and Dol. It was quite a meeting: Dol had never met either James Park or Janey, Keith had not seen his father for more than eight years and had not previously met Janey.

In March he was medically examined and found fit for full flying duties. His posting to Aboukir, Egypt, for 'technical duties' was therefore confirmed. Keith, Dol, their son Ian (now aged three and a half) and a nanny sailed for Egypt aboard a troopship on 5 May, arriving on the 16th. Park had for reading aboard ship an Air Ministry pamphlet restricted to squadron leaders and above on 'The Value of Egypt to the RAF' (June, 1921). The vital importance of the Suez Canal to imperial sea-links, it declared, was obvious. A large portion of British air power operated constantly in the East and until Britain's 'Eastern Dependencies' developed, technical supply and personnel must be provided via Egypt. Egypt was also Britain's principal base for cooperation with the Royal Navy in the Mediterranean and a convenient training area where men became acclimatized to conditions comparable to those found farther east. It was essential that 'the facilities for air work so laboriously built up' should not be impeded 'by any change of status of the country'.

In May 1923, when the Parks set sail, the Air Ministry had just compiled some 'Notes for RAF Officers Proceeding to the East for the First Time'. These gave sensible advice on the climate and on keeping clothes and quarters free of vermin; on diet, drinking and exercise. The various Egyptian stations were described. Aboukir, where Park was posted, was an aircraft and stores depot eighteen miles east of Alexandria. Although all service quarters were supposed to be fully equipped, the notes warned that it often happened that furniture was 'temporarily unavailable'. European goods were more expensive than in Britain, especially clothing, which must be examined carefully and regularly for 'objectionable insects'. On the other hand, sporting facilities were excellent and officers had privileges in regard to membership and fees. The colloquial tongue of the natives was easily picked up, though not essential, but bazaars should be avoided until the art of bargaining had been mastered. How this was to be done without experience, the notes did not say. All educated Egyptians spoke French, which Keith and Dol did not.

Park liked Egypt. The self-reliance, the 'make-do-and-mend' attitude and generally good team spirit of service life abroad were very much to his taste. He worked and played hard. After finishing the official working day, he would play tennis in the early evening for a couple of hours and then, after dinner, go back to the office. He was never one to hang about the mess, drinking and gossiping. He either rode, played tennis, went swimming, fishing or sailing (alone or with his family) or he worked. Almost every morning he got up in the dark and galloped towards the sunrise, turning back for breakfast only when the sun had cleared the horizon. But his health remained uncertain. On 20 September 1923, a few days after moving from

Aboukir to take up technical staff duties at the headquarters of RAF Middle East in Cairo, Park underwent a special medical examination. He was very thin and looked anaemic, the doctors reported. Park's answer was that he had been working hard recently, but was able to play a couple of sets of tennis without – he claimed – feeling exhausted. No more was said, for the moment, about his health.

In August 1924 a rebellion broke out in the Egyptian Army in the Sudan. Four aircraft of 47 Squadron (based at Helwan, south of Cairo) were sent down there, reaching Khartoum on the 18th, only six days after the first warning that they might be needed. In October Park was transferred to air staff duties at headquarters. The situation in Egypt seemed normal when on 19 November Sir Lee Stack, Sirdar of the Egyptian Army, was murdered in Cairo. Air patrols followed the delivery by the British High Commissioner of an ultimatum to the Egyptian government that it withdraw its troops from the Sudan. As in previous years, the presence of aircraft did much to prevent serious disorder. Sir Oliver Swann, commander of RAF Middle East, reported to the Air Ministry in December that before the delivery of the ultimatum he had discussed with the British army commander what action the RAF should take. They had agreed that aircraft should fly over the principal towns to show British power to the people and to observe if mobs were gathering. Strict orders were given to guard against sabotage and all personnel carried firearms and travelled only in pairs, on or off duty.

Park, of course, played only a minor part in these dramatic events, but they helped to prepare him for the important position he occupied in Egypt twenty years later. He was made aware of the uncertain balance existing between the several authorities in that country: British and Egyptian, civilian and military. His sensitivity to their interplay, his natural courtesy and readiness to listen patiently, and his evident liking for the customs and manners of Egypt enabled him to enjoy three successful spells of service there. Of more immediate significance, he earned the respect of Sir Oliver Swann who gave him his fullest support when the question of his health came to the fore again in 1925. He was brought before a Medical Board in June to ascertain his present medical category and the Board found him fit for full flying duties. However, he was examined yet again in September:

> This officer [the Board reported] has been flying for several years after being passed permanently unfit as pilot or observer. In view of his past history of neurasthenia and general debility together with his anaemic appearance it is considered that he would not stand stress.

As the future would show, this officer stood a remarkable amount of stress – not least that caused by the expression of this opinion. The president of the board decreed that Park was not to fly more than two hours a day nor above 5,000 feet nor to carry a passenger, though no restriction was placed on his performance of aerobatics.

Swann wrote to the Air Ministry in April 1926 on Park's behalf. He asked that his medical history be reviewed with the intention of placing him in a more favourable category or that he be regarded as a special case. Park, said Swann, was a very fine type of officer. He was a most skilful and keen pilot. Although his physique and powers of endurance were limited, he should not be handicapped by being placed in a low category. Swann accepted Park's statements about his medical record 'with the utmost confidence', but it was clear that there had been error or confusion somewhere. As a result of the report, Park, having done a good deal of flying in the past six years without ill effects or incidents, now found his activities very sharply curtailed and his promotion prospects, he believed, much prejudiced. In Swann's opinion, he had been over-restricted. Swann had more than once 'had the pleasure' of being transported by Park on cross-country flights and although he agreed that Park should not undertake flights requiring great powers of endurance, he urged the Air Ministry to ensure that his chances of promotion were not impaired and to permit him to carry out normal flying duties, in any type of aircraft, with or without passengers.

The Director of Medical Services at the Air Ministry commented on Swann's letter in May. He had studied Park's medical record and thought the root of the matter lay in Swann's remarks about his zeal. Many officers of great value to the service needed protection against their own enthusiasm. Since at least 1918, observed the director, Park had been suffering from the effects of diseases and strain incurred during war service, but he had reported sick only once in that time. His annual medicals, however, showed that he had never attained a high level of fitness. Swann was advised that Park's medical category was not below that required and did not impair his service prospects.

Nevertheless, it was decided to summon Park home in June. He decided to combine duty with pleasure by taking some leave and bringing his wife and children with him – a second son, Colin, had been born in March 1925. Sir Philip Game, Air Member for Personnel, interviewed Park and arranged for him to be examined by the Central Medical Board in London on 30 July 1926 to determine his present medical position. Once again, Park's career was at risk, but he cleared this hurdle comfortably and was graded A1B, fit for the full duties of his branch of the service. Instead of returning to Egypt, however, a chance meeting in London that summer was to land him a far more exciting job in England. From that time on, his career was safe and he moved steadily forward, out of the ruck.[5]

CHAPTER FIVE

A Little Golden Age

1926 - 1934

Hearts were young and life was good in the Air Defence Squadrons of ADGB . . . there was the time and the feeling and the spirit to perfect an art, the art of pure flying. It was a little golden age when the practice of war seemed to have lost its real meaning . . .

Peter Wykeham, *Fighter Command*

The first serious post-war attempt to construct an air defence system for Great Britain began in 1924. A committee formed in that year identified three needs (which were still to be causing Park daily concern in 1940). One, the need for a chain of command which would get the fullest and swiftest cooperation from the RAF, army and civilian components of the system; two, the need for early warning of approaching raiders; three, the need for rapid communications on the ground, with aircraft and between aircraft. The Air Defence of Great Britain (ADGB) was formed in January 1925 under the command of Air Marshal Sir John Salmond, whose chief of staff was Air Commodore F.V. Holt. ADGB had control of bombers as well as fighters, anti-aircraft gun zones and searchlight positions were marked out and an Observer Corps was formed. Its headquarters moved out of the Air Ministry to Uxbridge in Middlesex on 31 May 1926 and Salmond set Holt the task of finding him a staff.

One day in August, apparently quite by chance, Holt ran into Park at the RAF Club in Piccadilly. Holt asked him what he was doing and Park replied that he was in charge of the air staff in Cairo and had another six months to serve there to complete his tour abroad. Holt offered him a position on Salmond's staff and Park asked if he could take it up at the end of the year. For answer, he received orders one week later to report immediately for duty at Uxbridge. The Parks had only had half their leave and all their worldly goods were still in Cairo, but Dol, wrote Park, had been long enough in the service to 'follow the drum' without complaining. They packed up their seaside holiday and moved the children (together with their nurse, prams and a great deal of baggage) to an hotel near Hillingdon House at Uxbridge.

Park was put in charge of 'Operations, Intelligence Mobilization and Combined Training'. He was the senior of three squadron leaders and thus came fourth in the hierarchy after Salmond, Holt and Wing Commander J.S.T. Bradley, who was in charge of training. As the first holder of the post, Park found an empty office and blank files. It was, however, a great thrill to be in at the beginning, helping to create a new air defence system. He admired all his new masters: Salmond, Holt, Major-General E.B. Ashmore (in command of ground defences) and Brooke-Popham, the former head of the Staff College and now first commander of 'Fighting Area', the subordinate formation set up, also in Uxbridge, to handle all elements save the bombers.

The ideas about air defence set down on paper in 1926–7 had not changed in principle when war came a dozen years later. According to Park, the credit for this work lay chiefly with Holt and Ashmore, who drew upon their experience of defending London in the First World War. Fighter sectors, searchlight belts, anti-aircraft gun zones, balloon barrages and all the rest were created – though only on paper. Ashmore's equipment was even poorer than the RAF's, but he never lost heart although ground defence remained inadequate until long after the outbreak of war. Brooke-Popham's enthusiasm and hard work were vital to training and morale, helping to lay the foundations of Fighter Command. He was the first senior officer, in Park's opinion, to appreciate the value of scientists in the air force. Scientists were regarded with grave suspicion in the service and as late as 1938 Park knew of one commander-in-chief who refused to admit them to his headquarters. Park always insisted that Fighter Command was not created between 1936 and 1939; not even Dowding's driving force could have got it ready in time for war without the decade of effort before 1936.[1]

In November 1927, after fifteen months at Uxbridge, Park received the most highly-prized posting in the service – command of his own squadron. Later commands would bring greater responsibility, publicity and rewards, but none brought the same pleasure. This was the first time Park had had his own squadron for nine years; it was also the last time. Nevertheless, for sixteen supremely satisfying months he commanded 111 (Fighter) Squadron at Duxford in south Cambridgeshire and later at Hornchurch in Essex. The Squadron had just been re-equipped with the Armstrong Whitworth Siskin IIIA, a much improved version of the Mark III, the first British fighter of post-war design. 'Treble One' was already a famous squadron and ten years later would be the first to get the Hawker Hurricane. It was one of thirteen squadrons in Fighting Area and Park ensured that it was one of the busiest: in nine successive months it was three times top of the list in number of flying hours and second four times; it was third and fourth in the other months.

Park's career almost came to an abrupt conclusion on the night of 7 February 1928, when he crashed a Siskin at Duxford. He landed too fast, struck a ridge and turned over. The aircraft was totally wrecked, but Park suffered only cuts and bruises. Although shocked, he showed no signs of head injury and could recall the whole incident. He told the Court of Inquiry that he had only recently resumed night-flying after a lapse of ten years and, despite great difficulty in judging distance accurately in the dark, he had persevered. He confessed that for some time he had been unhappy about *motoring* at night, let alone flying. The Court might well have found Park's conduct irresponsible, but it accepted medical evidence that he suffered from 'night blindness' and even permitted him to make only local flights in bright moonlight, but he never did so. The incident shows Park's typical refusal to acknowledge any physical weakness in himself, but he was lucky neither to kill himself nor wreck his career.

By April 1928, the squadron was operating from its new home at Hornchurch. Park introduced a new work routine: day-flying was confined to mornings, and afternoons were spent servicing aircraft and preparing them for night-flying (cooperating with searchlights and anti-aircraft batteries). It proved an efficient routine and soon many pilots were qualified in night work. The squadron was to be inspected on 18 May by Salmond and Holt, so considerable time was spent practising a neat flypast. Unfortunately, the day proved wet and it was expected that Salmond and Holt would arrive by road. Suddenly, however, two Bristol Fighters emerged from 'the enshrouding gloom' (as the Operations Record Book put it) and landed with the great men aboard. They proceeded with the inspection as if the weather were perfect. Park admired their attitude and in later years made it a rule to carry out his own inspections in the same spirit.

Throughout May there was intense interest in the Sassoon Cup Race, a competition between fighter squadrons for a trophy presented by Sir Philip Sassoon, former Under Secretary of State for Air. Heats were run early in the month and the final was held at Hornchurch on the 24th. 'No.111 Squadron deserves congratulations,' reported *Flight*, 'for the excellent arrangements regarding viewing areas, car parking and the provision of tea in the Officers' Mess afterwards.' Park's ability to get these things right did not clear his path to the top, but an *inability* to cope, on such an important social occasion, would certainly have obstructed that path.

A few days later, four of his aircraft took part in 'observer exercises', each flying a predetermined circular course of five miles' radius, noting the time at which certain points were passed. These tests were carried out at high altitude and the time taken exceeded the Siskin's official limit of endurance, but only one had to land away from home.

Much work was done in June to improve formation flying, with the 'Battle Flight' event at Hendon in mind. On the 28th, ten Italian aircraft under the command of General Balbo (whose name would come to haunt Park in 1940

51

when appropriated by the 'Big Wings' advocates) were met at the coast by five of Park's Siskins and escorted to Hornchurch. They had flown non-stop from Rome and were to attend the Hendon display on the 30th. Four aircraft from 111 Squadron took part. Park himself flew in the grand finale – an attack upon an 'oil refinery'. In the Battle Flight event, the alarm was given that enemy bombers were approaching. The event was intended 'to demonstrate quick interception of enemy bombers' and was won by a flight of Park's Siskins. The time would come, in 1940, when his mastery of that skill won more than the applause of spectators at Hendon.

The first three days of July were spent perfecting the Quick Getaway for a display at Blackpool. According to spectators, Treble One gave the finest exhibition of formation flying and 'quick getaway' seen in their area. Later in July, the squadron took part in tactical exercises, intercepting and attacking bombers. In the proud words of its Operations Record Book, 'attacks devised by this Squadron proved very successful.' In August the Squadron practised locating night-bombers in cooperation with the Essex searchlights. These frequently caught and held the bombers until the Siskins were deemed to have shot them down (by firing a green Very light). Then came three weeks at Sutton Bridge in Lincolnshire for firing practice. All manner of equipment was tested during the year: cockpit heating, electrically heated clothing, oxygen apparatus, a new reflector sight and Radio Telephone (R/T) equipment, air-to-air and ground-to-air.

Park was promoted to Wing Commander on 1 January 1929, after exactly eight years as a Squadron Leader, the longest stint he spent in one rank. He left 111 Squadron in March, ending the happiest days of his career. In 1928 he had spent 158 hours in the air. Since the Armistice, he had topped the century only in one other year (113 hours in 1919) and never again would he fly so many hours under his own control. In the corridor of the Air Ministry Historical Branch there hangs a framed photograph of Park in full dress at the time when he commanded Treble One. He would probably prefer to be remembered there at that stage of his career rather than at any later, more eminent, stage.[2]

On leaving 111 Squadron in March 1929, Park was posted to Headquarters Fighting Area at Uxbridge for air staff duties. In that year and the next, he organized the flying programme for the pageants at Hendon. These were displays of the results achieved by a year of normal training. They were carefully organized and devised to show the RAF's skill in defence and attack, but as far as most spectators were concerned, they were simply magnificent entertainment.

Between July and September 1929, Fighting Area carried out combined exercises – with bombers, searchlights, anti-aircraft guns, the Observer Corps and army units – and also its own flying exercises, in daylight and darkness. New types of aircraft were brought into service and equipment of all kinds was tested. Operations rooms were improved. Proposals to introduce 'automatic plotting tables' were approved by the Air Ministry and negotiations with the Post Office were in train. Receivers would be installed at ADGB Headquarters and transmitters at Fighting Area Headquarters. Arrangements were in hand for circuits to link them with coastal observer posts. An Air Defence Landline Telephone Scheme was under study; the Wireless Telegraphy (W/T) organization was being revised and tested and R/T was planned for fighter squadrons.

On 5 March 1930, while driving to London, Park began to feel very ill. He went to bed and influenza was diagnosed next day. Even though he had been suffering from a heavy cold for a week, he had worked as hard as usual, often late at night. He spent a week in bed and then, after a couple of days back on duty, trying to behave as if nothing was wrong, took fourteen days' leave, but remained ill. A medical board granted him a month's sick leave and advised him to 'cut himself completely off from RAF work'. Air Vice-Marshal Hugh Dowding had been in command of Fighting Area since January 1930 and he reinforced the doctors' stern words to Park about driving himself into the ground. He heeded their advice – or concealed his exhaustion – for the next eight years before he was obliged to take another spell of sick leave.

Park returned to duty just in time to take part in tactical exercises in which Fighting Area's squadrons cooperated with a bomber squadron, a communications squadron and a couple of Fleet Air Arm units. 'Red Force' opposed 'Blue Force' and raids were so arranged that at least one passed through the territory of each sector, thereby permitting the fighters assigned to that sector to practise interception. The partnership between Dowding and Park was thus first forged ten years before the Battle of Britain.

Dowding was posted to the Air Ministry in September but the apparatus for automatically transmitting orders to fighter aerodromes (as installed between Fighting Area Headquarters and the Operations Room at Northolt) was by then fully tested. Defending fighters could now receive warning of approaching intruders over a much extended range: a gain of 3,000 feet in height and five miles in distance. The Northolt apparatus was to be extended so that it could handle two squadrons and similar equipment was to be provided at Kenley (in Surrey) and Hornchurch. The complete system, controlled from the operations room of Fighting Area Headquarters, consisted of an automatic telephone apparatus displaying orders in sector operations rooms and the pilots' rooms. There was also a daylight signalling panel on the aerodromes and warning orders were issued by signals blown on typhoon whistles.

During these months, Park played a vital part in the career of Arthur Clouston, who became famous in the thirties for his record-breaking flights to and from the Cape, Australia and New Zealand. Clouston, a New Zealander, went to England in 1930, hoping to join the RAF. Having failed his medical three times because of high blood-pressure, he made himself known to his fellow-countryman. Park, who had had his own troubles with medical boards, was sympathetic and arranged for Clouston to have yet another examination, which this time he passed. 'Wing Commander Park was my friend and saviour,' wrote Clouston, 'and I owe my career in flying entirely to him.' After four years in the RAF, Clouston was appointed a civilian test pilot at the Royal Aircraft Establishment, Farnborough, and enjoyed a distinguished career.[3]

In January 1931, Park became Station Commander at Northolt, an appointment which he held until August 1932. This was his fourth successive first-class posting since his return from Egypt in mid-1926. By August 1932, he had had six years in front-line home defence posts: excellent experience, one might have thought, upon which to build. However, he would spend the five years after August 1932 in positions which, while enjoyable and even prestigious, were far removed from fighters and home defence. Perhaps some policy was being followed, whereby he should acquire social polish and a broader outlook to go with his practical skills; perhaps not. Postings, then and later, were chancy things, dependent as much on the whims – or insight – of particular senior officers as on rational policy. His posting to Northolt certainly kept him in the eyes of important people: a communications squadron was based there which was entrusted with the carriage of the Chief of the Air Staff himself, and from time to time the Prime Minister was flown out of Northolt.

Park flew as often as he could, in as many different types of aircraft as he could, and was never deterred by cold or wet weather. Most of it was local flying, but twice he visited Scotland. He flew there in May 1931 to make preliminary arrangements for an air display at Renfrew in June, when he acted as officer in charge of flying. It was the most ambitious flying spectacle yet mounted in Scotland. Unfortunately, heavy rain on the Saturday forced them to cancel the day's show but Park sportingly agreed to give the Saturday show on Sunday. As many as 25,000 people attended, joy-rides were available and the bar and restaurant did splendid business.

He took part in an Air Ministry staff exercise at ADGB Headquarters in March 1931 and in April acted as chief umpire in a Fighting Area staff exercise at Uxbridge. Members of the Imperial Defence College visited Northolt in May and Park gave a lecture on the functions of the operations room. Instructors and students from the Staff College visited Northolt a week later and Park gave his lecture again. Several squadrons came to practise for the Hendon display. At that display, Park was in charge of the Set Piece event. Command air exercises were held at Northolt in July and a party of army officers came to observe. An Air Pilotage School was formed there in October and the first course, lasting a fortnight, began in November. The same pattern of exercises and visits was repeated in 1932.[4]

From Northolt, Park went to the Oxford University Air Squadron as Chief Instructor in September 1932. Sir Archibald Hope was one who learned to fly in that squadron and Park introduced him to 601 (County of London) Squadron, Auxiliary Air Force, which Hope joined in 1935 and commanded in 1940. Hope has pointed out that Roderic Hill, Guy Garrod and Keith Park all commanded the OUAS in the thirties and all three reached Air Marshal rank and were knighted for their services during the war. Evidently the Air Ministry selected only the most promising wing commanders for that position.

The university air squadrons were intended to encourage an interest in flying – attracting first-class recruits either for permanent commissions or as reserve or auxiliary personnel – but they were strictly civilian. No more than seventy-five pupils were accepted at one time and there was a long waiting list throughout the thirties. At Oxford, ground instruction was given in term-time at headquarters in the town and flying instruction at Upper Heyford (later at Abingdon). The annual summer camp was held on the Isle of Sheppey in north Kent, with flying taking place from nearby Eastchurch. The pupils attended in groups of twenty-five, for two weeks each group.

The Air Ministry issued a certificate of proficiency to pupils who attended at least one summer camp, carried out fifteen hours' flying (three solo) and passed ground courses. The certificate granted certain training exemptions to pupils who subsequently joined the RAF on a regular or auxiliary basis. Park administered the allowances for travel and messing and was responsible for the squadron's buildings, equipment and staff. He was required, in those days of austerity for the services, to exercise particular care over the consumption of power, both electric and gas.

He piloted an Armstrong Whitworth Atlas for the first time on 5 September 1932 and from then until he left the squadron, two years later, flew that aircraft and the Avro Tutor regularly. In November the squadron moved from Upper Heyford to a new aerodrome at Abingdon and Park persuaded the vice-chancellor (Dr F.J.Lys, the provost of Worcester College) to fly with him in an Atlas on the occasion of the move: Lys was thus the first vice-chancellor of Oxford to fly on official business. The flight lasted twenty minutes and Lys did not enjoy it at all. Park found this hard to understand. He himself was never happier – never more relaxed – than when he was in the air. The Atlas, escorted by five Avro Lynxes led by Squadron Leader F.J.W. Mellersh (Park's assistant), who had with him the university's registrar, was met at Abingdon by the Secretary of State for Air, Lord Londonderry, and Sir Geoffrey Salmond, now head of ADGB. Park and Salmond had to help Lys out of the Atlas, but after lunch he braved the November cold for a while to watch flying instruction in progress before returning to Oxford – by car.

In Hope's opinion Park was a good commander of the OUAS. An enthusiastic career officer and a first-class pilot, he set a proper example and attracted those who responded to a professional challenge. He was a strict disciplinarian and ensured, as far as he could, that the young men behaved like real officers at their summer camp. They were encouraged to make the RAF their career. Several did and nearly all became at least weekend fliers; some would serve under him again in 1940. Although his interests and sense of humour were not of the kind to appeal to 'young bloods', his straight ways, dignified manner and excellent war record appealed to the university authorities, not all of whom were enthusiasts for undergraduate aviation. Tom Gleave, a famous Battle of Britain pilot, was one of Park's assistant instructors in 1934. He liked Park and so did the pupils because he was such an imaginative teacher who believed in plenty of flying, including difficult aerobatic routines.

In July 1934, near the end of his time in Oxford, Park received the unusual distinction of an Honorary MA for his services to the University. The Public Orator, when presenting him for the degree, said that whereas his father had been a distinguished student of the earth – a geologist – the son's genius reached in the opposite direction. Park was described (in Latin) as 'a man noted for military skill, outstanding among heavenly charioteers for your consummate craftsmanship and bravery.' Park, always sensitive about his moderate school record, was gratified by this public recognition from one of the world's most famous universities. Thirteen years later, Oxford would pay tribute to him again.

Thus ended Park's busiest post war days as an airman. During the eight years between his return from Egypt and his departure for Argentina in November 1934, he amassed 917 flying hours at more than double the annual rate he was able to achieve either before or after. His two years at Oxford introduced him to an influential civilian world and the next two years in South America were to widen his social experience still further. In January 1935 he was promoted to Group Captain. From that high rank at his comparatively youthful age (in his forty-third year) he could hope to go on to important commands.[5]

CHAPTER SIX

South American Opportunity

1934 - 1936

In January 1933, Air Commodore Richard Peirse minuted Sir John Salmond, Chief of the Air Staff, on the question of air attachés. They should, he suggested,

> be selected from among officers who are in the first rank intellectually and socially. Their work is increasing annually both in importance and volume and they are therefore brought into greater prominence and closer touch with public men and affairs. Our credit in foreign capitals and countries must be in a large measure in the hands of our Air Attachés.

Salmond agreed and in July the term of appointment for air attachés was cut to two years in order to meet this new desire to employ only the best officers.

Group Captain R.B. Maycock, Air Attaché in South America, wrote to the ambassador in Buenos Aires in December 1933, making a case for an assistant. 'There is wealth here,' he wrote, 'and enthusiasm for modern aircraft, civil and military, but French and United States representatives outnumber me.' The Foreign Office sympathized, but the Air Ministry – despite its brave words – was reluctant to incur an extra expense that would, it thought, benefit mainly *civil* aviation.

Maycock informed the chargé d'affaires in Santiago on 19 July 1934 that Park – 'a very good fellow indeed' – would succeed him as South American Air Attaché. Aside from this unsolicited tribute, it is interesting to note how early Park had been chosen for this post. He therefore had several months to learn Spanish before he needed to use it. The Foreign Office informed Sir Henry Chilton, the Ambassador in Buenos Aires, that Park would be sailing for that city on 3 November, accompanied by his wife, but not by their two sons. Ian (then fifteen) and Colin (nine) were left at boarding schools in England. During the next two years, they would spend only the few weeks of their summer holidays with their parents in South America.

57

This posting owed much to the high standing of Dol's family in Argentina, although she had never been there. Her great-grandfather, Sir Woodbine Parish, had been Chargé d'Affaires in Buenos Aires from 1824 to 1832 and had concluded a treaty of amity and commerce between Britain and Argentina in 1825. Francis Parish, his third son and her grandfather, had been Acting Chargé in Buenos Aires and chairman of the Great Southern Railway. He had married Margarita Greenlaw in 1855 and their son, Woodbine Parish, Dol's father, had been a director of the Great Southern Railway. 'Our Woodie' became a Lieutenant-Colonel in the British Army. Like his father and grandfather, he devoted himself to fostering closer relations between Britain and Argentina, particularly in trade, investment and cultural exchanges.

Initially, Park was accredited to Argentina, Brazil, Chile and Uruguay, but soon he was also accredited to all the other independent South American states. In the whole continent, only the three colonial territories – British, French and Dutch Guiana (or Surinam) – lay outside his purview. He was to have an assistant, however, as a result of Maycock's support and the Air Ministry's growing awareness of the important work done by their attachés. Unfortunately, the man chosen as his assistant, Squadron Leader Peter Wood, proved not to be 'particularly industrious' (in the Air Ministry's words) and was retired at the end of 1938. Wood's idleness handicapped Park's efforts on behalf of British trade. Yet Park well understood that 'in these bad days', as a Treasury official wrote in July 1935, attachés had to act as 'business touts' and that his assistant had been expressly appointed to further the interests of civil, rather than military, aviation.[1]

On 1 March 1935 Park reported to the Air Ministry and to Sir Henry Chilton on his recent visit to the aircraft factory at Córdoba, in Argentina. The factory had become an important part of aviation in Argentina, he wrote, and increased local production of training and civil aircraft engines would intensify competition among foreign suppliers for a shrinking market. Córdoba had last been visited by an air attaché three years earlier, when it had still been under construction. Thanks to the generosity of Evans, Thornton (British aircraft agents in Buenos Aires), who lent Park their De Havilland Leopard Moth, the journey to and from Córdoba had taken seven hours; by express train it would have taken twenty-three.

The factory was easily spotted from the air, Park reported, and would make an excellent bombing target. It was far from any port (and therefore from all its imported raw materials), but road and rail links with Córdoba and thus with the rest of the country were adequate. There were no fewer than thirty-four separate workshops and offices, all arranged in neat rows with an eye to military precision rather than efficient aircraft production. Figures had been produced to show that factory-built aircraft cost less than imported aircraft, but Park refused to believe them. Even so, the factory had shown that it could produce adequate trainers and light civil types and therefore offered to British suppliers a market for instruments, accessories and raw materials. He recommended that training be offered in England to Argentine engineers and designers. The cordial reception he had received, Park concluded, suggested that few foreign attachés or diplomats visited Córdoba. The senior officers had entertained him to dinner and presented him with an engraved model of the first Argentine-designed aeroplane. They had also invited him to return later in the year.

A few days later, Park visited a military air base at Paraná. The lack of interest shown by British aircraft manufacturers in Argentina was, he recognized, a consequence of increased orders at home, but when those were filled another lull would follow and it might not then be possible to get into the South American market. Park advised the Air Ministry that Paraná was shortly to be re-equipped with a modern two-seat reconnaissance day-bomber. This decision to modernize offered Britain a clear opening, but Park feared – rightly – that the Americans would seize it. The Argentines, he emphasized, would no longer buy from prettily illustrated catalogues, even when printed in Spanish. Demonstration was essential. Paraná had not been visited by an air attaché since 1932 and no previous report had been compiled for air intelligence purposes. Evans, Thornton again lent Park their Leopard Moth. Unfortunately, a blocked petrol feed delayed him half an hour in starting his return journey. As he wryly admitted, this incident 'partly negatived the good effect of showing a modern British aircraft.'

In May 1935 Park reported on the military air units stationed at El Palomar, Argentina's largest air base. It had taken him longer, he said, to collect the information for this report than for any other base in Argentina because the Director-General of Military Aviation did all he could to hide its poor state of equipment and training. Money and labour had been freely spent and the administration, though inefficient, was more elaborate than elsewhere. The aircraft were clean, but their engines ran poorly because of inexpert maintenance despite 'a formidable set of printed forms and technical records in each hangar'. Flying discipline was negligible. 'It is quite invigorating,' Park remarked, 'to fly at El Palomar on a busy day when there are on occasion as many as thirty aeroplanes in the air over and around the aerodrome.' Park reported that he was pressing the authorities, tactfully he hoped, to consider elementary precautions, such as landing and taking off into wind. As for the fighter squadron based there, it carried out little gunnery or navigation training and never practised air fighting. 'The officers,' wrote Park, 'spend far too much time strutting about with their tin swords on when they should be either attending lectures or carrying out flying training.'

On 24 November 1935, Jean Batten – a New Zealand woman – landed in Buenos Aires. Flying alone in a Percival Gull monoplane, she was the first woman pilot to fly from England to South America. Enormous crowds turned out to greet her – among them Park, whose command of Spanish and imposing bearing were a great help in preserving some sort of order around her. He was dining with her one day at El Palomar when many of the officers suddenly stood on their chairs, placed one foot on the table, and drained their glasses. Miss Batten was startled, but Park explained that the bachelors were merely toasting her health. She smiled and everyone cheered. As Park pointed out, her visit provided one week of good publicity, whereas representatives of American aircraft companies were active every week and well supported from home.

There were men in the Foreign Office and in the Department of Overseas Trade who recognized the opportunities to which Park so forcefully drew attention, but the Air Ministry, committed to a major expansion of the RAF to meet the challenge of German rearmament, opposed all aircraft sales which it feared might hinder that expansion.[2]

Park's efforts on behalf of British aviation in Brazil were just as enthusiastic. In January 1935, the ambassador – Sir William Seeds – reported to the Foreign Office about flying displays given in Rio the previous September by HMS *Exeter* and USS *Ranger*. The American seaplanes had been obviously more modern than the British and the publicity was particularly bad because Brazil had been showing keen interest in purchasing new aircraft. Seeds therefore supported Park's proposals to offer free training in Britain to Brazilian service pilots as a means of fostering the pro-British sentiment which, according to Park, was evident in the Brazilian Naval Air Service. In March the Foreign Office invited the Air Ministry to do what it could. Eight months later the Air Ministry replied, offering to consider taking one officer. The Foreign Office was not impressed either by the tardiness or the content of this response; neither were Seeds and Park.

Seeds liked Park's pleasant manner as well as his energy and shrewdness. On 16 March, for example, in a despatch to the Foreign Office, he enclosed a note from his commercial secretary suggesting that Park be asked to urge Sir John Siddeley to find a more suitable agent in Brazil: the present man was at odds with the Brazilian Minister of Marine and this was costing the Armstrong Siddeley Company orders. Neither Seeds nor his commercial secretary felt able to influence Siddeley, but both were confident that Park could.

Park visited São Paulo in June 1935, having been informed that the firm VASP (Viação de São Paulo) was unhappy with the Pobjoy engines used in its two Monospar aircraft. He went thoroughly into the whole question, drawing upon reports by Maycock, the Consul General, the British Chamber of Commerce and his own enquiries and observations. The British manufacturer, he thought, took VASP's complaints too lightly. VASP shared an aerodrome with two other companies using American and German equipment and the Pobjoy failures had been widely publicized.

American influence was strong and growing. An engine repair shop was being built under the supervision of the Curtiss Wright Company, manned by

Brazilian civilians and military mechanics trained by Americans. They aimed at long-term sales by providing good servicing and Park warned that this would make it even harder for Britain to sell aircraft in Brazil. He cited the example of Brazil's Military Air Mail Service. The aircraft and engines used were American (Waco and Curtiss Wright), they performed well and the Brazilian authorities were therefore in favour of American equipment. Although the service was expensive, it offered a first-class training to aircrews and ground staffs and provided a rapid, economical means of communication in an enormous country which was short of roads and railways.

Park's admiration for North American energy and initiative, born during his term in South America, would mature during the Second World War. His readiness to express that admiration publicly, often linking it with criticism of British performances, was to irritate many senior officers in all three British services.[3]

Park also gave his attention to aviation affairs in Chile. In January 1935 he wrote from Buenos Aires to Sir Robert Michell, the ambassador, to ask if his assistant, Squadron Leader Wood, might be based in the embassy and concentrate on the west coast. Michell agreed, somewhat reluctantly, but soon found Wood's company congenial and reacted violently in May 1936 to Park's suggestion that Wood leave Chile for Peru. Michell considered Peru a 'useless' country and, having already resisted Park's attempts to get Wood even to visit it, was totally opposed to the idea that Wood should actually reside there. Park replied mildly. He was surprised, he wrote, that Michell objected to his making a recommendation to the Air Ministry about the employment of his own assistant, and sent Michell a copy of an Air Ministry letter clearly stating that Wood – like Park – had not been appointed to any one embassy, but equally to ten missions. As it happened, Wood was left in Santiago where he idled away the next two years before being retired. However, this incident showed Park's readiness to stand up to bluster even from influential officials; he would pass many similar tests during the rest of his career.[4]

In June 1935, Park spent ten days in Uruguay. The object of his visit, he reported, was to find out if Uruguay intended to re-equip her Army Air Service. Rumours to that effect had reached Buenos Aires and he now confirmed them. The Minister of Finance had told him at a dinner party that plans were being made to raise the money. Park had emphasized the merits of British aircraft and engines and kept local agents for British manufacturers informed. Here in Montevideo, however, as in Buenos Aires, rumours that the British Air Ministry had forbidden the export of military aircraft were so persistent that Park suspected foreign competitors were responsible.

Park had first visited Uruguay in February that year, when about half the air force was tackling a revolt in the interior. Four Tiger Moths apparently performed well: whenever they discovered a band of mounted rebels, they dropped bombs nearby, so that the riders were forced to dismount and hide. Their horses were then driven away by one aircraft while the others reported back to the commander of the government troops, who sent out his cavalry to collect the immobilized rebels. Uruguay, wrote Park, was too small to compete in military or naval terms with her neighbours and therefore her best means of defence was a substantial, efficient air force. He had discussed the point at length with Uruguayan military officers and although they said they agreed, only eighteen out of 950 were at present allotted to the air force.

Park spent a few days in Paraguay in November 1935, meeting the President, the Ministers for Foreign Affairs and War and visiting the headquarters of the armed services and several bases. The Chaco War with Bolivia had ended in June after three years of hard fighting. Although the advantage lay with Paraguay, both countries were exhausted. According to Park, the war had convinced the government of Paraguay that it must maintain a small, well-equipped air force and a civil airline linking Paraguay with the Atlantic coast. No budget for the services had appeared since 1932, although one was promised for the following January which would authorize expenditure on aircraft and ground equipment. Three years of war, however, had left Asuncion 'war swept' and more impoverished than any other city Park visited in South America. No previous air attaché had been to Paraguay and he was warmly welcomed in military and civilian circles. The Chaco War had been largely fought out on the ground, but Park summarized such aerial operations as there had been and concluded that the Bolivian Air Force, distinctly superior in terms of equipment, had missed a great opportunity to play an effective part in the war.

Park spent ten days in Venezuela in April 1936 and Edward Keeling, of the British Legation in Caracas, forwarded Park's report to the Foreign Office with the now-familiar comment that this was the first time any air attaché had visited Venezuela. With Keeling's help, he had met all cabinet ministers and many members of the diplomatic corps within two days of arrival. He also visited army and air force bases at Maracay and met the agents for British and American aircraft companies. Park thought the poor state of road and rail links should one day make Venezuela a good aviation market. The climate and terrain were suitable and there was money in Caracas. In the absence of a military attaché, he accepted an invitation to visit the military and cavalry schools at Maracay. The army, he reported, was organized, trained and equipped for maintaining internal order rather than frontier defence. The officers were poorly paid and disliked the current régime, which forbade them to draw pay and rations for more troops than were actually on strength.[5]

Throughout 1935, Park fought hard to wring from the Air Ministry an aeroplane for official use. Since his arrival, he wrote in April, he had flown in a variety of military aircraft with pilots who were by no means trained to RAF standards. Some of their landings had been 'indifferent' and on one occasion only his insistence on obtaining a map before take-off enabled him to locate a landing-ground at dusk for a pilot who had lost his way. His predecessor had flown with South American pilots two or three times and had then given up flying altogether for the three and a half years of his stay. But South America was enormous and many air bases were difficult to visit by road or rail. Moreover, it would be better for British prestige if the air attaché arrived by air. His American colleague had his own aircraft and deprecatory remarks were being made about Park's use of ground transport.

This request was refused, but in October Nevile Henderson, now ambassador in Buenos Aires, forwarded to the Foreign Office a second request which he strongly supported. It was true, wrote Park, that the capitals to which he was accredited were served by civil airlines, but his duties were not confined to capitals and internal airlines were non-existent. He could visit many more places by air, stay longer in each, and keep in flying practice, as a serving officer should. Michell (in Chile) seconded Henderson's support for Park's request and the embassy in Rio also wrote in favour:

> Miss Batten's recent flight has provided a brilliant and welcome advertisement of the excellence of British material, and the presence of a British aeroplane, piloted by a British officer in Brazil, if only for some three months in the year, might well have a more enduring if less sensational effect.

Despite this diplomatic support, now backed by the Foreign Office and the Air Ministry, the Treasury refused to sanction an aircraft. In fact, Park was forbidden even to pilot himself and during two years in South America he managed only fifty-nine hours personally at the controls.

Nevertheless, he travelled far more widely and frequently than any of his predecessors. He made a good impression among embassy staffs and commercial agents, British and foreign. Equally important, he was well liked at the numerous military and naval bases which he visited so assiduously. He obviously considered his job an important one and thereby conveyed the impression to his hosts that he thought them important too. He was eager to be taken everywhere and shown anything and always responded with an unforced enthusiasm which encouraged officers and men to talk freely about their common interest in aircraft, hangars, workshops, tool-boxes, landing-grounds, barracks, uniforms, sports facilities, rates of pay and difficulties in recruitment and training. It was at this time that he learned to inspect air bases swiftly and comprehensively. A few years later, his mastery of that art was so complete that he even demoralized flight sergeants in the Middle East and South-east Asia, one of whom advised his commanding officer, 'Tell him, Sir; tell him first. That way it'll cause less fuss than when he finds out for himself.'

Above all, Park had taken the trouble to learn Spanish and Portuguese and spoke both adequately. He was a good listener, unfailingly polite and, not least, he looked like a senior officer should: tall, slim, dignified and smartly dressed. His war record and his wife's South American connections were other advantages. Although Dol's Spanish was often wildly inaccurate, she had the confidence to use it fluently and such a cheerful personality that Latins found her more sympathetic than most women of the British communities. In personal appearance and fashionable dress she certainly compared with the best of them, but few cared to laugh out loud and tell jokes in public as she did. Park was not tempted either to patrol the cocktail circuits of the major capitals, waiting for work to find him, or to show the slightest condescension towards the officers he met, although he knew (and they knew) that South American aviation was primitive by the standards of Europe and the United States.

This unusual appointment also encouraged Park's latent interest in business, which would flourish, a decade later, on his return to Buenos Aires. During 1936 he had met the then obscure Juan Perón on several occasions. They would remember each other well enough to make their next meeting, in January 1947, a friendly reunion between the President of Argentina and an Air Chief Marshal representing Britain's most powerful aircraft company.[6]

PART TWO

1937 - 1940

CHAPTER SEVEN

Preparing a Defence

1937 - 1940

In December 1936 Lord Swinton, Secretary of State for Air, submitted to Buckingham Palace the name of Group Captain Park for His Majesty's consideration as Air Aide-de-Camp. Park had been selected to attend a course at the Imperial Defence College, wrote Swinton, and would therefore be serving in London. Swinton was informed that George VI 'entirely approves' his suggestion and early in January 1937 Park heard the good news, together with the information that the appointment carried additional pay at a rate of 10s 6d per day.

He attended the college at 9 Buckingham Gate, only a few yards from the palace which occupied so much of his time in that coronation year. The course was designed to further the education of a group of hand-picked officers of the three services, as well as some Dominion officers and civil servants. It aimed also to provide daily opportunities throughout a whole year for the practice of inter-service cooperation in staff work. Numerous experts were called in to lecture on their specialities: Sir John Reith spoke on broadcasting, Sir Alexander Cadogan on foreign policy, Clement Attlee on the higher direction of war and Hugh Dowding on air defence. That year, the students arranged a debate on Germany's colonial demands and their exercises included appreciations of war between Britain and Japan, Russia, Italy and Germany respectively.

Several survivors of that course had warm memories of Park. Sir John Balfour considered him 'a reserved, thoughtful and self-reliant person with a quiet sense of humour. The sort of man with whom one would gladly go tiger shooting – if one was in the habit of shooting tigers!' C.G. Hope-Gill wrote that 'that ardent spirit' was their star questioner: no lecturer got away without going through a veritable barrage of searching questions. He easily topped the 'Question Championship' in 1937, even though he was often away on the King's business.

In December, at the end of the course, Park was appointed to command

Tangmere, near Chichester, base for two squadrons of Hawker Fury fighters and one of Avro Anson reconnaissance/light bombers. For a few glorious weeks he enjoyed a last fling as a biplane pilot – flying the Hawker Fury – after three years virtually grounded. Then, in April 1938, he spent a week in hospital with acute streptococcal pharyngitis. That illness had immense consequences not only for Park, but also for Arthur Harris, later head of Bomber Command. In May the Air Ministry decided to send Park to Palestine; Harris was to go to Fighter Command as Senior Air Staff Officer, right-hand man to Sir Hugh Dowding. However, Harris wanted to go to Palestine and had a 'prolonged argument' with Cyril Newall, Chief of the Air Staff, about this decision. 'Eventually, by telling him that I had just got married and that my wife's trousseau was entirely tropical, I persuaded him to let my overseas posting stand.' It may be, however, that the result of a special medical examination of Park on 2 June swayed Newall more than Mrs Harris's new clothes. Park was found temporarily unfit for service abroad and sent on a month's sick leave, suffering from 'general debility'.

While on leave, Park learned that he was to go to Fighter Command in place of Harris. Harris's protest and Park's illness had together resulted in a decision to permit Harris to go to Palestine and Park to Bentley Priory. Had Harris, instead of Park, later gone on from Bentley Priory to command No. 11 Group, the conduct of the fighter defence in 1940 would have run along different lines. Similarly, the conduct of the bomber offensive would have been quite different without Harris's masterful direction. The original decision to send Park to Palestine shows that he was not in May 1938 considered a fighter specialist. Nor was he. Apart from his few months at Tangmere, he had not been close to front-line fighters since leaving Northolt in August 1932.

To complete his cure, Park learned that he was to be promoted. Owing to the 'voluntary and unforeseen' retirement of Geoffrey Bromet in May, a vacancy for Air Commodore had suddenly appeared and Newall recommended that Park be promoted on 1 July 1938 to fill it. He had been a Group Captain since 1 January 1935 and was twenty-sixth of 108 group captains at the time of his promotion. When a man reached that rank, he was eligible for promotion during the next four and a half years at six-month intervals. If not promoted, he would normally be retired once his current appointment ended. Park, then, still had a year – two chances – ahead of him when he became an Air Commodore.[1]

Fighter Command had been formed in July 1936 and its headquarters set up in Bentley Priory at Stanmore, Middlesex. As Senior Air Staff Officer, Park became in July 1938 second in command to Dowding and responsible for fighting efficiency. It was by far the most important position yet entrusted to him. He soon earned Dowding's confidence, however, and alarmed all who worked with him by his capacity for hard work, either in the office or in flying round the command's units or in sailing his boat at weekends off the south coast. Park was then just forty-six and at the height of his powers. With more than twenty years' service behind him, mostly in positions of authority and responsibility, he was a confident professional.

When he went to Bentley Priory, there was still resistance among some staff officers to the idea that its operations room should concentrate on broad direction, inter-group reinforcement and the dissemination of information, rather than on direct control. In defence exercises, it went against the grain with those officers not to interfere when the same picture appeared on the command's plotting table that was appearing on tables at the headquarters of individual groups and sectors. Dowding, fortunately, accepted that tactical control of the air defence could not be exercised from Bentley Priory, nor even, at times of hectic action, from group headquarters. He therefore encouraged the widest possible decentralization. Park grasped the structure of the command's planned method of operation and helped Dowding improve it. Long before he went to 11 Group in April 1940, where he and the men and women under his command bore the brunt of the Battle of Britain, Park had done much of the work necessary to make that group – and, indeed, the whole command – capable of prolonged and effective defence.

One of Park's chief concerns throughout his service at Bentley Priory was fighter tactics. At that time, the excellent Hurricane and Spitfire came into service, but so also did the Boulton-Paul Defiant – a two-seater whose sole armament was a four-gun turret firing to the rear. In June 1938, Sholto Douglas – Assistant Chief of the Air Staff – informed Dowding that he must form nine squadrons of these machines because 450 had been ordered. They had been ordered in the mistaken belief that the Defiant would emulate, as Edgar Ludlow-Hewitt, head of Bomber Command, wrote to the Air Ministry, the 'tremendous success of the Bristols in the last war'. But this overlooked the fact that the Bristol had relied primarily on its forward-firing armament whereas the Defiant fired only to the rear. Although Dowding expressed his anger at such an important decision being taken without his being consulted, Douglas argued that 'for work over enemy territory a two-seater fighter is best.' That might well have been true, but no successful fighter aircraft employed in the First World War (or, indeed, in any other war) left the pilot weaponless, facing forward, and required to fly in such a way that a gunner, facing aft, might bring his guns to bear upon a target which the pilot could not see. Donald Stevenson (Deputy Director of Home Operations) supported Douglas. Despite the fact that the Defiant, carrying two men and a heavy turret, weighed at least half a ton more than the Hurricane equipped with the same engine, Stevenson persuaded himself that the Defiant was 'slightly faster'. It was, in fact, markedly inferior at every point of comparison: level speed, rate of climb and manoeuvrability. Its inferiority to the Spitfire was even more pronounced. However, in response to growing doubts about the wisdom of the turret-fighter concept, Stevenson informed Dowding in June 1939 that he was to have six, not nine, Defiant squadrons. Dowding was still very unhappy: 'faced with the necessity' as he told Stevenson, 'of placing the Defiants where they will do the least harm', he wanted to use them solely for training, but this was unacceptable to the Air Ministry. In the event, only two such squadrons were actually formed and they suffered appalling casualties on the few occasions when they were used in the Battle of Britain.

Thus the first major issue with which Park was concerned involved Douglas, Stevenson and Ludlow-Hewitt. These three would cause him much heartache between 1938 and 1940. Against its will, Fighter Command was lumbered with an aircraft which it did not want, one which proved a liability in action. Park was given an early opportunity to see that Dowding and he would have to work hard to counter ill-advised interference in shaping Britain's air defence.

Park informed his staff on 11 October 1938 that the Air Ministry wanted a report on the action taken to meet the recent emergency, the Munich Crisis. What flaws had there been in the arrangements made? What improvements were possible? In Park's opinion, the command was short of aircraft. Five more regular and five more auxiliary squadrons were needed to give a total of thirty regular and ten auxiliary. More modern aircraft were needed: only five squadrons had monoplane fighters. There was no sector organization in south-west England or in the Edinburgh area. There was a shortage of aerodromes throughout the command and many of those available were inadequate. More labour was needed for guard duty, to fill ammunition belts and to repair bomb craters. More balloons and searchlights were needed and something superior to the Lewis gun was essential for aerodrome defence. Not least, more RDF (Radio Direction Finding, later 'radar') stations and wireless equipment were 'absolutely essential for the efficient operations of fighter squadrons in all areas of the United Kingdom.' The command's equipment, he thought, was so deficient in October 1938 that framing fighter tactics was an unreal exercise.

Park attended a meeting of the Air Fighting Committee at the Air Ministry in November to consider a report on tactical trials with high-speed aircraft. It raised questions which were to tax him during the Battle of Britain. How best, for example, should one attack enemy aircraft? How effective were various rates of fire? How dangerous was return fire from bombers? What formations should fighters use and what formations was an enemy likely to use? Another committee suggested to Park in December that guns be mounted at an angle to the line of flight. Park thought such a mounting could be useful for night-fighters. He was right: the Luftwaffe would employ upward-firing guns to devastating effect over Germany. At subsequent meetings, the 'optimum' range for fighter attacks was discussed and also their armament. Park asked, in vain, for heavy machine-guns (0·5-inch) instead of rifle-calibre weapons (0·303-inch). Again he was right:

the heavy machine-gun served the Americans well throughout the war whereas even the crack shots among Park's pilots in 1940 found it difficult to bring enemy aircraft down.

At the end of each training year, standard fighter attacks were revised and new ones prepared for the next year. On 29 December 1938 Park sent the commanders of 11 and 12 Groups a draft of the proposed instructions for 1939, together with details of tests he wanted the Air Fighting Development Establishment (AFDE) to carry out. The 'fire unit' was a section of three aircraft and although the AFDE considered a V-shaped formation the handiest, Park proposed to try more flexible methods: 'it is essential,' he said, 'that some latitude be left to the leader in the air in order to effect surprise.' But his hands were tied by an official ruling that single-seat fighters could only attack from directly below or dead astern.

A few days later, on 10 January 1939, he seized upon an invitation from the Air Ministry to criticize its *Manual of Air Tactics*. This assumed, he wrote, that an enemy would use the same methods as the RAF in dealing with raids, but the distribution and despatch of bombers was more difficult for Britain than for such a large state as Germany, whereas the problems of defence were simpler. Low-flying bombers (British or German) would not, as the manual suggested, enjoy 'comparative immunity' from anti-aircraft fire; all bomber formations would be at a grave disadvantage if they could be broken up and dive-bombers were particularly vulnerable to fighters. 'In Home Defence work,' Park argued, 'tactics do not interest the leader of a formation until he has been brought in sight of his target by the ground organization.' That target, he warned, might comprise fighters as well as bombers: 'The possibility of bombers having fighter escorts even in attacks on London should not be overlooked.'

He sent four copies of a new set of instructions, 'Fighter Command Attacks, 1939', to the Air Ministry in February. When submitting them to Dowding for approval, Park characteristically drew his attention to the officers who had actually done the work of sifting ideas, planning exercises and drawing diagrams. These instructions were designed to assist new squadron pilots to learn standard attacks upon bombers flying in formation. They assumed that increased fire power permitted decisive effect to be achieved at greater range. Park emphasized that they were not a set of *drills*: formation leaders must use their initiative in air fighting tactics. Good teamwork would be important and pilots would have to take advantage of blind areas, cloud and sun; above all, they should seek to surprise their opponents. Inevitably, however, elaborate precautions were laid down for peacetime training. These precautions, in practice, were so carefully followed that the principles of attack were overlooked. For example, day attacks were to be made only in formation and at specified, safe heights; all aircraft were to avoid cloud; pilots were not to change their aim after starting their attack-run and were not to lose sight of other aircraft either in their own formation or in the formation under attack.

71

Leslie Gossage, commander of 11 Group, wrote to Dowding in March 1939 to say that he had been asked at the Staff College if *annihilation of a few* was not preferable to the command's policy of the *interception of many*. No one, he had replied, doubted the desirability of annihilation, but the command lacked the means and the information to achieve it. The controller assigned enough aircraft to take serious toll of raids of which he had firm information, received early enough to enable him to position aircraft effectively. But if his information was uncertain and part of his force already airborne to deal with the unexpected, he would have to use what he could and reinforce as he could. He certainly could not keep strong patrols aloft in the hope of striking an annihilating blow because they might never get a chance to do anything. The whole matter of interception, thought Gossage, hinged on information. As it improved, so did the prospects for annihilation.

Dowding replied that the intention was to match machine with machine. If too many were sent up, they would be caught refuelling and rearming when a second wave came in; if too few were sent up, there would be losses for insufficient return. But ideal tactics could not even be practised because most squadrons had not yet had their monoplane fighters long enough to be familiar with them and too few target aircraft were provided to permit realistic interception practice. The command's work was always done in unreal conditions, except that training in small units brought out leadership qualities. The squadron, concluded Dowding, would remain the largest unit, though two or more might be paired against a large force. This exchange between Gossage and Dowding summarizes the principles Park followed and the problems he faced throughout his service in Fighter Command.

In August 1939 the Air Ministry asked Dowding if a fighter formation exceeding squadron strength could be mustered and operated as a single unit in battle. Wing Commander G.M. Lawson, a member of Park's staff, provided Dowding with the material for his answer. The squadron, in Lawson's view, was the largest unit able to climb, manoeuvre and attack effectively. A wing formation would have to split up and would in any case be impracticable in bad visibility or at low height. Time was also a vital consideration because an enemy should always be attacked as soon as possible. Lawson did not think that large bomber formations would hold together as tightly as the Air Ministry feared, once fighters attacked them. 'It might be possible,' he thought, 'to train our regular fighter squadrons in wing tactics in peace, but it is doubtful whether it would be practicable to maintain that high standard in war.' A year later, during the Battle of Britain, Park would exactly follow Lawson's line.

For some months after the outbreak of war in September, Dowding and Park had little fresh evidence to guide them in shaping fighter tactics. Then, in January 1940, Park received a note from Bomber Command on lessons learned as a result of recent Wellington raids. It stressed the need to fly 'shoulder to shoulder'; the tighter the formation the safer. He circulated it to the group commanders with a note urging them to instruct fighters to attack in formation, not singly. He was concerned at Bomber Command's report that German fighters were making *beam* attacks (from side on), using fixed forward-firing guns. This was a form of attack not seriously considered by Fighter Command in recent years because it was believed that the high speed of modern aircraft made full deflection attacks impracticable. Park still thought they were, for average pilots, though the attempt would be a useful distraction if combined with attacks from other quarters.

In February 1940 the Air Ministry sent Fighter Command a report by General Harcourt, commander of the French fighter units, on recent tactics. The report's principal disclosure was the paucity of interceptions achieved despite active patrolling. This was because France lacked an RDF system linked to a ground-to-air and air-to-air radio system. Harcourt stressed the importance of fighters keeping together during their approach to enemy formations: 'an attacking force which dashes into battle without a co-ordinated plan and proper control' would be ineffective. Park agreed wholeheartedly with this opinion.

Within a few more weeks, he would have ample opportunity to apply all the lessons on fighter tactics which he had studied since July 1938. Many principles were well enough learned in the biplane age, but others were new. During his term at headquarters few certain answers were found to questions so anxiously asked. Apart from experiments at the AFDE, the main source of information came from Home Defence Exercises. There were many of these and all involved Park closely.[2]

Bomber Command's reluctance to cooperate enthusiastically in these exercises caused Park much vexation during the year before the war. He wrote bluntly to Ludlow-Hewitt in December 1938, criticizing the absence from his instructions regarding monthly exercises of any mention of the need to test fighter groups in the control of their sectors and squadrons; nor was any awareness shown of the need to test the RDF and air-raid warning systems. Ludlow-Hewitt's list of objectives was concerned solely with his own bomber command. Park invited him to revise his instructions. For example, Ludlow-Hewitt permitted his groups to carry out raids by single aircraft, but Park reminded him that in monthly exercises civil aircraft and those of other commands were not excluded from the exercise area. Confusion could only be avoided by instructing observer posts not to report single aircraft. Single bombers would therefore not be reported to operations rooms and would not be intercepted by fighters; no one would benefit. Ludlow-Hewitt, greatly senior to Park, considered these criticisms out of order. Dowding, fortunately, did not – and he was senior even to Ludlow-Hewitt.

After the exercise in January 1939, Park wrote to two bomber group commanders, pointing out to one that he had attached an out-of-date map of the area covered by RDF stations to his operation orders and to the other that he was evidently unaware of the area covered since only two bomber raids had used it. The relevant information had been sent to Bomber Command Headquarters, but not forwarded to the groups. Such slackness contrasts sharply with Fighter Command's alertness under Dowding and Park.

Even the simplest matters baffled Bomber Command's staff officers. As Dowding minuted Park on 24 May 1939:

> I am a much misunderstood man! I have never asked that 'one particular type of aircraft' shall be used to represent friendly bombers. . . . My point is that *all* aircraft of any particular type shall be friendly or *all* enemy.

Park tried to explain this to Norman Bottomley, his opposite number at Bomber Command, the next day. Anti-Aircraft Command supported Dowding's stand, wrote Park, and he therefore insisted on this principle. Park added that although the Chief of the Air Staff had ruled that all Blenheim squadrons were to be used as friendlies, Dowding would forego the advantages of this ruling in view of Ludlow-Hewitt's objections. He yielded as often as he dared in an effort to exact genuine cooperation, but to no avail. As Park reported to the Air Ministry, bombers should start their approach 100 miles out to sea if the fighters and RDF system were to have realistic training, but Ludlow-Hewitt refused to permit his single-engined squadrons to proceed more than ten miles from the coast.

Park wrote again to Bottomley on 31 May. It was generally agreed, he said, that the Germans were unlikely to employ single aircraft by day against inland targets. Would he therefore stop using single aircraft in the exercises? In Bomber Command's opinion, replied Bottomley, the Germans might very well use single aircraft. He flatly rejected Park's criticism of his command's strategy and tactics. Park tried again on 8 June. The commanding officer of 2 Group, he wrote, who was so confident of the success achieved in target-finding by his crews, should remember that they were operating over country which they knew by heart. They might not find it so easy over foreign country in poor visibility. Sadly, this warning was disregarded by Bomber Command.

Park was also writing at this time to Bomber Command on behalf of the Research Station at Bawdsey in Suffolk. The superintendent, A.P. Rowe, wanted a copy of bomber raid schedules two or three days before the August exercise. They would be useful, he told Park, where large raids were planned, coming in from far out to sea. With advance warning, scientists would be able to send men to the RDF stations concerned in tracking and study the results. Park did what he could, but Bomber Command was unable to supply the information required and he therefore suggested to Rowe that a special exercise be arranged.

On 20 June Park issued instructions for 11 Group's exercise on 8–9 July

1939. Bomber Command would simulate an attack on southern England from east of Great Yarmouth under something like wartime conditions. The accepted limitations were that aircraft would approach from seaward not lower than 2,000 feet as far as territorial waters, raids would be distributed over the whole exercise area and not less than three aircraft would take part in each daylight raid. Attacking bombers would take evasive action from fighters and anti-aircraft guns in daylight and from searchlights in darkness. They would not attempt to evade fighters in darkness. No balloons would be flown above 500 feet and blackouts would be enforced from 1 a.m. to 4 a.m. in rural counties. No attempt was made to black out London and the south-east, the obvious target areas. Park sent a similar letter to 12 Group, which exercised on 13–14 July over northern England against an attack coming from east of Hartlepool.

A conference was held at Bentley Priory on the 24th to discuss the lessons of both exercises. Dowding considered the interception rate achieved by 11 Group (sixty per cent) reasonable. The rate achieved by 12 Group was lower because it started on interception technique later and RDF equipment in its area was less reliable. In neither group could low-level raids be consistently identified. There had also been unnecessary delay in allotting raids to sectors. Group controllers were to specify the tactical unit required (squadron, flight or section), but sector commanders were to choose the actual unit. Dowding and Park were gravely disturbed by the fact that too few bombers were made available for a realistic exercise – some observers thought it had been cancelled. Practice against large formations, obviously essential, was impossible before August 1939 because Ludlow-Hewitt refused to provide them.

A week after the August exercise, Trafford Leigh-Mallory, commander of 12 Group, submitted his report on it. Two points alarmed Park and his staff officers. Firstly, a low-level raid caught some of Leigh-Mallory's sectors by surprise and caused him to put up strong standing patrols for their protection. Park thought Leigh-Mallory overreacted, diverting too many fighters to local defence from their major task of intercepting bombers threatening vital industrial targets. And secondly, Leigh-Mallory's operations room was actually evacuated for ten minutes during a night attack. Dowding promptly directed Leigh-Mallory to ensure that in future no operations room, group or sector, was evacuated unless so damaged as to be useless. This was not the first time that Park and his staff had expressed disquiet about Leigh-Mallory's handling of his group and Park clearly had no high opinion of his ability long before their quarrels during and after the Battle of Britain.[3]

Exercises, like tactics, depended upon control and control depended upon operations rooms. Warrant Officer R.W. Woodley compiled a report on them in 1938. He described the equipment used in every room, outlining the procedures followed in each. Park was greatly impressed by Woodley's conscientious work and sent two copies to the Air Ministry in September. He asked that a certificate expressing approval of Woodley's work be placed in his record of service and six months later this was actually done. The Air Ministry also decided to keep Woodley's report up-to-date and enlarged to include descriptions of the equipment and procedures at command headquarters.

Park and Squadron Leader Raymund Hart, who had a distinguished career ahead of him as a technical expert, worked together on operations room problems: Hart on the equipment, Park on the practical layout. Hart had been attached to Bawdsey in 1936 to supervise RDF training and to act as a link between the scientists there and command headquarters. He convinced Park that the plotting on the general situation map was too elaborate. There were vital questions to be answered before the plot was useful. For example, were the indicated aircraft friendly or hostile? Were there duplications caused by reports from two or more RDF stations or Observer Corps posts? Park therefore introduced a second table on which could be displayed a clean 'filtered' – plot once queries had been settled. Only this filtered plot should be passed to the main table. Dowding rejected the idea of a second table when Park suggested it, so he secretly set it up in the basement at Bentley Priory and had power lines installed or reconnected to suit. For some time all that Dowding noticed was that 'his general situation map seemed to be much more readable and his Operations Room far more quiet and well-regulated.' When Park judged the time right, he unveiled his basement secret and Dowding was convinced.

After the outbreak of war, Park was more anxious than ever to improve and standardize interception procedures throughout the command – now extended by the formation of 13 Group (under Richard Saul) to cover the eastern coasts of northern England and Scotland. He proposed to try out 'certain new items of equipment' that had been designed at Bawdsey or at the Royal Aircraft Establishment in the sector operations room at Biggin Hill, long regarded as an experimental station for interception methods. In November 1939 he invited the group commanders to suggest improvements. Gossage and Saul responded promptly; Leigh-Mallory – following a prod from Park – sent a brief, formal reply.

The Air Ministry had advised Park in December that it was considering using women from the Women's Auxiliary Air Force, instead of men, in operations rooms. They performed the duties of plotters and tellers admirably and would be properly protected in underground rooms. In forward-surface-rooms, however, they would be required to remain on duty and work with extreme accuracy during action; it would not be practicable for them to take cover and the Air Ministry was reluctant to employ them in such exposed places. Watches in underground rooms should be composed entirely of women, otherwise they would think they were being supervised as potentially unreliable. Park replied on 10 January 1940. He agreed that WAAFs made satisfactory plotters and tellers and had no objection to women in forward areas. They were no less protected there than on other stations nor did he believe that women in mixed watches would feel 'supervised'. Although he did not know how women would react to air attack, he believed the presence of men would give them confidence. But he was worried in case women were permitted to resign or be transferred out of operations rooms whenever they chose: the continuity of routine would be broken and security jeopardized. He also wanted three women to replace two men because 'women are less able to stand up to the physical strain than are airmen.'[4]

Radar was vital to the effective functioning of operations rooms and Park kept in constant touch with the latest improvements. In October 1938 he reported to the Air Ministry that Mr Rowe, superintendent at Bawdsey, had told Dowding that considerable progress had been made since August by RDF stations in counting aircraft approaching from seaward. Until August, they could distinguish between one, two or three and over three up to fifty miles away; between fifty and eighty miles, they could only distinguish between one and more than one. They were now capable of much better, but progress was handicapped by the lack of large numbers of aircraft to use in trials. Since Dowding placed great emphasis on such trials, Park hoped the Air Ministry would arrange for sufficient aircraft to be provided.

An informal arrangement was made between Rowe and Hart for a small group of scientists to move to Bentley Priory in the event of war. A team moved there for the summer exercises of 1939 to observe the operation of Park's filter room and proved so helpful that Dowding asked for a section to be permanently based in his headquarters. At the same time, a second group was sent by Rowe to observe group controllers dealing with the information provided by the radar chain. They concentrated on control procedures, equipment and techniques for controlling aircraft during an actual interception attempt. This team was released from Bawdsey under pressure from Park and became the Operational System Research Section.

The two sections were established at Bentley Priory by September 1939 and a scientist from Bawdsey called Larnder was appointed to lead the combined team. The unusual step of appointing civilians to an operational headquarters was taken because radar was a new device and the analysis of results was best conducted by scientists (who happened to be civilians). Rowe and Larnder found Park helpful and sympathetic in dealing with the Air Ministry and Bomber Command. They were deeply concerned in the summer of 1939 with the problem of counting aircraft and were grateful to Park for his efforts to obtain the necessary cooperation, even though these were not always successful.

In December, Park told Dowding that group and sector controllers regarded RDF as 'black magic'. They accepted its reports as totally accurate and this accounted for some failures to intercept. Their over-reliance on it was 'our fault' because no information had been issued about its limitations. He proposed to circulate a note compiled from material supplied by Hart out of his long experience with the RDF chain. Dowding agreed and Park's note appeared on 13 December. The chain of coastal RDF stations between the Isle of Wight and Aberdeen had been hastily erected, he wrote, with 'scratch equipment', now being replaced as quickly as possible. There were still gaps in the coastal coverage and stations could not report aircraft flying below 1,000 feet. Group and sector controllers were to bear in mind these limitations in the system: range and position were accurate to within about one mile; height was accurate to within plus or minus 1,000 feet in the Thames estuary and plus or minus 2,000 feet elsewhere; up to three aircraft could be accurately counted, but more than three could mean as many as nine and more than nine *any* number over nine; the time lag was about ninety seconds from the sighting by the RDF operator to the plot appearing on group and sector tables. A research section had been set up at command headquarters to devise improvements and Park went out of his way to commend Hart's contribution, although as late as 8 March 1940 Dowding wrote that 'RDF is very capricious and unreliable, but it is better than nothing, as being the best evidence we have of what is going on over the sea.'[5]

Throughout Park's time at Bentley Priory, questions about sector organization and the number of squadrons to be allotted to each sector were regularly under discussion. Leigh-Mallory sent him a memorandum in October 1938 on the air defence of England north of London. It was based on the assumption, as Park told Dowding, that Britain would continue to be defended by two-gun biplanes rather than eight-gun monoplanes. It emphasized local defence at the expense of area defence and showed no appreciation of the advantages gained by the extension of the searchlight area and improved wireless communications. To implement his plan, Leigh-Mallory wanted twenty-nine of the country's forty-one fighter squadrons, leaving only twelve for London – the most vital area – not to mention Portsmouth or Bristol. Park had spoken to him, but without effect, and suggested that Dowding do so. Dowding agreed. Leigh-Mallory's memorandum, he told Park, 'shows a misconception of the basic ideas of fighter defence.' Unfortunately, Dowding did not seek his replacement.

Park wrote to Gossage and Leigh-Mallory in November 1938 to say that Dowding inclined to transfer Debden sector to 12 Group in order to relieve congestion in Gossage's operations room. When 13 Group was formed in 1939, it would assume responsibility for northern Britain, leaving Leigh-Mallory 'a light task' unless he was given Debden. But Leigh-Mallory replied that he did not want Debden 'because it means becoming actively involved in the defence of London, which it is felt should be the concern of one commander only.' Park told Dowding that Leigh-Mallory's real reason for

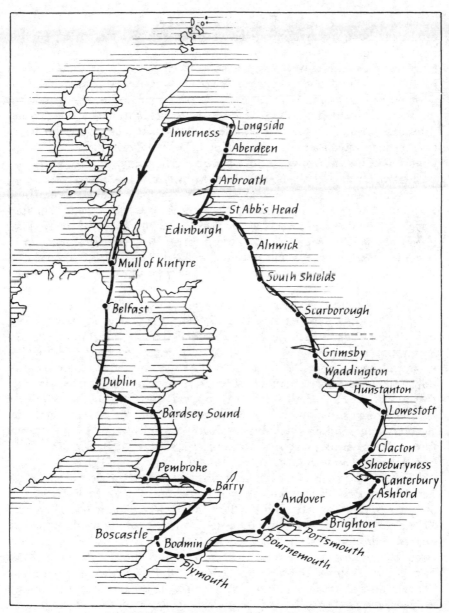

4: Park's round-Britain flight, April 1919

refusing Debden was that he feared it would weaken his claim to keep Church Fenton sector (covering most of Yorkshire and Lancashire north of the Humber). He had admitted to Park that if Church Fenton went to 13 Group, as intended, he would then like to have Debden. As for Gossage, Park continued, it would be 'unnatural' to expect him to give up part of his command, but members of his staff had admitted the difficulty of controlling six sectors and fifteen squadrons. Yet 'they lightheartedly talk of controlling ten sectors with twenty-eight squadrons.' As it happened, Debden would form part of 12 Group and Church Fenton part of 13 Group until August 1940. Debden was then transferred to 11 Group and Church Fenton to 12 Group.

Dowding asked Park in November 1939 if Duxford should not come into 11 Group, but Park thought the groups would be better balanced if Duxford stayed in 12 Group and Dowding accepted his opinion. Unwittingly, Park had made the most fateful decision of his career. If Duxford had gone to 11 Group, Douglas Bader would have come under Park's direct command in 1940. Bader would then have had neither the opportunity nor the inclination to discuss fighter tactics with Leigh-Mallory and it is probable that there would have been no 'big wings' controversy.

Park had ample experience of Leigh-Mallory's independent methods long before the Battle of Britain. In September 1939, for example, Dowding asked his group commanders not to issue special group orders in addition to command battle orders. Drafted by Park, these covered the movement of units from one station to another. It had to be remembered, wrote Dowding, that squadrons might be freely moved up and down the line in accordance with changing situations and it was important that they should not find themselves in a group where orders which they did not understand were in force. He instanced special action orders issued by Leigh-Mallory on 5 September and ordered him to cancel them.

Leigh-Mallory, however, was unabashed and wrote to his sectors on the 26th about the disposition of their squadrons. Park drew Dowding's attention to this letter. If Leigh-Mallory had his way, Park wrote, Digby and Wittering would be overcrowded, refuelling and rearming would be slowed and adjoining sectors underworked and weakened. Dowding agreed and wrote a long, carefully argued letter to Leigh-Mallory. 'I have delegated tactical control almost completely to Groups and Sectors,' he said, 'but I have not delegated strategical control, and the threat to the line must be regarded as a whole and not parochially.' Leigh-Mallory was to remember that units at Duxford, for example, might be urgently needed for the defence of London. Moreover, the organization could not handle more than three squadrons at one aerodrome or four under one sector controller, but Leigh-Mallory proposed, in certain circumstances, to have five squadrons at Digby and no fewer than seven at Wittering. 'I would only ask you,' ended Dowding, 'to remember that the Fighter Command has to operate as a whole.' Suitable assurances were offered and accepted and the incident closed. Keeping

Leigh-Mallory in line with the rest of the command proved an endless task and one which defeated Dowding and Park.[6]

Problems of aerodrome and coastal defence caused Park continuous concern. Quite apart from the difficulties of obtaining and installing sufficient anti-aircraft batteries to protect vital targets, he faced even greater difficulties in attempting to *coordinate* the several elements in the defence (aircraft, guns, searchlights, ships in harbour, radar and the Observer Corps) to ensure that enemy aircraft would be challenged promptly and friendly aircraft would not.

Park was warned on 6 October 1939 via agents in Berlin that a major German offensive against British shipping was timed to begin in mid-October. Air attacks would be launched in great strength, now that a convoy system – providing large, slow-moving targets – had been introduced. Together, Dowding and Park drafted a signal to put their sectors on guard against such attacks and Park required one squadron from each sector in eastern England to be at readiness throughout daylight hours from 12 October. During the next few days, he sent numerous signals: on liaison with Coastal Command aircraft; the movement forward of fighters to action stations; the identification of friendly aircraft; the code-names for convoys, and the signals that vessels would display. Even though no offensive against British shipping took place in October 1939, Park's work was not wasted. He, and the defence system, were given a gruelling exercise to help prepare them for the tests ahead.

Apart from his general concern with the defences of the south and east coasts, Park was particularly concerned with defence of the Thames estuary. He was involved in such matters as the location of guns, balloons and searchlights and negotiations with other commands and naval authorities about their dispositions, effectiveness and the problems of aircraft working with them (as opposed to confusing them or being in danger from them). There was nothing 'phoney' about the period September 1939 to April 1940 as far as Park was concerned. In that time, he gained valuable experience in operating under war conditions systems and ideas conceived in peacetime. As well as the expertise he took to the conduct of the Battle of Britain, Park gained experience of operations over water in cooperation with the Royal Navy and land-based anti-aircraft guns that he would later put to good use in Egypt and Malta. It was also during the 'phoney war' that he was introduced to the dangers of employing the fighter defence force in France.[7]

Park wrote to the Air Ministry in December 1939 about the employment of fighter squadrons in the event of an invasion of the Low Countries. The British Air Forces in France had proposed a programme of patrols for two of Gossage's squadrons which could only be carried out if they operated from French aerodromes and if a servicing wing was established there for them. Dowding, said Park, refused to accept this reduction in his forces. The squadrons might operate over France, but must return to England each evening. It soon became clear, however, that bad weather – apart from rearming and refuelling – made a maintenance base in France necessary. Park recognized the thin end of a wedge: should Germany launch an offensive in the west, Britain's fighter defence force would be drained away to France. As a result of his efforts to coordinate British and French fighter cover over Channel convoys, he was already aware that France's air defence system was rudimentary and her fighter force inadequate.

Fighter Command would be required to fill the breach, although its resources were insufficient even for home defence. Ever since May 1939, Park had been forwarding to the Air Ministry monthly statements of the 'mobilizable' squadrons in the command: the effective number available, their state of re-equipment with the latest aircraft types, their progress in flying training and the shortage of spares and tools for maintenance work. Between the outbreak of war and 1 February 1940, he reported, eighteen new squadrons had begun forming, but only two (both Gladiator biplane squadrons) were fully equipped. The other sixteen were all deficient in armament, wireless or electrical equipment.

Dowding followed up this report in a letter to the Air Ministry on 10 February. Not only were these new squadrons unready for service, he wrote, but additional duties had been incurred since September 1939. Six squadrons had been sent to France, four more were earmarked for France, four set aside for trade protection under Coastal Command and two each provided for service at Wick in northern Scotland, the Aberdeen coast and a new sector at Middle Wallop in Hampshire. For the protection of the country's vitals, Dowding concluded, the situation was roughly as it had been on the outbreak of war, despite the creation of eighteen new squadrons.[8]

Throughout his service at Bentley Priory, Park's relations with Ludlow-Hewitt of Bomber Command were uneasy. In their differences over the conduct of peacetime exercises, Park was usually defeated or thwarted, but after the outbreak of war he prevailed in an important dispute concerning the bomber liaison section at Fighter Command Headquarters. In October 1939 Park asked Ludlow-Hewitt to upgrade and enlarge that section. Squadron Leader R.W. Stannard, the senior liaison officer, supported Park. Ludlow-Hewitt, however, received the request with his usual coldness. When Park got Hazleton Nicholl (Air Officer in charge of Administration at Fighter Command) to repeat the request, Ludlow-Hewitt recommended the employment of four junior reservists under a squadron leader.

Park tried again on 16 December in a letter to the Air Ministry. Before the war, he wrote, the activity of British bombers over the sea had been restricted, both in number and distance, but much longer journeys were now commonplace and involved irregular reappearances. The liaison section must therefore monitor the movements of all service and civilian aircraft leaving or returning to Britain. The work called for continuous concentration by experienced men because the penalties for mistaken identification were obvious. He questioned Ludlow-Hewitt's wish to replace the section's present flight lieutenants by junior officers; their duties compared more than favourably with those of the coastal and naval liaison sections, where no suggestion of a reduction in rank had arisen.

This letter fell on fertile ground. An Air Ministry official recorded on 15 January 1940 that it put the matter in 'the fairest way': Fighter Command was responsible for air defences and was thus in a far better position than Bomber Command to judge the section's needs. The section was enlarged and made responsible for coordinating and controlling the movements of both Coastal and Bomber Commands. Shortly before Ludlow-Hewitt was relieved of his command, on 3 April 1940, the whole establishment was transferred to Fighter Command.[9]

Park was admitted to hospital on 8 March 1940 and an appendectomy was performed the next day. He was allowed up after a week and sent on three weeks' sick leave, much against his will, but Dowding threatened (perhaps not in jest) to have him arrested if he appeared at Bentley Priory before 12 April. Park endured his leave as best he could and on 13 April received one of the most pleasant shocks of his life: he learned that he was to succeed William Welsh as commander of 11 Group on the 20th. Welsh had succeeded Gossage in that post as recently as 12 February.

In April 1940 it was not obvious that 11 Group, rather than 12 Group, would shortly bear the brunt of national defence. France, Belgium and Holland had not then been invaded, much less conquered, and until those disasters occurred, air attacks on England would have to be made from German bases and Leigh-Mallory's territory (the Midlands and East Anglia) would be their natural target. Nevertheless, 11 Group – charged with the defence of· London and the south-east – had always been considered the senior group and treated accordingly in the provision of the latest equipment or aircraft and the ablest personnel. In the appointment of Park as new commander of 11 Group, therefore, Leigh-Mallory was undoubtedly passed over in favour of a junior officer and his feelings were presumably injured. So, too, were those of Gossage (removed from 11 Group after only five months of wartime service) and Welsh (who held that group for barely two months). In wartime, countless changes in command are made, usually quickly and usually without regard for personal feelings. Park would learn this bitter lesson himself in November 1940. Meanwhile, Dowding and his masters at the Air Ministry jointly decided that Park was a man fit to be entrusted with command of the senior fighter group. Following the German conquest of Western Europe, command of that group became the most vital position in Britain's front-line defence.[10]

CHAPTER EIGHT

A 'Possible but Unlikely Evacuation': Dunkirk

1940

For almost two years, Park had helped to prepare an air defence for Britain but his first test as an operational commander had nothing to do with that defence. On 10 May 1940, three weeks after his arrival at the Uxbridge headquarters of 11 Group, the Germans launched an invasion of France, Belgium and the Netherlands. Within two more weeks, Park found himself improvising protection for Allied armies besieged in and around Dunkirk and trying to cover their retreat to England.

During the first eight months of the war, one of Dowding's major headaches, fully shared with Park, had been the despatch of home defence fighters to France to help resist just such an invasion. Dowding and Park were concerned about supply as well as policy because the production of Hurricanes and Spitfires was no more than two of each per day at the end of 1939, and over the first four months of 1940 output averaged only six fighters per day. However, as long as France, Belgium and the Netherlands remained unconquered, England lay beyond the range of the Messerschmitt Bf 109 and Park agreed with Dowding that unescorted bomber raids could be defeated. But neither had any illusions concerning the losses which Fighter Command would suffer if German fighters were based on the coasts closest to England.

Six British fighter squadrons were already in France on 10 May and within a few days of the invasion Dowding had lost the equivalent of six more squadrons from home defence; another four squadrons were fighting over France each day and returning, if they could, to English bases each evening. the pressure for still more assistance, wrote Dowding, was 'relentless and inexorable' and on 15 May he obtained permission to appear before the War Cabinet and ask for it to be checked. Later that day, he wrote to Park:

> We had a notable victory on the 'Home Front' this morning and the
> orders to send more Hurricanes were cancelled. Appeals for help will

84

doubtless be renewed, however, with increasing insistence and I do not know how this morning's work will stand the test of time; but I will never relax my efforts to prevent the dissipation of the Home fighter forces.

Dowding's suspicion that the impact of his appeal would not last proved well founded. Park asked him on the 17th if in future *whole* squadrons could be sent abroad. This, he said, would avoid the present situation whereby fourteen flights of different squadrons were operating as composite squadrons at home and overseas under leaders who knew only half the pilots and airmen they commanded. Although Dowding sympathized, the crisis was so grave that he could do little. This fragmentation of squadrons made Park's task harder during the desperate days that followed.

A meeting at the War Office on 19 May discussed the problem of the 'possible but unlikely evacuation of a very large force in hazardous circumstances' through Dunkirk, Calais and Boulogne. Unlikely as the need may have seemed then, plans were made to effect a withdrawal, which was just as well because they were implemented as soon as formulated. Sholto Douglas minuted Newall that day on the difficulties of covering an embarkation. It had already been seen, he wrote, what comparatively few German bombers could do in daylight to render a base practically untenable. But the moon was rising and would soon be full: weather conditions throughout the twenty-four hours would be such that bombers could easily recognize a port of embarkation.

Dunkirk was farther from English bases than Calais or Boulogne and therefore more difficult to cover by short-range fighters, but when those ports fell on 25 and 26 May, Dunkirk became the only hope of escape. Already hampered by the fragmentation of his squadrons, Park's difficult task was now made even harder.

On 23 May, he had learned of a new hazard to British fighters: British destroyers. They were firing indiscriminately at all aircraft and the Admiralty informed Dowding that 'our destroyers fire at any aircraft that comes within range whether they make our recognition signals or not.' Park was distressed by this disregard for measures of cooperation worked out with the Admiralty over the past year, but worse followed. He received three Admiralty messages via Dowding during the evening of the 23rd complaining that fighter defences over Boulogne were inadequate – this after two fighters had been shot down and two damaged by Royal Navy ships earlier in the day. British bombers were also prevented from attacking German land targets by fire from British destroyers.

By 26 May the Allied armies had disintegrated or fallen back so rapidly in the face of a powerful German advance that Vice-Admiral Bertram Ramsay, Flag Officer Commanding Dover, was ordered to implement Operation Dynamo 'with a view to lifting up to 45,000 of the BEF [British Expeditionary Force] within two days, at the end of which it was probable that evacuation would be terminated by enemy action.' Ramsay was in charge of the embarkation of troops and Park had tactical control of the fighter cover. Coordination between fighters, bombers and reconnaissance aircraft was handled at Hawkinge, conveniently close to Ramsay's base at Dover and with good communications to Park's headquarters at Uxbridge.

Park explained to his controllers and staff officers on 26 May the system he intended to use. Both flying and ground personnel would be given short periods of heavy duty, he said, followed by long release in surroundings of reasonable comfort. The available force would be divided into two parts, to work mornings and afternoons, proceeding direct from their permanent bases on their first patrol and landing at a forward aerodrome to re-arm, refuel and have lunch or tea. They would, if possible, return to their permanent base after their second patrol and unless the crisis was very great they would then be released for the day.

For his efforts to protect the embarkation, Park was assigned sixteen squadrons (some 200 aircraft, including – for the first time in operations over Europe – Spitfires) out of Dowding's home defence force, now whittled down to thirty-six squadrons. The remaining twenty were used as a reserve to keep up the strength of Park's force and to protect vital targets in the Midlands and the North and also coastal shipping and the fleet. Although only three fighter squadrons were never engaged over Dunkirk, Park was short of men and machines for the task on hand. The area to be protected lay at least fifty miles from his nearest bases; fighters operating outside their planned defensive system could receive no help from radar and were obliged to rely on wasteful, exhausting standing patrols; and the limited fuel capacity of his aircraft permitted only forty minutes at most on the actual patrol lines. Even when resistance in Calais and Boulogne ended, Park was unable to cover Dunkirk properly because the area defended by the Allied troops had a perimeter extending for ten miles and the shipping employed in the rescue operation was liable to attack anywhere on the Channel crossing.

Consequently, although his fighters were present on patrol lines throughout 27 May (the first full day of withdrawal), they were heavily outnumbered. They could not prevent the Luftwaffe from reducing the town of Dunkirk to rubble, but they prevented its concentration on the targets that mattered most: the harbour moles and ships. Despite the damage done, the port never became untenable. At 2 a.m. on the 28th, Newall informed Dowding that that day was 'likely to be the most critical ever experienced by the British Army.' An hour later, he ordered him to ensure the protection of Dunkirk and its beaches from first light until darkness by continuous fighter patrols in strength. It proved impossible to obey this order, however, because the twin demands of continuity and strength could not both be met. Experience had already shown that weak patrols were ineffective and neither the aircraft nor the pilots were available for constant patrols, as long as Dowding conserved men and machines to counter the even graver danger of an invasion of England.

It was only after urgent and repeated requests that Park secured Dowding's permission to employ squadrons two at a time and abandon attempts at continuous coverage. Unlike many senior officers, Park had kept in flying practice and was therefore able to pilot his own Hurricane over Dunkirk. His observations, and conversations with his pilots, convinced him that stronger patrols, even at longer intervals, would prove more useful. Aircraft losses were reduced, there were more successful combats and bomber formations were broken up, thus reducing the effect of their attacks.

From 28 May, Park was allowed to use his squadrons as he thought fit. He employed as many as four at a time on the 29th, even though this meant leaving longer intervals between patrols. Three out of five large raids in the afternoon were intercepted, but the other two caused serious damage. Estimates of the victories achieved by these large formations were, however, exaggerated and it may be that pairs of squadrons would have done as well and also permitted more frequent patrols. Attempts to synchronize the presence of fighters and the movement of ships failed.

Richard Peirse, Vice Chief of the Air Staff, found time to write to Dowding on 30 May. Sinclair, the Secretary of State for Air, had asked Balfour, the Parliamentary Under-Secretary, to visit some fighter stations on the 29th and would like to hear how Dowding intended to mitigate the conditions of fatigue which Balfour had observed. Dowding replied as politely as he could. Most of Balfour's criticisms, he said, covered matters which were the subject of anxious discussion between Park and himself. They arose from the need to fight a battle over Dunkirk while at the same time maintaining other units in readiness to meet a possible attack on England. He had already arranged with Park to take advantage of a lull in the air fighting to let the most heavily engaged units take some leave. He also wanted to get the scattered squadrons back to their home bases as soon as possible. There the matter rested, but it illustrates the gulf between Dowding and Park on the one hand, and Sinclair and Balfour on the other, a gulf that widened as the year advanced.

Rain and low cloud hindered all aircraft on 30 May, but during the next two days Allied troops were heavily bombed. These attacks, as well as German command of the Dunkirk roads by shore-based gunfire, obliged the British to suspend daylight evacuation on 2 June. From then until the operation ended on the morning of the 4th, evacuation was restricted to dawn and dusk each day and Park was able to concentrate his forces much more effectively during those periods. The last Hurricane to fly over Dunkirk was Park's. The extreme danger now facing Britain did not alarm him: he felt, in fact, strangely exhilarated, as did so many Britons at that time. The Germans, he thought, must soon attempt an invasion somewhere in south-east England, and the defensive system which he had worked so hard to help perfect in theory would now be his to direct in practice. Below him was an empty sea and German-held beaches. The British Expeditionary Force had left behind 68,000 men (40,000 of them taken prisoner) and over

200 ships of all sizes had been sunk. But 340,000 Allied troops had been rescued, a figure to compare with 'up to 45,000' hoped for when the operation had begun.[1]

Without the courage of numerous seamen, amateur as well as professional, who crossed the Channel time and time again in over a thousand vessels to carry soldiers to safety, there could have been no 'miracle' at Dunkirk. The courage of many soldiers ashore, especially units of the French First Army holding the perimeter's bridgehead, was equally vital. So, too, was the fact that the German advance was halted for three days, partly to allow recovery from the effects on men and machines of heavy fighting, partly to preserve precious tanks for the next phase of the battle against France and partly because Hitler was persuaded by Göring to entrust the major assault to the Luftwaffe. Its attack was as much an improvisation as the RAF's defence: close-support units were disordered by days of headlong advance and both air and ground crews were exhausted. Moreover, the Luftwaffe's medium bombers were now operating at extreme range from their German bases. Many of them were withdrawn from the assault to prepare for the next stage of the French campaign even before the evacuation ended. The generally cloudy weather on most of the nine days of the evacuation, together with the huge pillars of smoke rising from burning oil tanks and warehouses in Dunkirk, also hindered the Luftwaffe. Nevertheless, essential to the operation's success was the part played by Park's fighter pilots, assisted by the crews of Bomber and Coastal Commands, in denying the Luftwaffe supremacy over the target.

Sadly, the RAF's efforts were much criticized at the time. Vice-Admiral Ramsay submitted a report to the Admiralty as early as 18 June, exactly two weeks after the operation was concluded.

> Rightly or wrongly [he wrote] full air protection was expected, but instead for hours on end the ships off shore were subjected to a murderous hail of bombs and machine-gun bullets. . . . In their reports the COs of many ships, while giving credit to the RAF personnel for gallantry in such combats as were observed from the ships, at the same time express their sense of disappointment and surprise at the seemingly puny efforts made to provide air protection during the height of this operation.

Ramsay had nothing to say about British destroyers firing on British aircraft nor, in his haste to report to the Admiralty, did he have time to contact Dowding or Park to see if he was presenting the facts fairly. Many combats had taken place out of sight of soldiers and seamen who could hardly be expected to appreciate the fact that, although they were still being bombed, the attack was less heavy than it would otherwise have been. His hasty strictures coloured Admiralty opinion about the RAF's powers and determination throughout the war and played a part in some tense situations encountered by Park in Malta and Egypt.

The Admiralty published Ramsay's report in July 1947. Ramsay was dead by then and the Admiralty, although admitting that some parts of his report were 'necessarily distorted', refused to correct them on the grounds that they represented naval feeling at the time, 'when many of the true facts about the general RAF operations were not known to the Flag Officer, Dover.'

More than a quarter of Britain's fighter force had been lost over France even before the evacuation began. When it ended, Dowding had only 331 Spitfires and Hurricanes available for operations and all his squadrons were disorganized. One hundred and six fighters were lost over Dunkirk and 80 pilots, in exchange for perhaps 130 enemy aircraft. During the whole French campaign, 453 fighters were destroyed or abandoned and 435 pilots, many of them experienced regulars or men trained in peacetime, failed to return. Although Luftwaffe casualties were heavier, the German recovery was helped by the release of 400 aircrew prisoners after France surrendered towards the end of June 1940.

Park himself came out of the disaster of the retreat from France with his reputation enhanced. His readiness to visit the scenes of fighting and the aerodromes in Kent from which his men flew attracted favourable notice throughout Fighter Command and he was quick to congratulate ground crews as well as pilots on their efforts. Many of his pilots had little experience in handling high-speed monoplanes, let alone in using them effectively as weapons of war. All of them, whether they admitted it or not, had been alarmed by the odds they faced in the air and upset by the bitter criticism received on the ground from seamen and soldiers. Park expressed, loudly and clearly, complete confidence in them. He had shown that he was able to keep his fighters efficiently employed, improvising at short notice a constant shuttle of patrols. He had acted quickly, sensibly and calmly in a situation for which there were no precedents. It was at this time that he formulated a basic principle for the conduct of the Battle of Britain: that it was better to spoil the aim of many German aircraft than to shoot down a few of them.[2]

The Dunkirk evacuation did not end Fighter Command's commitment across the Channel. Air Marshal Arthur Barratt, head of the British air forces in France, advised the Air Ministry on 4 June that France was rallying and that German losses were perhaps greater than had been supposed. It was essential, he thought, that a great many fighters be sent to France as soon as possible. Barratt enclosed with his letter one signed on 3 June by General Vuillemin, commander of the French air forces. Vuillemin went farther even than Barratt in his appeal for help: he wanted the support of at least half the fighters presently based in England. Churchill signalled Reynaud, the French Prime Minister, on 5 June: 'You don't seem to understand at all that British fighter aviation has been worn to a shred and frightfully mixed up [by the demands of Dunkirk].' Nevertheless, he still had hopes of using British fighters to help the French to rally. As late as 8 June he informed Reynaud that 'We are giving you all the support we can in this great battle short of ruining the capacity of this country to continue the war.' On the 12th, however, Douglas told Barratt that the game was practically up and that he must prepare to withdraw.

Park's offensive spirit and self-confidence were unimpaired by the disasters in Europe. On 20 June, for example, he asked Dowding for permission to modify some Hurricanes to carry small bombs and to use them and Blenheims in night raids on enemy aerodromes. Permission was refused. On the 30th he wrote to Brooke-Popham, who was acting as chairman of a committee collecting information of tactical value arising out of the recent air fighting. When Brooke-Popham could spare the time to visit Uxbridge, Park promised to explain 'the system I evolved for operating a large number of fighter squadrons over France, and at the same time protecting the south of England. . . . These two roles were not easy to reconcile, but we managed the task.'

On 22 July he submitted to Dowding a report on operations over France between 10 May and 4 June. A copy was sent to the Air Ministry, but Dowding added a chilling disclaimer: 'The report is of interest, although I cannot endorse all the opinions expressed.' Surprised and annoyed, Park asked for details of his criticisms. Douglas Evill, now Dowding's Senior Air Staff Officer, replied that Dowding did not wish to correspond with Park on this subject, but would be glad to discuss it some time at Bentley Priory. More urgent concerns prevented such a discussion and Park never learned what Dowding thought was wrong with his report.

The report covered one problem which pressed harder during the Battle of Britain: the problem of radio frequencies. It was impossible to group all Park's squadrons on a common frequency and there was rarely time to change incoming squadrons over to the frequency of their new sector. Trouble was caused when squadrons on different frequencies *had* to work together because R/T control was impossible. Park urged that R/T silence be maintained by all pilots except for important information and that R/T communication from the ground also be kept to a minimum, both to prevent the enemy from overhearing and to avoid blocking essential communication between aircraft in the air. Devoted efforts by unsung technicians throughout the summer of 1940 eased these problems and went far towards ensuring that the experience so dearly bought over Dunkirk was later used to thwart an invasion of England.[3]

CHAPTER NINE

The Battle of Britain: Meeting Them

Churchill now broke silence. 'There appear to be many aircraft coming in.' As calmly, Park reassured him. 'There'll be someone there to meet them.'

Richard Collier, *Eagle Day*

On 26 June, twelve days after the Germans entered Paris, Park urged Dowding to transfer the Debden sector from Leigh-Mallory's care in 12 Group to 11 Group. The weight of attack on London and south-east England now likely from French bases was greater than he could resist without that reinforcement. For the same reason, he urged that Tangmere sector remain under his command and not be transferred to 10 Group, then forming for the defence of the south-west. Although information about raids was passed from one group to another, there was never the same coordination as when the interception fell entirely to one group. Dowding agreed: Park kept Tangmere and received Debden on 10 August.

From that date, Park controlled seven sectors and, as a rule, twenty-three squadrons. Leigh-Mallory commanded about fourteen squadrons distributed around six sectors to the rear of Park's group and was responsible for the defence of the Midlands and East Anglia. Sir Quintin Brand commanded 10 Group (which became operational on 17 July) and had some ten squadrons in four sectors to protect South Wales and England west of Portsmouth. In the north lay 13 Group, under Richard Saul. He had up to fourteen squadrons (not all complete or fully operational) with which to guard Tyneside, Clydeside, Scapa Flow and Northern Ireland.

The underground operations room at Uxbridge, Park's headquarters, had been completed in 1939. It was similar to that at Bentley Priory, except that the map showed only the group's area, with some adjoining land and water, and the tote board showed only the group's squadrons, plus any on loan from neighbouring groups. Park received his radar information from Bentley

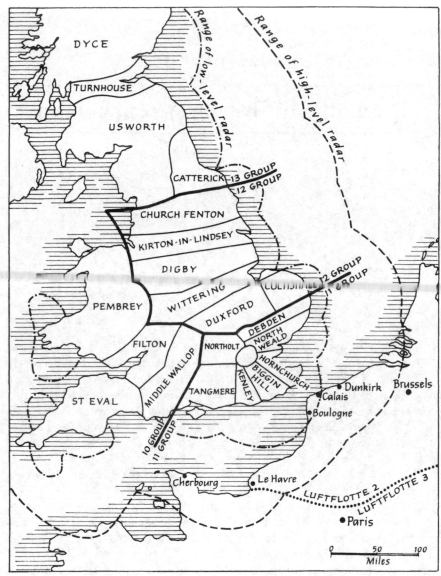

5: The Battle of Britain: Air Defence sectors

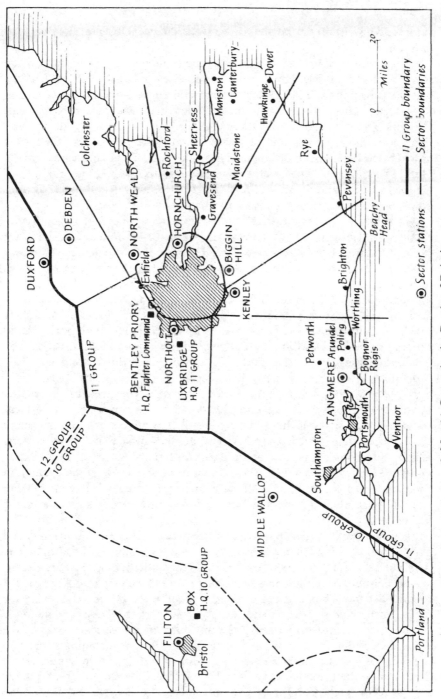

6: No. 11 Group in the Battle of Britain

Colchester

DEBDEN

DUXFORD

NORTH WEALD

Enfield

HORNCHURCH

Rochford

Sheerness

Gravesend

Maidstone

Manston

Canterbury

Hawkinge

Dover

Rye

Pevensey

Beachy Head

BIGGIN HILL

KENLEY

Brighton

Worthing

Arundel

Poling

Bognor Regis

Petworth

TANGMERE

Ventnor

Portsmouth

Southampton

11 GROUP

BENTLEY PRIORY
H.Q. Fighter Command

NORTHOLT

UXBRIDGE
H.Q. 11 GROUP

12 GROUP

10 GROUP

11 GROUP

10 GROUP

MIDDLE WALLOP

FILTON

Bristol

BOX
H.Q. 10 GROUP

Portland

0   Miles   20

Sector boundaries

11 Group boundary

⊙ Sector stations

Priory and his visual or aural plots direct from tellers in Observer Corps groups in his area.

All operations rooms were laid out to the same pattern. On a dais sat the senior controller, flanked by assistants and liaison officers. Each place on the dais was provided with communications to squadrons, to aircraft in the air and to all other units and headquarters to which messages needed to be sent. Wireless operators sat in cubicles behind the dais in contact with airborne fighters. Radio cross-bearings of sector aircraft were plotted and the results passed to the main operations room. The senior controller could see at a glance plots of hostile raids as well as the movements of his own fighters, the state of the local weather and the state of readiness of his squadrons. He could also see how much petrol and oxygen his airborne fighters had left.

As the battle progressed, Park showed remarkable speed in responding to changes in German tactics. Although the Luftwaffe held the initiative throughout, and Park was obliged to fight entirely on the defensive, he was never off balance for more than a few hours. His choices were rational and his means as effective as could be expected. He would not otherwise have retained his command, for Churchill himself visited Uxbridge several times and, as Park wrote, 'never interfered with the conduct of operations'. It is unlikely that Churchill would have interfered directly whatever Park did, but he would certainly have sent Dowding a tart note had he not thought Park up to his job.

Like Dowding, Park believed that the squadron was the fighting unit. This belief underlay Fighter Command's structure. From the moment that orders were given by group controllers to sector controllers, they were to be executed by squadrons ordered off singly, in pairs or in larger formations from adjacent stations. Once airborne, they were controlled from the ground, by direct contact with their sector controller, and guided towards incoming raiders. When squadrons operated together from different sectors, each remained under the control of its own sector. As soon as raiders were sighted, squadron commanders took charge and no further attempts were made to contact them from the ground until it was reported to the sector controllers that the action had ended.

Group controllers had to distinguish between major raids and feints and keep as many aircraft as possible ready for action. Major raids had to be met with 'sufficient' opposition (bearing in mind the limited resources) and aircraft should neither waste their fuel on mere patrol nor be caught on or near the ground. Several balances between likely alternatives had to be struck every day of the battle. The reward for successful guessing was to delay once more the penalty for unsuccessful guessing. Group controllers were at the heart of the defensive system. Within minutes of the appearance of incoming aircraft on the cathode ray tubes at the coastal radar stations, group controllers would see displayed on their operations tables all the information coming from Bentley Priory. It was mainly on the basis of this information that they decided what action to take.

That information was supplemented by radio traffic analysis, the use of direction-finding to pinpoint the location of Luftwaffe bases, prisoner interrogation and the examination of captured documents. The most famous intelligence source was the Ultra operation at Bletchley Park in Buckinghamshire, where German radio signals that had been enciphered by an Enigma machine were intercepted and translated. Enigma provided Dowding with information about the Luftwaffe's organization, order of battle and equipment. It was unable to tell him whether the RAF would outlast the Luftwaffe because it was silent on the losses and effective strengths of Luftwaffe units and the size of reserves, nor could it forecast changes in German methods and objectives because communications between Berlin and formations in France were by landlines. 'For all his major decisions,' concluded the official history of British Intelligence in the Second World War, Dowding 'depended on his own strategic judgment'.

In the day-to-day fighting, however, Enigma provided Park with an increasing amount of intelligence about the timing, size and targets of particular raids, even if the intelligence often arrived too late to be of immediate operational value and the Luftwaffe frequently made last-minute changes of plan. Park also received precious information from many careless German pilots, who paid little heed to radio security. Such interceptions supplemented other signals, radar and reconnaissance intelligence to help him determine the composition of enemy formations, their likely targets, assembly points for returning home and routes to follow. Even so, the pace of events throughout the Battle of Britain was so rapid, the options available to the Luftwaffe so many and the disparity in numbers and combat experience between the rival air forces so great that Park's daily judgments were crucial to the battle's course.[1]

Park had presided over a conference of squadron commanders at Northolt on 14 June to discuss air fighting tactics. Everyone had agreed upon the need for squadrons detailed to work together to plan their tactics on the ground. They discussed the composition of formations at length: should squadrons be employed singly, in pairs or in larger groupings? Even before the Battle of Britain began, Park was familiar with the arguments for and against the use of 'big wings', arguments which became bitter late in 1940. Everyone also agreed that R/T discipline was poor and Park directed that 'a brief but pungent' instruction be drawn up to curtail needless chatter.

He then invited suggestions for the best method of separating German bombers from their escorts. He reminded everyone of the danger of dispersing fighter strength too widely and observed that anti-aircraft fire might prove valuable in breaking up formations. He invited criticism of arrangements made and facilities available for operating fighters. It was vital, he thought, to see that pilots got proper rest and relaxation and therefore ruled that not more than two squadrons be based at one sector station; a third should be moved to a satellite airfield. Finally, Park had reminded his squadron commanders of a principle which he would stress over and over again once the battle began: their aim, he said, was the destruction of enemy *bombers* and action against fighters was only a means to this end.

On the same day – 14 June – Park informed his sector commanders that the Luftwaffe would probably soon begin attacks on 11 Group aerodromes in an attempt to cripple the ground organization. Should these attacks succeed, the Germans would be able to dominate southern England and repeat the conditions that obtained in Poland. Everyone must understand, he emphasized, that there was no intention of evacuating to bases elsewhere. This would merely play into German hands by severely hampering squadron control and servicing. Eleven Group would continue to operate its fighters however intensive the attacks. While attacks were actually in progress, personnel not performing essential duties would take cover, but others would carry on servicing aircraft and manning ground defences. Before the battle began, then, the decision to defend coastal Sussex, Kent and Essex had been taken and Park wholeheartedly supported it. Some pilots in 1940, and some commentators since, thought it foolish to hold coastal bases. Some even advocated a complete withdrawal to bases north of London, outside the range of German fighters, where British fighters could gain operational height undisturbed before speeding south. In the event, Park's pilots were often obliged to climb under their opponents and were therefore at a serious disadvantage.

Nevertheless, he believed it necessary to hold the foremost line. There had as yet been no daylight raids on British towns and villages and the reaction of their inhabitants could not be known. There were also important military and industrial targets in the south-east. Moreover, 11 Group's withdrawal would have been interpreted by many as a sign of impending defeat, while the consequent flight from the area would have cleared the way for a German assault – by parachute, if not by sea. Although Park was deeply concerned to safeguard the lives of his pilots and ground crews, he recognized a greater need to defend every acre of England against whatever odds the Germans imposed. If the south-east were to be defended, it followed that Park must engage at odds, promptly, and maintain reserves to use as and when he recognized the development of a heavy attack. His watchwords were speedy challenge, repeatedly offered. The time needed to assemble large formations would have permitted German raiders to reach their targets unmolested, and those formations would have absorbed reserves needed to challenge other raids.

One of his most persistent instructions concerned the need to attack bombers head-on. They were vulnerable in front, he wrote: poorly armoured, lightly armed, flying in tight formations (without room to manoeuvre) and led by the best pilots. 'Attack the ones in front,' he urged. 'If you shoot them down, the formation will break up in confusion. Then you

96

can take your pick.' Such attacks allowed the least time for accurate shooting, the danger of collision was high, fighters were exposed to coordinated fire from rear-gunners as they overshot and enemy escorts could be well placed to join in. For these reasons Dowding refused to approve head-on attacks as a standard tactic, but many brave and skilful pilots responded to Park's exhortation. Myles Duke-Woolley was one who did and survived to recall the fighting:

> I will say the old Hun certainly tried hard, but they *did not like* that head-on business. One could see the leader carrying on straight, but the followers wavering, drawing out sideways to the flanks, and in some cases just plain leaving the formation.

Such tactics would only serve in daylight, of course, but Park was also concerned throughout his time at Uxbridge with attempts to counter night attacks. On 14 June Wing Commander Vasse, of the Air Fighting Development Unit (formerly Establishment), sent him a paper on night-flying control. Sector controllers, he thought, must place pilots behind and below enemy aircraft and on the same course. It was no use putting them in the *vicinity* of raiders and asking them to search visually. Above all, controllers must not ask pilots for their positions. Having been directed all over the place, often above cloud and flying on instruments, they had no idea where they were. It was the controller's job, said Vasse, to keep track of them. Park agreed and a few days later circulated Vasse's paper together with new instructions of his own to all sectors. When enemy aircraft carried out a large number of night attacks, he wrote, group and sector plotting tables quickly became cluttered with tracks, making group control impracticable. When this happened, the group should order 'sector control' in the congested area and sectors would put up standing patrols when controlled interception became impossible.

Dowding remarked at the end of June that the use of searchlights provided the only hope of picking up enemy aircraft at night until AI [Airborne Interception, by radar] improved. Park thought so too, but on 25 July he wrote to Dowding about recent experience with single-engined fighters at night. Results had been 'not less satisfactory' than with the twin-engined Blenheim, which was too slow and the pilot's field of vision too restricted. He recommended that three sections of each Blenheim squadron be re-equipped with single-engined night-fighters. He recognized the inconvenience, from the point of view of maintenance, of operating two types of aircraft in one squadron, but more interceptions would be made. He was told that the Beaufighter, a twin-engined machine specially designed for radar-controlled interception at night, would soon be available. Unfortunately, it suffered many teething problems and achieved little in Park's time at Uxbridge.[2]

During July, the 'Channel War', like the Dunkirk evacuation, posed problems for Park that he could not solve. Whenever a convoy was at sea, the Luftwaffe attacked at its own convenience and obliged Park to mount a standing patrol overhead during daylight. At one time early in July, as many as seven coastal convoys were in passage around British coasts between Swanage in Dorset and the Firth of Forth: all open to attack and all difficult to defend, given the short range of British fighters and the brief warning provided by radar. Although unescorted bombers were easily driven away, tiring patrol work from primitive forward airfields continued day after day. Casualties caused by fatigue were already noticeable and Park became aware of a problem that plagued him until December – when to withdraw experienced but tired men from the front line and replace them with fresher pilots who were novices in the savage world of aerial combat.

Operations over water soon revealed the need for a properly organized system of rescuing ditched airmen. They were at first entirely dependent on ships which happened to be nearby. Specially equipped search aircraft and high-speed launches were needed as well as aids to help pilots stay afloat and mark their position until help arrived. In these respects, the Luftwaffe was better placed than the RAF. It had float planes for rescue work, combat aircraft carried inflatable rubber dinghies and aircrew were provided with fluorescine, a chemical which stained the sea bright green. By the end of July, Park and Vice-Admiral Ramsay at Dover had borrowed from the army some Lysander aircraft to work systematically with rescue launches and the use of fluorescine had been copied. Gradually, but not until long after the Battle of Britain was over, a comprehensive air–sea rescue organization was created in August 1941.

On 29 July 1940 Sholto Douglas signalled Fighter, Bomber and Coastal Commands to order strong counter-measures against E-boat bases, enemy coastal aerodromes and gun emplacements. These measures should be so planned as to hit aerodromes just after German aircraft had landed following attacks. Douglas Evill minuted Dowding about this signal next day, having discussed it with Park and Bottomley, the Senior Air Staff Officer of Bomber Command. E-boat bases could be attacked when reconnaissance reported that the boats were there, he said, but attacks on aerodromes were unlikely to be profitable because they were too well defended. Attack following a large raid would be particularly tricky. German activity over Calais was constant and it was impossible to tell when a large raid had actually begun until it moved out from the coast. By that time, it was within five minutes of Dover. From the moment such a raid became obvious until the moment it re-crossed the French coast was seldom more than thirty minutes. In order to catch enemy aircraft on the ground after their attack, bombers would have to be given executive orders as soon as an attack even seemed likely. They would need to be at fifteen minutes' notice in order to reach their objectives in time and kept indefinitely at that notice.

As for Park, continued Evill, he would find it difficult straight after an attack to find enough fighters to cover a counter-offensive. He was using about six squadrons against large attacks and needed three more to cover his advanced landing-grounds while those six were refuelling and rearming. Finding three or four more to escort bombers would absorb his entire force. Park had pointed out, moreover, the difficulty of controlling and coordinating three or four squadrons hastily detailed for escort from different aerodromes. It would therefore be 'unwise and probably impracticable', concluded Evill, to attempt a counter-attack in strength. A deliberate attack at a chosen time, preceded by thorough study and reconnaissance of harbours or aerodromes, offered more fruitful prospects. The note of reality thus introduced by Evill, Bottomley and Park into Douglas's orders was one that had to be repeated all too frequently during the summer and autumn of 1940.[3]

Evill wrote to Park on 6 September. The past month of intensive fighting had passed week by week through several distinct phases, he said, and it was obviously important that the authorities responsible for higher policy should be as fully informed as possible about this fighting. At present, Park's headquarters was 'carrying the whole force of the enemy attack'; in his sector and group operations rooms there was 'experience and information not available elsewhere' and Evill would therefore welcome a note on recent operations. What, he asked, have been the main features of the enemy dispositions and tactics from phase to phase? What effects have these had on the success of British squadrons in interception and combat? Did Park recommend any changes in organization? Evill knew that he was very busy and expected only a short report, but he would like it soon.

Park sent his report within a week. Evill, an intelligent and sensitive man, had guessed that Park, if asked tactfully, would do more to oblige than one could reasonably expect of someone carrying his present burden. Dowding thought it a good report and forwarded it to the Air Ministry with his comments on 22 September. He agreed with Park on the need to supplement the means available for reporting raids by using fighter reconnaissance aircraft to observe the composition of enemy formations during their approach and report direct to group headquarters. However, when Douglas minuted Cyril Newall, Chief of the Air Staff, on Park's report and Dowding's covering letter, his tone was critical throughout and in particular he seized upon the brevity with which Park discussed the problems of night-fighting. There had, however, been very little night-fighting prior to 10 September, when the report ended. Douglas, moreover, was usually the chairman of an Air Ministry committee specifically set up to consider night-fighting problems, but that committee never asked Park for his views.

The report covered the period from 8 August to 10 September and Park divided it into three phases. The first was from 8 to 18 August, the second from 19 August to 5 September and the third 'which is now occupying all my

Group's attention by day and by night' had begun on 6 September. In the first phase, the Germans had used massed formations of bombers escorted by fighters flying much higher. 'These tactics,' wrote Park, 'were not very effective in protecting the bombers.' Attacks on coastal targets in Kent were intended to attract British fighters and so clear the way for heavier attacks on ports and aerodromes on the south coast between Brighton and the isle of Portland Bill. Park's main problem had been to identify the principal attack, as opposed to feints, bearing in mind 'the very unreliable information received from the RDF stations after they had been heavily bombed.' To counter attacks on coastal targets, it was necessary to keep most 'readiness' squadrons at forward aerodromes and group controllers had to be extremely vigilant to protect them from attack while grounded. Even in the first phase of the battle, Park had stated his cardinal principle: 'to engage the enemy before he reached his coastal objective.'

His general plan had been to employ Spitfires to engage high-flying German fighters and to direct Hurricanes against bombers. Stern attacks worked well against fighters, but not against bombers, so Park had advised pilots 'to practise deflection shots from quarter astern, also from above and from below against twin-engined bombers.' Casualties were relatively higher than during the French campaign because of 'the fitting of armour to enemy bombers' and a shortage of 'trained formation and section leaders' in the British force. Even so, results had been satisfactory. He thought the proportion of enemy aircraft destroyed to British losses had been about four to one during the eleven days from 8 to 18 August.

In fact, it was less than two to one, although the Luftwaffe lost more than five times as many aircrew killed as the RAF during that time. Whatever the true figures, the defence had undoubtedly proved too good for the offence and a break of five days from intensive operations followed the Luftwaffe's major effort made on 18 August. On no other day would either side suffer a greater number of aircraft put out of action, which is why the eminent historian Alfred Price nominated the 18th 'the hardest day' of the Battle of Britain.

The Luftwaffe should have concentrated on knocking out radar stations and Fighter Command's coastal aerodromes, thus easing the way for subsequent penetration as far as London. Well directed attacks, boldly pressed home, would have wrecked the early-warning system. Sector aerodromes and dispersed aircraft could then have been attacked at leisure and landline communications disrupted. The Germans, in short, could have achieved aerial supremacy over south-east England despite Park's skilful handling of the defence. He once told Johnnie Johnson, the top-scoring Allied fighter ace of the war, that he dreaded more than anything a persistent attack on his sector stations. He could not have intercepted successfully from ground readiness and standing patrols were no answer. There were plenty of *aerodromes* in south-east England that Park could have used, but they were not equipped to communicate direct with his headquarters. 'Without signals,' he said, 'the only thing I commanded was my desk at Uxbridge.'

The attack on radar stations on 12 August showed what could be done. Dover, Pevensey and Rye were all put out of action, though emergency systems enabled them to resume reporting within six hours. They were difficult targets to destroy, but the Germans failed to realize that they were worth the effort. On this occasion, a large raid was built up (unseen by the Kent and Sussex radar stations) which hit the Isle of Wight hard and knocked out Ventnor radar station. Even in this crisis, Park remembered the German tactic of introducing new fighter formations to cover the withdrawal of a large raid. He therefore held back some fighters so that when Bf 109s were reported flying west near Beachy Head, he was able to intercept them and so prevent the situation over the Isle of Wight from getting worse.

Next day, 13 August, Park had good warning from radar that a big raid was approaching and responded with an effective blend of enterprise and caution. On his extreme left in Suffolk, he put up small formations over two aerodromes. At the same time, still on the left, he ordered up two Hurricane squadrons and a Spitfire squadron. These aircraft were divided between a convoy in the Thames estuary and forward aerodromes at Hawkinge and Manston. On the right, he ordered a section of Tangmere's Hurricanes to patrol their base and the rest of the squadron to patrol a line over west Sussex from Arundel to Petworth. He also ordered a squadron of Northolt Hurricanes to take up a position over Canterbury from where he could switch them in any desired direction. Finally, he reinforced his left with most of a Spitfire squadron from Kenley and his right with another Tangmere squadron. These dispositions left him with about half his Hurricanes and two-thirds of his Spitfires uncommitted, a fair provision for contingencies in view of the large forces at the Luftwaffe's disposal. As the Germans reached the Sussex coast, in two escorted formations, Park chose the right moment to send in the Hurricanes waiting over Canterbury. One formation was intercepted near Bognor, the other near Worthing by one of the Tangmere squadrons; neither reached its target.

The effective resistance offered in south-east England led Göring, head of the Luftwaffe, to believe that fighters must have been withdrawn in substantial numbers from the north. Therefore, on 15 August large raids were sent from bases in Norway and Denmark towards the north-east. They were beaten back and their failure was vital. Had they succeeded, Dowding's defences would have been dangerously stretched thereafter. When the crisis came early in September, he could not have concentrated his dwindling reserve of trained pilots in Park's command. On the other hand, he could not know that the attempt on the north would not be repeated and was obliged to retain a strong force there and in the Midlands. It was a matter of seeking a balance between real and potential dangers. As

101

it happened, some pilots in 12 Group felt themselves underemployed and it was there that the notorious 'big wings' controversy originated.

On 19 August Park summed up the lessons of recent fighting in one of his numerous instructions to his controllers. He was convinced, he wrote, that the Luftwaffe could be thwarted as long as sector aerodromes remained in service, inflicting steady losses, and the temptation to swap fighter for fighter was resisted. But too many pilots were being lost over the sea in hot pursuit of retreating aircraft. Such losses grieved Park more than any others: retreating Germans were beaten Germans, at least for that day, and if they could be forced to retreat every day it mattered little to him that their lives and machines were spared, because Britain's defences grew stronger every day. The battle would be won if Fighter Command remained in being until autumn weather prevented a seaborne invasion. And yet, on the very next day, Park signalled Hornchurch to commend the 'fine offensive spirit of the single pilot of No. 54 Squadron who chased nine He 113s [actually Bf 109s] across to France this afternoon.' He went on to ask everyone at Hornchurch, and at all his other stations, to beware of the German practice of putting up strong fighter patrols over the Straits of Dover to protect aircraft returning from raids. It is a revealing signal. He had just given strict orders that this chasing was not to be done. When it was, he made the best of it, mixing praise for the pilot's courage with advice on the dangers involved, and avoiding a heavy rebuke. He had himself been a fighter pilot and could still handle the latest types; he understood that the young men who fought in them must be led rather than driven.[4]

In the second phase of the battle (19 August to 5 September in Park's reckoning), the Luftwaffe turned their attacks from coastal shipping and ports to inland aerodromes, aircraft factories, industrial targets and 'areas which could only be classified as residential.' Just as Park had taken stock during the five-day lull following the 'hardest day' on 18 August, so too had the Germans. From 24 August smaller bomber formations were employed, escorted by fighters ordered to stay close to their charges. These tactics made it difficult for Park's pilots to obey his orders to attack bombers and avoid fighters. Worse, the use of a larger number of smaller formations impaired the radar warning: plots were more complicated and British fighters liable to be dispersed in several directions, leaving gaps for a carefully prepared penetration. As the Luftwaffe raided further inland, Park called upon 10 and 12 Groups to provide cover for aerodromes and aircraft factories near London. He was thus able to meet the enemy further forward in greater strength, while his neighbours protected vital targets behind his fighters.

On 25 August he drew his controllers' attention to a new German tactic. Bombers had recently been coming inland escorted by fighters flying at the same level. By detailing some British fighters to go high, to engage escorts which turned out not to be there, controllers were permitting these bombers an easier run. He was acutely aware that his pilots were anxious to get as high as possible before engaging the enemy and that single squadrons had sometimes faced large formations. Both problems were exacerbated by cloud and consequent errors in reports from the Observer Corps. He therefore ordered formation leaders on 26 August to report the approximate strength of enemy bombers and fighters, also their height and position, as soon as they sighted them. Such reports, given promptly, would allow Park to see to appropriate reinforcement.

It was also on 26 August that Park reminded Dowding of a report he had produced on 8 July which had drawn attention to the fact that the heaviest casualties had been suffered by reinforcing squadrons from the north, which had been formed only after the outbreak of war. This, he said, was still the situation. He asked that only highly trained and experienced squadrons be sent south to exchange with depleted squadrons. He had compared the fortunes of three 13 Group and two 12 Group squadrons transferred to his command at various dates in July and August. The former were credited with forty-three aircraft destroyed at a cost of two pilots missing and two wounded; the latter had brought down only seventeen aircraft and lost thirteen pilots in exchange. Park attributed this pronounced disparity to the fact that Richard Saul of 13 Group always chose experienced units for service in the south whereas Leigh-Mallory did not.

'Contrary to general belief and official reports,' wrote Park in September, 'the enemy's bombing attacks by day did extensive damage to five of our forward aerodromes, and also to six of our seven sector stations.' Manston and Lympne were unfit for operations 'on several occasions for days' and Biggin Hill was so severely damaged that for over a week it could operate only one squadron. Had the Luftwaffe continued to attack these sectors, 'the fighter defences of London would have been in a parlous state during the last critical phase when heavy attacks have been directed against the capital.' Sector operations rooms suffered both from direct hits and damage to landlines. They all had to use emergency rooms, though these were too small and poorly equipped to cope with the normal control of three squadrons per sector.

In Park's view, the Air Ministry's arrangements for labour and materials to repair damage to fighter aerodromes were 'absolutely inadequate' despite 'numerous letters and signals during the past four weeks.' On his own initiative, he employed whole battalions of soldiers to fill in bomb craters and clear away rubble. Predictably, the Air Ministry objected to this unofficial arrangement and the incident still rankled with Park twenty-five years later: 'I was severely criticized by the Air Ministry at the time for accepting Army assistance. Had my fighter aerodromes been put out of action, the German Air Force would have won the battle by 15 September 1940.'

When forwarding Park's report to the Air Ministry on 22 September, Dowding claimed that only two aerodromes were unfit for flying for more than a few hours and that the works organization coped well enough. Did Park exaggerate the damage done and the weakness of that organization? His criticisms, so forcefully expressed, caused offence in the Air Ministry, weakening Park's standing there and making it easier for Douglas to win support for his conviction that Park should be replaced. But Dowding had come round to Park's opinion a year later, when he submitted his own account of the battle to the Air Ministry. It must be 'definitely recorded', he wrote, that the damage done was serious and had been generally under-estimated.

During the eighteen days of Park's second phase (19 August to 5 September), the Luftwaffe lost more than three aircraft for every two British aircraft destroyed and nearly five times as many German airmen were killed. Statistically, Fighter Command was doing well. Not only were Luftwaffe losses much heavier, but British fighter production and repair made good most of the command's losses. At that rate of exchange, however, the command would collapse while the Luftwaffe was still in being. Quite apart from the 106 British pilots killed, nearly as many were badly wounded out of a total strength of about one thousand and the output of the training system failed to match the casualties suffered.

Park issued a terse instruction to his controllers on 7 September, pointing out that on one occasion the previous day only seven out of eighteen squadrons despatched had intercepted the enemy. Some controllers were ordering squadrons intended to engage bombers to patrol too high. When group control ordered a squadron to 16,000 feet, its sector controller added another couple of thousand and the squadron did the same, hoping to avoid danger from above. The result was that bombers were getting through every day at 15,000 feet. In fact, said Park, most of them were intercepted only after bombing, on their way home. The low interception rate worried him because Dowding had told him that morning that invasion was officially considered 'imminent'. Park made his dispositions for the day with continuing attacks on sector stations in mind, ordering squadrons to patrol well back from the coast in anticipation of another assault on battered aerodromes. He then left Uxbridge to confer with Dowding at Bentley Priory. Unfortunately, these dispositions helped clear the route to London for the Germans, who launched a massive attack upon the capital late that afternoon.[5]

Only seven men were present at the meeting: Dowding, Park, Evill and Nicholl of Fighter Command, Douglas and a group captain from the Air Ministry and an NCO shorthand-typist to take the minutes. Dowding explained that he had convened the meeting in order to decide the steps to be taken to 'go downhill', if necessary, in the most economical way to permit a rapid climb back. He assumed a situation arising in which efforts to keep fully trained and equipped squadrons in the battle would fail. His policy had been to concentrate a large number of squadrons in the south-east, with stations on the fringe brought in at Park's request on the worst days. As squadrons became tired, these were taken out of the line and fresh ones put in from one of the three reinforcing groups. If the present scale of attack continued, however, this replacement policy would become impossible. So Dowding wanted to make a plan now to cover what he would do in that event. Although he would not amalgamate squadrons if he could help it, he might have to rob rear squadrons of their operational pilots to make up shortages. It seemed that enough pilots would be available, but the problem was to turn them into *combat* pilots. The Germans must not be allowed to know how hard hit the command was and Dowding would therefore keep 11 Group up to its present numbers, come what may, but he could not increase the number of squadrons in that group.

Douglas asked if he were not being pessimistic in talking about going downhill. Dowding disagreed, emphatically. Park, he said, was at this moment calling for reinforcements to five squadrons which had themselves just come into the line. But there was no shortage of pilots, Douglas replied, and when Dowding began to explain the skills needed of a fighter pilot, he assured him that the command would be kept up to strength. Douglas's lack of comprehension baffled Dowding, but Evill now intervened. Total casualties for the four weeks ending 4 September were 348, he said, and since the three Operational Training Units had turned out only 280 fighter pilots in that period, a net loss of 68 resulted, quite apart from accidents and illness.

For the moment, Douglas fell silent and Park remarked that casualty figures in 11 Group were nearly 100 a week and that there was indeed a pilot shortage. That day, he said, nine squadrons had started with fewer than fifteen pilots and the previous day squadrons had been put together and sent out as composite units. Dowding interrupted him. 'You must realize,' he said, speaking directly to Douglas, 'that we *are* going downhill.' After a pause, Park continued. It was better to have twenty-one squadrons with no fewer than twenty-one pilots in each than to have a greater number of under-strength squadrons in 11 Group. Some squadrons were doing fifty hours' flying a day and while they were flying – and fighting – their aerodromes were being bombed; while they were on the ground, they could not get proper meals and rest because of the disorganization and night raids.

Douglas suggested opening another OTU. This would be done if casualties remained heavy, although if the whole of August was considered, the command's strength was being maintained. Dowding pointed out that the true picture only emerged from the figures after 8 August, when large-scale attacks had begun. He had to assume that present scales of attack – and casualties – would continue. Another OTU, repeated Douglas, would ensure that pilot strength was maintained. But to be effective, Evill interjected, it would need to be in action very quickly; and, added Dowding, it would itself be a drain on the command for personnel.

Park then described his scheme of sector training flights. They had been needed, he said, because OTU pilots were unfit to fight until they received extra training. But training flights had now been cancelled because all experienced pilots were needed for fighting and all stations were dispersed because of bombing. He suggested that pilots should go from their OTUs straight to squadrons in the north for extra training and that squadrons in the south should receive only fully trained men from the north to fill their gaps. Dowding argued that he must always have some fresh operational squadrons to exchange with 11 Group's most tired squadrons. The two schemes could run parallel, replied Park. His idea of importing pilots, rather than whole squadrons, would only take effect when a squadron's strength fell to fifteen pilots. Dowding agreed.

The next day, 8 September, Nicholl informed the group commanders that all squadrons had been divided into three classes. Class A were those in 11 Group, to be maintained at a minimum strength of sixteen operational pilots. Some squadrons in 10 and 12 Groups were also designated Class A, but their pilot strength (likewise a minimum of sixteen) might be operational or not. Class B squadrons might include up to six non-operational pilots in their quota of sixteen and Class C squadrons would retain at least three operational pilots. Command Headquarters would inform 10, 12 and 13 Groups daily of the number of pilots required of them for allotment to 11 Group. Evill wrote to Douglas on the 9th, enclosing a copy of this letter.

Douglas replied on the 14th. The draft minutes of the conference reminded him, he said, of a music-hall turn between two knock-about comedians in which one, usually called 'Mutt', asked foolish questions. He appeared to be cast in that role in these minutes, he said, claiming that they misrepresented him. 'However, life is too strenuous in these days to bother about the wording of minutes,' he continued. Evill answered the same day, politely rejecting Douglas's charge of minute-faking. They were, he said, in almost exactly the words recorded at the time by the NCO shorthand-typist. He also rejected Douglas's argument that there were too many Class C squadrons. They might each have to produce five operational pilots per week, said Evill, as well as perform their own operational tasks.

Park had long shared Dowding's opinion that Douglas was a man of limited capacity. They believed that their plans for making the best use of available resources were sound. Evill and Nicholl, experienced and able officers, fully supported them. Dowding and Park had neither the taste nor the time for Air Ministry politics, least of all during a major crisis, and consequently they quite failed to realize that their unconcealed contempt for Douglas's contribution to the meeting on 7 September placed them in grave danger. Douglas attended no more meetings at Dowding's headquarters, away from his home ground in the Air Ministry, where supporters were plentiful and he could usually act as chairman. The next meeting which Dowding, Park and Douglas all attended took place six weeks later – at the

Air Ministry, with Douglas in the chair – and he did not then find life too strenuous to bother about the wording of minutes, as Park learned to his cost.

Douglas never accepted a distinction between simple flying ability and vital fighting experience. On 31 October, for example, he would write that the pilot position had undergone a 'kaleidoscopic change' in the last week or two: 'in the case of Fighter Command we are actually faced with a surplus.' Two days later, Evill reported more realistically to Dowding on the pilot position as at 31 October. At the end of July, he wrote, there had been sixty-two squadrons and 1,046 operational pilots; at the end of October, there were sixty-six and a half.squadrons, but only 1,042 operational pilots. Total wastage in those three months was 1,151 pilots: twenty-five every two days. During October, 231 pilots had been lost to the command, during a month when the weather had been exceptionally bad and combat losses as low as could possibly be assumed for any winter month. The command, Evill concluded, was 'at about the lowest ebb in operational pilots' at which it could function. Early in 1941, the Air Ministry would publish an account of the battle in which it claimed that Fighter Command's squadrons were stronger at the end than at the beginning. Dowding and Park rejected that claim, vigorously and publicly.[6]

At about 5 p.m. on 7 September, while Park was still in conference at Bentley Priory, the Luftwaffe launched a massive daylight attack on London. During the next hour and a half, more than 300 bombers (escorted by 600 fighters) set fire to docks, oil tanks and warehouses along the banks of the Thames east of the city. They also blasted numerous densely populated streets. Park's senior controller, John Willoughby de Broke, said later that Park was adept at sensing German intentions. He would let his controllers set the stage and then make decisions which could only be based on instinct or experience. Unfortunately, that afternoon he was not, for once, in his operations room. The very fact that the Germans chose a new target, one not hitherto attacked in daylight, contributed to the surprise achieved. Although the eventual challenge was vigorous, costing the Luftwaffe more than sixty aircraft destroyed or damaged, London was hit hard and Fighter Command lost twenty-four pilots killed or injured.

Park managed to reach Uxbridge shortly before the raid ended and, after a hasty discussion with his controllers about their handling of the fighters in his absence, left for Northolt, where he kept his Hurricane. From there, he flew over the blazing city to see for himself the extent of the disaster. Appalled by the sight of so many fires raging out of control, he reflected that the switch of targets would not be just for a single day or even a week and that he would have time to repair his control systems and so maintain an effective daylight challenge to enemy attack. He did not fear either a civilian panic or unmanageable and intolerable casualties in consequence of the new German policy, and yet Fighter Command was helpless at night. This was graphically demonstrated that very night. By 8.30 p.m., not long after Park landed, the Luftwaffe had returned. For the next seven hours, wave after wave of bombers flew over London, finding fresh targets in the light of the fires started by their comrades in daylight. They bombed at their leisure, unhindered either by anti-aircraft fire (of which there was little and that ill-directed) or by night-fighters (of which there were few and those ill-equipped).

In Park's mind, 7 September was always the turning point. Three years later, he flew to London from Malta and gave his first press interview on the Battle of Britain. He explained how close the Germans came to victory and how they threw it away by switching their main attack to London. In 1945 he broadcast from his headquarters in Singapore on the fifth anniversary of the battle, an anniversary by then established as falling on 15 September. Park still regarded the crucial moment as the change of target eight days earlier. Then and later he said that he would never forget the courage of his outnumbered pilots. Their morale was so high, he thought, because they believed they had done well at Dunkirk. They believed also that persistent opposition would eventually discourage the Luftwaffe and they knew that, in any case, they had no choice. It was common knowledge that numerous barges were being assembled in enemy ports and that the British Army was insufficiently equipped to resist German soldiers should they get ashore in force. In September 1949 Park claimed that on the day when the invasion scare was at its height, 7 September, he was ordered by the Air Ministry to prepare to demolish every aerodrome in south-east England. He refused. Resistance, he said, was impossible without them and he was determined to resist to the end. The effect on morale of the mere issue of such an order would be wholly bad. Churchill himself telephoned Park at Uxbridge that day to tell him of the invasion alert. He had not seemed particularly perturbed and neither was Park. Provided that his fighter force could still be controlled from the ground, he did not fear an invasion attempt because he believed that the German fighters could be held off by part of his force, leaving the rest free to shoot down bombers and transport aircraft at will.[7]

Park completed his report on the third phase of the battle (6 September to 31 October) on 7 November. He instructed his sector controllers on 10 September to employ squadrons in pairs: they must not be 'flung into battle singly to engage greatly superior numbers.' Having seen for himself that some squadrons still flew in close v-shaped formations of three aircraft, he ordered them to fly in loose, line-abreast formations of four aircraft. Experience had shown that the latter formation allowed pilots to keep a much greater area of sky in constant view and so be able to offer each other quicker support. Whenever squadrons split up in action, he wrote, pilots should try to keep in pairs because a solitary pilot could not guard his own tail and sooner or later must be shot down.

His squadrons were now working under extreme difficulty because of the heavy damage caused earlier to installations and landlines. Sectors were still controlling squadrons from emergency operations rooms, and telephone links between group, sector and Observer Corps centres were unreliable. The wide dispersal of squadrons to satellite airfields and the damage to station organization caused a marked slowing down in refuelling, re-arming and maintenance of aircraft and equipment. The extra motor transport required by dispersal had not been received and internal telephone links at sector stations were often broken. Luckily, attacks on aerodromes were now carried out mainly at night or at high level by day and caused little additional damage. Fully equipped alternative operations rooms, located well away from sector aerodromes, were being brought into use throughout Park's group during September.

Since August, he had been using single Spitfires to supplement radar and visual information by shadowing raids and reporting their movements. These 'Jim Crows', as they were known, provided valuable information for sector controllers, but it could not reach group controllers in time to help them. Too few machines fitted with VHF Radio Telephone equipment were available. At length, a special unit was formed at Gravesend and an R/T station set up at Uxbridge to receive direct reports from aircraft on patrol. No sooner had the unit begun work than the Air Ministry moved it to make room for night-fighters. It went to West Malling just in time to be grounded by heavy rain. Despite these setbacks, the unit supplied information, especially about high-flying intruders, that was beyond the capacity of radar or the Observer Corps. After four of its unarmed Spitfires were shot down in the first ten days of October, Park urged the Air Ministry to double its strength and provide him with interceptors capable of protecting 'Jim Crows'. Although Dowding supported him, nothing had been done by December.

During the morning of 15 September Park received a visit from Churchill, accompanied by his wife and one of his private secretaries. He had no wish to disturb anyone, he said, but as he happened to be passing, he thought he would call in to see if anything was up. If not, 'I'll just sit in the car and do my homework.' Naturally, Park welcomed the Prime Minister and his companions and escorted them down to the bomb-proof operations room, fifty feet below ground level. Churchill sensed that something important might happen that day. (Park's wife had the same sense: when he apologized at breakfast for forgetting that 15 September was her birthday, she replied that a good bag of German aircraft would be an excellent present.) Once they were in the operations room, Park tactfully explained to Churchill – not for the first time – that the air conditioning could not cope with cigar smoke. As the day's dramatic events unfolded, the Prime Minister was therefore obliged to observe them with no better consolation than a dead cigar between his teeth. He had met Park several

109

times and regarded him highly, recognizing (as he wrote after the war) that his was the group

> on which our fate largely depended. From the beginning of Dunkirk all the daylight actions in the South of England had already been conducted by him, and all his arrangements and apparatus had been brought to the highest perfection.

Although Dowding exercised supreme command, 'the actual handling of the directions of the squadrons,' Churchill continued, 'was wisely left to 11 Group.'

Soon after the visitors were seated in the 'dress circle' of the operations room, Park received a radar report of forty-plus aircraft over Dieppe, but no height was given. Then came another report of forty-plus in the same area and several squadrons were despatched to climb south-east of London. More squadrons were alerted to 'Stand By' (pilots in cockpits, ready for immediate take-off) and the remainder were ordered to 'Readiness' (take-off within five minutes). Having decided that a major attack was intended, Park had to guess its most likely targets, for his squadrons could not be everywhere. As always, he would concentrate on engaging bombers before they reached those targets, seeking to break their formations and cause them to jettison their loads into the sea or over open country.

Churchill remembered Park walking up and down behind the map table, 'watching with vigilant eye every move in the game . . . and only occasionally intervening with some decisive order, usually to reinforce a threatened area.' Churchill now broke silence. 'There appear to be many aircraft coming in.' As calmly, Park reassured him. 'There'll be someone there to meet them.' Soon all his squadrons were committed and Churchill heard him call Dowding to ask for three squadrons from 12 Group to be placed at his disposal in case of another attack. He noticed Park's anxiety and asked: 'What other reserves have we?' 'There are none,' Park replied. Exactly four months earlier, at the Quai d'Orsay in Paris, Churchill had put the same question to General Gamelin, Commander in Chief of the Allied army in the West, and had received the same answer. However, Park had a far stronger grasp of his problems and resources than that unfortunate Frenchman. Nevertheless, as Park wrote later, Churchill 'looked grave'. In fact, his squadrons were often wholly committed and Park's anxiety on this occasion was exacerbated by wondering just where and when the reinforcements from 12 Group would turn up.

Churchill asked if Park could yet judge the results of his pilots' efforts. He answered candidly that he was not satisfied that the maximum number of raiders had been intercepted. It was already evident, however, that the Germans had caused serious damage. By this date, Park had learned to cope with one of a commander's heaviest burdens, the burden of waiting: waiting to learn if his dispositions had been correct or if he had made an error that would cost the lives of his own men or if he had failed to seize an opportunity to harm the enemy.

While Park and Churchill wondered and waited, the Germans had made their greatest bid for victory in daylight. The attack on London was made in two stages, one in the late morning and the other after an interval of about two hours. If the Luftwaffe were to use its full bomber force, maximum fighter protection would have to be provided all the way out and home. Consequently, there was no scope for feints which would consume fuel and reduce both the number and endurance of escorts. The German shortage of fighters compelled the division of the attack, so that some could be used twice and so that the second attack could, with luck, catch many of Park's fighters on the ground, re-arming and refuelling.

Masses of German aircraft were observed by radar about 10.30 a.m., but they remained on the French side of the Channel. Park and his controllers therefore had time to work out a sequence of action and ground defences were fully alerted. Only then, almost as if they were waiting for these preparations to be completed, did the Germans advance. The attack proved so straightforward that Park's fighters were fed into battle as and when it suited him. He employed eleven squadrons and then asked for help. Brand sent one squadron, Leigh-Mallory a wing of five squadrons. With admirable judgment, Park threw in five more of his own in time to meet the enemy over Rochester, after five of his original eleven had engaged farther forward. He had asked Leigh-Mallory's wing to guard his aerodromes north of London. Instead, it flew straight to London and helped to break up the German formation. Bombs were scattered at random and as the raiders turned for home, they found four of Park's squadrons waiting for them over Kent and Sussex.

After a welcome lull the Germans launched their second attack. The clouds had become heavier, the radar warning was shorter, Park's fighters were later off the ground and the combat was more intense. As before, Leigh-Mallory contributed a wing of five squadrons and they, together with two of Brand's squadrons, gave an excellent account of themselves over London, although Park's pilots intercepted two of the three principal German formations before they reached the capital. Once turned, they were hotly engaged, as the first wave had been, over Kent and Sussex.

Two days later, observing that air superiority had not been attained, Hitler postponed his invasion 'until further notice'. In the opinion of the official history, 'the decisive factor was the series of actions fought by Air Vice-Marshal Park on the 15th of that month.' But this was not apparent at the time, wrote Churchill, 'nor could we tell whether even heavier attacks were not to be expected nor how long they would go on.' Visiting Park again a few days later, he got the distinct impression 'that a break in the weather would no longer be regarded as a misfortune.' The threat of invasion remained real for weeks. An analysis of decrypted Enigma signals revealed on 16 October that 'invasion preparations are actively proceeding or indeed becoming intensified' and some date after the 19th was considered likely.

The first decrypt to suggest that invasion had been postponed appeared on the 27th and it was not until 5 November that Churchill felt able to tell the House of Commons that 'all these anxious months, when we stood alone and the whole world wondered, have passed safely away'; invasion was no longer an imminent danger.

Park had issued orders on 18 September to deal with an invasion attempt. His fighters would protect naval forces and bases, cover operations by Bomber and Coastal Commands, distract dive-bombers from attack on ships engaging enemy vessels and destroy enemy aircraft carrying troops or tanks. They would attack barges and landing craft and protect British troops from dive-bombers. Army and RAF personnel would jointly defend forward aerodromes. Demolition of installations and withdrawal would take place only as a last resort, 'pending the arrival of Army mobile forces, when the aerodromes will be immediately recaptured'. As for inland aerodromes, they were to be held 'at all costs and not evacuated'. Group control would be maintained as long as telephone links with sector operations rooms were intact. Should group control become impossible, sector commanders would take charge. Should sector control fail, senior officers would act on their own initiative. The invasion would be defeated in seventy-two hours at most, but during that time pilots and ground crews must expect a hard time.[8]

The great increase in the number of enemy fighters employed late in September and the onset of cloudy weather made the task of obtaining accurate information about the composition of raids more difficult than ever. It was practically impossible to distinguish fighters from bombers when operating at high altitude and yet it was necessary to do so. Otherwise, fighter sweeps – which were not attacked – would turn out to include a large proportion of bombers. Park's high-level reconnaissance patrols did what they could to determine the composition of raids, but from 21 September he was obliged to resort to wasteful and exhausting standing patrols as well.

Dowding, in his comments of 15 November on Park's report, drew particular attention to the fact that standing patrols had been resumed. He noticed a tendency to think that the danger from daylight attacks had passed and that chances could be taken in south-east England in order to strengthen forces elsewhere, at home and abroad. But the higher state of readiness now required, and the need for keeping patrols actually in the air before the start of an attack, meant that Park's squadrons were under severe strain even though their actual losses were low.

The need for long patrols at high altitude made Park acutely aware that some pilots were simply not fit enough for this work. He was therefore keen to see that as many as possible were released for exercise and recreation whenever bad weather ruled out flying. He wanted more facilities, equipment and transport for them, also regular hot meals and more comfortable accommodation at dispersal points. Those in the London area should be billeted off their aerodromes in order to get undisturbed sleep. Regular 'guest' nights should be reintroduced and the provision of 'string bands, in order to remove some of the drabness of the present war' would be well worth the effort.

Park was conscious of the need to keep pilots amused and comfortable as well as fit, especially during the coming winter when bad weather and long hours of darkness would curtail flying, but he was also conscious of the fact that too many were novices both as pilots and as fighters. Many squadrons, he complained, being quite untrained in defensive tactics, were completely broken up by inferior numbers when attacked from above. They failed to make intelligent use of cloud and simply got lost in it, they were unable to conserve their oxygen or to maintain a good rate of climb. Some squadron and flight commanders were too old and staid for combat. The RFC lesson, he wrote, that peacetime qualifications for promotion – age and seniority – were irrelevant for combat pilots had to be learned again. Early in October a check revealed that the average age of squadron commanders was nearly thirty and Park was determined to move 'old and tired' men to ground duties or flying training and promote younger men before the 'spring offensive' of 1941.[9]

On 26 September Douglas informed Dowding that on the afternoon of the 24th twelve Blenheims of Bomber Command had been sent to attack minesweepers in the Channel. Fighter cover had been asked for, but had apparently failed to make contact with the Blenheims. Douglas wanted to know why. On the morning of the 24th, he continued, a single Anson of Coastal Command had been sent to attack E-boats and had itself been attacked by enemy aircraft. Had fighter escort been provided? If not, why not? Douglas did not ask Coastal Command why a single, vulnerable Anson had been used on such a dangerous mission.

Evill investigated both incidents at Dowding's request. During a heavy raid on the 24th, he reported, instructions came from Douglas for fighter protection of an operation he was mounting involving both Bomber and Coastal Commands. The latter refused to take part, but Bomber Command agreed to go ahead. Although Park was very busy, three squadrons were sent to the right place at the right time. Only one pilot, however, was able to attack when German fighters dived on the Blenheims. Evill thought this illustrated the weakness of a mass of fighters tied at low altitude to direct support of slow-flying bombers. Many German fighter pilots would have agreed heartily and Douglas himself would eventually grasp the point, during 1941. As for the Anson affair, Evill regarded it as 'an enterprise whose value may perhaps be questioned.' The request for an escort, which failed to find it, had come from Stevenson, Director of Home Operations.

In his reply to Douglas, Dowding observed that 'the arrangements made by No. 11 Group were all and possibly more than might have been expected of them under the circumstances.' Douglas, abandoning his usual peremptory manner for the moment, kept silent. Portal, however, did not. Then head of Bomber Command, he wrote on 6 October to inform Dowding that he entirely appreciated the difficulty of coordinating bombers and fighters in busy times and emphasized the 'very amicable relations' between No. 2 (Bomber) Group and Park's group, adding that he was unaware of the reason for Douglas's signal of 26 September since neither he nor the commander of 2 Group had complained about the escort provided for the Blenheims. Both Douglas and Stevenson had the duty of scrutinizing the conduct of Fighter Command, but on this as on other occasions that scrutiny lapsed into dangerous interference.[10]

Until the end of September, Park was confident that his fighters were superior to their opponents. During October, however, in fighting at great heights – above 25,000 feet – he thought the Germans 'vastly superior' because their two-stage superchargers maintained higher engine power. The Mark II versions of the Spitfire and Hurricane were not the answer, in his opinion. Fighters capable of at least 400 m.p.h. with a ceiling of at least 40,000 feet were needed. They also needed heavier armament. A combination of two cannons and four machine-guns would be ideal, he thought: cannons for a more destructive blow against bombers, at the expense of a rapid rate of fire, and machine-guns to deal with fighters, when quick bursts were essential. He wanted more attention paid to improving cockpit heating and preventing air leaks, because at high altitude the smallest leak had a paralysing effect if it played upon any part of the body. In an attempt to counter intense cold, pilots were wearing thick, heavy clothing, which made it difficult for them to respond quickly to an emergency.

Park would have left the command before these matters were attended to, but progress was made in October in re-equipping aircraft with VHF R/T equipment. This made it possible, he explained, for squadrons to operate on separate frequencies when detailed to separate tasks or to operate on a common frequency when working as pairs or in larger units. He reminded command headquarters on 5 November that each sector station in his group would soon have two day squadrons equipped with VHF, but this would leave one squadron on HF at six stations. While one was on HF, the whole system must be retained, employing many personnel and landlines. Operational flexibility, he pointed out, was very restricted because HF squadrons could not be put on the same frequency as VHF squadrons. There was only a fifty-fifty chance that when two squadrons were ordered off in company that they would be able to communicate with each other. Park therefore asked for the highest priority in fitting VHF equipment in the third squadron at stations in his group. Once this much superior equipment was generally installed, the employment of large formations by Park's successor became a feasible tactic.

On 21 October Air Vice-Marshal L.D.D. McKean, head of the British air liaison mission in Ottawa, informed Park that Billy Bishop, one of the most famous pilots of the First World War, had been greatly taken with Park during his visit to England early in October. McKean enclosed press cuttings in which Bishop, now an Air Marshal in the Royal Canadian Air Force, said of Park: 'He impressed me more than any man I have ever met.' Park thanked McKean for the 'amusing' cuttings reporting Billy's 'excellent propaganda' and sent both Bishop and McKean copies of his report on air fighting in September and October. McKean thanked Park on 22 January 1941. It was the first time, he said, despite numerous applications to the Air Ministry, that he had received anything of real value concerning operations:

> I was immensely struck by the way you were always thinking ahead of the Hun, and I would add that from what I have heard from other sources there can be no question of the tremendous reputation your Group has gained in first-class efficiency.

Unfortunately, Park was less adept at thinking ahead of the Air Ministry and by the time he read McKean's praise had long been dismissed from his command.

Despite his losses and strains in the great daylight battles, Park was eager to mount an offensive at the first opportunity. He told his sector commanders on 21 October that the Germans could not assemble and launch mass raids from north-west France later than ninety minutes before sunset if they hoped to return to base in daylight. He therefore proposed to use that period to surprise them by making strong sweeps over their airfields. Dowding had ruled against such sweeps, as Evill politely reminded Park on 2 November, but Douglas – who replaced Dowding on 25 November – was anxious to 'lean forward into France' and now ordered Park to look into the possibility of escorting bomber raids as well as making fighter sweeps. On 20 December, a few days after Leigh-Mallory replaced Park at 11 Group, two Spitfires attacked a German airfield at Le Touquet. This attack marked the start of the counter-offensive, one that Park had very much in mind weeks before his dismissal.[11]

He also had night operations very much in mind from September onwards. His Blenheims proved quite unsuitable and at the end of October the Air Ministry decided to form two night-fighter wings, of two squadrons each, at Gravesend in Kent and Rochford in Essex. Park looked forward to the introduction of the Beaufighter, specially developed for night-fighting, and the opportunity to carry out intensive training. But his sector operations rooms, working almost continuously, were not free for long to practise controlling night-fighters and exercises in remote areas were of little use. Many more Beaufighters fitted with AI Mark IV radar equipment were needed, he wrote, but both aircraft and equipment suffered so many technical failures that only the most devoted nursing by day enabled them to function at all by night.

On 12 November Park issued instructions for the operation of the two night-fighter wings. Tactics, he said, were 'those of a cat stalking a mouse rather than a greyhound chasing a hare'. He went on to discuss the type and number of aircraft to use for differing conditions, their control and operation, area of patrol and cooperation with ground defences – guns, searchlights and balloons. He would have made a good night-fighting organizer. He certainly covered the subject shrewdly and in detail in his report of 7 November and in these instructions. Douglas, so quick to comment on the absence of such coverage at a time when there had been little night activity, refrained from comment now. If Dowding and Park had to leave their respective posts in November and December 1940, would it not have made sense for one or both to be assigned to the night defence problem? It would have been beneficial to divide the problems of day and night defence: they required different aircraft, aircrews, tactics and methods of control.[12]

Park wrote to Squadron Leader Max Aitken (son of Lord Beaverbrook, then Churchill's Minister of Aircraft Production) on 7 November, sending him a copy of his account of operations in September and October. He drew Aitken's attention specially to his paragraphs on aircraft performance. Aitken replied on the 10th, having shown those paragraphs to his father: 'Actually, I have been talking "height" to him for some weeks,' he wrote. Park was delighted to hear that Beaverbrook was interested in the problem of providing high-altitude fighters for the spring offensive. 'I hope by then,' he replied, 'to have a few additional squadrons and to make it really offensive, instead of struggling against superior numbers over home territory.' Park wrote again to Aitken on the 14th. Dowding had telephoned, he said, and was angry that Beaverbrook had seen the report before it was officially submitted. Park had answered that he had sent it to Aitken because he had a lively interest in the subject, but 'that did not placate him, and you may expect to see me selling newspapers on the corner of Piccadilly and Haymarket any day now. If so, you will at least know that I got fired in a good cause.' Within days of penning this pleasantry he had in fact been fired; so, too, had Dowding.

In mid-November, Park sent a report to Wing Commander Sir Louis Greig, Sinclair's secretary, on the unsatisfactory situation in regard to works services and transport facilities at the majority of his fighter stations. These were all matters that had been raised for months past, he wrote. Though always very sympathetic, he continued,

> Higher Authority has proved quite incapable of meeting the most urgent requirements of the fighting units, which leads one to suppose

that the existing machine is beyond the stage of requiring a little
lubrication, but requires a sledge hammer.

The Duke of Kent, recently appointed Welfare Officer in Park's group, 'is
quite incensed at the general discomfort and lack of facilities he has had
pointed out at every station he has visited.'

A fortnight later, on 27 November, Park wrote to Greig again, thanking
him for his help in improving living conditions at fighter stations. He had
landed at Biggin Hill a few days earlier, 'and to my surprise found there the
Director of Works, accompanied by many experts, busily taking down notes
and conferring with the Station Commander.' The Duke, however, 'appears
to have lost interest now that he has heard that I am leaving the Group,' but
Park would try to revive his enthusiasm.

He sent copies of his September–October report to several senior officers,
emphasizing that it was fuller and more interesting than his earlier reports.
Leslie Gossage, his predecessor at 11 Group and now Air Member for
Personnel, thanked Park for a copy on 26 November. 'You leave behind you
a record of fine achievement,' he wrote, 'and have given the country an
overwhelming sense of security during the hours of daylight and, maybe, by
night too, before long!' Park replied next day:

> As the senior members of my Group Staff deserve the lion's share of the
> credit for our successes, I am taking the liberty of showing them your
> letter, because they have not had much recognition apart from my own
> thanks at the end of each phase of the operations.

He was glad that the pilots had received immediate and liberal recognition,
but there were many officers and men spread around his twenty-six fighter
stations whose gallantry, good judgment or hard work had so far been
ignored.

Gossage thought the lack of recognition was a result of the command's
preoccupation with the battle, but Park disagreed. During the past seven
months, he told his senior staff officers on 10 December, recommendations
for non-immediate and periodic awards had been called for. With few
exceptions, those from station and squadron commanders had been
forwarded by Park to command headquarters with his strong recommendation. 'After considerable delay' and 'after having been pruned', they were
forwarded to the Air Ministry. Park knew that Dowding took a hard line on
honours and awards even for acts of gallantry and rarely considered them
justified for continuous hard work: public recognition meant little to him and
he disdained its appeal to others. In such matters, among others, Park was a
more imaginative and sensitive commander.[13]

Park served out his last days in the command under Douglas's orders. He
attended a group commanders' conference at Bentley Priory on 29

November. Douglas announced that he was keen to get away from a purely defensive outlook and, when weather permitted, wanted sweeps carried out over Calais by one or even two wings (of three squadrons each) to 'practise squadrons in working in large formations.' Park said that his squadrons had been operating occasionally in this way and showed great enthusiasm for the work. He was asked by Douglas to get in touch with Bomber Command to see if these fighter sweeps could be combined with any of their operations.

On 3 December he sent Douglas a report on air fighting in November. G.M. Lawson, Group Captain (Ops.), minuted Evill on the 11th about 'another excellent report' from Park. His group had 'dealt with the changing tactical situation in an able manner.' The air–sea rescue system, as Park pointed out, was unsatisfactory. Coordination between 10 and 11 Groups was admirable, but it remained to be seen whether 12 Group's wing could be operated efficiently in future. Park had again omitted to include the number of pilots wounded and injured with the figure of those missing and killed. Hence his picture of air combat was too favourable, as in his earlier reports. Like Lawson, Evill drew Douglas's attention to the weakness of the air sea rescue system, which must be improved if the command were planning more offensive action. Evill did not think Park's reaction to the resumption of attacks on convoys was as spontaneous as he implied, but his measures were certainly successful and his controllers almost always reacted quickly enough when estuary shipping was threatened. Although the control of reinforcing squadrons was being made easier by the introduction of VHF, a real solution was mainly a matter of inter-group cooperation. Evill agreed with Park that little had been done to examine training methods in the groups with a view to selecting the best ideas and bringing them into general use. He also agreed that training was essential to the success of night interception. While these comments on his last report were before Douglas, in mid-December, Park was packing his bags for exile in deepest Gloucestershire.

The Battle of Britain was, in fact, a *campaign* lasting 114 days, from 10 July to 31 October. Over such a long period, there were many changes of strength in the respective forces, caused by efforts to increase rates of production and repair as well as by destruction and damage. There were also marked differences between the numbers of aircraft available on station, combat-ready or unserviceable at any one time. This is why no two books on the subject use the same figures. In round figures, however, the Luftwaffe usually had about 2,250 aircraft combat-ready: 1,250 bombers (including 250 dive-bombers) and 1,000 fighters (including 220 twin-engined fighters). Opposing this force, Fighter Command in July had 750 *effective* fighters (450 Hurricanes and 300 Spitfires), of which 600 were combat-ready. These forces increased by nearly ten per cent in August and September. Over the whole campaign, Fighter Command lost 537 aircrew killed and as many again badly injured out of some 3,000 aircrew who made at least one sortie. The Luftwaffe lost almost five times as many men killed (2,662) and more than

6,000 wounded or captured. The British lost ten fighters for every nineteen German machines destroyed: 1,023 for 1,887 in total.

Park was a practical airman, at home in the cockpit of a Hurricane even at the age of forty-eight. He was one of the few officers of high rank in any of the world's air forces in 1940 who flew modern fighters. He flew more hours (eighty-three) that year than in any year since 1934 and except in 1941 he never logged so many again. It was not until 3 May 1940 that he flew a Hurricane for the second time (his first flight was in July 1938), but thereafter he flew one regularly. He wanted to see for himself conditions on the ground as well as in the air and to hear what pilots and ground crews had to say. He had often flown around on his own over France in 1918 for the same reason: to see for himself what his men were doing. From 3 May until 24 November he piloted a Hurricane on sixty-one occasions: twice a week, on average, during those seven hectic months. He took every chance he could to escape from his 'mahogany bomber' (his office chair) and climb into a Hurricane. When he died, Air Commodore E.M. Donaldson, a Battle of Britain pilot, wrote: 'All of us worshipped him. Not only because he was an outstanding commander, but because he also set a tremendous example of courage in the air.'

Park had taken with him to Uxbridge a detailed knowledge of Fighter Command's structure and also the knowledge that reckless expenditure of precious Hurricanes and Spitfires might lose the war in a few hours. His experience of the previous two years, however, had taught him to curb his natural instinct to attack. He knew that he must refuse to commit his meagre force until he was in a position to deliver a crushing blow against an enemy weakened by many vain attempts to bring him to premature action – and he knew that that happy position was not even in sight. Week after week, throughout the whole campaign, Park showed uncommon strength of mind in resisting pressure from both senior and junior officers to use larger forces than he thought proper. That resistance cost him his job once the battle was over.[14]

CHAPTER TEN

The Battle of Britain: Big Wings

One day in February 1940, while Park was still at Bentley Priory, Leigh-Mallory 'came out of Dowding's office, paused in mine and said in my presence that he would move heaven and earth to get Dowding removed from Fighter Command.' Dowding did not hear about this incident until 1968, when Park revealed it to the New Zealand press. 'I had no idea,' said Dowding, 'that there was such a feeling of enmity towards me on Leigh-Mallory's part . . . what a wretched position for him to place Park in.' Leigh-Mallory 'made it quite clear to me,' added Park, 'that he was very jealous of my group, which was in the front line [after Dunkirk].' Dowding wished Park had kept him more personally informed about his difficulties with Leigh-Mallory:

> I know now that he tried to fight it out for himself. He would, and he deserves praise for that. But I might have been able to help him more. When the time came for me to intervene it was too late . . . too late for both of us.

Dowding, however, had several opportunities to observe Leigh-Mallory's inadequate handling of his group even before war began, and during the Battle of Britain Park did, in fact, draw Dowding's attention to Leigh-Mallory's sins of omission and commission long before it was too late for him to intervene.

'By persistently declining to give cover to my sector aerodromes . . . in late August and early September,' wrote Park, 'No. 12 Group jeopardized our victory in this crucial battle.' This serious charge was made long after the war, when Park had had plenty of time to reflect and choose his words carefully; when, moreover, his conduct of the battle had been amply vindicated not only by most historians but also by an overwhelming majority of the pilots concerned. Leigh-Mallory, killed late in 1944, was unable to speak in his own defence, but few historians or pilots have spoken for him.[1]

Throughout the summer of 1940, Leigh-Mallory found it increasingly difficult to accept his place in the rear, behind the front line. Then, at the very end of August, he suddenly found in the 'big wings' idea of Douglas Bader what seemed a way of making a direct contribution to the battle. Bader had lost his left leg below the knee and his right leg above it when he crashed an aircraft in 1931. He was obliged to leave the RAF, but returned when war broke out, demonstrating the courage and skill needed to become a fighter pilot despite his grave handicap. In February 1940 he was posted to a squadron in 12 Group and by June had been given command of a squadron in Norfolk which moved to Duxford on 30 August. Everyone who served with Bader admired his achievements and rapidly became familiar with his trenchant criticism of British fighter tactics. According to Bader, a wing of three or more squadrons should take off from aerodromes in 12 Group as soon as news was received that a raid was building up over France. Having had time to gain vital height, the wing should intercept the enemy in force as it crossed the English coast. Park's squadrons should then join in and harry the departing raiders. Bader quite understood that a wing could not operate from 11 Group aerodromes because the time needed to assemble and climb to a safe height was too short.

Like Leigh-Mallory, he was irked by his place in the rear. His frustration no doubt sharpened his advocacy of a means by which he could become more closely involved in the battle. He could – and should – have served his turn in the front line, but Leigh-Mallory refused to permit him to go south and he did not ask to go. Bader rejected the strict ground-to-air control system devised by Dowding, Park and their advisers, service and civilian. It was this lack of team cooperation, as much as the enthusiasm for big wings, which agitated and confused the defence system.

Sholto Douglas supported the use of big wings. Unlike Leigh-Mallory, Douglas had been a fighter pilot, but since 1918 had spent most of his time in administration or teaching. As long before as 11 August 1938 he had told Donald Stevenson that he thought it 'immaterial in the long view whether the enemy bomber is shot down before or after he has dropped his bombs on his objective.' His intention was *not* to prevent bombers from reaching their target, but to punish them so severely that they would be reluctant to return. Leigh-Mallory agreed: targets should be left to their ground defences, he thought, and a concentrated attack made on the enemy – if necessary, after he had bombed.

Douglas and Leigh-Mallory received valuable assistance from a Member of Parliament, Peter Macdonald, who was adjutant of Bader's squadron. 'Boozy Mac', as he was known, busied himself in the House of Commons in support of big wing tactics and at the suggestion of Harold Balfour, Under-Secretary of State for Air, saw the Prime Minister himself. Neither Dowding nor Park had any idea that a squadron adjutant was using political influence behind their backs.[2]

Park wrote to Evill on 27 August. Thanks to the good cooperation of Sir

Quintin Brand, he said, he never had any difficulty or delay with 10 Group either in obtaining or providing quick reinforcement. Although Leigh-Mallory had recently offered assistance, his squadrons had not in fact been placed where requested. Station commanders who had been informed that 12 Group squadrons were assigned to protect their aerodromes felt insecure when ordered to send squadrons forward to intercept on the coast. Park hoped Evill would agree that to accept offers of aid and not get it was apt to shake confidence. He had neither the time nor the facilities, he went on, to check if 12 Group squadrons were ordered to patrol aerodromes that were bombed. He could only say that in one instance they had not patrolled North Weald until long after the bombing was over, and in the cases of Debden and Hornchurch, Park could get no confirmation that Leigh-Mallory's squadrons had ever been seen.

He had therefore instructed his controllers not to accept direct offers from the north. When assistance was needed, they were to ask command controller. Would Evill advise his staff to expect such requests? Park's controllers would need to know if the request had been agreed to, when the aid would be forthcoming and if that aid was subsequently diverted from the area under threat so that Park could make other arrangements. The next day, Evill informed command controllers that Park 'has represented that it may on occasion be more satisfactory to him' if temporary reinforcement of his group were arranged by command and not, as hitherto, between the groups concerned. This support, Evill instructed, 'is not to be diverted from the allotted task' without further reference.

These arrangements cannot have been made without Dowding's knowledge. As Commander-in-Chief, it was surely his duty to enquire promptly and closely into the incidents which gave rise to them. North Weald had been bombed on 24 August and no aircraft from 12 Group had appeared in time to defend it. Two days later, a squadron from Duxford which had been expressly ordered to patrol over Debden had failed to appear and this sector station had been damaged. On 30 August Biggin Hill was hit by raiders unchallenged from the air, even though Park had appealed for help. Were his controllers seeking help too late? Were Leigh-Mallory's men responding too slowly? By the end of August, according to Park's senior controller, Willoughby de Broke, relations with their opposite numbers in 12 Group were no longer good.

On 30 August, however, Bader claimed an astonishing victory in an air battle west of Enfield. Ten Hurricanes attacked no fewer than 100 enemy aircraft and routed them: twelve destroyed, several more damaged and not so much as a bullet-hole suffered in exchange. Evidence in support of this claim is hard to find, but Leigh-Mallory was convinced and agreed with Bader that several squadrons operating as a unit would achieve even more spectacular results.

In the late afternoon of 7 September, one of the critical days of the battle,

Bader's wing was summoned to patrol over North Weald. As usual, he interpreted this order broadly and went in search of action. By the time he found it, his wing had lost all cohesion and although his squadron alone claimed as many as eleven aircraft destroyed, in exchange for the loss of one pilot, he admitted to Leigh-Mallory that the operation had failed in its self-appointed task, quite apart from its failure to guard North Weald. Leigh-Mallory, however, was impressed by Bader's victory claims and encouraged him to continue using a big wing. On 9 September he assigned two more squadrons to him, following another freelance sweep which again claimed a spectacular bag of downed Germans and which was again carried out in defiance of orders to patrol Park's aerodromes.

On 17 September Leigh-Mallory signed a report on wing patrols carried out by squadrons of his group. Experience had shown, he said, that mass attacks on London and the south-east involved large numbers of fighters as well as bombers. When asked to protect 11 Group's aerodromes, he therefore considered it 'wholly inadequate' to send single squadrons and employed instead a wing of up to five squadrons. Five such operations had now taken place. All told, they had claimed 105 German aircraft destroyed, another 40 probably destroyed and 18 damaged. These causes for celebration, 163 of one kind or another, were offset by the loss of only six pilots killed or missing, five wounded and 14 aircraft destroyed. Victory claims by Bader's wing were notoriously high: twice as many victims for each squadron as were claimed by other squadrons, whose claims, it is now known, were already exaggerated.

Dowding replied to Leigh-Mallory's report on 23 September. 'I read a great many combat reports,' he wrote, 'and I think I am beginning to pick out those which can be relied on and those which throw in claims at the end for good measure.' Evill forwarded the report to the Air Ministry the next day. The claims, he said, could only be regarded as approximate. There were good reasons for letting it be widely known that Fighter Command was bringing down enormous numbers of enemy aircraft, but the Air Ministry was well placed to know the actual figures, allowing something for those lost in the Channel or crashing in France. It must have been clear to someone in the Air Ministry, and hence to Douglas, that the claims made by Bader's squadrons were beyond all likelihood. Douglas chose to accept the claims without question. As for Park, he noted on his copy of Leigh-Mallory's report: 'Did these Wings engage before targets were *bombed*?'

Douglas informed Air Vice-Marshal Saundby, Assistant Chief of the Air Staff (Tactics), on 24 September that he had received 'a number of criticisms recently from several sources' about Park's tactics. Squadrons, it was alleged, went up with no clear idea as to how many other squadrons were in the air and no instructions as to how they were to cooperate with them. What we want, said Douglas, is 'some plan . . . some sort of broad coordinated plan of action'. Saundby instructed Group Captain H.G. Crowe, Deputy Director of Air Tactics, to enquire and report, which he did on 1 October. Squadrons, said Crowe, did sometimes go up with no clear idea how many other squadrons had been detailed to attack nor how they were to cooperate with them. When they were despatched singly from separate aerodromes, it was difficult to rendezvous before making contact with the enemy. Crowe pointed out that Park did in fact detail a proportion of his force to deal with high-flying escorts and that he did have a broad plan for dealing with large raids. When VHF radio became available, wing leaders would be able to speak to each other and squadrons within a wing would be able to communicate: the means to coordinate attacks and alter dispositions to suit changing circumstances would then exist. Saundby passed Crowe's report to Douglas with a note advising him to read Park's report on air fighting in August and September – and *especially* to read Leigh-Mallory's report on wing patrols.[3]

Park, meanwhile, had written to Dowding on 29 September. When it appeared likely that the scale of attack would be too heavy for him to break up and turn unaided, he had arranged for Brand to provide up to four squadrons in support. Those squadrons were not requested unless it seemed likely that aircraft factories or sector aerodromes west and south-west of London were probable targets. Similarly, when Brand needed help, he asked and Park provided, unless he was heavily engaged. The arrangement had worked smoothly for the past two months because Brand agreed with Park that

> it is more essential to get a small number of squadrons quickly to the point requested than to delay whilst his squadrons are forming up in wings, which would mean their arriving at the scene of battle after vital objectives have been bombed and the enemy was retreating. The latter action undoubtedly secures a bigger 'bag' of enemy aircraft but does not achieve our main aim, which is to protect aircraft factories and other vital points from being bombed by day.

Arrangements with Leigh-Mallory, by contrast, were unsatisfactory. Actions by his group had confused the Observer Corps, Park's sector controllers and fighter squadrons. Twice in August his group had failed to cover sector aerodromes north-east of London while Park's squadrons were engaging the enemy between the coast and their targets. Those aerodromes were bombed and consequently all requests for aid from Leigh-Mallory had since been submitted to command controller in the hope that squadrons would be sent to and remain in the areas required. During a recent attack, Park had asked if 12 Group squadrons were patrolling between North Weald and Hornchurch as requested, so that he could concentrate his own squadrons south of the Thames. He had been told that the squadrons were down in Kent, somewhere near Canterbury. There had been several occasions when the Observer Corps reported raids in east Kent to which fighters were directed, only to find themselves facing British fighters.

Evill commented on this letter for Dowding on 5 October. Leigh-Mallory, he said, *did* send one or two squadrons to help Park when urgently needed. As a rule, though, he sent them in big wings. 'It is, of course, entirely wrong that these formations should be permitted to rove without control over 11 Group's sectors, and I presume that you will wish this stopped.' It seemed to Evill that all Park's requests concerning aid were 'entirely reasonable except that they tend to ignore the value of utilizing the large formation when time permits.' Park's squadrons, thought Evill, had been affected by constant fighting against heavier numbers. There were times when the position could be reversed, however, and Park should give more recognition to this possibility and so organize things that he could deliberately use Leigh-Mallory's strength.

Dowding forwarded a copy of Park's letter to Leigh-Mallory on 8 October, asking him to comment. As for the bombing of North Weald and Hornchurch, replied Leigh-Mallory the next day, the request had been made too late for his squadrons to reach the attack area at the height of the enemy aircraft. As for the point about a small, early reinforcement rather than a large, later one, if he were permitted to send up his wing when German activity was boiling up over the French coast, there was ample time to get down to the Hornchurch area. And as for Park's proposals to avoid confusion, Leigh-Mallory did not agree that he should send his squadrons to the area and at the height requested because the requests came too late; nor did he intend to stop forming up a mass of five squadrons before despatching them. He admitted that his wings had appeared in east Kent, but only when called down by Fighter Command or when drawn down in the course of action. Evill and Lawson checked and rejected this assertion.

The experience of Myles Duke-Woolley illustrates some of the practical problems of wing tactics. One day, late in September, he was leading his Hurricane squadron (based at Kenley, in 11 Group) on a standing patrol over Canterbury. He got everyone up to 31,000 feet and then, looking north, saw a black mass far below coming from the direction of London. He recognized it as 12 Group's wing. It is worth noticing that Duke-Woolley spotted the wing miles away and had a decisive height advantage over it even as far south as Canterbury, despite Leigh-Mallory's advocacy of Duxford as a base from which to gain safe altitude before flying into Park's area. The wing looked so determined that Duke-Woolley turned in behind it as a voluntary top-cover. His squadron was using a loose German-style formation, in accordance with Park's instructions, and Hurricanes were not supposed to fly as high as 31,000 feet. The wing, failing to recognize the Hurricanes and thinking it was about to be attacked, orbited. Duke-Woolley, thinking it was preparing to intercept a raid, followed suit. For some minutes there was complete stalemate until the wing began to run short of fuel – having taken so long to assemble – and retired in good order northwards. A fortnight later, Duke-Woolley learned that his patrol report had got around and was received with 'huge delight' by ground crews and pilots throughout 11 Group. The incident underlines the fact that radio communication between unaffiliated squadrons was still impossible at that time.

There was a feeling among some pilots, wrote Park to his sectors on 1 October, that the only way to defeat enemy raiders was to employ fighters in wings of three or more squadrons. This note was intended to explain 'why such formations have been used off and on during the past five months, yet have not been made the standard method of grouping our fighter squadrons in home defence fighting.' During operations over Europe, Park wrote, squadrons had at first been employed singly. When opposition increased, they had been used in pairs. Occasionally, when squadrons were seriously under-strength, they had been used in wings of three. There had been time then to arrange them into pairs or wings, but now – for home defence – that time was not available. Actually, despite the favourable conditions for operating wings over Europe, Park had found that the best results were obtained by pairs of squadrons. Whenever possible, two pairs would patrol the same area: one at high altitude to engage fighters, the other about 5,000 to 8,000 feet lower to engage bombers, which had not in those days been provided with close escorts.

Experience during August and September, he went on, showed that a formation of three squadrons had great difficulty in assembling above cloud at rendezvous points and keeping in touch when passing through cloud. Instead of devoting time to searching for the enemy, each squadron had to pay the closest attention to maintaining contact with the other two. In fact, it took longer to assemble a wing of three squadrons and climb it to operational height than to assemble and climb two pairs. Nevertheless, in clear weather and when the enemy attacked in two or three waves, there was often time for squadrons on the flank of the attack to be sent as a wing to meet the third wave or to catch retreating aircraft from earlier waves. It was not practicable for three squadrons to work on a common R/T frequency until VHF was available in all squadrons, whereas pairs could and did work successfully on a common frequency. Experience had shown, Park concluded, that the pair was the most satisfactory formation, but squadrons should continue to study and practise fighting in wings of three because those tactics would probably be used more often when the British offensive began.

Two copies of this letter went to every fighter squadron, one to every sector controller and three to Bentley Priory. Even if his pilots did not agree with all his arguments, they could not complain that they were kept in the dark about their commander's thinking. They were paid the compliment of a reasoned analysis of questions which concerned them deeply. Park had no objection to the employment of aircraft in any particular formation, large or small. He insisted constantly on the need to keep in mind weather, time and the variety of challenges posed by the Luftwaffe.

Park wrote to Dowding on 10 October. He wanted 12 Group to take a larger share of the fighting, but owing to more cloudy conditions and to the higher speed and altitude of present fighter-bomber attacks, interception was impossible unless squadrons had perfect R/T communication and worked directly under a sector controller who had in front of him all available information from reconnaissance aircraft, sighting reports by patrols, Observer Corps and gun site reports. They could only take advantage of this information if controlled from sectors close to London. Effective sector control required squadrons to live and work in a sector for weeks, so that there was complete understanding between formation leaders and sector controllers. To achieve this, 12 Group squadrons would need to be exchanged with squadrons presently in 11 Group. The only alternative, Park thought, would be for Leigh-Mallory to provide a wing of three squadrons to work under the control of Biggin Hill or Kenley for a short period each day. This would involve a great deal of flying time, to and from 12 Group, as well as refuelling before or after patrol in 11 Group.[4]

While Park was working out a method of cooperating with 12 Group, the Air Ministry was producing a critique of his tactics. On 14 October Stevenson produced for Douglas some notes on the operation of fighter wings. Based on Leigh-Mallory's report of 17 September, they followed his line: fighters had been meeting the enemy on unequal terms in number and height; they should be operated in tactical units large enough to deal with their opponents and so controlled that they were not caught at a disadvantage; the efforts of squadrons had not been effectively coordinated; squadron leaders had had few opportunities to discuss or concert operations with other squadron leaders; and fighters had often been ordered to patrol too low and to engage enemy formations from below. Stevenson recommended that the minimum unit used to meet large formations should be a wing of three squadrons. When necessary a force of two wings should be used. It would be known as a 'Balbo' in memory of an Italian politician and airman who had led large forces of Italian aircraft. In order to ensure 'sympathetic and effective' control of the wing, one of its squadron commanders should 'supervise' that control from the sector operations room.

It would frequently happen, thought Stevenson, that Balbos would pass out of R/T range of their sectors. 'When this happens it may be confidently expected that weather conditions will be such that large enemy formations will be clearly visible from a distance and vectoring therefore will be unnecessary.' Not to mention impossible. Should Stevenson's confident expectations be dashed, something which he called 'Esprit de Wing' would guide pilots. He ended by announcing that the Chief of the Air Staff (Newall until 25 October when Portal succeeded him) intended to hold a conference in his room on 17 October 'to discuss major tactics by fighter formations, and to hear a report on the progress of night interception.' Dowding, Park, Leigh-Mallory and Brand were asked to attend.

Together with his notes, Stevenson circulated a covering letter in which he wrote that Park's report on the fighting in August and September did not say whether squadrons were vectored into battle singly, in pairs or in larger formations, nor did he say what role was allocated to the squadrons in a general action. Stevenson also circulated a copy of Leigh-Mallory's report: 'It will be noted that no less than 105 enemy aircraft were destroyed at a cost of 14 of our fighters (6 pilots of which were killed or missing).'

Park, having received Stevenson's letter and notes, asked him on 15 October to circulate two recent instructions in which he summarized the results of 'our five *months* experience in the employment of wing formations.' Since Stevenson had included in the conference papers details of results achieved by 12 Group, Park asked him to circulate the results achieved by himself and Brand, using pairs. They were better overall, even though the groups' primary task was to protect London, aircraft factories and sector aerodromes and not to secure a 'maximum bag' of enemy aircraft after they had done their worst.

It was a small meeting, by Air Ministry standards: only twelve men and two secretaries. Douglas presided in the absence of Newall, who was indisposed. Leigh-Mallory brought Bader and the appearance of so junior an officer (a squadron leader) at so senior a meeting may well have been unprecedented and certainly astonished Dowding and Park, among others. Although Leigh-Mallory was surely justified in encouraging the acknowledged leading spirit of wing tactics to put his case, a pilot with regular front-line experience should also have been invited to attend and comment, for or against Bader's arguments. But neither Park nor Brand thought of taking a pilot to this meeting and naturally Douglas, Stevenson and Leigh-Mallory did not suggest that they should. In the event, to produce Bader at the meeting proved a masterstroke, establishing the claim of Douglas and his friends to be patrons of bold, new ideas.

Douglas asked the meeting to consider three propositions. One, that enemy formations should be outnumbered when encountered. Two, that fighters should go into battle with a plan of action, so that escorts were engaged by one part of the force and bombers by the rest. And three, that fighters should, if possible, have a height advantage. Douglas's long speech showed no sign of being informed by a reading of Park's reports or his numerous instructions in which these and many other matters of anxious, daily concern had been exhaustively analysed. Eventually, Douglas stopped talking and invited comments.

Park spoke first. According to Bader, he looked tired. No doubt he was and no doubt he looked worse than he felt – he was normally pale and thin and had been in hospital before the start of the battle; he had also been at the heart of fighter defence for more than two strenuous years. Despite his tiredness, he spoke cogently, making many telling points. Yet he spoke in vain. Why was he unable to persuade those at this meeting whose minds were not already made up? Some, such as Slessor, who after his retirement spoke out boldly against this 'unhappy (and wholly unnecessary)' meeting, were mindful of their own prospects of advancement. Portal, however, had reached the top of the tree. True, he had no experience of fighter defence and his tenure of Bomber Command had been brief, but he knew Park of old and evidently preferred the opinions of Douglas and his friends. They were better educated than Park; more polished, more urbane. An austere man, serious and ambitious, Park struck many people as humourless and vain. Portal was a man of similar stamp and it may be that, privately, he admired more vivid personalities, such as those of Douglas, Leigh-Mallory and (later) Harris. For the rest of the war, all three conducted their various commands as they pleased, outfacing Portal whenever he challenged them. Not the least of Park's problems in winning over those at the meeting was the fact that he was Dowding's man, put into 11 Group ahead of Leigh-Mallory. In Churchill's opinion, 'jealousies and cliquism' were rife in the Air Ministry. Dowding, as is well known, was hated there and sooner or later one of the many attempts to get him out of Bentley Priory must succeed. When that happened, Park must also go. His apparent fatigue provided the neatest justification for dismissing him.

Everyone present at that meeting (except Bader) knew, or ought to have known, that the reality of air defence was more complicated than Leigh-Mallory supposed. The argument that his aircraft, based in the rear, had time to get into position if scrambled as soon as it was learned that a raid was building up and that it should make the initial interception while Park's squadrons pursued retreating raiders, was impracticable. Radar could not give accurate information about the number and height of approaching aircraft; German aircraft did not select one target for each raid and head straight for it; Park's squadrons would have been in even greater danger of being caught on the ground and less able to gain combat altitude once German aircraft were actually overhead; and, above all, it was not certain that the all-out fighter-to-fighter contest resulting from Leigh-Mallory's tactics would end in British favour. Nor did it. In that contest, despite its escort duties and many operations at extreme range, the Luftwaffe had a distinct edge, losing 873 fighters (single- and twin-engined) in exchange for 1,023 British fighters.

Leigh-Mallory asserted that he could get a wing of five squadrons into the air in six minutes and that it could be over Hornchurch at 20,000 feet in twenty-five minutes. (In fact, on 29 October the Duxford wing was to take seventeen minutes to leave the ground and a further twenty before it set course from base – this after two months' constant practice. Moreover, because it absorbed five squadrons from a relatively weak group, important targets in East Anglia and the Midlands were left short of fighter cover.)

Portal asked how this local concentration affected Leigh-Mallory's responsibility for the defence of his whole area and was assured that 'satisfactory arrangements' had been made. Leigh-Mallory looked and sounded impressive at that meeting. His views were simple and appealed most to those who knew least about the battle: large formations, boldly led, would have smashed the Hun, whereas the cautious defence doggedly offered by Dowding and Park allowed him to get away with it and preserve bombers for the current night offensive which was causing so much distress and alarm.

On 21 October Park sent to the Air Ministry a list of amendments to the draft minutes of the meeting 'with the urgent request that these be embodied because I cannot agree to the important statement which I made being omitted.' Stevenson's notes contained 'misinformed criticism' of his handling of fighters and Park therefore enclosed a rebuttal together with his amendments. But Douglas did not agree to the inclusion of Park's statement, nor did he think remarks Park had made on the Duxford wing's failures to do as it was asked 'appropriate to the minutes of a meeting of this kind.' Park was told that his statement would be excluded 'both on account of its length and because it is held to be out of keeping with the rest of the minutes which are intended more as an *aide mémoire* than as a detailed report of the discussion.'

Park's copy of Stevenson's notes is liberally annotated with the major points of his rebuttal. One: pairs, not single squadrons, were constantly used. Two: effective coordination was achieved with Brand. Three: group and sector conferences were frequently held for the exchange of views. Four: fighters were not told to patrol at heights which put them at the mercy of high-flying German fighters. Five: they were told to gain height over their own base or rear patrol line. Six: it was impossible to operate wings of three squadrons in 11 Group as a rigid rule and the wing was in any case too clumsy for home defence fighting. Douglas and Stevenson undoubtedly misrepresented Park's handling of the battle, but no amount of protest did more than slightly rock the boat. On 6 November Brand thanked Park for sending him a copy of his paper on recent results of the employment of the Duxford wing. 'They do not surprise me,' he said, 'and I am fully in agreement with your conclusions regarding the operations of No. 11 Group.' He sent Park a copy of his own amendments to the minutes which, like Park's, were rejected on Douglas's orders.[5]

Park wrote to Leigh-Mallory on 20 October. He would be delighted, he said, to have the Duxford wing's assistance, provided that it patrolled where requested until engaged, so that he would know where to dispose his own squadrons to the best advantage. It was also necessary for him to know the wing's position in order to inform the Observer Corps and Anti-Aircraft units. Otherwise, they would be confused by the appearance of unexplained fighters and unnecessary air-raid warnings would be issued. If Park knew when the wing had taken off, he would inform Hornchurch, which could fix the wing's position if aircraft of Leigh-Mallory's VHF-equipped squadron were fitted with Hornchurch's fixer crystals.

But Leigh-Mallory refused to agree to Park's suggestions, believing he could maintain good R/T communication and fix by Direction Finding (D/F) the position of his wing south of the Thames. At noon on 25 October Leigh-Mallory asked permission to send it into Kent. Park agreed at once and asked the wing to patrol at 25,000 feet between Sheerness and Maidstone for half an hour unless the enemy were sighted. The wing was already in the air, climbing over Duxford, and took about thirty minutes from the time of request to reach Sheerness. During about one hour while it was in Park's area, he received only six position reports from 12 Group and none after the wing had crossed the Thames. Park therefore asked the Observer Corps to report its track to his headquarters and sectors. Near Gravesend, it broke up on sighting a pair of Hurricane squadrons above it to the east and everyone went home. As a result of this fiasco, Leigh-Mallory agreed to try the procedure Park had suggested on the 20th.

Even so, the wing's performance remained unimpressive. On 29 October Leigh-Mallory was asked at 10.30 a.m. to provide his wing against approaching German fighters. It left the ground at 10.47 a.m., but did not leave the Duxford area until 11.07. Consequently, it failed to intercept the German formation. Three separate raids followed, all reaching England shortly after noon. Park put up eight squadrons to oppose them, but the wing could not help because it was landing at Duxford about that time. In the late afternoon came the day's heaviest attack. Park had seventeen squadrons airborne and the Duxford wing was instructed to patrol between Maidstone and Sheerness and then to intercept two raids crossing the Thames estuary and heading for Essex. This instruction, however, was disobeyed. Hornchurch could not get through to the wing because of continuous R/T traffic between it and Duxford. When it was seen that the interception must be missed, Leigh-Mallory was asked to order the wing to sweep through north Kent and intercept other raiders. Instead, he recalled it because of a report that the weather had deteriorated at Duxford. An attack on aerodromes in East Anglia began just as it was landing.

Lawson, Evill's chief assistant at Bentley Priory, commented on these operations. In the morning, he wrote, the wing had taken too long to assemble over Duxford and should have gained height while flying south; it had been ordered off in good time, while the enemy was actually crossing the coast. The last attack had showed that it was almost impossible for the wing to be controlled by either group when operating in the south. Park had now arranged for an 11 Group section of fighters to accompany it while it was in his area, working on an R/T frequency which would enable it to be plotted on his operations tables. Not only had the wing failed to intercept on the 29th, but it was immobilized when required to operate in its own area to repel attack. Evill drew Dowding's attention to Lawson's report. The attack on the East Anglian aerodromes, he wrote, had been cleverly timed to take advantage of the defence's preoccupation with the big raid on Kent and had caught Leigh-Mallory unprepared; he must not neglect his own responsibilities in future.[6]

Douglas wrote to Dowding on 3 November, enclosing a copy of some notes Balfour had made following a visit to Duxford. It was clear, thought Douglas, that the differences between Park and Leigh-Mallory, 'so patent at the conference which we held on 17 October', had not been resolved. Although Douglas appreciated Park's difficulties, he inclined to support Leigh-Mallory and thought Park had a subconscious aversion to another group fighting in his area: 'The word "poaching" has, I am told, been bandied about.'

Balfour had written that his visit confirmed what Sinclair himself had gathered from Duxford a week earlier. The wing had had no contact with the enemy since the end of September, even though it had carried out at least one operational sortie a day in suitable weather. The system which made them late could be altered, said Balfour, were it not for Park's resistance, but he was jealous of the wing's being likely to shoot down 'his' Germans. There was knowledge, continued Balfour, of the conference held on 17 October 'to study the particular question of support by 12 Group for 11 Group,' but no improvement had been seen. Bader said that his flight commanders and pilots had personal friends in 11 Group who were entirely sympathetic to the wing viewpoint and regretted that it was being ignored and wasted. Moreover, 11 Group pilots were being shaken in morale by being so constantly outmatched. However, Bader and his unit looked forward to the renewal of mass daylight raids. Given their wing formation, maximum advance information and reasonable time to get height and position, he was 'absolutely certain' of taking 'enormous tolls'.

Dowding asked Evill to comment on Balfour's report. Four points were raised, in Evill's view. One, that 12 Group was not allowed all available radar information. Two, that Duxford had been denied Observer Corps information. Three, that the Duxford wing was not called upon by Park until too late. And four, that in consequence opportunities to destroy German aircraft had been lost. Evill commented on each point in turn. Firstly, he himself, had issued orders on 11 October about the importance of passing initial radar plots to groups without waiting for tracks to form. Secondly, a practice had grown up whereby Bromley was passing information to Colchester for Duxford's benefit. It had been stopped by the Southern Area Commandant of the Observer Corps – not by Park – because it was interfering with the essential function of handing over tracks between one observer area and another. Thirdly, Evill thought the early history of the Duxford wing would now be difficult to discover, but a study of operations on 29 October showed that the wing was called out *too* promptly on that occasion, without justification, and it happened again on 5 November. Fourthly, the wing would have been effective a month before against mass attacks which were slowly built up. Now, however, it had less to bite on. It absorbed the energies of four or five squadrons which had to be kept at readiness and concentrated if there was to be any hope of successful attack. Even so, it was too slow to form up and diverted too much of the strength of a weak group from the defence of its own area.

Dowding drew on this minute for his reply to Douglas, dated the same day, 6 November. He agreed that the wing was causing so much friction that he had decided to control the combined operations of the two groups from his own headquarters. He informed Douglas that Balfour's conclusions were wrong. In his letter, Douglas had said that Balfour hoped Bader would not be disciplined 'for having been so outspoken.' Dowding replied that Balfour, having himself been in the service, should know better than to listen to Bader's accusations and put them all down on paper with the 'pious hope' that he would not get into trouble. In Dowding's view, 'a good deal of the ill-feeling which has been engendered in this controversy has been directly due to young Bader [he was then thirty], who, whatever his other merits, suffers from overdevelopment of the critical faculty.' His amazing gallantry, Dowding concluded, would protect him from disciplinary action, if at all possible.

So, too, would his friends. Dowding had taken no action against Bader, but fears persisted that he might, so Portal himself wrote to Dowding on 17 November to say that Sinclair 'has directed' that no reproof be offered to Bader. Balfour, an experienced politician, might have listened a little more critically than he did to Bader's ever-wagging tongue. He knew that Bader had not served in 11 Group, the front line; he might also have visited any one of a number of 11 Group aerodromes to check his assertions, particularly about low morale. He did not and neither did Sinclair.[7]

On 15 November Dowding forwarded to the Air Ministry Park's report of the 7th on raids in September and October. Park's emphasis on the delay caused by using wings, wrote Dowding in a covering letter, was central to the argument. If a system could be devised to get large formations off the ground and up to the necessary altitude before raiders arrived, well and good, but Dowding saw no way in which it could be done 'short of keeping four or five squadrons continuously on patrol at 15,000 feet during the hours of daylight, and I do not consider this to be practical even in the winter.' He sent Leigh-Mallory a copy of his comments and asked for his reply to Park's analysis of Balbo operations in October. Ten operations took an average time of fifty-six minutes to reach Sheerness and spent an average of twenty-four minutes on patrol, destroying a total of one fighter. Moreover, on only a few days was the weather considered fit for the wing to operate, whereas on several days that were unfit for Leigh-Mallory's squadrons, Park's were operating at high pressure. Leigh-Mallory merely ignored the weather question and repeated his assertion that the wing was summoned too late.

Park's daily task was to analyse and sift incomplete or misleading evidence, to distinguish between real and feint attacks, to offer opposition at the right time, height and place and not merely to maintain a *reserve* of aircraft, but to organize a continuous *flow* of aircraft, into and out of the front line. During the First World War, it was said that Admiral Jellicoe could lose the war in an afternoon. Throughout the Battle of Britain, it was no less true that Park and his controllers could have done the same. Jellicoe, in fact, was put to the test only once, whereas Park was tested on many days. German pilots often complained that British fighters were elusive. It was a notable tribute to Park that they remained so. Concentration of force, an excellent military principle, did not apply in this battle, as Alan Deere – one of Fighter Command's outstanding pilots – made clear in his account of it. That principle applied over Dunkirk and Park then insisted on it more strongly than Dowding. Over England, however, the need was for a wide ranging, persistent defence and the use of large formations was often inappropriate. Johnny Kent, another outstanding pilot, emphasized the fact that with the radio sets then in use squadrons in large formations were usually on different frequencies and could not speak to each other. And Ginger Lacey, the most successful British pilot in the battle, considered the big wing 'a cumbersome and time wasting' method of getting aircraft to the killing ground. 'We also believed,' he added, 'that if you did not get to the enemy bombers before they bombed you were only doing half your job.'

To allow the Germans to attack targets at will was the negation of air *defence*, however many aircraft might be shot down afterwards. Had such tactics been followed in 1940, the sector control system would have been destroyed. With control gone, the wing would have been hard pressed to find the enemy. The Luftwaffe *wanted* Park to put up large formations to deal with a mass attack over one area while another equally large force attacked elsewhere. He denied them the opportunity to take decisive toll of his fighters because he realized that Fighter Command would win if it remained in being until the onset of winter weather prevented an invasion in 1940. By the time good weather returned – at least six months later – Fighter Command would be stronger and the British Army would be reorganized and re-equipped. Neutral countries, particularly the United States, would observe that the Nazi menace was not invincible and might see in Britain a rallying-ground.

In February 1956 Douglas was given an opportunity to comment on a draft of Basil Collier's official history of this period, *The Defence of the United Kingdom*. He argued that causing heavy casualties and therefore using large forces was one way to diminish and end an assault. Interception prior to the enemy's reaching his target obliged the use of small forces and the risk of defeat in detail. In the short run, the effect of bombing was minimized by interception, but in the long run the best answer might be to withhold attack until large fighter forces were massed. 'Of course, I realize that Dowding and Park were under pressure from the government to try and break up the attacks before they reached their objective at any cost, and that they could not afford to disregard this pressure.' Thus thought Douglas, but this political reason weighed less with Dowding and Park than the military reason Douglas, Leigh-Mallory, Stevenson and the rest thought constantly in terms of a single raid on one target. Had that been the normal pattern of the attack, it would certainly have made sense 'to withhold attack until large fighter forces were massed', but the Germans did not make it so easy for the defence.[8]

Shortly before 25 November, Park learned that he was to be relieved of his command. Richard Saul, of 13 Group, wrote to say how sorry he was 'in view of the magnificent achievements of your group in the past six months; they have borne the brunt of the war, and undoubtedly saved England. My sympathy is entirely with you.' It was a shock, Park replied, but a far greater shock to learn that Leigh-Mallory would succeed him,

> in view of the little support that No. 11 Group has had from No. 12 Group ever since away back in May. Your group and No. 10 Group have always sent properly trained squadrons to relieve war-weary squadrons from the front line. Moreover, your group has always cooperated in helping out with junior leaders and providing properly-trained pilots required to replace wastage. On the other hand, a number of the pilots provided from No. 12 Group were rejected by squadrons because they had not been trained after leaving OTU.

Park felt that if a change had to be made, the job should have gone to Saul, who knew the stations and the country. He himself had flatly refused a position in the Air Ministry:

> As I was told that the only reason for my leaving No. 11 Group was because I had carried the baby long enough for one man and was due for a rest from the responsibility I do not quite see why I should be stuffed into a very busy office job at the Air Ministry.

He went instead to a Flying Training group, where his precious experience was passed on to those most in need of it, but that had not been the Air Ministry's original intention. The Ministry was 'a most cumbersome and ill-working administrative machine', in Churchill's opinion, and Park was well out of it.

Dowding, himself replaced by Douglas on 25 November, was partly to blame for the misery inflicted on Park. He should have realized that the disagreement between Park and Leigh-Mallory was serious and enforced better cooperation. Two senior commanders should not have followed such contrary tactics without Dowding taking action. As the historian Gavin Lyall wrote, it was 'hard luck' on Park, but 'hesitancy in command can cause casualties other than those in battle.' Dowding had held his command for more than four years, a very long time as service appointments go. Park, however, had held his for only seven months and was ten years younger than Dowding. 'To my dying day,' he said in 1968, 'I shall feel bitter at the base intrigue which was used to remove Dowding and myself as soon as we had won the battle.' Leigh-Mallory, recalled Park, showed no generosity in victory: 'He did not even bother to attend to the usual formality of taking over from me, so I handed over to my Senior Air Staff Officer.'

On 4 December Park was received by the King at Buckingham Palace and made a Companion of the Most Honourable Order of the Bath (CB). As soon as the news was announced, congratulations poured in. They were so many and so warm that the pain of dismissal must have been eased. Leslie Gossage, his predecessor at 11 Group, congratulated him

> on an award which has seldom, if ever, been more richly deserved. The consequences of what you have achieved may prove wellnigh incalculable in the history of the world and my admiration for the way in which you have met and overcome the serious and novel problems which have so frequently confronted you is unbounded.

Gossage knew that Park was anxious about awards for those who had served him so well and was able to assure him that they would be promulgated, now that Park had his award.

Evill was also quick to congratulate Park:

> You know, I think, that I have admired immensely the way in which you have commanded and led your group through the battles of this summer and autumn – and regret your departure. You dodged all our telephone calls last week, hence this letter.

Park's response to Evill's letter shows his resilience. He swallowed his hurt at what he considered an unjust dismissal, knowing full well that to sulk in his tent – to continue dodging telephone calls – would lead him swiftly to the Retired List. He began to fight back:

> Maybe I shall be able to help Fighter Command [he told Evill] by raising the standard of the FTS pupils that we send to the OTUs. To that end I wish one of your staff could write to me direct at No. 23 Flying Training Group and let me know where our weakness lies. I cannot promise an immediate cure for every fault, but I should like to know in what direction I can assist Fighter Command to defeat the enemy in 1941.

During December several members of Park's staff wrote both to congratulate him on his CB and to express their regret at his departure. To all of them Park replied personally, finding something different to say in every letter. Among those who wrote was Wing Commander T. Menzies McNeill (Intelligence) who recalled that Park always drilled into him good leadership and teamwork: 'I have never heard one grouse in 11 Group; it has been a team led by an amazing commander.' Group Captain G.M. Lawson, throughout the battle one of Park's wisest supporters at Bentley Priory, also wrote and Park replied that he very much regretted leaving, 'but I am told I must have a spell of training duty after the past strenuous seven months. I feel quite fit and was looking forward to the spring offensive for which we are now preparing.' Wing Commander Victor Beamish, C.O. of North Weald and one of Fighter Command's outstanding personalities, expressed his regret at Park's departure: 'This feeling is reflected from all ranks, and we all wish to serve under you in future.' Group Captain Cecil Bouchier, C.O. of Hornchurch and a special friend of Park's for years, wrote the most emotional of the letters he received at this time. When Park came to 11 Group, he said, 'we gained the one man above all others in our Service who by his own infinite efforts and personal example would not only ensure ultimate victory but inspire it.' Bouchier found it difficult to express his personal feeling of loss at Park's going: 'the feeling that so much heart is going out of the group'. Apart from RAF officers, Park received congratulations from Vice-Admiral Ramsay at Dover, Major General F.G. Hyland (who commanded an anti-aircraft division at Uxbridge), two men who had served with him in 48 Squadron during the First World War and several civilians.

Park thus spent his last days at Uxbridge wading through a pile of letters both congratulatory and commiserative. The 'translation' of Dowding and Park, in the careful words of Denis Richards, an official historian, 'to quieter spheres, though doubtless wise in itself, was not perhaps the most impressive immediate reward that might have been devised for the victors of one of the world's decisive battles.' As a change from writing letters of thanks, Park was able to offer one congratulation of his own: to Richard Saul, who took Leigh-Mallory's place at 12 Group.[9]

Although Park never thought so, he was lucky to leave Fighter Command when he did. Like Göring and Hitler, Leigh-Mallory and Douglas loved to see lots of aeroplanes in the sky – as soon as he took command of 11 Group, Leigh-Mallory wrote to Douglas advocating a formation of *108* aircraft. Park would have conducted operations over France in 1941 more skilfully than did Leigh-Mallory, but casualties would still have been heavy because the Spitfire and Hurricane were short-range, defensive fighters, needing all the help they could get from radar and the Observer Corps if they were to match the latest marks of the Messerschmitt Bf 109 and the formidable Focke-Wulf Fw 190 (introduced in July 1941). Fighter Command would never again be tested as in 1940 and no one can know how Douglas and Leigh-Mallory would have fared under pressure nor whether Portal could have influenced them. It is perhaps as well that they were not called upon to conduct a prolonged defence against a foe better equipped and more cunning even than in 1940.

An alarming instance of Leigh-Mallory's incompetence was seen on 29 January 1941 when he decided to conduct a paper exercise using the circumstances of an actual attack on Kenley, Biggin Hill and Hornchurch on 6 September 1940. His intention was to prove correct his opinion on the use of large formations. The exercise was carefully set up and Leigh-Mallory totally mismanaged it. The raid was not intercepted inbound and both Kenley and Biggin Hill were 'bombed' while their aircraft were still on the ground. Thomas Lang, one of Park's controllers, first revealed this story and it is supported by a copy of the exercise in Park's papers. When Lang explained Leigh-Mallory's several mistakes to him, he replied that next time he would do better. In fact, there was no next time. He later told Lang that 'if there are any more major battles over England I shall control all of them.' He went on to declare, echoing Douglas, that if a large-scale raid approached, he would permit it to bomb its target and intercept it in force on the way back to France. The enemy, he believed, would be so badly mauled that there would be no more raids.

Alan Deere thought that Fighter Command's aim in 1941 was the same as that of the Luftwaffe in 1940: to entice fighters into the air where they could be destroyed. The British bombers were, in effect, bait – and not a particularly attractive bait because they were too few and too lightly armed to threaten seriously any target the Luftwaffe wished to defend. Johnnie Johnson found, when leading big wings over France, that they were difficult to control in action because pilots got in each other's way. When he climbed his wing through layers of cloud, more time was spent looking for friendly aircraft than seeking targets in the air or on the ground. He learned from his own experience that Park had been right: three squadrons could be worked together, more could not, and a pair was the ideal formation.

As early as 12 February Douglas was unhappy. 'Our idea,' he reminded Leigh-Mallory, 'was to go over the other side and leap on the enemy from a great height in superior numbers; instead of which it looks as though we ourselves are being leapt on.' Evill strongly agreed. A very difficult task was being attempted with pilots who were not nearly well enough trained, he told Douglas in March. The level of training in 10 Group was very low and even lower in 11 Group because too high a state of readiness was being maintained. 'It is out of all reason,' he exclaimed, 'that we should be imposing such a serious handicap on ourselves.' Evill's distress was shared by Douglas's Wing Commander (Tactics), who thought squadrons should be carrying out surprise attacks on each other and practising regaining formation after being split up; instead, they were so busy holding formation that they were unable to keep a good lookout.

In May 1947 Air Marshal Sir James Robb issued a despatch on Fighter

Command operations between 1 November 1940 and 31 December 1941. They had had three objectives. Firstly, to wrest the initiative from the enemy for the sake of morale and tactical advantage. This objective, Robb thought, had been achieved. Secondly, to cooperate with Bomber and Coastal Commands in preventing the enemy from withdrawing flying units to the Eastern Front after the attack on the Soviet Union in June 1941, Robb thought the Germans had kept much the same force in the west after June as before. And thirdly, the operations had been intended to oblige the return of forces already withdrawn to the Eastern Front. This, Robb admitted, did not happen. Overall, he concluded, temporary air superiority had been achieved 'at a substantial cost to ourselves', but this achievement had had no decisive military value. As in the First World War, it was too readily assumed that an advance should be made simply because it had become physically possible. Consequently, Fighter Command lost more pilots and inflicted far fewer casualties in 1941 than during the Battle of Britain and achieved no comparable strategic advantage.[10]

CHAPTER ELEVEN

The Battle of Britain:
The Whirligig of Time

And thus the whirligig of time brings in his revenges
                                                    Twelfth Night

Park survived his dismissal from Fighter Command by more than thirty-four years. During that time, his conduct of operations in 1940 received much praise, public and private, from those involved as well as historians. The appearance of the Air Ministry's account of the battle in March 1941 marked the first stage in his rehabilitation, although he was not yet to enjoy his 'revenges'. The *Daily Herald*, in a review published on the 28th, drew attention to the fact that Dowding's name was not mentioned. Criticism from such a source could be ignored by the Air Ministry, but Churchill himself made the same point in a minute to Sinclair on 3 April: 'Your admirable pamphlet,' he wrote, 'is remarkable for the fact that it avoids mentioning the name of the Commander-in-Chief in this battle.' If any name had been mentioned, replied Sinclair, the highest possible tribute would have been paid to Dowding; tributes would also have been due to Park and others. If these had been named, the public would have been disappointed if some of the most famous pilots had not been mentioned. Churchill was unimpressed by this argument and Sinclair thereupon became anxious to produce an illustrated edition of the pamphlet. Although Dowding's name was unmentionable, his picture could appear; so, too, could those of others. Eventually this was done and by August 1943 a new Air Ministry account had been published in which both the names and faces of Dowding and Park appear.

Meanwhile, Park sent copies of the original pamphlet to his friends and to those whom he hoped would prove to be friends. Among the latter was Lord Beaverbrook, who thanked him fulsomely on 2 April: 'Of all the letters I've received in half a century, your note gives me the greatest joy. I shall frame it

140

in my heart. And will you please come to town one day soon so that I may give you thanks again.' This was the first of many letters exchanged between Park and Beaverbrook, who wrote to Park again on 12 April recalling 'the splendid period in your life when you successfully defended Britain against the overwhelmingly powerful German Air Force.' Major Desmond Morton, Churchill's Personal Assistant, thanked Park on 3 April for sending him a copy of the pamphlet. Churchill, he said, hoped to meet Park again soon and Morton added that he himself looked forward to dining with Park when next he came to London. The Duke of Kent, 11 Group's Welfare Officer, sent Park a handwritten letter of thanks on the 18th. There had been many changes in the group, he wrote, and everyone was waiting 'rather anxiously' to see the result. 'I have been all over the country,' he ended, 'visiting fighter stations and none have ever been as bad as 11 Group were last November.'

Group Captain Harcourt-Smith, a member of Park's staff now serving at Bentley Priory, was delighted to receive an inscribed copy of the pamphlet: ' . . . how proud and grateful we as a staff were to serve you in those historic days. Remarks made to me then and since by many of the group are happy proof of their loyalty to you and of their unshakable faith in their captain.' He, like Bouchier, would get his wish to serve under Park again. Wing Commander Douglas-Jones, another former member of his staff, echoed Harcourt-Smith's sentiments: ' . . . fortunately for our country, the Battle of Britain had been won before you left for your next command. It will take no less a man than yourself to restore 11 Group to its former high standard.' Finally, Wing Commander Lang, who had sent Park the results of Leigh-Mallory's disastrous paper exercise in January, summed up: 'I think you will always be referred to as AOC No. 11 Group.'[1]

On 4 October 1941 Park composed a letter to Portal but did not send it. During the next three weeks he revised and polished it until a need for peace of mind, to say nothing of his stationary career, compelled him to put it in the mail on the 24th. The previous December, Park wrote, he had been told that the reason Portal had removed him from 11 Group was that he needed a rest from active operations. But from remarks Portal had made to the Duke of Kent in December and information given to Park by Douglas, it appeared that the real reason for his removal was the receipt of unofficial reports that he had failed to cooperate with Leigh-Mallory.

Throughout the battle, Park continued, 11 Group had received full cooperation from Brand and Saul, but 12 Group 'appeared to withhold its cooperation' in respect of relief squadrons, temporary reinforcements and reinforcement pilots. At a conference which Portal had attended (the 17 October meeting), Leigh-Mallory had claimed that his wings were effective against fighter raids, that they could be tracked and controlled by R/T south of the Thames and that there had been no delay in their arrival over the Thames at 25,000 feet within thirty minutes of Park's request. Accurate records had been kept of the wing's movements in October and November and, as Park reported, these claims were found to be incorrect. He was not asking to be reinstated in his old command, Park ended, but 'I do, however, wish to clear my name of the damaging unofficial reports that I failed to cooperate.' One day, he hoped to return to an operational command and his ambition was 'to command the biggest bomber group containing the biggest bombers carrying the biggest bomb load to smash the Huns into final submission.'

Portal replied at once. There had never been any question of 'removing' Park from his command in December; he had been relieved 'because we considered it unwise and unfair to allow you to continue to bear for another year the heavy strain which must fall upon the AOC No. 11 Group.' It was 'common knowledge', continued Portal, that Park and Leigh-Mallory held 'conflicting views' on the handling of fighters, but Portal assured Park that he had left his command with the honour and credit due to him for his splendid service. Portal did not recall discussing these matters with the Duke of Kent or anyone else and hoped that Park would disregard idle gossip'. Park, pleased with this prompt and encouraging response, replied that Portal's personal assurances had 'removed a heavy weight off my mind'. He had, he admitted, been very tired at the end of 1940, but was 'fitter now than I was even in the leisurely days at the IDC [Imperial Defence College] and count the days to the time when I can have another crack at the Hun.'

On the day that Portal wrote his welcome letter to Park, 26 October, a full-page account of the Battle of Britain, written by Dowding, appeared in the *Sunday Chronicle*. Dowding had had no hand in the production of the Air Ministry's pamphlet on the battle and thought it tended 'to exaggerate the ease with which the most dangerous assault which has ever been made on this country was beaten off.' Park's part in the battle, Dowding continued, ' . . . should be more widely known. His initiative and resource in countering each new move on the part of the enemy, and his leadership of the gallant men whom he commanded, were beyond all praise.'

Next day, he sent Park a copy of the article. He had already in July told Park that he was composing an official despatch on the battle. 'I think I shall do you justice,' he had written. 'Your part in the Battle has never been properly recognized.' Now, in October, he welcomed the opportunity of paying a more public tribute. 'Don't trouble to answer this,' wrote Dowding. 'I just thought you might like to see the article as I mentioned your name.' Naturally, Park replied at once. He was grateful for Dowding's praise, the more so because he had recently heard that Leigh-Mallory was still 'relating with relish' his own account of the previous October's meeting and Sinclair's alleged opinion that big wing tactics would have brought victory more easily.

The fact that in January 1942 Park was pulled out of Flying Training Command and sent to Egypt – at a time of acute crisis for the British Empire, the Soviet Union and the United States – is evidence that his abilities were remembered. In July he went to Malta and there too he showed that he would never allow bombs to fall unchallenged upon military or civilian targets in the hope of securing good results in subsequent aerial combat. According to a radio broadcast he made on 12 September 1942, published on the 15th in the *Times of Malta*, neither the passage of time nor another operational command had improved his regard for that 'batch of armchair critics' who planned to attack the Germans *after* they had bombed.

Private and public praise, as well as demanding work of vital importance, had by then fully restored Park's self-esteem. Nevertheless, he would have been delighted to learn that he was regarded with respect by the Germans – and even more delighted to learn that they shared his low opinion of Leigh-Mallory. Early in 1944, Air Ministry Intelligence obtained and translated some German appraisals of leading British and American personalities. Park, it was said, had earned the title 'Defender of London'. Efficient and courageous, he was no theorist and thought little of staff work, although he despatched it capably. Leigh-Mallory, however, was considered 'a pedantic worker with a preference for administrative questions, who gives his subordinates little room for personal decisions. He is therefore known as "The Flying Sergeant".'

Park was obliged to retire from the RAF at the end of 1946, but the man responsible for that decision – Lord Tedder, Chief of the Air Staff – took the earliest public opportunity to offer Park the highest praise. In February 1947, at the annual dinner of the New Zealand Society in London, Tedder spoke about Park to a gathering that included the Prime Minister and a galaxy of senior officers in all three services. 'If ever any one man won the Battle of Britain, he did,' said Tedder. 'I don't believe it is realized how much that one man, with his leadership, his calm judgment and his skill, did to save not only this country, but the world.'

Long after the war, in May 1951, Sir Robert Watson-Watt asked Park (then living in New Zealand) to help forward a claim which he and ten members of his old radar team were prosecuting before the Royal Commission on Awards. 'You would, of course, have been high among the friends on whose oral evidence we lean heavily if you had not been so far away,' wrote Watson-Watt, but he would value Park's written testimony on the part radar played in his wide-flung war. 'I am glad to have this excuse for remembering and renewing the contacts with yourself which formed such a very pleasant and encouraging part of our work for the RAF and for Fighter Command in particular.' Park, surprised to learn that Watson-Watt and his team had not already been granted handsome awards, welcomed the opportunity to say that 'I do not think we could have won the Battle of Britain without the aid of radar. Similarly, we might have lost the siege of Malta if it had not been for radar.' In April 1952 Watson-Watt told Park that his letter had done the trick. Its effect was such that the chairman said he did not need to hear any other VIP evidence 'and we are satisfied that yours was the most important evidence by far on the operational value of radar.' Watson-Watt added: 'I am proud to have had the privilege of helping you in the great tasks which you so brilliantly carried out in defence of civilisation.'[2]

Air Chief Marshal Sir Philip Joubert, however, was not among those who praised Park or his conduct of the Battle of Britain. In his book *The Fated Sky* (1952), Joubert made the case for big wings and Park answered him in the New Zealand press. Joubert returned to the attack in another book, *The Third Service* (1955). Leigh-Mallory, wrote Joubert, 'had a brilliant brain, and his character was determined and cool. . . . He "could run rings round Park" intellectually.' Park 'was not a great commander but at least he was a successful one. . . . [He] was a good pilot and an intelligent man, but highly strung. He also suffered from a very sensitive ego which did not help him in his relations with other people.' Mrs E.M. Rich, Park's personal clerk at South Cerney in 1941, sent him a copy of a letter (not published) which she had written to the editor of the *Sunday Express* in September 1955, defending him against Joubert's criticism. She had had the privilege of working for Park for ten months, she wrote, and never found him 'highly strung'. He was, in fact, absolutely calm whatever the situation. Park thanked her for her support, but said 'I am really tired of all this controversy [raised by Joubert] in support of his old school friend.' Lord Beaverbrook also wrote to Park, hoping that he approved of the *Sunday Express*'s answer to Joubert. Park replied that he thought the answer very fair; he had not wished to advertise Joubert's book and had therefore refused to comment until a 'snappy reply' from Lady Park appeared on the front page of the London evening papers. Told that he could not let her fight his battles, he had then made a short statement. Finally, a former flight sergeant in the Signals Branch at Uxbridge wrote to say how much he resented Joubert's criticism, knowing from his own experience what Park's personal example meant to everyone who served under him: 'As long as any members of 11 Group are still alive, we will actively repulse any criticism of you.'

A year later, on 20 September 1956, the *News Chronicle* made a feature of its review of Johnnie Johnson's book, *Wing Leader*. He contradicted Joubert and his opinions had added weight, the newspaper thought, because Johnson was still a serving officer and 'undoubtedly would not have been so emphatic unless he knew his views to be those of the majority of the Air Ministry.' Leslie Hunt, a plotter at Uxbridge in 1940, sent Park a copy of the article and asked why he had not written his own account of the controversy. Park replied that he did not wish to hurt the friends and relatives of living officers, but he would recount his version of the story for Hunt's private information. Hunt, he said, was at liberty to publish it after Park's death, if Park had not then written his own account.[3]

In September 1957 an article on the Battle of Britain by Sir John Slessor, by

1a. (*left*) Purser Park, of the Union Steam Ship Company,
relaxes on the Avon, Christchurch, in 1913
1b. (*right*) Captain Park, MC and Bar,
Flight Commander in 48 Squadron, Royal Flying Corps, in October 1917

1c. Major Park, Commanding Officer of 48 Squadron,
with his Bristol Fighter at Bertangles (near Amiens) in 1918

2a. 48 Squadron's aerodrome at Bertangles, seen before the German air raid on 24 August 1918

2b. (*left*) Bertangles, August 1918: Park 'standing on the ruins of his hut burned down in a fire caused, I believe, by a kerosene stove' (Stanley Rycroft)

2c. (*right*) Park (centre) with members of his crew and ground staff and the Handley Page 0/400 twin-engined bomber in which he completed his round-Britain flight, April 1919. No one knows why it was called *Last Days*

3a. (*left*) Dorothy Margarita ('Dol') Park in 1928
3b. (*right*) Calm before the storm: Park and his second son Colin
photographed by Dol while sailing off England's south coast in the summer of 1939

3c. 'My dear old "Hurricane" [OK1] that I flew throughout 1940 when commanding No. 11
Fighter Group. She still does over 300 m.p.h. and remains a faithful "charger".' (September 1941)

4a. (*left*) Air Vice-Marshal Douglas Evill, Senior Air Staff Officer at Bentley Priory during the Battle of Britain, by T. C. Dugdale
4b. (*right*) Air Marshal Sir Sholto Douglas (Dowding's successor as head of Fighter Command) and Sir Archibald Sinclair (Secretary of State for Air) in February 1942

4c. (*left*) Dowding with three of the most famous Battle of Britain pilots in September 1942: from the left, Wing Commanders Max Aitken and 'Sailor' Malan and Squadron Leader Alan Deere
4d. (*right*) After the Battle, 21 December 1940: Park at his lowest ebb, dismissed from Fighter Command

5a. Park at the wheel of his 'fire engine' (a red MG) with Portal and an unidentified Group Captain in the back, Malta, 25 November 1943

5b. On 7 February 1945, his last day in Cairo, Park presents an Avro Anson to King Farouk of Egypt at Almaza airport

6a. Park talking to a Burmese ground crew man at Ramree Island in April 1945

6b. Park, Mountbatten and Slim in Ceylon, July 1945

7a. Slim, Park and Power cheerfully await Mountbatten before attending the ceremony marking Japan's formal surrender in South-East Asia, Singapore, 12 September 1945

7b. Tea in Singapore: Dol and Keith at ease, December 1945

8a. (*left*) The Parks arrive in Auckland, February 1948, Dol wearing one of her granddaughter's nappies as a turban
8b. (*right*) City Councillor Park in the 1960s, wearing his 48 Squadron badge

8c. Park and his friend Arthur Parrish standing in front of a painting of Gallipoli in the Auckland Officers' Club, May 1973

then a Marshal of the Royal Air Force, appeared in the BBC journal, the *Listener*. Both in that battle and later in the defence of Malta, wrote Slessor, Park 'proved himself to be a magnificent Commander of Fighters. Future generations of Englishmen should recognize that we owed our salvation . . . in no small measure to Keith Park.' Sir John Salmond, under whom Park served in the Air Defence of Great Britain at Uxbridge in 1926–7, wrote to tell Park how 'extremely pleased' he was to hear Slessor 'refer to your invaluable services in the very highest terms and emphasizing the enormous contribution you personally made to winning the battle.' For once, however, Park rejected praise. He had quarrelled with Slessor in 1936 over his public criticism of 48 Squadron; he and Slessor were in constant and often acrimonious contact between 1944 and 1946; Park believed that Slessor had engineered his premature retirement from the RAF; and, not least, he thought the warmth of Slessor's tribute false. Sir Leslie Hollinghurst, who served with Park in the Far East and became a close friend, also thought the tribute did not ring true. It was, he said, 'a clear case of a guilty conscience'.[4]

Stanley Lee, who served with Park in the depressing days after the First World War, wrote to him from London in November 1957. He had left the RAF in 1946 as an Air Vice-Marshal and had since published six books, mostly biographies. Although many accounts of the Battle of Britain had appeared, wrote Lee, 'we have yet to hear from the commander who actually fought and won the main battle.' He suggested that Park either write his own account or engage Lee to write it for him. He himself had the background necessary to understand the issues, but he had not been in Fighter Command in 1940 and so had no personal axe to grind, although he was already on Park's side. 'I should aim deliberately to present you as the Air Force Commander who, more than anyone else, held the fate of this country, and indeed of Europe and the world, in his hands over those vital weeks of 1940.' Park replied at once. The publishing firm of Hutchinson's, he wrote, had made him an offer in 1946 to publish his war experiences if he wrote them up, but business pressures had kept him from getting anything done. Lee's suggestion interested him and he promised to bring a great deal of material to England on his next visit in August 1958.

By July he had had second thoughts. Officers write books after a war, he told Lee on the 14th, to justify their own actions. Park's had been dealt with by important persons and there was no need for him to try his hand. 'No doubt the intriguing that Joubert and Douglas did at the Air Ministry in collaboration with Leigh-Mallory would make exciting reading, but it would not enhance the reputation of the Royal Air Force and would delight their critics in the Navy and Army.'

Lee prodded, Park fended. He wrote three times in July 1960, urging Park to provide material. His part in the story was being overlooked, Lee said, and when he died his papers would be destroyed or pass to some other writer 'who, however conscientious, will not produce your story as truly and authoritatively as if you had been there to guide and supervise.' Park answered him on 3 August. 'I have never felt strongly the need to produce a book to explain my actions in the Battle of Britain. Now that others have fully endorsed my fighter tactics, e.g., Wykeham, Deere, Johnson etc., (apart from Dowding's despatch), I feel no urge to make explanations to anyone.' Lee made a last effort. It was not a matter of justifying his conduct, he wrote, but of the chief figure in a vital episode of British history putting the facts on record as he saw them. If Park would not send documents, would he cooperate if Lee went out to New Zealand for a couple of months? 'You see how important I think your story is.' But Park resisted and Lee gave up.[5]

In April 1958 Dowding had written to tell Park that his old operations room at Uxbridge was to be closed and that he, Dowding, had unveiled an inscription to mark the occasion. The room was manned for the last time, some of the raids of 15 September 1940 were repeated on the table and after Dowding spoke, the last serviceable Hurricane and a Spitfire flew overhead. Warrant Officer Leonard Lyons, a former general-situation map supervisor, was among those present and recalled that after the battles were over, Park would come down from the control room and talk to the plotters. 'He was very friendly with everyone and rank was nothing with him.' He was, said Lyons, a gentleman.

Lord Willoughby de Broke, Park's senior controller at Uxbridge, also wrote to him about this occasion. It was long since they had met, he said, but their old association 'and, if I may say so, friendship as well' came to mind so vividly and he had heard on all sides expression of regret that Park was not present.

> May I say [he continued] that one of my most treasured possessions is the copy of your 11 Group Despatch which you so kindly sent me when you gave up command of the group and I retired to the Air Ministry. I was very sorry to have done this, but I just felt I couldn't bear to be continually lectured by your successor as to how the Battle of Britain ought to have been fought!

Park replied that he would have loved to have been there and would always be grateful for the honour and excitement of commanding the fighter forces at that time, but 'a great deal of the personal satisfaction has long been destroyed by the scheming and deceit of envious senior officers in No. 12 Group and at the Air Ministry after we had won the battle.'[6]

In June 1966 Park wrote to Harry Saltzman to say how delighted he was to see that Saltzman intended to produce a film of the Battle of Britain. He drew attention to the role of 10 Group, castigated 12 Group and Brickhill's biography of Bader, sent Saltzman a copy of an article he had written for

Icare (the journal of the French airline pilots' association) in 1965, and referred him to the books written by Deere, Johnson and Wykeham and Dowding's despatch. Ben Fisz, replying on Saltzman's behalf, said he believed that Park's tactics were correct and assured him of a square deal in the film. 'As an ex-member of the Polish Air Force, I have been a great admirer of yours.'

Almost two years later, in May 1968, Air Commodore James Wallace (the film's publicity officer) informed Park that Rex Harrison was due to play him in the film. On 2 July he wrote again, however, to say that Trevor Howard had replaced Harrison because his other commitments clashed with a changed production schedule. Park, however, had already heard that Harrison was out and leapt into print. He speculated in the *New Zealand Herald* on 4 July that the film would cover up 'a dirty little wartime intrigue' and that Harrison's late withdrawal was a protest. His outburst attracted a great deal of attention and Wallace hastened to reassure him. The script was based on Wood and Dempster's *The Narrow Margin*, he told him. 'This excellent book is generally accepted as the Bible of the period and I am taking the liberty of sending you a copy.' Park expressed his thanks, adding that it was indeed a balanced account, agreeing with Johnson and Deere.

Dowding, meanwhile, had been taken to the studios at Pinewood to see some of the filming. It was hoped that he would subsequently report favourably to Park. Dowding spoke to Howard, who listened attentively and promised that his portrayal would be worthy of Park. Dowding then watched a scene from the film in which Park and Leigh-Mallory (played by Patrick Wymark) argued for and against the big wing in Dowding's office. But it was Dowding (Laurence Olivier) who drew attention to the 'essential truth': 'we're fighting for survival. And losing. We don't need a big wing or a small wing. We need pilots . . . and a miracle.' A miracle which would be granted when the Germans switched their target from aerodromes to London. After his visit to Pinewood, Dowding wrote to Park to set his mind at rest. He had talked to Howard on the airfield at Hawkinge, a place with deeply felt memories for both Dowding and Park. It may have been these, going back long before the Battle of Britain, as well as the sight of Spitfires in the air once more, that inspired Dowding to offer this tribute to his old companion in arms: 'If it hadn't been for Keith Park's conduct in the battle, and his loyalty to me as his Commander-in-Chief, we should not be here today.'

Trevor Howard himself wrote to Park on 12 July 1968. He had had talks with Dowding and with his biographer, Robert Wright, who had briefed Howard on the 'inner history and the personal background':

> after all that Lord Dowding has told me [he continued] I feel very strongly about the difficult position in which you found yourself . . . I

shall be making every effort to portray you as your many friends would wish. We all have your interest greatly at heart, and I am most conscious of the responsibility that is mine in preserving your good name in the magnificent role that you played in the Battle of Britain.

Thomas Lang attended the film's première in London on 15 September 1969 and wrote about it to Park a few days later. Dowding received a standing ovation and Lang thought the action shots superb, 'although one could have had more of your troubles with Leigh-Mallory.' Lang and Willoughby de Broke had recently attended a dinner with Balfour. They both knew he was a Douglas/Leigh-Mallory man, but the evening proved delightful: 'we spoke of you with admiration, telling stories of our adventures in the Ops Room, the problems of getting the "Balbo" moving and wondering why we could not really receive his [Leigh-Mallory's] willing cooperation.' In October Lang sent Park a copy of his letter to *The Times* (19 September 1969) telling the story used by Wright in his biography of Dowding (page 212) of Leigh-Mallory's demand for an explanation of the shooting down of an enemy aircraft into 12 Group territory by an 11 Group fighter.

Meanwhile, Park had agreed to write an article for the *New Zealand Herald* on his reaction to the film at which he would be guest of honour at a charity première in Auckland on 20 October. He told his wife, by then suffering from the disabling lung condition emphysema, how pleased he would have been if only she could have gone with him. Dol then did 'a darn stupid thing', as she wrote to her niece, Betty Neill: she said she *was* going. 'Betty, it must be three years since I've been out in public and I'm TERRIFIED – but determined to go.' She was carried from a car to her seat and back again and thought the film wonderful. Park thought it entertaining, but pointed out that the scene in Dowding's office did not take place whereas the real confrontation at the Air Ministry – which was much more dramatic – was not depicted. He presumed it was omitted to save the faces of surviving officers and politicians. Beaverbrook, too, was conspicuous by his absence: another omission that would not have displeased the Air Ministry.[7]

Peter Townsend, one of the battle's most famous pilots, wrote to Park in July 1968 to say that he was at work on a book about it (published in 1970 as *Duel of Eagles*). He had not written earlier because he only saw the battle 'through the windscreen of my Hurricane' and needed to read widely in order to see it in perspective. 'You were one of the outstanding figures in this victory,' said Townsend. 'As one of your squadron commanders I realized that even at the time, but now I know much more.' He arranged for a research assistant to visit Park and tape his comments. Park rejected the suggestion made to Townsend by Bader that the battle should have been controlled from Bentley Priory. The clearest distinction had always been drawn between Bentley

Priory's strategic role (to control the entire defence system – radar, the Observer Corps, air-raid warning, balloon barrages, the supply of fighters and pilots for the whole command, the rotation of squadrons, liaison with other services and with the government) and the tactical role of group commanders (to conduct the fighter battle). For Bentley Priory to have attempted the tactical as well as strategic control of around fifty squadrons on a front extending from the Wash to the Bristol Channel would have been impracticable. Swift and flexible response to a variety of challenges was difficult enough from Uxbridge and its sector stations, even though they were equipped and trained to provide it.

In 1970 Alan Deere published a study of the tactics employed in which he came down firmly on Park's side. He sent a copy to Slessor, who thought it 'an extremely interesting and absolutely sound memorandum'. Slessor's only criticism of Dowding's handling of the battle was that Leigh-Mallory 'should never have been allowed to take the line he did':

> I like to think that if I'd been in Stuffy's [Dowding's] place I would (i) much earlier have told L-M to shut up and get on with commanding his Group in accordance with what he knew quite well was my policy and (ii) when the conference was mooted have told Sholto Douglas . . . that I would not agree to it and that if he or L-M or anyone else did not like the way I was commanding, they could bloody well find someone else to command. To my mind it was intolerable that a C-in-C should have been subjected to it – and I was there and heard the whole thing. Keith Park (another rather difficult customer I'm afraid) was first-class throughout and it put him in a very difficult position. He was an *extremely* good Fighter AOC – as he proved again in Malta later – but I'm afraid that was his upper limit.

There were, however, men who shared Slessor's regard for Park's ability as a fighter commander who did not find him so limited in other capacities. Sir Kenneth Porter, for example, who went to Uxbridge in May 1940 as a signals officer and regularly attended Park's morning meetings with his heads of department, thought Park an excellent man to work for: acute, decisive and with a wide range of sound knowledge of the problems facing each department. Although Park was not himself a signals expert, Porter found that he rarely had even to complete an explanation before he had grasped the point. Everyone who worked for him admired and respected his professional knowledge and judgment, though he was not a warm man: he was never off-duty, never relaxed and seemed to have no interest outside his work. He was ambitious and vain, thought Porter, and ruthless to those whom he felt did not measure up. Very shortly after Park's arrival at Uxbridge the Senior Air Staff Officer was despatched and others went too.

He was always accessible, preferably by telephone, but very blunt if he thought he had been disturbed unnecessarily. He made great use of the telephone himself and was likely to turn up anywhere in his group, usually at inconvenient moments and invariably with a shrewd idea about what was going on – or not going on. He had no interest in the trappings of his rank; there was nothing fancy about his office and he made no ceremonial entrances or exits: he was there to work and so was everybody else. His forecasts of likely German actions were excellent, and though they owed something to Ultra information, Porter was sure they owed more to his good judgment.

Porter knew Leigh-Mallory as well as he knew Park and had no doubt as to the gulf between them. Leigh-Mallory was outstanding only in pomposity and deeply concerned with appearances – his own, that of his office and headquarters and his relations with other officers. He had nothing like Park's clear and detailed understanding of the defence system. Douglas also lacked the necessary knowledge of that system and had even less experience of handling fighters than Leigh-Mallory. His understanding of the system never became sound, for he was a man loath to take instruction.

One of Park's great qualities in 1940, which Tom Gleave (yet another famous Battle of Britain pilot) has stressed, was that he could fly modern aircraft and understood how they worked. Too many senior officers at that time were quite ignorant about aircraft performance and the needs of their pilots, but Park had studied both. He was 'a typical fighter pilot,' wrote Gleave, 'in thought, action and approach to problems.' A very active man, physically and mentally, he was able to make decisions quickly. He did not flap or bluster, but he could be immovable if he thought he was right.[8]

The ascetic side of his personality impressed several observers. Derek, the present Lord Dowding, always felt a distance between himself and his father and sensed that same remoteness in Park. Derek was a Battle of Britain pilot and last met Park in Egypt in 1944, finding him, as always, austere: not a man to confide in or to seek friendship with, though he was unfailingly courteous. His hospitality was plain and simple and he lived more like a monk than an Air Marshal. Desmond Scott, a much-decorated Typhoon pilot who met Park in 1944, thought he would have made a fine bishop: he greatly admired him for speaking kindly even of Leigh-Mallory. Donald Wiseman, his personal assistant at Uxbridge in 1940, said that Park once told him that he would have been happy to make his career in the Anglican Church had he not found his way in the RAF.

As far as Wiseman could see, there was no one – at least, no one who ever came to Uxbridge – with whom Park was at ease, ready to gossip away about old times or non-military subjects even for half an hour. Wiseman doubted if he was 'unbuttoned' with anyone outside his wife and family. He had a strong personality and was well able to inspire men, appealing greatly to all who were themselves efficient and conscientious. Park was 'going round his men', as Wiseman pointed out, a couple of years before Montgomery made himself known in this way. His concern for ground crews and operations room staff was as obvious as his concern for the morale and comfort of his pilots.

Although himself a devoted regular officer, he showed no condescension towards 'amateur' airmen (auxiliaries, reservists or enlisted men). It was he who drew Wiseman's attention to the tireless work of the civilians who repaired or extended telephone communications: in fact, everyone who laboured or suffered in the whole defence team, at whatever level, mattered to him. Park was a bold delegator, partly because he expected his subordinates to cope with responsibility, partly because he did not care for office work, even though he was good at it. His regular flying, usually alone and always in dangerous areas, caused agitation both at Bentley Priory and at the Air Ministry, but he refused to give it up. At heart he was a fighting commander, a leader who understood how important it was for a man in his position to obtain a clear picture from those at the 'sharp end'. He earned their respect by his presence and by his evident knowledge of everyone's job.

Sandy Johnstone (a pilot) underlined this last point. He recalled meeting Park at Westhampnett in October 1940. His directness and informality made a refreshing change from the behaviour of most senior officers. Park obviously knew what was being done or attempted and wanted to hear what Johnstone had to say. He was a good listener, sympathetic to real grievances, but quick to jump on anything trivial. He went to no end of trouble to explain what he was trying to do at headquarters. Another distinguished pilot, Michael Crossley, supported Johnstone. Few other senior officers, he wrote, took the trouble to visit squadrons or understood what they were told if they did. Crossley never heard anything but good words about Park at Biggin Hill. 'He would say exactly what he meant in perfectly straightforward, loud and clear language, and we all had the greatest confidence in him as a leader. To hell with what jealous contemporaries might have thought about him, he was OUR boy all right.'

Crossley's enthusiasm would be warmly supported by George Westlake, who recalled a day in August 1940 when his engine cut dead somewhere over the Isle of Wight amid a great many aircraft, British and German. He promptly spun down to about 10,000 feet and since no one had followed him, he decided to attempt a landing at Westhampnett. Everything went so well that he reckoned he could even land wheels down. Unfortunately, 'a bloody great line of poplars' appeared at the last moment, causing him to wreck his Hurricane though he himself escaped unhurt. He was ordered to report to Park at Uxbridge next morning. After he had told his story, Park asked him how many aircraft he had shot down. 'One, Sir,' Westlake proudly announced. 'Pity,' replied Park. 'Now your score is exactly zero, isn't it?' He then quietly took Westlake to pieces – for not baling out, for trying to land wheels down without engine power, for hitting the poplars and, in short, for being an idiot. Finally, he told him not to rush back to Tangmere. Westlake, thinking he had been grounded, almost collapsed. 'No,' said Park, 'take the morning off and read the papers in the Mess. I'll be in at lunch-time and you can buy me a beer.'

I not only bought him a beer [Westlake recalled] he bought me a few, then he asked me to join him for lunch and to this day I simply cannot remember who else was there. As far as I was concerned, I could only see the great Keith Park – what a man. From that day on, I worshipped him . . . [9]

PART THREE

1941 - 1946

CHAPTER TWELVE

Flying Training Command

1941

Park became head of 23 Group, Flying Training Command, at South Cerney near Cirencester, Gloucestershire, on 27 December 1940 and remained there for just over a year. Throughout that time there was a great need for pilots. But the creation of more Service Flying Training Schools (SFTSs) and Operational Traning Units (OTUs) swallowed many pilots for instructor duties. Even though a major programme of expansion abroad as well as at home was in hand, this meant a *smaller* immediate output because the first trained men had to be ploughed back into the enlarged system as instructors. The schools were also very short of adequate training aircraft, especially twin-engined machines. About one in seven of the aircraft in use when Park arrived in the command was an obsolete Hawker Hart biplane. Clearly, training plans depended upon aircraft being found for them: any and every aircraft 'not wholly unsuitable' was pressed into service. The aircraft shortage was matched by a shortage of spare parts and cannibalism of unserviceable machines and improvised local manufacture of essential parts became common.

Flying training was an important task for Park, a proper use of his long experience in the front line and his known ability to get the best out of ground crews and pilots. Instructors, pupils, hangar and clerical staffs in 23 Group soon learned that they had an active, practical man in charge of them. It seems, moreover, that his group – if not the entire command – was in need of a vigorous shake. When he arrived at South Cerney, he was astonished to learn that the schools were working at only two-thirds capacity and following peacetime routines more than fifteen months after the outbreak of war. Some staff officers were unaware of the fact that Britain had come close to defeat in 1940 as a result of the shortage of pilots in Fighter Command.

Park's group was responsible for seven SFTSs, as well as the Central Flying School at Upavon in Wiltshire and the School of Air Navigation at St Athan, Glamorgan. The Aeroplane and Armament Experimental Establishment and the Blind Approach Development Unit, together making up the RAF station at Boscombe Down in Hampshire, were transferred to 23 Group in July 1941. All these units lay in south-west England, within a rough square bounded by Gloucester, Oxford, Salisbury and Bristol, except for the SFTS at Cranfield (north-east of Bletchley) and St Athan (west of Barry). Single-engined types – Harts, Fairey Battles and Miles Masters – were in use at two schools. The other five used the twin-engined Airspeed Oxford: 'the biggest basket that has ever been in the air', according to Arthur Clouston, a great test pilot. 'The controls are not balanced, and it is quite unstable,' he reported; but this instability made it an excellent trainer because 'a pilot who can fly the Oxford well can fly almost anything.'

By the end of January 1941, Park had visited every unit in his group, some of them twice. Whatever regrets he had about leaving Uxbridge, he was at least able to console himself with plenty of flying, over the same beautiful countryside where he had learned to fly more than twenty-four years earlier. By 10 July, when his only surviving log book ends, he had already flown over fifty-eight hours that year: a better rate than he had managed in 1940 and more hours than he had flown in any year since 1934. Apart from his beloved Hurricane OK1, he flew every other type that came his way and on 5 June he took the Duke of Kent as passenger in a De Havilland Hornet Moth, flying from South Cerney a few miles north to Bibury and back.

Upon reflection, he could see a bright side to his present position. He had left Uxbridge warmed by numerous expressions of regard from men in all ranks of society, in and out of the services, and had been decorated by the King in person at Buckingham Palace. He was still a group commander, with a wide measure of independent authority, ample opportunity to fly and, best of all, an urgent task ahead of him. During 1941, it became clearer every day that the war would be long and hard and Park had increasing reason to believe that he would return, sooner or later, to the front line. Meanwhile, he would seek victory in what Balfour called 'The Battle of Training'. Victory in this battle, wrote Balfour, was essential to victory elsewhere: in the Atlantic, in the desert and over Germany. This was work that Park could put his back into.[1]

He presided over the first of his weekly conferences with the group's staff officers on 6 January and began by announcing that his headquarters were untidy and dirty; the whole building needed redecorating to make it a fit place to work in. He also said that he would not have two fires burning in his office when other people were shivering with no fire at all. The station orchestra would be re-formed at once and would play during lunch in the Officers' Mess. Turning to larger problems, he thought the local defence position a muddle and had therefore sent the group defence officer to command headquarters (at Shinfield Park, Reading) to find out what was supposed to be done in the event of invasion. As for accidents, he appreciated that a great deal of time must be spent on investigation, but too much of his time was being taken up by *non-flying* accidents. Discussion followed, and would continue throughout the year, on the difficulty of finding Relief Landing Grounds (RLGs) for night-flying training.

A week later, at his second conference, he opened an attack on paperwork that would also continue throughout the year. The most serious item of business at this meeting, however, concerned the shortage of flying instructors. Park had written to headquarters on 12 January, complaining that the Air Ministry had demanded over the past week forty-five experienced instructors from his group for posting overseas. The remaining instructors, themselves inexperienced, were overworked. Park's AOC-in-C, Air Marshal Lawrence Pattinson, was sympathetic and forwarded this letter to the Air Ministry. Park told his staff officers to tell the instructors the worst so that they could prepare for it; British people, he said, liked to know what was expected of them.

On 2 February Park had signals sent to ascertain at what time the first aircraft left the ground at each station that morning. Although it was light at 8.05 a.m., he was amazed to learn that the first machine took off at his own school only at 9.45 a.m. English weather being what it was, he said, the country could not afford to have pupils hanging about on the ground on a fine morning through slack organization. As for matters arising from previous meetings, he was still pressing for more efficient methods of handling files, for a reduction in paperwork, for the delivery of pieces of wrecked German aircraft (big enough to include swastikas and crosses) to each school and for better methods of dealing with cold engines.

Little attention, he observed, had been paid to the possibility of renewed attacks on aerodromes, including training schools, as a prelude to invasion. The previous year, when fighter aerodromes had been attacked, they had been 'shockingly caught out': no alternative arrangements had been made for carrying on with routine administration – feeding and watering, accommodation and transport – from outside the station. Consequently, several stations had been seriously disorganized for weeks while hasty dispersal took place and temporary systems were improvised. Park also said that he was unimpressed by the ground instructional equipment in his schools. It was extremely dull and unimaginative; some of it was so old that he had used it himself in 1916. Good diagrams, modern models and instructors with flair and initiative were needed. By 'initiative' he meant the enthusiasm to scrounge what was wanted from wherever it could be found.

He urged all staff officers to impress upon units the importance of initiative. Following his own advice, he had obtained from Canadian Air Force headquarters in London detailed information, including a film, on coping with heavy snowfalls. Despite bad weather, accidents must be reduced given the shortage of training aircraft (quite apart from the deaths and injuries suffered by pupils), but the shortage of spare parts was actually graver than the aircraft shortage. It was an ancient fallacy, Park said, that by increasing the number of aircraft at a training school one automatically increased the number of flying hours; the prime need was for spares.

Another hindrance to training was unserviceable aerodromes. Tarmac runways were the answer, but Pattinson, said Park was 'definitely prejudiced' against them, much preferring grass. When he and Park visited Cranfield, Park pointed out that training would have been impossible there for the past two months without sealed runways, because the grass would have been reduced to mud or frozen ruts. A question then arose about procuring a Hurricane for the use of staff officers to get around the group as Park insisted they should. He remarked that he had had to overcome considerable obstruction from higher authority when bringing his own Hurricane to South Cerney. Fortunately, 'higher authority' had eventually recognized that it was not possible to separate him from his Hurricane, short of dismissing him the service.

Various ways of reducing the demand for advanced trainers were investigated during the winter of 1940–1. The use of Hurricanes instead of Masters in the second half of courses was introduced as an experiment, on Park's suggestion, at Hullavington in February. A marked improvement was noticed at fighter OTUs and the use of Hurricanes as trainers spread until it was found, in August, that the accident rate was too high. The Hurricane's short endurance was held responsible for pupils having to make forced landings; the standard of instruction was poor; and more maintenance staff were needed for a mixed establishment of advanced trainers and single-seat fighters. The use of Hurricanes therefore died out.[2]

Early in March, South Cerney was visited by the artist Sir William Rothenstein, who enjoyed a roving commission from the Air Ministry to draw a selection of airmen of various ranks and employment and to write a few words about each man. Rothenstein came to sketch Park and described him as 'tall, elegant, with penetrating blue eyes and clear-cut features, his face sensitively lined', adding that he was then 'bringing his active mind to bear on the training of pilots.' So, too, was Pattinson, who produced in March a paper on flying training after discussions with Park and other group commanders. There was a danger, thought Pattinson, that training at maximum pressure might produce quantity at the expense of quality, as had happened in the First World War. This would result in high casualties during both instruction and operations. The command was handicapped by a shortage of suitable aerodromes, aircraft, spares and instructors with recent combat experience. It was still capable of producing many of the pilots who would be needed later that year, in his opinion, but only if it was now brought up to strength. Park agreed that training must be regarded as part of the impending campaign. Unfortunately, many instructors were 'pitiably inexperienced' in night-flying and barely competent in daytime; all were overburdened. As for their aircraft, Masters were in 'enthusiastic production' at a new factory in Swindon, he told Pattinson, but the Wasp-engined version was very fast and heavy on the controls; pupils would find it tricky to handle.

Meanwhile, the Director of Flying Training at the Air Ministry, the Hon. Ralph Cochrane, had begun an enquiry into the organization of Pattinson's command because reports had reached him that 'inherent resistance to change might be greater than its eagerness to try experiments for improving training.' During April, therefore, Group Captain Gordon-Dean investigated the capacity of SFTSs and reported in May that by organizing a school so that the load was spread evenly over aircraft, instructors, pupils and maintenance staff, it should be capable of handling 288 pupils. Gordon-Dean proposed working by day in a system of five-hour shifts, each instructor having six pupils. Pattinson, however, wanted each instructor to have only four pupils and required of him only eighty hours flying per month. But it was clear to Cochrane, as it was to Park, that the schools could work harder and in June seven of the twin-engined schools began to handle 240 pupils, as opposed to 200, and the eighth, at Little Rissington in Park's group, began an experiment in working to Gordon-Dean's shift system. Hampered mainly by a late start, bad weather and numerous changes in instructors, it nevertheless worked well.[3]

William Welsh, Park's predecessor at Uxbridge, replaced Pattinson early in July and held a conference at his headquarters on the 31st to take stock of defence arrangements. Most of the command's personnel were unarmed airmen: 9,000 in 21 Group, 14,000 in 23 Group and 16,000 in 25 Group. Welsh said they must aim at regular defence training for all ranks and asked when it was being done. Park replied that he found it difficult to find the time: his group was doing fifty-seven per cent more flying for each machine than in the previous year; no one was hanging about, everyone worked eleven hours a day. Welsh said the WAAFs must know their allotted places, even if they were only to keep under cover. Park, by now entering into the spirit of this less than serious discussion, suggested that they form first-aid parties, act as messengers and carry food to the men on guard.

Welsh held a more serious conference a week later, attended by Guy Garrod, Air Member for Training at the Air Ministry. As usual, Park urged the construction of permanent runways to reduce wear and tear on men, machines and aerodromes. He expressed his fear of a return to the conditions of 1918, when new pilots had needed intensive squadron training before they could be employed on operations, and drew attention to the increasing strain on ground personnel – clerical staffs, who were too often taken for granted, as well as hangar staffs. Garrod agreed with his comments.

A few days later, Welsh visited the airfield at Brize Norton and Park subjected him to close questioning. Why had the maximum permitted boost for take-offs in Oxfords been lowered? When would sodium flarepath equipment be supplied? Why was the instruction book still in the proof stage? Welsh having agreed to look into these matters, Park flew him to Netheravon, where he asked Welsh why Fighter Command OTUs had been allotted Masters ahead of the school there (still burdened with Harts and Battles) and whether Netheravon could have an advanced course for naval pilots. Finally, Park recalled Garrod's statement at the conference on 6 August that the Dominions must take a proportion of inexperienced instructors. There was, he observed, no sign of this in the September postings and he asked Welsh to see what he could do.

Park then took a week off, which he spent with his family at Itchenor, near Chichester, in the cottage which he and Dol had bought soon after returning from South America. It was intended as the family's permanent home, convenient for the sailing they all enjoyed. Dol gave him a copy of A.B. Austin's recently published book, *Fighter Command*, to commemorate, as she wrote on the inside cover, 'our summer leave, all four together at the cottage.' They all spent Christmas 1941 there, but that was the last time Keith, Dol and their sons would be together for at least five years.

Welsh wrote to Park in September with a proposal to ease his problems over night-flying. Since he had too few Relief Landing Grounds of his own, his only hope was to make use of operational aerodromes on nights when they were not required. He asked Park to make a list of those within easy reach of schools and Welsh would seek permission to use them when they were free. Once permission had been granted, he proposed to run night-flying on a mobile basis: all the places they would want to use had the appropriate equipment already installed and they need only send out ground parties to man the flares. Park responded enthusiastically, as he usually did to a demand for improvisation. By moving from place to place, it was possible to get in far more night-flying than would otherwise have been the case.

At a conference on 22 September Welsh announced that the Air Ministry had decided to increase the length of courses up to eighteen weeks for the winter and revert to twelve the following summer. Schools should aim to turn out pilots with eighty-five or more hours instead of seventy-two as at present. Park welcomed the news. There would be more time for night-flying, cross-country and instrument work, he said. He agreed with Welsh that short, snappy navigation exercises were better than long ones. Pupils, he thought, should be taught to drive cars. This was a skill which few had mastered (owing to wartime licence and petrol restrictions, apart from the price and scarcity of private cars), but such practical training in coordination and judgment of speed and distance would be invaluable, especially in avoiding taxiing accidents.[4]

Towards the end of 1941, as the overseas schools came into full production, Park could see his job disappearing from under him. He had served his exile with good grace and was anxious about his future. Various moves were afoot in the Air Ministry: Garrod suggested that Park return to Fighter Command as Air Officer in charge of Administration, but nothing came of that suggestion. December, however, proved to be his last effective month of RAF service in England. Except for brief visits home he was continuously abroad from January 1942 until August 1946 and the following month retired from the service. There had been a real job for him to do in Flying Training Command, one for which he had the experience and the personality. He threw himself wholeheartedly into it and when it was done, he was given an important operational post – to his profound relief.

It was clear from the middle of 1940 that if the war were to be won at all, it would be slow work. Good men could not be wasted, allowed to burn themselves out, as Park would have been prepared to do. Portal knew his quality and presumably also knew from his medical record, if not from his own knowledge, that Park's physical reserves were slender. Whether by design or chance, he would be given alternating positions, front and rear, throughout the war: Fighter Command, then training; Egypt and Malta, then Egypt again (more training); finally, Allied Air Commander, South-East Asia, the most demanding position he ever held. By 1946 he was very tired indeed. Had he spent 1941 in Fighter Command, close to Douglas, attempting a job for which the tools were not then available, he might not have lasted the course. In 1941 he showed the energy, enthusiasm, attention to detail and grasp of principles that had carried him to Bentley Priory at a critical moment and would now, at an even more critical moment, carry him to Egypt. On Boxing Day it was learned that Park was to proceed early in January to take up his duties as AOC Iraq. However, a few days later he instead received orders to go to Egypt whilst Champion de Crespigny, AOC of 25 Group, was despatched to Iraq in his place.[5]

CHAPTER THIRTEEN

Malta Besieged

1942

In January 1942 Park sailed as far as Sierra Leone aboard the *Viceroy of India* and then flew on to Cairo. It was the first time in more than twenty-three years that he and his wife had been separated and, except for a couple of fleeting visits by Park to England, they would remain separated for the next two and a half years. A young New Zealand pilot, John Mason, travelled on the same ship and recalled an occasion when a Major ordered him and some other pilots to leave the boat-deck, where they had been sunning themselves, because that deck was reserved for senior officers. When Park was informed, he at once told all the senior officers that 'these young gentleman have faced and will face dangers that none of you will ever meet. They will share any facilities on board this ship equally with you.' Needless to say, added Mason, this arrangement lasted only until Park disembarked.

The critical importance of Egypt as the main base for the British war effort in the Middle East led to the despatch of a small mission of air and army officers to Cairo at the end of 1941 to examine its air defences. Douglas Evill, Senior Air Staff Officer at Fighter Command, led that mission. The Chiefs of Staff, he said, had in mind an 'Air Defence Commander of the Delta Area': an Air Vice-Marshal who would be in a position similar to a fighter group commander in Britain, handling day- and night-fighter squadrons, anti-aircraft guns and searchlights, supported by a radar chain and an observer system. This was the job assigned to Park as AOC Egypt and it may be that Evill, who thought highly of him, recommended him for it. A unified defence system was gradually built up in the Nile Delta, though Park never had as many aircraft, guns or searchlights as planned. As in England in 1940, he had few opportunities to mount an offensive of his own. The danger of an all-out daylight assault on Egypt was high and Park spent many anxious hours trying to bring the defensive system up to the standard he remembered in England.

Park's six months in Egypt served to refresh his experience in fighter defence problems and to introduce him to new problems in handling a wide variety of aircraft of limited capability over a vast extent of land and sea. Although the Axis powers did not launch a serious daylight assault on Egypt, night raids were frequent and apart from challenging these, Park's aircraft were constantly busy mine-sweeping, hunting submarines, escorting convoys and carrying out photo-reconnaissance along shipping routes from Crete to Libya and the approaches to the Delta. As usual, Park was constantly on the move, visiting the units under his command. On 28 May, the *Evening Standard* paid a handsome tribute to him at a time when the Battle of Britain was long over and he had yet to earn fresh laurels in Malta. According to this newspaper, Park was the top airman in Egypt and Arthur Coningham – another New Zealander, known to his friends as 'Mary' (Maori) – was the top airman in the Western Desert. With these two colonials, Tedder had 'about the best team of fighting leaders we could put in the field'. Park was 'probably our greatest expert in the operational command of fighter aircraft . . . a good talker and reckoned to be one of the best brains in the RAF.'

A single sheet of handwritten notes headed 'Egypt 1942' survives among Park's papers. One day at the end of June, he drove out of Cairo towards Alexandria, passing several airfields that he had developed and stocked during the previous six months:

> As I drove past I felt a little reflected glory in the fine achievements of the DAF [Desert Air Force] because my command had been able to give them such sound administrative backing as our Army fell back on Egypt. I also reflected on what grand bombing targets these airfields offered to the Luftwaffe. . . . Looking back over the war as a whole, I believe that if the Luftwaffe had obtained even temporary air superiority during the critical months from June to September 1942, our Army could not have held Rommel at El Alamein. On the other hand, his Army had no respite from air attacks by day or night against his single road and single rail track communicating with his base ports.

From 26 May, when Rommel began his offensive against the Eighth Army positions at Gazala, until 30 June, when his spearhead reached El Alamein, the British position deteriorated rapidly. Four hundred miles of coastline were surrendered. Between Gibraltar and the untried and still incomplete defences at El Alamein – a distance of over 2,000 miles – Malta was the sole British base. This 'unsinkable aircraft carrier', anchored a mere sixty miles south of the Axis aerodromes on Sicily, had already suffered heavy air attack. On 2 July, the eve of Park's transfer there, Churchill told Parliament that there was at that moment 'a recession of our hopes and prospects in the Middle East and in the Mediterranean unequalled since the fall of France. If there are any would-be profiteers of disaster who feel able to paint the picture in darker colours, they are certainly at liberty to do so.'

Yet, at the time when Churchill spoke, the very success of Rommel's offensive averted the invasion of Malta. Operation Hercules, as the invasion plan was called, had been postponed at Rommel's request on 23 June. During the next few days, he reached out for what seemed the available prizes of the Nile Delta and the Suez Canal. Had they fallen, the surrender of Malta would have followed without the need for a costly invasion. This proved to be one of the war's most fateful decisions because Rommel was still outflanked along his lines of communication by the naval–air base of Malta. The Afrika Korps should therefore have stayed put on the Egyptian border until its seaborne supplies from Italy and Greece were safeguarded by the capture of Malta. The failure to take the island led directly to Rommel's defeat because half his supplies were destroyed by attack from Malta.[1]

Park handed over command of AHQ Egypt on 8 July and assumed command of RAF Malta on the 14th in place of Air Vice-Marshal Hugh Lloyd. In January 1957 Park recalled his arrival there. He flew to Malta in a Sunderland, he said, arriving at dawn during an air-raid. After circling around for a quarter of an hour, he told the pilot to go in and land because everyone aboard was cold and hungry. Lloyd was very angry: the Sunderland might have been shot down, he said, and should have stayed away. On the way from Kalafrana to Sliema, Lloyd 'puffed out his chest' (according to Park) and said 'now you will see how Malta can take it! Aren't we brave?' 'I think you are dumb,' Park replied, 'why don't you stop the bombing and get on with the war instead of sitting back and taking it?'

Within a fortnight daylight bombing had been stopped and an offensive begun. Park, however, arrived when the worst of the blitz was over and when sufficient Spitfires were at last available to give the defence a chance. Beaverbrook sent Park his warmest congratulations on his new appointment:

> Once more you are in the post of danger [he wrote on 21 July]. And once more my confidence is complete that you will emerge triumphant. The lustre of you and Dowding grows always. You have your place in the history of the country, both of you. It is not unlike the place that is given to the narratives of Drake and Hawkins.

Dol Park, stuck in England, kept a scrapbook of press cuttings and photographs of her husband's deeds in Malta. In the dark months before the victory at El Alamein, Park was made much of by the press. His role in the Battle of Britain was recalled and lavishly praised; it was even recalled that as Air Aide-de-Camp to the King he had ridden in the coronation procession 'on a charger which he said was the finest horse he had ever ridden.' Park was 'Malta's Man of the Moment' and large pictures of him appeared on the front pages of weekly magazines. He was frequently photographed in the cockpit of aircraft, above such captions as 'The Air Marshal Who Cannot Be Kept Down'. Cartoons on Malta's stubborn defence were popular. For example,

Hitler catapulting his bombers against a Maltese Cross high in the sky, from which they bounced off and crashed. As is often the way with the British, a stubborn defence against odds appealed greatly. Naturally, photographs and stories of the Maltese 'taking it' and 'carrying on' as stoutly as the British made good propaganda.

'Laddie' Lucas, a distinguished fighter pilot, served briefly under Park in Malta. Park struck Lucas as an assertive, self-confident man with a strong personality, who believed in going out to meet the enemy and played an important part in changing the spirit of the military machine in Malta. Bold offence, rather than stolid defence, became more frequently emphasized. In Lucas's opinion, Park was well liked by his squadron commanders, for his visibility, professional knowledge and readiness to listen, although once he had heard and considered his pilots' views, he then dictated tactics and would brook no opposition. His dislike of paperwork was also popular and, best of all, his recognition of the need to prefer the welfare of those at the 'sharp end' (on the ground as well as in the air) to the administrative convenience of staff officers.

Park enjoyed his time in Malta. As in the Battle of Britain, he had a wide measure of personal control over a major campaign in which air forces were decisive. He was very conscious of his image in Malta: ceaseless aggression in military operations, ceaseless visits to units and civilians. As an observer remarked, he was the first Air Vice-Marshal anyone had seen doing his rounds on a bicycle. He would arrive at an aerodrome by other transport and then, because of the desperate petrol shortage, pedal his way from squadron to squadron. Soon, however, he obtained a small MG sports car, painted bright red. The sight of Park threading his way through cratered streets in his 'fire engine', as it was popularly known, lifted morale everywhere in the island. He enjoyed driving it, but it also gave him a cheerful, even jaunty image – in welcome contrast to the gloomy manner of too many other senior officers – and he always picked up walking servicemen if he had a spare seat. Lieutenant Commander E.W. Whitley, then serving as a fitter in a Swordfish squadron, recalled one such lift but not what he and Park talked about: 'From my position, he was almost God!' Whitley admired the way Park got about on his own, 'without a tribe of staff officers following, seeing for himself what was going on.'

Like Montgomery, Park was a calculating showman, whose flamboyance was for public consumption only. In private, he was not at all a man to gossip easily. Sandy Johnstone was a pilot in Malta at this time and compared Park's red MG with his white overalls in 1940: both were trademarks, intended to single him out instantly. Moreover, he always appeared in immaculate uniforms, contrasting painfully with the shabbiness of most Malta servicemen. Johnstone believed that Park's success depended heavily on his readiness to listen and then redistribute as his own ideas those which he picked up. In this respect, he resembled Eisenhower. Park greatly valued the

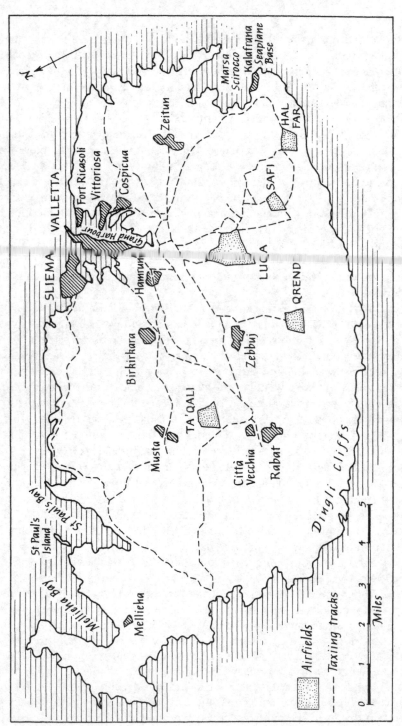

Mellieha Bay

St Paul's
Island

St Paul's Bay

Mellieha

Musta

Birkirkara

TA'QALI

Citta
Vecchia

Rabat

Zebbuj

Dingli cliffs

SLIEMA

VALLETTA

Fort Ricasoli
Vittoriosa
Cospicua

Grand Harbour

Hamrun

Zeitun

Marsa
Scirocco

Kalafrana
Seaplane
Base

HAL
FAR

SAFI

LUCA

QREND

Airfields

Taxiing tracks

0   1   2   3   4   5

Miles

7: Malta

regard of his aircrews and carefully fostered it. For instance, he always managed to conjure up a full bottle of gin for 'Father's Prayers' (his meetings with squadron commanders) and circulated it freely to dispel inhibitions about talking with the boss. He learned more than he would have otherwise and the officers felt more comfortable with him.[2]

On 19 July 1942, within a week of his arrival in Malta, Park signalled details to HQ RAF Middle East of his immediate operational needs. He was particularly concerned about the shortage of aviation fuel, aircraft spares and experienced pilots. As Lloyd had said, Malta was no place for beginners: there was no fuel for practice, no safe practice area and no time for tuition. These signals were passed to Norman Bottomley, Deputy Chief of the Air Staff, who wrote to Park on the 24th. A number of 'somewhat violent and hasty signals' from Park's predecessor, he said, had expressed dissatisfaction at 'occasional misfits who have passed through the sieve.' Some of the complaints were justified, Bottomley admitted, but others 'tended to fray the nerves and jar the susceptibilities' of people who were doing their best for Malta. The position had recently improved, 'and I am sure you will be unwilling to let it deteriorate in any way'. Park picked up his cue and on 13 August signalled his thanks to Bottomley for a good bunch of replacement pilots.

Park issued his 'Fighter Interception Plan' on 25 July. Until lately, he wrote, Malta's squadrons had been greatly outnumbered by enemy raiders. This had caused the adoption of a defensive system whereby squadrons were sent into the air by the sector controller and provided with a running commentary about approaching raiders. It was left to formation leaders to decide where to patrol and when to attempt interception. Squadrons normally flew south of the island after take-off to gain height, returning when they saw anti-aircraft fire and making their attacks (as a rule) after the enemy had bombed his target and was free to take evasive action while retreating under cover of a fighter escort.

The fighter forces were now, however, a match for those of the enemy said Park, and so the time had come to end daylight attacks. A plan would now be introduced with the object of intercepting raids north of Malta, before they crossed the coast. The sector controller was to ensure that his first squadron got its height up-sun and then intercepted the enemy's high fighter cover. The second squadron was to intercept the bombers' close escort or the bombers themselves, if unescorted. The third squadron was to make a head-on attack on the bombers about ten miles north of the coast, followed by a quarter attack, to force them to jettison their bombs into the sea. If a fourth squadron was available, it would tackle any bombers which broke through the forward fighter screen. The plan had been explained orally to all concerned. It required reliable radar warning and alert pilots. Take-offs must be much quicker than in the past, control must be accurate and clear, and squadrons must obey orders immediately. Wireless discipline must be strict and pilots must not open fire at long range, thereby alerting the enemy and wasting valuable ammunition. Last but not least, sea rescue services must have sufficient high-speed launches and be thoroughly trained in their work. Park emphasized that all pilots were welcome at any time of the day or night in the visitors' gallery of the operations room and their suggestions for improvements in procedure would always be considered.

After two weeks of his 'Fighter Interception Plan', Park expressed himself pleased with the results. Only four aircraft had been damaged or destroyed on the ground as compared with thirty-four during the first two weeks of July. Most raids had in fact been intercepted north of Malta and handled so roughly that the enemy was resorting to high-flying fighter sweeps which were intended to regain air superiority and so clear the way for a resumption of bombing raids. Given radar's short warning and the inaccuracy of its high altitude information, fighters were easily able to arrive over Malta with a height advantage. Park had decided, however, to restrict patrols to 20,000 feet. This would oblige the enemy to come down to an altitude which suited the Spitfire more than the Bf 109 if he wanted to fight, and any bombs dropped from above that height could scarcely be aimed.

Unfortunately, Lord Gort, the Governor and Commander-in-Chief of Malta, nourished a bitter resentment of the RAF for its failures, as he saw them, during the French campaign in 1940 and his relations with Park were, at best, tense. Park was responsible for all air operations, but Gort had an overriding authority in the event of an invasion attempt. He complained continually about the drain on petrol stocks caused by any operation not directly concerned with protecting Malta. The Air Ministry, for example, required Park to use his Beaufort torpedo-bombers to strike at Rommel's supply lines and to assist Allied convoys by threatening the Italian Navy. In Park's view, these strikes and threats could only be carried out if he also prevented daylight raids on Malta by attacking Axis aerodromes in Sicily and southern Italy. Gort, however, resisted this escalation of effort: Malta's aircraft and fuel would be consumed, he argued, and the island exposed to invasion, unhindered from the air.

By the middle of 1942, four Special Liaison Units (SLUs) had been set up in the Middle East to handle Ultra information: one in Cairo, another with the Eighth Army, a third with the Desert Air Force and a large one in Malta to look after the needs of all three services. The Malta SLU was housed deep in the rock next door to the naval and air headquarters. Whenever two or three Axis ships were loaded in Naples or Taranto for despatch to Rommel, Kesselring, Germany's Commander-in-Chief South, would inform him by signal what supplies were loaded, at what time and date the ships would sail and the course they would follow. These signals were intercepted and decoded at Bletchley Park and the information sent to Park and Admiral Sir Henry Harwood, commander of the Mediterranean fleet. Both were meticulous in observing Ultra's rules to prevent the enemy realizing his signals were being picked up. Park, for example, ordered his aircraft to patrol in areas just close enough to where he knew a convoy would be to ensure that it could be spotted before British ships arrived to attack it.

On one occasion in the summer of 1942, a dense fog came down shortly after a convoy left Naples. It could neither see nor be seen by Park's aircraft. Hoping the fog would lift, he delayed the operation as long as he dared, but when the convoy neared the African coast, he acted. British ships and aircraft turned up in the right place at the right time and sank the Axis vessels, but not before one of them reported this suspicious accident. The British intercepted Kesselring's signal to Berlin demanding an inquiry, but the Germans thought Italian informers responsible and the British encouraged this opinion. Apart from the sinkings achieved, with or without secret assistance, the combined operations of British ships and aircraft forced the Axis into lengthy diversions in attempting to supply Rommel. Convoys would put back to port three or four times simply at sight of reconnaissance aircraft.[3]

Although the air battle was turning in Malta's favour, the siege was tightening. On 29 July Air Marshal Arthur Tedder (then AOC-in-C, HQ Middle East) asked the Middle East Defence Committee whether Park should continue to attack Axis vessels sailing from Sicily to Tunisia in view of Malta's fuel shortage. Harwood thought that 'Malta's fate was entirely dependent on the August convoy. If that failed to get through, nothing would enable a convoy to get through in September.' Aircraft and ships should therefore strike as hard as possible at enemy supply lines while they still could. Park agreed entirely. He had been the very apostle of defence in the summer of 1940, but now he believed that offence was essential. It was a matter of priorities: unless his aircraft seriously impeded the build-up of Rommel's forces, the Eighth Army might be defeated again and the fall of Malta would follow that of Egypt, no matter how prudently its fuel, ammunition and food stocks had been conserved.

Operation Pedestal, as the August convoy was named, was an Allied operation of prime importance. The Germans prepared to attack it by shifting almost the whole of their long-range bomber force from Crete to Sicily and assembling torpedo-bombers in Sardinia and the island of Pantelleria. All told, some 540 Axis aircraft were gathered for the attack whereas Park had only 155 serviceable aircraft. Another major threat was the presence of the powerful Italian fleet within easy striking distance of the Sicilian Narrows, where the convoy would be at its most vulnerable.

The convoy, of fourteen merchant vessels under the escort of thirty-six warships, entered the Mediterranean during the night of 10/11 August. By the time the severely damaged tanker *Ohio* was hauled into Grand Harbour on the morning of the 15th, nine of the merchant vessels had been sunk and seven of the escort sunk or damaged. It is surprising that so many got through, including the vital tanker. Had the Italians played their part with the same tenacity as the Germans, none would have reached Malta. Vice-Admiral Weichold, German Commander-in-Chief in the Mediterranean, wrote later that to the European observer the British losses seemed disastrous, but the Axis had failed to prevent crucial supplies from reaching Malta and thereafter that island was able to prevent equally crucial supplies from reaching Rommel. The arrival of five merchant vessels in Malta represented, from the Axis viewpoint, 'a strategic failure of the first order'.

Park's report on Pedestal characteristically singled out several officers for praise in reconnaissance or air fighting. He also had praise for those whose achievements were personal: the pilot making his first landing in darkness, the Wellington crew on its first operation. Throughout recent months, he added, army personnel had been employed filling runway craters, building aircraft pens, helping to arm, bomb-up and refuel aircraft, driving lorries, steamrollers and motorcycles, controlling traffic and removing wrecked aircraft. This assistance had been vital before and during Pedestal. Given the limited experience of most crews and his shortage of aircraft, Park was glad that the Italians had performed so timidly.

Sinclair, Secretary of State for Air, signalled congratulations to Park on behalf of the War Cabinet and Park, in turn, congratulated the squadrons concerned in protecting the convoy. He signalled Portal, Chief of the Air Staff, so say that if air superiority over Malta could be maintained, the island's fuel reserves had now been extended from four to fourteen weeks because his aircraft used less fuel on planned strikes than on defensive patrols. After the arrival of the ships, he put on a first-class dinner, despite the strict rationing still in force, for the masters and captains of the merchantmen and their escorts, one of whom said afterwards:

> Nowhere was I more heartened than when entertained by Air Vice-Marshal Park, who was a great host and sent us back spiritually elated in the conviction that the RAF would always be a move or two ahead of the Axis and that the great aerial ordeal of the people of Malta is in the limbo of the past.[4]

As soon as the *Ohio*'s precious oil was unloaded, Park sought permission to resume offensive action. He was informed that attacks on southbound shipping and training directly related to that task should take precedence over petrol conservation in the immediate future. But an unduly defensive, even defeatist, attitude had taken hold upon ruling circles in Malta and Gort regularly voiced his fear of ending 'in the cooler'. He therefore resisted offensive action and gave way only under orders from Cairo and London. He sought constantly to limit Park's freedom of action, rejecting his opinion that the whole point of garrisoning Malta was to attack shipping and so weaken Rommel.

Such attacks were, however, costly and difficult to organize, as Park informed Gerald Gibbs, his old deputy at 11 Group and now Director of Overseas Operations at the Air Ministry. He understood that crews were *detailed* for torpedo-bombing and suggested that in future only volunteers be employed on this dangerous duty. The German example of regarding dive-bomber crews as the cream of the service and granting them special privileges might well be followed. The number of hours currently laid down as the tour of duty for a torpedo-bomber crew (200) was so high that no crew had 'any prospect' of surviving it; to stick to that 'altogether excessive' figure would merely result in attacks not being pressed home or the destruction of good men. Gibbs promised to do what he could, both to reduce the tour and to provide more and better aircraft and more experienced aircrews.

The fuel shortage remained grave and on 9 September Park was ordered by the Air Ministry to cut consumption from 250 to 200 tons per week. Throughout September he personally made daily checks on consumption, reporting his figures to Gort, to Cairo and to London. He disagreed strongly with the policy of cutting down to stretch supplies: 'What a pity Whitehall has to remove sting of wasp,' he signalled on the 27th, 'to extend its miserable existence a couple of weeks instead of finding ways and means of running more honey into the nest.' Malta was as short of food as of fuel and on the 26th Gort had informed Cairo that essential stocks could not be expected to last beyond the second week of December.

The next day, Major-General Ronald Scobie (GOC Troops), who had attended the Imperial Defence College with Park in 1937, wrote from Malta to Lieutenant-General Archibald Nye (Vice Chief of the Imperial General Staff) at the War Office. 'The RAF here are grand,' he said, 'with a fine commander in Park. They have their opposite number in Sicily completely down at the moment. . . . Relations between the services are very good and cooperation is excellent.' Although the army was not yet suffering from a shortage of food, the civilians – on a lower ration scale – were feeling the strain. Scobie found them friendly, but pointed out that it would be embarrassing if they turned against the British: there were 270,000 of them.

At the end of September, Gort complained direct to Portal about Park's failure to show him important signals. 'I know very well what your difficulties are,' wrote Portal to Park on 4 October, 'and I find it extremely hard to believe that you have been in the least uncooperative, but for the sake of peace, show Gort too much rather than too little in the future.' Park replied that he was surprised to hear of Gort's complaint. Although he had often complained about Tedder, Lloyd and others, he had 'affected an outward display of friendliness' towards Park. Sadly, Gort believed the RAF had let him down in 1940 and Park agreed with Lloyd that he was 'an embittered and disappointed General'. It was not cooperation but 'complete subservience' that he wanted. His Chief of Staff (Captain Guy Russell, RN) was 'a Prince of snoopers' and though Gort was undoubtedly brave, he had a morbid fear of being taken prisoner and offensive operations were anathema to him.[5]

On 11 October the Axis powers began a last attempt to neutralize Malta and so end the constant harassment of their supply route between Sicily and Tunisia. The attack lasted nine days, though on a diminishing scale. The proportion of fighters to bombers steadily increased and high-flying fighter-bomber sweeps became common – both indications, as in the Battle of Britain, that the attack was failing. Most raids were intercepted over the sea and few were pressed home; only moderate casualties were suffered on the ground and little serious damage was done. As always, Park had emphasized the need to concentrate on bombers and his victory was complete: even during the battle there was only one night when his aircraft did not carry out shipping strikes; it was a night when no Axis ship came within range of Malta. A German report, composed two years later, considered this battle the last turning-point for German air power in the Mediterranean.

Park was overwhelmed with congratulations from the highest quarters, Gort surprised him by expressing his delight in the most generous terms. Sinclair congratulated him on the brilliant exploits of his squadrons; Portal and Freeman, Vice-Chief of the Air Staff, were also well pleased. One tribute that touched him deeply came from Michael, Bishop of Gozo, who told 'Mr Park' that in spite of the bombing of Sannat village, when sixty-two people were killed or injured, 'we know that we are efficiently protected from the air. May God help and bless your work among us.' In military terms, Park's achievement in October 1942 bears no comparison with his work on many occasions in 1940, but it was admirably *timed*: most of the war news from elsewhere was bad and Malta provided welcome relief.

From Malta came only good news: the Axis powers did not invade, their aircraft were vigorously attacked and the tally was always in British favour. There was a constant emphasis in the cricket-starved newspapers on scores: daily, weekly and over the whole campaign. 'Malta (Tea Score): 17 Down' is one example from 14 October. The Germans, wrote Colin Bednall in the *Daily Mail* on the 16th, were 'using up still more of the planes which they would like to turn against British towns this winter . . . and here they are meeting probably the world's finest combination in air defence – frontline Spitfires, radio-location and Air Vice-Marshal K.R. Park'. A large photograph of him filled the front page of *Picture Post* on the 31st and Park sent Beaverbrook a copy, together with an account (now lost) of 'the Second Battle of Malta'. Beaverbrook was delighted, he replied, 'to have from you this fascinating and dramatic letter. In these days, every word that comes out of Malta has an extraordinary interest for us.'

News Review (London) published a full-page article about him on 5 November, written very much in the nauseous style of a modern interview with a pop star: 'I went in search of him, found a man with frank blue eyes . . . He lit a pipe, smoked as he talked in a softly modulated voice: "I love flying. Truly I love flying," he said.' Park spoke about a red triangular banner given him by a New Zealand merchant captain who arrived in Malta with the last convoy. It had belonged to an artilleryman who wanted Park, an ex-artilleryman, to have a memento of that phase of his career. On the wall of his office was a shield presented to him by the people of Malta and over his desk hung a model of a Wellington bomber given him by Malta's gunners to remind him of Wellington, New Zealand. Although the Germans had just destroyed the balcony of his house and all the windows were broken, he seemed undismayed and talked about his days in South America and his plans for sailing after the war.

A new aerodrome at Qrendi was opened by Gort on 10 November and the first aircraft was flown off by Park himself. Before his flight, Park emphasized the great assistance received from the army in constructing aircraft pens in record time and thanked the Maltese contractor and his men for overcoming persistent shortages of transport, material and labour. 'Malta,' he said, 'has shown the world how a brave population can take heavy bombing, and is now going to show the enemy how hard it can hit back.' He then took off in his Hurricane, OK2, 'amid the cheers of the assembly and to the delight of the children,' not to mention the press reporters and photographers who were encouraged to attend. Park had often observed Churchill at close quarters in 1940 and from that master of the art had learned the value to a people under siege of bold, confident words. He had also learned that a leader should be seen as well as heard.[6]

The brave words used at Qrendi were not empty. Even before the first unmolested convoy arrived in Malta on 20 November, indicating the end of the year-long siege, Park was giving important assistance to the Allied landings in North West Africa under the command of General Eisenhower. He never liked to hear that Malta was 'a bomb sponge' (though it did receive nearly 13,000 tons of them). On the contrary, he vigorously asserted that Malta was a fortress, tying up superior enemy forces and also making a direct contribution to the land campaigns of Montgomery and Eisenhower. Despite endless worry over shortages of every commodity he never lost sight of his ambition to make of Malta 'an offensive springboard'.

It was in November that Park first fitted some of his Spitfires with two 250-lb bombs each. The racks were made in the dockyards out of metal salvaged from wrecked aircraft and these Spitfire-bombers did so well against ships, airfields, factories and railway trains that he even used them for night attacks. Although bombs had not apparently been fitted to Spitfires before, this was no gimmick. Enemy fighters were not coming up to challenge 'normal' Spitfires, but if they were carrying bombs they could not be ignored. Park had learned this lesson in October 1940. His ingenuity, aggression and eagerness to help did not pass unnoticed. During November,

Eisenhower (in Algiers) expressed himself 'most grateful for the splendid support afforded by air operations from Malta' and Montgomery praised Park and his men for their assistance to the Eighth Army throughout the advance westward from El Alamein.

The months of October and November were glorious for Park. Following the lavish praise he received for his repulse of the October attacks, and while his men were making effective strikes in support of Allied thrusts from west and east, Trenchard himself wrote to Park:

> You are magnificent and I hear great things of what you and ail your people are doing. It is splendid. The news coming from North Africa is good. . . . I do congratulate you enormously. The work of your people ground strafing in broad daylight and your torpedo-bombing of Rommel's convoys have been magnificent and must have very materially helped Tedder and Coningham in the Middle East.

To an old RFC officer, praise from no other man, not even the Chief of the Air Staff himself, could compare with praise from the immortal Boom, 'Father of the Royal Air Force', who personally singled out for particular encouragement practically all the officers who reached the top in the Second World War.

The ultimate accolade followed: Portal signalled Park on 22 November to offer his heartiest congratulations, together with a misquotation from Browning's *The Patriot* on the announcement of the well-deserved award to Park of a knighthood – 'Roses, roses all the way . . . And myrtle mixed in my path.'

At dusk on 16 November a convoy codenamed Stoneage had sailed from Port Said and reached Grand Harbour intact early on the 20th. Vice-Admiral Arthur Power commanded the escort and recorded in his diary on the 22nd that 'the Malta fighters were magnificent' during the approach to the island. Park signalled his congratulations on the successful completion of a vital task and Power quoted 'this very kind' signal in a message of his own to all ships under his command. Power went ashore on the 27th and met Park and Scobie. The following day he wrote in his diary: 'I saw Park RAF and don't like him: also Scobie who is V.G.1'. Scobie and Leatham (Vice-Admiral Malta) were excellent friends, thought Power, and Park was quite out of it.

He, meanwhile, had flown with Tedder and two American Air Force generals to Algiers to discuss with Eisenhower the creation of a unified air command, responsible for all aerial operations in the Mediterranean. He described his visit to Algiers in a letter to Beaverbrook on 30 November. Most cafés were shut, the shops had little for sale, he had seen no taxis or buses during his two days there and the working classes looked hungrier, thinner and worse-clad than even the Maltese who had lived under siege for a year. No accommodation had been booked for Tedder and Park, but eventually Park had managed to get them two rooms at the GHQ hotel.

Park's was lavishly furnished, except that it had no bed; Tedder's, however, had three and Park had explained to their servant in his best schoolboy French that Tedder was an abstemious man and could one be moved into Park's room? It took two applications to senior American staff officers to get this done before midnight. The incident was typical of Algiers, he thought, 'everyone appears to be full of enthusiasm, talking incessantly and attending innumerable conferences – no agenda, no decisions and therefore no need for any minutes'. The whole atmosphere reminded him of *Alice in Wonderland*.[7]

In November Mr C.E.O. Wood, an Air Ministry engineer with whom Park had been friendly before the war, visited Malta to inspect the aerodromes. Park said of him on 1 December that he had galvanized the Air Ministry Works Department and 'almost succeeded' in getting labour and transport out of the local government. Wood was still there at Christmas, despite a flock of Air Ministry signals requesting his return, and gave Park a beautiful inscribed paper-knife which he used for the rest of his life. Wood also did what he could to have pierced steel planking supplied for Malta's runways, taxi tracks and dispersal points. No praise could be too high, he told the Air Ministry, for the way Park and his staff tried to overcome the lamentably slow progress managed by the works services, but Ta'Qali and Hal Far remained unserviceable after heavy rain, and accidents caused by inadequate surfaces were much too frequent.

Lieutenant-General Nye wrote to Scobie from the War Office on 3 December. It has been 'simply thrilling' to read of Malta's successes against shipping; these, thought Nye, had contributed greatly to Rommel's defeat. 'If you read the English newspapers,' he added, 'you rather get the impression that Rommel was beaten solely by the brilliance of our generals. That, of course, is very good publicity, but it is very bad history!' Another general, Eisenhower, was equally impressed by the efforts of Park and his men. In a telegram to Churchill on the 5th he said: 'Daily reports show that Malta is straining every nerve to help us, and I have nothing but praise for the work Park has done.'

Gort and Power were less impressed. 'He is very bitter against RAF,' wrote Power of Gort on the 16th, 'apparently it started in the "France" days and increases.' Power was having an unhappy time with Park. On 1 December they had driven together round the aerodromes and Power found Malta 'saturated' with aircraft, a condition which seemed to displease him. That night he dined with Park and Scobie: 'Park is rather too much Park; Scobie is obviously not in sympathy with Park but tolerates him and won't have a row unless it is essential.' On 13 December Power blew off a fine head of steam into his diary: 'Park is entirely insincere – he does not understand the naval aspect and is very unsatisfactory to deal with.' Power's diary is full of critical comments on all operations and it is rare for him to praise anyone or anything; Park is by no means his only or even chief object of distaste. There are, for example, several references to Churchill's 'most foolish boastful manner'.

Early in December, some Mosquitos were promised to Park by the Air Ministry which might, he was told, replace a Spitfire squadron. Park, however, fought hard to keep his Spitfires because he foresaw that the Mosquitos would not last long. Nor did they: of the fifteen which arrived, eight were grounded for lack of spares by the end of January. Cairo offered him some Wellingtons, but they arrived in such a poor state that their frequent engine failures were likely, he said, to impair the morale of crews flying them. He reiterated his demand for new machines from England, together with ample spares and qualified ground staff to service them. Gradually, he got his way. In the last three months of the year 921 men were sent to Malta and another 282 were promised for January. Clearly, Malta's days as a besieged fortress were over. On Christmas Day, Park received a signal from Eisenhower: 'My admiration for your deeds past and present is exceeded only by my appreciation of your invaluable support.' That support would be much stronger in 1943 as Malta was transformed into a powerful offensive base.[8]

CHAPTER FOURTEEN

Malta Offensive

1943

'Malta has been transformed into one vast aircraft carrier,' wrote Richard Capell of the *Daily Telegraph* in January 1943. 'In the messes one hears the latest gossip from Cairo, Gibraltar, Algiers. Someone was only last week in West Africa or Washington.' Park, at the hub of this activity, continued to attract favourable attention. Eisenhower informed Portal on 5 January that if 'Eastern Air Force could be placed under Park or another [officer] of equal experience and ability in Mediterranean warfare, we would have, for the immediate problem, a most happy solution.' Sinclair wrote to Portal (who visited Malta late in January): 'Tell Park how much I wish I could pay him a visit myself and congratulate him on the brilliant and varied exploits of his Squadrons.' Gerald Gibbs was in Malta at this time and Park drove him round the aerodromes for a couple of days, 'but there was little I could suggest to my old chief – he knew the job from A to Z. Gibbs reported to the Air Ministry on 8 January that ample skilled labour (army and civilian) permitted good runways, pens and accommodation to be provided and essential operations rooms, stores and workshops to be built safely underground. Given a small increase in maintenance personnel, Malta was capable of operating very large air forces efficiently.

Vice-Admiral Power, unfortunately, remained displeased. He thought the RAF's over-the-sea performance 'practically useless' and as for the Maltese, 'they think Europeans are getting more than their fair share of what is available. . . . Politically, Malta is not sound: a firm hand may be wanted any day.' He entertained Park and Gibbs to dinner on 8 January. Gibbs was dismissed as 'a poor creature, no brains and unattractive' and although Park was admitted to be in good form, he recorded: 'there is no depth in the man.'

Peter Wykeham, who served in Malta as a squadron commander for about seven months from Christmas 1942, thought rather better of Park. He was certainly vain and too fond of his own speeches, but Wykeham admired him for his record in the First World War and for his handling of 11 Group as well as for his work in Malta. Because Malta was besieged until near the end of 1942, there was no getting away from duty, no opportunity to get rid of 'dead wood', and so the maintenance of morale was particularly important. Park's obvious bravery and readiness to go everywhere at any time were much remarked upon and Wykeham thought him an excellent commander both on the ground and in air matters.

In January 1943 Park reminded his squadron commanders, not for the first time, that Malta's soldiers played a key part in keeping aerodromes operational. They were based in the island to defend it in the event of invasion, but unless or until that happened, they had no opportunity to play an active role in the war except in manning anti-aircraft batteries. They had been employed in many jobs which were really airmen's work and Park insisted, very firmly, that his senior officers stop junior officers from making fun of the army's passive role: such 'fun' did not help Park when he was pressing for the 'odd ounce of bread to be added to the daily scale of rations'.

This firmness owed much to his recent memories of good work done by soldiers during the Battle of Britain and to a desire to preserve friendly relations with Scobie. At the end of January he asked Cairo if more airmen could be sent to Malta to take over duties presently carried out by soldiers; Scobie wanted to devote more of his men's time to army training and Park sympathized. However, Cairo replied that the Chief of the General Staff would inform Scobie that assistance to the RAF in Malta must continue to take priority over army training. Scobie accepted the situation and also recognized that the siting of anti-aircraft guns and searchlights were matters for Park to decide. Gort, however, did not; neither did Vice-Admiral Leatham, when deputizing for Gort as Governor. It took a blunt instruction from the Chiefs of Staff in London to bring him to heel.

Park's career almost ended in January 1943. He was en route to Cairo in a lone Beaufighter when five German bombers were seen. Park ordered his pilot to attack, but return fire knocked out the Beaufighter's port engine, leaving it to fly back over 160 miles of open sea on the strength of the other one. Quite unabashed, Park organized a sweepstake with the other two men aboard on whether or they would make it and if not, how far short they would fall. When Park eventually arrived in Cairo, he received from Sholto Douglas (his old enemy in 1940) a richly deserved admonition. Nevertheless, it was an escapade of which he remained foolishly – or endearingly – proud, to judge by the currency it obtained in South-East Asia and in New Zealand. And he continued to risk his neck. In June 1943 there was a tremendous panic, recalled Clifford Piper (a Spitfire pilot) when Park went missing in his Spitfire for an alarmingly long time. The degree of concern, said Piper, reflected the men's appreciation of his uncommon ability to combine firm authority with a pleasant manner: 'he didn't fuss or bully you.'[1]

In February 1943 Park had four aerodromes with a capacity to operate fifteen squadrons, but even before the outline plan for Operation Husky (the invasion of Sicily) was complete, a new aerodrome was being built and the others extended. In ten months the equivalent of more than 120 miles of fifteen-foot-wide road was laid in Malta, in runways and roads. By early July Park was able to operate thirty-five squadrons, some 600 aircraft. It took constant hard work and careful planning to build up an air force of that size from starvation level in November 1942. In particular, there was the need to book shipping space for supplies and technical stores months in advance at a time when changes in the planning for Husky were numerous.

Arthur Coningham, head of the Desert Air Force, addressed senior Allied officers in Tripoli on 16 February. Park obtained a copy of his address, underlined many passages, and would follow Coningham's principles in South-East Asia as well as in Malta and Egypt:

> The Soldier commands the land forces [said Coningham], the Airman commands the air forces; both commanders work together and operate their respective forces in accordance with a combined Army–Air plan, the whole operation being directed by the Army Commander. The Army fights on a front line that may be divided into sectors, the Air front is indivisible. . . . An Army has one battle to fight, the land battle. The Air has two. It has first of all to beat the enemy air, so that it may go into the battle against the enemy land forces with maximum hitting power. . . . In plain language, no soldier is competent to operate the Air, just as no airman is competent to operate the Army.

Tedder also believed the Air front indivisible, despite the difficulties of combining a single Air Command with two Land Commands (one British, one American) and an independent RAF with an air force that was part of the United States army. Mediterranean Air Command, as it was called, came into existence on 17 February, the day after Coningham had enunciated his principles. It comprised Middle East Air Command (under Douglas, in Cairo), North West African Air Forces (under Lieutenant-General Carl A. Spaatz, USAAF) and Malta (under Park), all commanded by Tedder in Algiers. Tedder did his best to ensure that the armies received full aerial cooperation, but he would not countenance the control of aircraft by those armies. In Malta, Park made all operational decisions concerning aircraft, subject only to Tedder's direction. Tedder trusted his judgment and initiative; had he doubted either, Park would long since have been removed from such a crucial position. Eisenhower shared Tedder's confidence and even Montgomery trusted Park, because he was a New Zealander and therefore, in Montgomery's opinion, steady and sensible as well as brave.

Malta was to be a major operational base, recorded Power in his diary on 1 March, and everyone was more cheerful. Park, however, remained very difficult and 'important'. Bonham-Carter, who had succeeded Leatham as Vice-Admiral (Malta) was taking a much firmer line with Park, 'but nothing can change the man, he is a twister.' Power nevertheless lunched with Park on 4 March and was then taken round his aerodromes and underground workshops. He spend an enjoyable hour over the island in a Beaufighter – a treat arranged by Park – and a few days later had the opportunity to study the state of training of Park's torpedo-bombers: 'very feeble' he thought. But on the 20th Park visited Power and they discussed methods of impeding a German evacuation of Tunisia. He was really first class, wrote Power, and a plan of action was agreed. This is one of Power's rare favourable comments on another officer and the only one on Park.

Park had issued instructions for the spring offensive on the 11th. All commanders, he wrote, were to remember that 'sweat saves blood and brains save both.' He emphasized the need to train hard during lulls between battles and to recall not only past experience but to think up new tactics and practise them. Malta's role was to achieve air superiority over Sicily, to undertake reconnaissance throughout the central Mediterranean, to protect friendly shipping and to attack enemy land and sea communications. Accurate navigation was essential, since so much work must be done over the sea, and take-offs and landings at dusk and in moonlight must be practised. He urged all commanders to plan every mission or exercise carefully and to discuss it critically afterwards, not only with each other but with the army and navy if they had been involved. Commanders must realize, he ended,

> that they are not performing any favour but an essential duty by taking an active interest in the messing, housing, clothing and recreation of their airmen. The ground staff are just as susceptible to the 'team spirit' as aircrews and their interest and enthusiasm are to be fostered and not left to some 'old sweat'. New ideas are always welcome at my Headquarters.[2]

'It will take more than Rita Hayworth to cheer me up in these days,' confided Power to his diary on 2 May. For several weeks he had been concerned about Bonham-Carter, who was deeply depressed, sleepless, and even contemplating suicide. Power admitted that he had himself felt that way recently, but on the 7th he, in turn, succeeded Bonham-Carter as Vice-Admiral (Malta), handing over 15 Cruiser Squadron the same day. Bonham-Carter collapsed completely and had to be shipped home.

Park, meanwhile, was sternly rebuking his squadron commanders. He had observed aircraft at the Hal Far airfield taking off in all directions regardless of the wind, mess parties were carrying on too late at night and the airmen's disparagement of British soldiers and Maltese civilians was continuing. Sadly, Park's efforts to support Gort failed to sweeten relations with him and on 1 June Power recorded a 'very stormy' Defence Committee meeting at which Gort 'went for B of B [presumably 'Battle of Britain'] for all he was worth.' In Power's view, Park 'deserved all he got. He is just a conceited idiot, I fear.' But Tedder, a demanding commander, considered that Malta's airmen maintained under Park 'the standard of intense, devoted exertion which had charaterized Lloyd's regime' and even Air Chief Marshal Joubert, one of Park's severest critics, was to admit in 1955 that he 'had done great work in Malta during a most difficult period.'

Park's life was not all work and quarrels, however. One visitor to his home recorded that a first impression of him 'is one of handsome remoteness, dignity, and a cold aggressive efficiency'. But he had a lighter side: after dinner in his quarters, he would sometimes put a short plank, sea-saw fashion, over a smooth log. Guests were invited to stand as still as they could with one foot at each end of the plank. It could not be done for long and 'guests crash in all directions. The AOC purrs.' W.G.G. Duncan Smith also saw the more humorous side of Park. He had been posted to Malta to take command of a wing in preference to a local officer of Park's choice, and he felt that Park regarded him with suspicion, particularly since he had served on Leigh-Mallory's tactics staff at Bentley Priory. At dinner one night, however, Park caught his eye, smiled, and said: 'As an ex-Leigh-Mallory boy, Duncan Smith, we won't hold it against you if you help yourself to another glass of my port.'[3]

Vast numbers of VIPs and 'not very IPs' were finding their way to the island by June and drinking the Officers' Mess dry. Park's tolerance gave way on the 26th and he signalled Tedder's deputy to say that during the past week forty-five officers from Africa had visited Malta *excluding* VIPs and their staffs. Many arrived without warning and most without evident duties; it would have to stop. AHQ Western Desert had moved to Malta on the 18th, followed by other formations, and Park was finding it difficult enough to arrange transport, meals and accommodation for those who needed to come and arrived when expected. At that time, he had nearly 16,000 officers and men, including civilians, under his command.

One welcome visitor was Trenchard, who arrived on 6 June. He was taken by Park to observe a 'normal day' at several aerodromes and spoke to the men in workshops, hangars and mess tents. An even more welcome visitor was King George himself, who arrived in the cruiser *Aurora* on the morning of 20 June and left that evening. He now invested Park with the insignia of Knight Commander of the Most Excellent Order of the British Empire (KBE), the award which had been announced the previous November. Gort received a Field Marshal's baton and the King later visited several aerodromes, accompanied by Park. The last of the welcome visitors was Sinclair, who was brought to Malta from Tripoli by one of Park's Liberators on 24 June and left next morning. Park had hoped to entertain Sinclair, but Gort insisted that a Cabinet Minister must stay with *him* and expressed 'surprise and annoyance' at not receiving a personal signal about Sinclair's visit. Park wrote to Sinclair on 5 July, telling him that he had found room for another three fighter-bomber squadrons, which brought his total to thirty-five, as well as a small force on Pantelleria. Montgomery had recently arrived and was in great form: 'I like him very much and find him easy to work with'; Admiral Cunningham had also arrived, 'complete with a large staff', and would shortly be followed by other principal commanders.

On 12 June Portal informed Park that Drummond and Slessor were shortly to be promoted to Air Marshal. Since both had been junior to Park, Portal wanted him to know that their promotion did not mean that he had been passed over. On the contrary, said Portal, 'I have the highest opinion of your ability as a commander.' 'There is always some luck in these things,' he added, 'and you happen to be filling (with great distinction) a post which cannot justifiably be upgraded.' He hoped Park would not interpret this letter as an intimation of early promotion, 'but I do want to reassure you about the opinion which the Secretary of State and I hold of you.' Despite this cautionary conclusion, it was clear to Park that if Operation Husky went well, he would be in the running for another important position. Could he now look forward to a major role in the invasion of Italy or the invasion of France, or would he be made a Commander-in-Chief?[4]

The Allied invasion of Sicily, which began on 10 July 1943, was a natural sequel to the final defeat in May of the Germans and Italians in North Africa. The African campaign, fought largely for control of the Mediterranean, could hardly be considered won as long as Axis aircraft, ships and submarines were able to threaten communications between Gibraltar and Suez from bases in Sicily. The same argument applied also to Axis bases in Sardinia, Corsica and Crete, but Sicily was held to be the principal danger and its conquest could lead directly to an assault on Italy. Operation Husky was the first major landing in the Second World War of seaborne troops against a fully defended shore and air superiority was clearly essential. More than 4,000 aircraft ensured that superiority for the massive surface forces employed: 160,000 men were landed in the first wave, with 600 tanks, 14,000 vehicles and nearly 2,000 guns. They were transported to Sicily by an Allied armada of 2,600 vessels under the command of Admiral Cunningham, who described Operation Husky as 'the most momentous enterprise of the war' to that date, because the Allies were 'striking for the first time at the enemy in his own land.' The control of all air forces based on Malta, Gozo and Pantelleria was exercised by Park's newly constructed operations room. He controlled day- and night-fighters, night intruders, tactical reconnaissance, fighter-bombers, shipping escort and air-sea rescue as well as the air defence of those islands. The operations room functioned smoothly and presented a picture of friendly and hostile aircraft movements within a hundred-mile radius of Malta; it also plotted shipping convoys within a fifty mile radius. Here indeed was the pay-off for all the work done at Bentley Priory and Uxbridge. Malta was the forward headquarters of those who directed the invasion and its combined war rooms recorded, hour by hour, the constantly changing situation on the ground, at sea and in the air. It was largely owing to Park's energy and experience that those preparations, in a war-torn island, were completed in time. By 17 August, after a campaign lasting less than six weeks, Sicily had been captured.

As soon as the campaign was over, Park recorded certain lessons learned during Operation Husky. Given good ground organization, he wrote, aircraft serviceability need not decline as soon as intensive operations began. A central point of operational control was essential for the efficient management of a large invasion. Squadrons needed a short period of intensive training prior to such an invasion, and it could be carried out in the area concerned without forfeiting tactical surprise. Squadron commanders need not be briefed until the day before D-Day, but wing commanders needed four or five days' warning. An area within four miles of friendly shipping should be declared a 'Gun Defended Area' up to 10,000 feet and although fighters should be safe outside that area, gun crews still needed much more training in aircraft recognition. Whenever possible, ships unloading troops and equipment should lie close to the beaches, where fighters could protect both. Night-fighters could be controlled by Ground Controlled Interception (GCI) stations mounted in tank-landing craft and such stations were of great value as forward links to base control.

In his administrative report, Park recommended that units coming to the assembly-point for major operations should be self-supporting. He was most impressed by the American units, which arrived complete with their own food, water and cooking facilities. Their system could well be copied by British units. Park was to become confirmed in his admiration of American methods over the next two years. Many RAF units did not know their own strength, in men or material, whereas American documentation was excellent. On the whole he was pleased with the plans made and carried out, although he observed more than once that enemy resistance to the landing was unexpectedly light and this spared the system from a searching test.

Park ended his report by quoting a signal received from Eisenhower. It was obvious, Eisenhower had said, that the invasion could scarcely be classed as feasible had it not been for the 'constructive accomplishments of the whole Malta Command during the past year.' These things could not be published, but he wanted Park and his men to know of his obligation to them. The success of the operation, Park had replied, was sufficient reward. (A pleasing tailpiece to the history of friendly relations between Eisenhower and Park comes in the fortunes of a jeep named Husky, presented by Eisenhower to Park in July 1943. Almost twelve years later, that vehicle was presented to the people of Malta by the RAF and at the wheel was Flight Sergeant Emanuel Aquilina, who had driven it during the war; it is now a major exhibit in the National War Museum.)

One day in August, Park flew his Hurricane from Luqa airfield on Malta to La Marsa, near Tunis, arriving while Flight Sergeant Tet Walston, a photo-reconnaissance pilot, was on duty. The landing strip was the nearest to

Tedder's headquarters and so Walston had seen many senior officers passing through. He recognized Park and helped him to unload his luggage from the underside wing storage. Park told him that he had popped in en route from seeing an old friend on Pantelleria and they had gone shrimp fishing together. Suddenly he said: 'Do you like shrimps?' 'Very much,' replied Walston, whereupon Park opened one of his bags, took out some shrimps packed in ice and wrapped in a waterproof cloth, told Walston to get a container and gave him at least half. Not surprisingly, Walston was impressed by Park's friendliness.

On 3 September 1943, the remains of a Gloster Gladiator named 'Faith' were presented by Park to Sir George Borg, Chief Justice of Malta, who accepted them on behalf of the people of the island. Park gave a brief account of the part 'Faith' had played in Malta's defence. When Italy had declared war, he said, Malta had had no fighter defences. However, the RAF had obtained three Fleet Air Arm Gladiators and for several months these biplanes, named 'Faith', 'Hope' and 'Charity', together with a handful of Hurricanes, had performed prodigiously. 'Faith', the only survivor of the trio, had been recovered from a scrap pit where it had been dumped in busier days and restored to something recognizable before the ceremony.

As has long been known, the story is much exaggerated. The Italian challenge in 1940 was not serious, nor were the three names used in that year. It seems that some imaginative journalist invented them in 1941 and embellished the record of honest service performed by the Gladiators. The machine Park presented bears no sign of battle damage and probably survived the siege in a crate. The descriptive plaque which he had made assigns it the number of a Gladiator destroyed on 26 June 1940. It seems unlikely that members of Park's staff deceived him and more likely that he sanctioned, or even inspired, this formal acceptance of a myth.[5]

On 1 September Park had written to Freeman (Vice-Chief of the Air Staff) to say that Tedder had granted him ten days' leave in England. He asked permission to call on Freeman to discuss his future. While in London he was given no indication of his next move and October passed without his hearing anything firm. Tedder opposed Portal's wish to appoint Park head of the Tactical Air Force in Coningham's place and on 15 October Portal tried to persuade Tedder to accept him:

> I know that Park has certain mannerisms which some people find a little irritating but I must say that in my opinion, for what it is worth, he has one of the finest records among the officers of his rank as an Operational Commander in this war. We cannot get away from what he did in the Battle of Britain under Dowding, or the way he kept Malta going through its darkest days. I know of no officer on whom I would rely more to get the very utmost out of the units which he commands, and I know from personal observations how his units trust him, and how all his subordinates work for him.

Tedder replied at once, on 17 October. He entirely agreed, he wrote, about the magnificent work Park had done. 'I did consider him very carefully for the command of TAF. What surprised me was the adverse reactions I got from different directions and levels when I put abroad the report that Park was relieving Coningham.' Park had been very severely stretched during the past year, he continued, 'and has for the moment lost some of his ability to coordinate with other people and services.' As for Major-General J.K. Cannon, USAAF, the man Tedder wanted to command the Tactical Air Force, he had more practical experience of air support to the army than any available RAF officer, including Park, and – as Tedder had already told Portal – 'I think we must now give the Americans their turn.'

Deferring to Tedder's opinion, Portal decided on the 24th to send Park to Delhi as Air Officer in charge of Administration in India. Sinclair sought Churchill's permission the same day. Churchill had asked Sinclair not to make any change in the Mediterranean Air Command until the reorganization he had in mind was further considered, but Sinclair asked him to allow this exception. Park, said Sinclair, 'has a record of fine service in this war, culminating in the direction of the air operations for Husky from Malta. Now the war has slipped away from him and he is wasted in Malta.' Churchill, however, refused to allow Park to be sent to India.

During December it was decided that Lieutenant-General Ira C. Eaker be made first Commander-in-Chief of the newly formed Mediterranean Allied Air Forces (MAAF) with his rear headquarters in Algiers and his advanced headquarters at La Marsa in Tunisia. Douglas was unwilling to serve under an American officer whom he considered his junior and Portal therefore offered him Coastal Command, a position acceptable to him, in place of Slessor, who became Eaker's deputy and also C-in-C RAF Mediterranean and Middle East (MEDME), with his headquarters at Caserta, near Naples. Park, strongly recommended by Tedder, was promoted to Air Marshal, appointed AOC-in-C Middle East, and sent to Cairo for the third time in his RAF career. He wanted the job, Tedder told Portal, and would fit in well with the new organization. Promotion to Air Marshal and appointment as Commander-in-Chief were two substantial steps forward. Park's new position was undoubtedly an important one. It would require a talent for establishing and preserving workable relations with numerous Allied air forces. He would also have to look after vast and widely scattered resources in men and materials, to identify and uphold the RAF's best interests when dealing with British or Egyptian military, naval or civilian authorities. Nevertheless, there could be no disguising the fact that Park had not obtained one of the principal operational commands for the next stage of the war. With his record as a successful front-line commander in England and Malta, he had had high hopes of a third such command. But the war was far from won in January 1944 and Park was determined to show in Egypt that he still had the energy, powers of leadership and flexibility of approach to intractable or unexpected problems to justify another recall to the most dangerous front.

An editorial in the *Times of Malta* on 4 January 1944 marked his imminent departure (he flew to Cairo on the 6th). Park, it said, left Malta carrying with him the good wishes and gratitude of the people. During the period of his command, the Axis aircraft which had 'enlivened the day and made hideous the night' since June 1940 had been finally defeated. He had been provided with the tools and the men, but these would have been useless without his own skill and judgment. This renowned leader of the Battle of Britain demonstrated the effectiveness of the air cover for convoys to Malta. He was a born fighter and commander of men, a fearless leader and a man of courage and vision. Under Air Vice-Marshal Sir Keith Park, Malta had become a proud base for attack and had made the first breach in the Fascist fortress of Europe.[6]

CHAPTER FIFTEEN

Egypt

1944

Sholto Douglas summarised the duties of RAF Middle East in December 1943. They consisted of operations in Turkey and the Aegean, convoy protection and the defence of bases in the eastern Mediterranean, operational training in Egypt, Cyprus, Palestine and South Africa, internal security and inter-service cooperation in Palestine, Syria, Iraq, Persia, the Sudan, Aden and East Africa, operations from bases in Arabia, Somaliland and East Africa in cooperation with Indian Ocean units, maintenance work for all air forces in the region and, not least, the preservation of the Middle East as an 'entity'. It would remain, thought Douglas, a focus of RAF activity 'in any postwar structure that can now be foreseen.' Its geographical location at the intersection of three continents must make it of paramount importance in relation to any air-route developments, of which the foundations were then being laid. In Douglas's opinion, the idea of placing Middle East under the control of MAAF for all purposes was 'unworkable' and would lead to 'inefficiency and friction'. Operations in the Mediterranean must remain under MAAF's control, but Middle East should be permitted the greatest degree of administrative autonomy.

Slessor took up his dual appointment as Eaker's deputy at MAAF and C-in-C MEDME on 12 January 1944 and for the next year would do his considerable best to limit that autonomy. As soon as he arrived in the Mediterranean, Slessor decided that Park was inadequate and wrote at once to tell Portal this. Park had been given a position of great importance, he wrote, but was simply not up to it:

> He has an excellent record as an operational group commander and is very conscientious about getting round his units and so on. But he has no experience at all of dealing with these semi-political problems, and is not really interested in them as far as I can see, and I think is probably inwardly conscious of his limitations in this regard. I have never had any official contacts with him before and frankly am rather alarmed at finding

what a very stupid man he is; and I am very much afraid that unless we take some steps about it we shall lose our position in the Middle East and the control of policy will drift increasingly into the hands of the Army – who would be only too delighted to assume it. . . . I am, of course, not suggesting that you should remove Park. That would be impossible [he conceded] just after he has been appointed.

He had therefore thought hard about how best to help Park and decided that he needed the help of a first class civil servant.

I am really uneasy about the situation [he concluded], with him here alone with Toomer who, though a good solid staff officer [he was Senior Air Staff Officer], has not the experience, character, brains or personality to fill the bill on the political as apart from the purely RAF side.

Slessor's criticisms, as he admitted, were based on a very slight knowledge of Park, although he and Park had already differed sharply in 1936 over the handling of 48 Squadron in August 1918. Slessor was new to his own job, which should have been absorbing his whole attention. Park, moreover, had much more experience of Egypt than had Slessor, and while at Malta had been in touch with Middle East affairs, as Tedder reminded Portal when advocating Park's positing to Cairo – and Tedder was that rare bird, an officer of whom Slessor approved. Slessor's letter was addressed to Portal, a man who had known Park well for over twenty years and was better placed to evaluate him than Slessor. Park was not a man to yield any essential RAF interests to the army or to the navy and his record in Malta (and later in Kandy and Singapore) showed him more than ready to bat for his own service.

Perhaps Slessor's interest in 'semi-political problems' was excessive; he was, after all, a serving officer with military duties and the temptation to meddle outside those duties was particularly dangerous in sensitive regions which Slessor knew only slightly and could rarely even visit. Nor did Slessor say what it was that Park should do that he was not doing. Presumably the expression of contempt for Toomer, no less than Park, was not lost on Portal, who would be aware of Slessor's tendency to hold dismissive opinions. No assistant was sent out to Park, who made no important mistakes and was not relieved of his command. (Indeed, his next job was to carry even greater responsibility.) Nor did Slessor find it impossible to work with Park during the next three years, though he rather often failed to get his own way. There were other senior officers, British and American, who did not find Park over-placed for his talents either in Egypt or in the Far East.

Coralie Hyam was personal secretary for four commanders of RAF Middle East between 1942 and 1946 – Linnell, Douglas, Park and Medhurst – and regarded Park as by far the ablest. He was an efficient despatcher of business and a good delegator. This left him free to travel round his units, which he loved to do, but it also gave his subordinates great responsibility: there was no other way for him to learn if they were up to their jobs – nor, indeed, for *them* to learn this – and he was ruthless with those who failed. Miss Hyam thought Park very even tempered. He had great self-control and did not shout or even raise his voice when angered or placed under pressure. He was approachable to all ranks and very straight, never finding someone else to deal with such unpleasant jobs as telling people they would not be promoted; in such areas he did not delegate.

He would quietly visit ships passing through the Canal and find a word of comfort not only for the wounded and sick but also for those being sent home for 'Lack of Moral Fibre'. Whereas Douglas imported a large team of friends and clients to the Middle East, Park arrived alone and made do with the staff on hand, unless and until he needed to remove any of them. When he went to Ceylon in 1945 it was the same. During Douglas's regime, as many as five aircraft were reserved for his personal use, even though he was no longer a pilot. Park, still able to fly himself, retained only two. His aircraft were available for the use of other senior officers when he did not need them.

Flight Sergeant Tet Walston was working in Flying Control at Heliopolis in January 1944 when Park arrived from Malta in a Lockheed Lodestar to take up his appointment. The CO, recounted Walston, was naturally anxious to make a good impression and assembled the most respectable-looking part of his entourage. Park shook hands with the senior officers of the welcoming party and then 'strolled over to have a little chat with the airman who drove the crash tender', thereby astounding everyone present. He went into Flying Control to report his arrival and, catching sight of Walston, casually asked him how he had enjoyed the shrimps. Walston savoured the aftermath. His CO withdrew from the procession following Park and whispered: 'You never told me you knew the C-in-C,' to which Walston was able to make the classic reply: 'You never asked me.'[1]

On 15 January, his first full day in command, Park held the first of his daily conferences with his senior staff officers. The next day, he told his staff of his wishes in regard to dealing with the Americans. They were helping Britain to win the war, he said, and close cooperation with them was essential. The political or postwar aspects of particular problems were to be dealt with 'by the people at home'. He made it clear that he intended to visit units every week and that far too much paper was coming to him. Once a matter had been discussed and agreed, he *assumed* that the necessary action followed. If it did not, he would know what to do. He was not to be presented with a sheaf of papers to wade through and ruled that henceforth the officer most concerned with the particular case must provide a short brief as well as the papers. One piece of paper crossing his desk at that time gave him pleasure, however: a message from Field Marshal Smuts (another man of whom Slessor approved): 'Please tell Keith Park with what pleasure I have heard of his promotion to chief air command in Middle East. It is a most fitting honour

189

and recognition for his great work in Malta. All good luck for the great job ahead.'

Park thanked Beaverbrook on 30 January for his congratulations on his new appointment. 'This is a vast and sprawling command,' he wrote, 'with only one area where we are conducting active operations, but I find it most interesting.' He was delighted to have with him again Beaverbrook's son, Max Aitken. During 1944, he often sailed in Alexandria harbour with Aitken and another squadron commander, John Grandy. There was more time for socializing, Park was readier to gossip and Grandy thought him more relaxed than he had been in 1940.

Since times were easier, the Parks decided they would like to be together again. Park wrote to Sinclair on 10 February to ask permission for Dol to come to Cairo and do welfare work. When Lady Tedder had been there in 1942, said Park, she had had a full-time job doing welfare work, but since her departure little had been done. Several army generals had their wives with them and they looked after the soldiers' welfare, but there were no senior RAF officers' wives in Cairo. Sinclair, however, refused to permit Dol to go on the grounds that once it was done at the top it would be hard to resist lower down. In April the question was reviewed again. Slessor conceded that there were arguments in favour of Lady Park going out to Cairo, but had resolved that she should not be allowed to *fly* out. At the end of May, the War Office withdrew its objection to wives joining husbands 'if it is definitely in the national interest' and if the husband was stationed overseas until the end of the war or longer. However, the Air Ministry rejected both principles.

At Park's suggestion, Dol asked Beaverbrook to help. He wrote to Balfour, the Under-Secretary of State for Air, on 23 May. 'You know that Park is a great friend of mine,' said Beaverbrook, 'and I would like to help. Can you direct me please?' Balfour replied the same day. He had learned of a considerable correspondence between the Parks and Sinclair on this matter. The position was that she could go to Cairo, but not until the Home Office ban on travel was lifted and he could give her no indication of when that would be. 'I hope this will set her mind at ease,' Balfour concluded, somewhat optimistically. Beaverbrook advised Dol to tackle the Home Office. This she did and by early August, after six months of determined joint effort, she was in Cairo.[2]

One of Park's main tasks in Egypt was aircrew training. As well as meeting British needs, he was responsible for training the nationals of occupied countries. Yugoslavs were a particular problem because part of the air force remained loyal to the King while part had gone over to Tito. In Slessor's view, Tito's desire for an independent Yugoslav air force was 'a manifest absurdity . . . professional discussion of technical details of air force organization with a Balkan brigand will not be easy.' Nor was it: General Franjo Pirc, Tito's senior airman, tried to renege on an agreement signed with Park on 29 March. As Park signalled Slessor on 2 April: 'Pirc says cannot risk Tito's wrath otherwise must shoot himself but promises to do so in own country not Middle East.' The Soviets, added Park, had offered Tito his own squadron if the British failed to meet his wishes.

Both Park and Slessor were reluctant to give aircraft to guerrilla groups, believing private air forces undesirable, but 173 Squadron was assigned to meet transport requests for 'any sound military purpose'. In Park's opinion, Colonel Prendergast, Deputy Commander of Raiding Forces in the Middle East, was doing valuable work in March against coastal shipping in the Aegean and needed transport for his staff officers to get around scattered forces in Syria. Force 133, however, he thought inefficient. Normally under Prendergast's command, it was in fact a poorly organized group, composed mainly of Greek partisans assisted by British officers. It also concerned itself with attacks on Aegean shipping, but suffered losses on three successive missions. Park proposed to send an officer to liaise with Force 133, though he recognized that 'it is difficult to get these people away from their cloak-and-dagger methods.'

Nevertheless, given his enthusiasm for improvisation, Park delighted in properly organized cloak-and-dagger work. Operation Zeppelin, for example, was a combined services operation intended to persuade the Germans that a large invasion of the Balkans was being prepared in North Africa, between Tobruk and Derna. The most obvious sign that the operation had succeeded came when the Germans reinforced the eastern Mediterranean in May and June despite the Allied invasion of Normandy on 6 June; but Zeppelin also concealed a *withdrawal* of Allied squadrons from the Middle East to assist in that invasion. Park's contribution included arranging aircraft and glider displays on Cyrenaican airfields, a balloon barrage over Tobruk and an increase in R/T traffic designed to persuade the Germans that Operational Training Units in Palestine were being used as a cover for front-line work. He also used heavy bombers in daylight to give the impression that they were troop-carrying (they were in fact flown by pupil pilots experiencing a welcome – and unexplained – break from night-flying). Operation Turpitude was a follow-up to Zeppelin, involving 'Colforce': a build-up of army and air force strength in northern Syria. The RAF was to move various squadrons and armoured cars into the Aleppo area in the hope of making the Germans think an invasion of Turkey was imminent. Park even fed false information about Colforce into his staff meetings to keep the deception pure.

Despite Slessor's opinion that he lacked interest in political affairs, Park was quick to react when Slessor neglected to send him reports and minutes of Middle East Commanders-in-Chief meetings, and asked Slessor to ensure that these papers were sent to him, whether he was in Cairo or elsewhere. Temporarily chastened, Slessor asked him on 1 April if he should say anything at a forthcoming press conference which could help partisans in

Greece, Yugoslavia, Hungary, Rumania and Bulgaria. Park suggested that Slessor stress the dual role of air power: to bomb Germans and to supply partisans. The Air Ministry, however, refused to permit Slessor to mention partisans. When representatives of *Life* magazine and Britain's *Paramount News* visited Cairo in April, Park was also forbidden to mention them.

He returned to Cairo on the 3rd from a four-day tour of the Canal Zone and the Western Desert that covered 1,700 miles. He visited units of all kinds, chatting with the men for half an hour at each one. He asked them to gather round in an informal group and told them that their work was valuable, encouraging them to 'stick at it' despite the loneliness of their bases. Then he sketched the general war situation, inviting questions which he answered in plain, straightforward terms. Park made the tour by air, taking regular spells at the controls. He also navigated an air-sea rescue launch in heavy seas, bringing it safely into harbour, and rode in a DUKW landing-craft.[3]

On 18 April, while Park was visiting units in East Africa, King Farouk suddenly proposed wholesale changes in the Egyptian government. The British civilian and service chiefs quickly forced him to back down and even considered deposing him. Park, back in Cairo, signalled Slessor on the 23rd to say that there was no danger of riots and that if Farouk were deposed the Egyptian Army would support his successor. On the 25th he added that Slessor's reference to the Egyptian political situation at a meeting attended by Americans had caused annoyance in Cairo; Lord Killearn (the British ambassador) would be most perturbed, said Park, if he learned that his remarks to service chiefs had been passed on to the Americans. Slessor thanked Park for keeping him informed about the crisis and assured him that he would not tell the Americans anything they should not hear. Although he liked Americans, Park was acutely aware that the Wafd, a powerful upper-class nationalist movement in Egypt, wanted rid of the British after the war – if not during it – and was ready to play upon the well-known sympathy of Americans for nationalist aspirations everywhere in the Middle East. Britain's position in Egypt was a strange one: she exercised *de facto* rule, though Egypt was not constitutionally part of the British Empire and, indeed, was technically neutral throughout the war.

On 27 April Park replied to Killearn's request for his observations on the Royal Egyptian Air Force. A squadron was operating under Park's control, but he could not truthfully say that it was proving useful. There were maintenance and administrative problems, although the Egyptian authorities were helping him to overcome them. The squadron would soon be moved to Mersa Matruh, where it would be employed on shipping protection and help as much as the squadrons manned by Greek and Yugoslav allies. Aircraft lost from this squadron should be replaced, Park thought, but a second squadron should not be raised at British expense.

Killearn sent a copy of this report to the Foreign Office, inviting support for Park's views, and the Foreign Office, in turn, invited that of the Air Ministry.

Early in June Killearn asked Park whether surplus Hurricanes should be transferred to the REAF. Park thought they posed no threat to British interests in Egyptian hands and such transfers would discourage the Americans from stepping in with offers of their own surplus aircraft. Killearn agreed and offered his support in recommending these views to the Air Ministry. In October the Air Ministry wrote to the Treasury about its discussions with Park concerning the supply of aircraft to the REAF. He and his predecessor had made 'a number of arrangements of which we at the Air Ministry were not fully apprised', intended to keep the Egyptians flying British aircraft and to encourage them to take over certain ground duties to release RAF manpower for service elsewhere. The Air Ministry emphasized that all Park's actions and promises to the Egyptians were supported by Killearn and by the Foreign Office and asked for retrospective Treasury approval – which was given, most reluctantly, in January 1945.[4]

Ira C. Eaker, head of Mediterranean Allied Air Forces, wrote to Park on 27 April to express his gratitude for 'the many kindnesses shown us while in Cairo'. On the way home, he had stopped at Benghazi and learned of 'your earnest desire to get some Mustangs at an early date to accompany the Marauders, cut down losses and punish the Germans.' Eaker had discussed this request with Slessor, who assured him that Park was to get the next Mustang squadron probably by mid-May. These fighters, replied Park, would not only cover Marauders and Beaufighters on shipping strikes in the Aegean, but also carry out trials with rockets. Men and machines were constantly being transferred to the front line from Park's command because he and Slessor agreed that they should be used as offensively as possible.

Late in July Park visited Eaker and Slessor at Caserta. His relations with Slessor were then in a friendly phase (Slessor having recently thanked him for his 'very helpful collaboration' in building up the Desert Air Force) and on his return to Cairo he found waiting for him a warm letter from Eaker. Park wrote to thank him for his generous remarks about Middle East's contribution to MAAF.

> When I came here six months ago [he continued], I found a big operational force, especially single-engined fighters, that had not enough to keep them occupied. As fast as MAAF have been able to absorb them, I have been pleased to send these squadrons along to where they can engage the enemy instead of sitting in a back area to engage an attack that might never come. We have done the same with Coastal and Bomber Squadrons of which we had quite a large number six months ago. As our operational commitments have shrunk, our Training and Maintenance organizations have been built up so that we still control about 150,000

193

enlisted, also civilian, personnel spread over a dozen countries comprising the Middle East Command.[5]

Killearn informed the Foreign Office on 31 July that Park was seriously disturbed because he was not getting the calico and yarn needed to meet his parachute commitments. Egypt wished to purchase cotton goods from the United States, but was unable to do so because London refused import licences. In view of assurances given to the Egyptians that British forces would not make cotton purchases except for urgent needs, and bearing in mind the very large offtake for parachutes, Park considered that Egypt's request for imports was reasonable. He had asked Killearn to recommend this in the strongest terms and he readily did so. The political dangers were real, said Killearn, and he doubted if they were appreciated in London. A Foreign Office official minuted on 2 August that Park had made a good case, based on the demand for supplies by parachute drop to guerrillas and partisans in the Mediterranean area, but it was not until 22 September that the Air Ministry advised Park that parachute production could be reduced from 30,000 to 12,000 a month, because of Canadian supplies and a more favourable war situation.

Meanwhile, moves were afoot to send Park to Australia. During 1944 the Royal Australian Air Force was plagued by quarrels between its two most senior officers, Air Vice-Marshals Jones (Chief of the Air Staff) and Bostock (Commander of Operational Forces). The Prime Minister, John Curtin, discussed the problem with General MacArthur in June. The only satisfactory solution, Curtin thought, would be the appointment of an officer senior to both. MacArthur replied that it was a problem for the Australians to solve; should such an officer be appointed, he would cooperate with him. On 4 August the Australian War Cabinet agreed that Park's services should be sought. Curtin visited London later that month and approached both Churchill and Portal in an attempt to secure Park. Nothing was concluded, however, and on 28 September Stanley Bruce (High Commissioner) informed Curtin that Park was 'earmarked' for an important RAF command. However, Sinclair would not stand in his way if he wished to accept an Australian invitation. MacArthur then told Curtin that it was too late to make a change. As Frederick Shedden (Secretary of the Department for Defence) pointed out, the Americans liked to play off Jones and Bostock against each other. A man of Park's stature, in overall command, would have asserted the RAAF's views much more effectively. On 31 October Curtin told Bruce that 'it would now appear inadvisable' to seek Park's appointment. Park's views, assuming that he was in fact consulted, are not known.

In August Dol had at last managed to join him in Cairo and for the next two years usually accompanied him on tours to non-operational areas. Her cheerful manner and abundant energy, fortified by a nursing background and personal experience of service life, fitted her admirably for welfare work. As she often pointed out, she was the mother of an RAF Corporal and an Army Lieutenant as well as the wife of an Air Marshal. Dol proved herself an extremely active welfare worker in the Middle and Far East and in New Zealand for many years after the war, until her health gave way.

On 27 October the Parks flew to South Africa for a fortnight at the invitation of Field Marshal Smuts. Park visited South African Air Force bases to study training methods and spoke to the press about his respect for Sir Quintin Brand (born in South Africa), who had so loyally supported him in the Battle of Britain. He praised the fighting qualities of South African airmen, commented favourably on their rugby and speculated that an international air police force might be formed after the war. To his great delight, he met several mining geologists who had either studied under his father or knew his work. A trip down a gold mine reminded him of the ingot James had brought home from Maunahie. On 13 November he and Dol were back in Cairo, having also visited Rhodesia and Kenya. Park had asked Slessor if there were any queries he wished him to raise in South Africa, but Slessor refused to work through Park if it could be avoided.[6]

Slessor wrote to the three Middle East Commanders-in-Chief on 19 November about the command and coordination of operations involving all three services. The debate evidently became unduly warm as far as Slessor and Park were concerned because on the 27th Park wrote to 'My dear Jack' to say that he would do as he suggested and destroy their most recent exchange of letters. Park assured him that he 'did not suggest or intend to imply' that Slessor should never write personally to the other Cs-in-C, but he did ask that comments on the Cs-in-C Committee 'and especially criticism of my actions' should go through normal channels – to Park himself – and not direct to the army and navy members. Since Slessor had agreed to do this, the matter was closed.

One of Park's first tasks on coming to Cairo, he told Slessor, had been to improve relations with the Mediterranean Allied Air Forces. His staff officers felt that MAAF had stripped them of resources and disparaged their efforts. Feelings ran high in Cairo, but Park set himself to calm them and his staff responded loyally, as Eaker and Slessor both acknowledged. MAAF, however, remained 'ungracious and unhelpful' and by the end of October, Park's staff had lost all sense of security. Slessor's failure to consult or even to inform Park about postings was an acute grievance; he also sent instructions direct to Park's subordinate formations and dealt directly with the British Embassy in Cairo on matters which were Park's responsibility.

Park signalled the Air Ministry (and repeated the signal to Slessor) on 24 November. Both Tedder and Douglas had told him, he said, that the main reason for placing Middle East under MAAF was to permit a closer coordination of operations then taking place at both ends of the Mediterranean. Eaker and Slessor had testified to the wholehearted support given them by Park during the year, but conditions had now changed: MAAF's concern was operations, Park's was training, maintenance and reinforcement for several commands as well as MAAF, also with internal security problems which could best be handled in Cairo. Park therefore believed the time had come for Middle East to be placed directly under the Air Ministry.

Slessor agreed that the organization of the RAF in the Mediterranean and Middle East should now be reviewed. It had always been intended, he said, that as soon as possible after operations against Germany ended, the main directing headquarters of the RAF should once again be in Cairo. Meanwhile, however, Slessor argued that MAAF should continue to control Middle East, even though he admitted that Park's position was 'slightly anomalous' in that he had a Commander-in-Chief between him and the Air Ministry, whereas his army and navy counterparts dealt directly with the War Office and the Admiralty respectively – and Park had a far wider responsibility than either.

Slessor wrote to Park on 3 December in an unusually conciliatory tone. Policy control, he repeated, should return to Cairo as soon as the German war ended. Middle East 'should clearly exercise far more responsibility and deal more directly with the Air Ministry than an ordinary subordinate HQ.' It had always done so, Slessor thought, and he was sorry to hear that Park's staff felt there had been 'undue interference'; he would instruct his own staff to intervene only in matters where 'coordination and a common standard' were essential. Matters of higher policy should be reserved for discussion between himself and Park. He looked forward to seeing Park soon because these discussions on paper at long range were never satisfactory.[7]

In the 1945 New Year's Honours List Park was made a Knight Commander of the Most Honourable Order of the Bath (KCB) and on 2 January Beaverbrook again sent his warmest congratulations. 'It will be a matter of the widest satisfaction,' he said, 'that this public recognition has been given to what you have done for the British cause in the past two years.'

One of Park's last duties in Cairo was to hand over an aircraft to King Farouk. This simple ceremony formed the centrepiece of a saga that began in 1939 and lasted until 1951, when agitation over payment for spare parts was finally resolved. Should Farouk be presented with or permitted to purchase an old or new aircraft and of what type? The political and financial ramifications proved labyrinthine. An Avro Anson was mooted in October 1943, the gift of which was authorized in December; instructions for shipment were given in July 1944.

Park wrote to the Air Ministry on 2 December 1944 to say that the Anson would shortly arrive in Egypt for Farouk. He was a good friend to the RAF, said Park, and took a keen interest in his own air force. It had therefore been suggested that Park make an official presentation of the Anson. The Commanding General of the USAAF in the Middle East had personally presented an American aircraft to the Emperor of Ethiopia in August and a great occasion had been made of it. If the Air Ministry agreed to Park doing the same for Farouk, it would help if he could read out a message from King George or from the Foreign Secretary, Anthony Eden, who had recently made a very favourable impression in Cairo.

The Foreign Office, however, was gravely concerned about American reaction to Farouk's aircraft: *presentation* might be construed as *export*, infringing an agreement with Washington and offending senators who might say that Britain could only afford such a gesture because she had so much Lend Lease equipment. The presentation might, perhaps, go ahead, but there could be no message from the King or the Foreign Secretary. On 5 December a Foreign Office official minuted: 'The civil air war with the USA is now virtually on'; it was suggested that while Britain worried about not offending the Americans, they would step in and give Farouk one of their own aircraft. Two days later, a brilliant solution was advanced: why not put the aircraft at Farouk's *disposal* 'until the time when we can present him with a better one'? No *gift* would have been made. Killearn was advised that he might present the Anson on the RAF's behalf, but without publicity, because another Anson was meanwhile being *sold* to the Regent of Iraq.

Park wrote to the Air Ministry again on the 10th. They were aware no doubt that a similar Anson, intended for the Regent of Iraq, was arriving in Cairo about the same time as Farouk's but that that aircraft was being purchased by Iraq. In view of the gift of an aircraft by the Americans to the Emperor of Ethiopia and the British gift to Farouk, would it not be wise, even at this late hour, to waive the cost of the Regent's aircraft and make a ceremonial presentation to him? He pointed out that the Regent was bound to learn that Farouk was getting an Anson free while his had cost £10,000.

Much Foreign Office debate ensued on a new tack: that Egypt wished to buy a second Anson for the use of court officials. After prolonged discussion, it was agreed that this might be permitted. Moreover, it could be put about that Egypt was buying an Anson and therefore the Iraqis need not be upset. Unless, of course, they could count to two. On 7 February 1945, his last day in command of Middle East, Park visited the REAF and marked the occasion by presenting (at Killearn's request) an Anson to Farouk 'as a birthday gift'. Foreign Office officials, having decided that news of the ceremony could not be entirely censored, passed anxious days and nights until it became clear that the Americans had not noticed it. A short paragraph had appeared in *The Times* on the 8th, but not in a prominent position and mercifully there had been no photograph.

Major-General Ben F. Giles (Commanding General USAAF, Middle East) wrote to Park on 5 February to express his appreciation of Park's 'untiring efforts to get things done in the most efficient and friendly manner possible.' Giles recommended Park for the award of the U.S. Distinguished Service Medal, but instead he received the Legion of Merit in the degree of

Commander. His 'willing cooperation', in the words of the citation, had helped the Americans to acquire land for airfield construction. He had readily handed over technical installations, provided supplies and materials and agreed to the removal of RAF units to facilitate American operational control of airfields. Park's liking for Americans and their methods, his experience in managing enormous air forces scattered about many countries (not all of them able or willing to espouse the Allied cause enthusiatically) and, by no means least, his gifts as an operational commander fitted him well for his next, last and greatest service appointment: Allied Air Commander-in-Chief, South-East Asia.[8]

CHAPTER SIXTEEN

South-East Asia Command:
The Winning Card

1945

. . . properly organized air supply . . . was to prove the winning card in
that theatre.
Bernard Fergusson, *The War Lords* (ed. Michael Carver)

On 17 September 1944 Portal informed Sinclair that the Americans had
withdrawn their objection to a British Air Commander-in-Chief of South-
East Asia Command (SEAC). Churchill had agreed to the appointment of
Leigh-Mallory, who had headed the Allied Expeditionary Air Force during
the invasion of Normandy. At about 9 a.m. on 14 November Leigh-Mallory
left Northolt for India in an Avro York. Shortly after midday, while flying in
cloud through a snowstorm, it struck a ridge in the Belledonne Mountains,
some fifteen miles east of Grenoble. The York somersaulted down a steep
rocky slope, disintegrating as it went. Everybody on board was killed. A
Court of Inquiry into the accident found that the weather had been very poor
on the day of the accident, but that Leigh-Mallory 'was determined to leave
and he is known to be a man of forceful personality'; Portal added that he had
had no need to make such haste, risking his crew as well as himself and his
wife: 'the desire to arrive in India on schedule with his "own" aircraft and
crew overrode prudence and resulted in this disaster.'

On 21 November, when it was clear that the York was lost, Lord Louis
Mountbatten, Supreme Allied Commander, SEAC, had informed Portal that
he and Richard Peirse (the man Leigh-Mallory was to have succeeded) agreed
that a new appointment should be made as soon as possible. Meanwhile, Guy
Garrod (Peirse's deputy) took over and Peirse returned to England. Slessor
was offered the job, but preferred to return to the Air Ministry as Air
Member for Personnel. As late as 26 January 1945, Park signalled Garrod to
congratulate him on his appointment as Peirse's successor, which had been
announced in the Cairo newspapers. On the following day, however, Sinclair

told Garrod that he was to succeed Slessor at Caserta and that Park was to be the Air C-in-C, SEAC. Garrod was reluctant to leave and Mountbatten reluctant to release him, but they both gave way; Park signalled Garrod on 31 January to thank him for his best wishes. For a second time in the war, Park's career was thus crucially affected by Leigh-Mallory.

Douglas Evill (Vice-Chief of the Air Staff) instructed various Air Ministry officials on 11 February to help Park obtain as much information as possible about air staff matters in SEAC. Portal himself discussed with Park the RAF's postwar policy in India. On 14 February he was received by the King at Buckingham Palace and invested with the insignia of the KCB. Later that day he attended a meeting at the Air Ministry and at 10 a.m. on the 17th he and Dol left Northolt – by Dakota – and flew via Malta and Cairo to Calcutta, to take part in an important conference with Mountbatten and all the other principal Allied commanders in South-East Asia.[1]

In welcome contrast to the shortage of men and materials which had plagued him at Uxbridge in 1940 and Malta in 1942, Park found himself master of vast resources in his new command. The tasks ahead of him, however, were hardly less daunting. He had arrived at Uxbridge and Malta in times of crisis and once again, as soon as he took his place at a conference in Calcutta on 23 February 1945, he was immediately required to make a major decision. It was a decision which had to be made, moreover, before Park had had a chance to become familiar with either his new duties or his new resources. However, he did not hesitate. Quite simply, he agreed to supply General Slim's Fourteenth Army from the air throughout its advance on Rangoon.

It was an immense undertaking, calling for the greatest supply operation of the war. Park's aircraft would sustain an army of more than 300,000 men, fighting in a country mostly unsuitable for aerial operations. But Park agreed to carry nearly 1,900 tons of supplies every day from 20 March and a little over 2,000 tons every day from 1 April. If the Japanese could be beaten in the central Burmese plains around Mandalay in a short campaign, the port of Rangoon might fall before the monsoon began in June and the reconquest of Burma would be practically complete. The penalty for failure would be severe: if Rangoon was not taken by June, Park's transport squadrons would have to continue supplying the Fourteenth Army throughout five months of steady rain.

Christopher Courtney, Air Member for Supply and Organization, reported to Portal in March on his tour of South-East Asia. He doubted if the major part being played by Allied air forces in that theatre was generally appreciated. Slim's army was almost entirely maintained by the American Combat Cargo Task Force, and the British 221 Group provided most of his artillery support. One heard constantly, said Courtney, about the difficulty of supplying the army by a single poor road, but it was not in fact *used* for that purpose. One continually heard also that a brigade had captured a village and

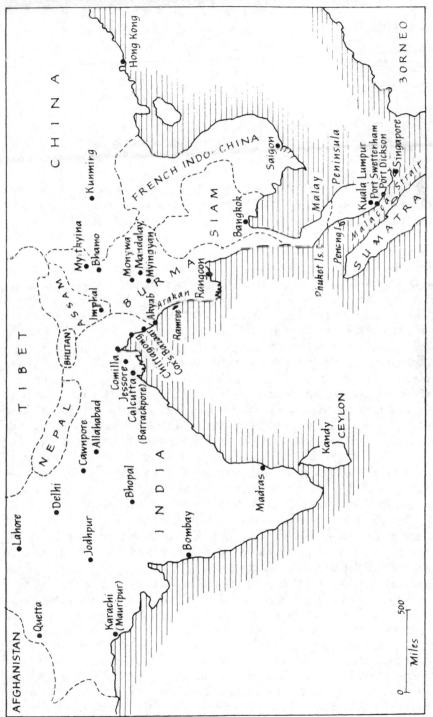

8: South East Asia Command

counted so many dead, when in fact it was the RAF which had overcome the opposition, causing most of the casualties and leaving the army to walk in and occupy the place.[2]

Park made a short speech to his new staff at his headquarters in Kandy, Ceylon, on 2 March. He thought it wise when going to a new command, and this was the sixth he had had during the war, to meet the staff and explain his methods and ambitions. One function of a higher formation, he said, was to simplify paperwork and organization so that lower formations, where the fighting was done, did not get confused. He had already landed at five airfields in ACSEA (Air Command, South-East Asia) and at two of these the commanding officers had said they did not know who their masters were. ACSEA was, necessarily, a complex machine, but COs should know their place in it. A second major function was to concentrate on essentials. 'You never saw such a volume of paper passing as at Middle East HQ when I went there in January 1944,' he recalled. 'We reduced it by half, missed nothing essential (indeed, we had more time for it), got round the units more and kept fitter.' The further one got away from units in the line, he said, the greater the tendency to become inflexible and fall into routine responses.

On his appointment to this job, Park continued, he was called home to the Air Ministry for 'consultations': these consisted of dashing from one department to another during six hectic days and collecting a deal of paper. He had thought it a bind until he realized how much the Air Ministry knew about the command; it was eager to help and contrary notions must be forgotten. 'Bellyaching signals' could easily be dictated at the end of a long day, he said, and anyone who felt the need to blow off steam should carry on dictating them – but leave them to be read through the next morning before despatch. He knew he sounded like a schoolmaster, but the Air Ministry's goodwill was important and he for one would try to set an example. Finally, Park appealed to everyone to have teamwork in mind: at headquarters, throughout the command, and with the army, the navy and the Americans.

Having delivered himself of these admirable sentiments, Park spent a week touring his enormous command with the intention of putting them into practice. He had a reputation for going to see what was actually happening in any units under his command and would fly many thousands of miles during the next year from his headquarters in Kandy (later in Singapore) to Quetta in the north-west, the Cocos Islands in the south and Hong Kong in the north-east. Given the primitive or isolated conditions under which most units operated, exacerbated by intolerable heat and dust alternating with intolerable rain and mud, Park's obvious concern for the living and working conditions of all ranks fitted him well for what must then have been, in both senses, the RAF's most demanding command. By the end of March, he had already travelled over 17,000 miles in all types of aircraft, motor vehicles and watercraft. His wife had the same desire to see for herself and had visited many hospitals, sick quarters, canteen and welfare centres in Ceylon and India. Her cheerful support helped to keep him going.

During his first tour, Park examined all matters, great and small. At Barrackpore (near Calcutta), for example, tools were spread carelessly around workshops; at Jessore, there had been only three ENSA shows in eighteen months; and at Digri, proper engine handling, good training and experience had increased Liberator bombloads by up to 800 lbs, but there were no means of making hot coffee for long flights and no fans for ground crews working in very high temperatures. He inspected the casualty evacuation service at Comilla, across the Ganges, observing that aircraft were being refuelled while stretcher cases were still on board; in view of the fire risk, this should not be done. Unlike some officers, junior or senior, Park never carried out his inspections as formalities, completed at a brisk trot. He took the time and trouble necessary to notice what was going on. Fecklessness always angered him. For example, a squadron newly arrived from England complained that it had had no beer ration although stocks lay in Comilla two miles away. At Chittagong, an American base, he saw a jeep fitted with VHF radio which took over aircraft control on the ground, directing taxying, thus freeing the control tower to concentrate on traffic in the air; could not similar arrangements be made for busy RAF airfields?

He went to Akyab in Burma for talks with the Earl of Bandon (AOC, 224 Group) and thence to Monywa to meet an old friend, Stanley Vincent (AOC, 221 Group). Only four Spitfire squadrons were available to cover the whole area of operations of the Fourteenth Army, Vincent told him, and many pilots were very tired. If the Japanese used their fighters properly, losses in transport aircraft would be heavy. Park also visited the headquarters of the US Tenth Air Force at Bhamo in north Burma and called at Myitkyina East to watch the despatch of supplies across the Hump to China. As at all American stations, he was greatly impressed by the amount of equipment available, domestic as well as military, and the efficient methods employed. When he returned to Barrackpore, he learned that the aeroplane in which he was to fly to Kandy had been sent empty down to Calcutta from Delhi. This thoughtless waste of space exasperated him: if a little initiative had been shown, a whole planeload of personnel committed to the crowded railway service from Delhi to Calcutta could have been given a pleasant surprise.

Overall, his tour confirmed the reports of poor conditions in his command which he had read in England. It was still not possible to buy razor blades, toothpaste or soap except at fantastic prices; beer (so-called) from Indian sources was rationed to three bottles a month; there were no canteens at most forward aerodromes, no sports facilities and the mail service was at best irregular; there were few wirelesses, books, newspapers, rest rooms or cinemas. In the South Pacific, where transport difficulties were as taxing as in Burma or India, Australian and American forces had numerous live shows arranged for them right up to the front line. But virtually nothing was done in

South-East Asia, where at least seventeen per cent of personnel were ineffective because of sickness caused by the alien climate and bad conditions. 'I have frequently heard officers, and especially senior officers, boasting that we look after our men better than the Army,' he wrote on 24 March. 'It seems to me that some units pay less attention to the well-being of their men than we did to our horses when I was a junior officer. It was a matter of pride in those days that we got the very best rations and fodder for our men and horses *and* a bit extra just for luck.'

In Burma – as in Britain, Egypt, and Malta – Park showed himself a forceful, resolute and highly visible leader. Although his responsibilities were heavier than ever and his forces far more widely scattered, Park's long, lean figure and smiling face were soon familiar to many and he was no less ready to sit with a group of pilots at dispersal, discussing operations and listening to opinions or complaints. Flight Lieutenant Peter Ewing, a Mosquito pilot in 221 Group, recalled his surprise at Park's consideration for his men. Ewing was awarded the DFC and Park took the trouble to write personally to congratulate him and then again to send him a piece of DFC material, knowing that Ewing would find it difficult to obtain. Most important, Ewing emphasized that under Park more determined efforts were made to keep everyone informed about the overall progress of the Burma campaign.

That campaign was going well and during March it was recognized that the time had come to look beyond Rangoon and plan for operations in Malaya. The problem was how to exploit the present advantage without large reinforcements from Europe. Park therefore encouraged action to release manpower from his own rear areas by disbanding redundant units, reducing establishments and making non-combat zones bear the brunt of shortages. The base organization in India and Ceylon was severely trimmed in order to build up the strength of the advanced striking forces for the battles ahead. The reoccupation of Burma, he said, was largely a land battle to recover territory and destroy an army, but after Rangoon was taken, the emphasis would be upon seaborne and airborne assaults intended to seize bases for the capture of Singapore and the reopening of the Malacca Strait.[3]

Park wrote a ten-minute talk in March on the air forces in SEAC for use by the BBC, which he would send to the Air Ministry if Mountbatten approved. 'I really think it is one of the best I have read,' replied Mountbatten, 'and quite first-class and it has my wholehearted backing.' The Air Ministry approved the text with certain changes. Where Park had written: 'I know from personal observation that this is not generally known in the United Kingdom nor in fact outside the South-East Asian theatre,' he was required to say: 'I know that at home exploits of the Allied Air Forces are followed with keen interest and admiration.'

Meanwhile, on 20 March, he had written to Beaverbrook. He had just completed a tour around Burma, he wrote, and learned for the first time how dependent the army had been on air support for its victory in the battle for Mandalay. Undisputed aerial superiority enabled close support squadrons to concentrate on accurate firing and also permitted the carriage of whole divisions up to the battle zone, together with the bulk of their supplies Flying over forward areas, Park was struck by the congested roads, uncamouflaged dumps and Mechanical Transport parks right up to the front line, whereas on the enemy side no Japanese dared show a leg by day. He was so impressed, Park concluded, that he had written an account for the BBC to tell the world. On 29 March the account was broadcast by All-India Radio; the BBC, however, never did broadcast it. This confirmed Park's suspicion that the words foisted on him by the Air Ministry were simply not true: there was both ignorance and lack of interest in Britain about what was going on in South-East Asia. His brief, authoritative account of well organized and highly successful attempts to expel invaders from British territory, written with a British audience in mind, were rejected by British radio.

Nevertheless, his efforts to publicize the work of the air forces in SEAC gradually bore fruit. On 17 April he told transport squadrons of Eastern Air Command in Arakan that on the Western Front 'the Armies of Liberation are advancing under the protecting wings of the Air Forces. But here in Burma our Armies are advancing *on* the wings of the Allied Air Forces.' These words (later to be much quoted, usually without acknowledgement) were taken down by a reporter and broadcast over All-India Radio on the 24th. Beaverbrook informed Park on the 26th that the astonishing part played by air transport in Burma was becoming clearer to the British public. Although attention was inevitably fixed on the final stages in Europe, the swift succession of Burma victories was another cause for rejoicing. 'Nor is it without remark,' he added, 'that the increased pace of the Burma Campaign has coincided with your own arrival in that theatre of operations.'[4]

Park's relations with Lieutenant-General Sir Oliver Leese, GOC-in-C Allied Land Forces, South-East Asia, soon became uneasy. He received a signal from William Dickson, an Assistant Chief of the Air Staff at the Air Ministry, on 25 March informing him that Leese had signalled the War Office to say that he would need more transport aircraft to ensure decisive success in Burma. Dickson told Park that he was surprised by this statement because the Air Ministry had met in full Mountbatten's request for transport aircraft. Park replied that the air forces had lifted every ton of the amount agreed with the army and that Leese should be told by the War Office to follow the normal procedure of complaining about another service only through Mountbatten and with the knowledge of that service. He assured Dickson that the closest cooperation existed between Slim, the various corps headquarters and the air forces – and hoped that when Lesse moved his headquarters from Calcutta to Kandy, as Mountbatten and Park had asked him to, they would get the same cooperation from him.

On 4 April Park reported to Portal. Fighting spirit, he said, was equally good in both British and American squadrons, but the Americans had more and better equipment and more ground transport. Since they served only a two-year tour and got more air transport for local leave, they were fresher as well as more comfortable than the British. Park's groups suffered from a lack of experienced administration officers and the many changes of organization in the last six months had caused much confusion. Maintenance units were overloaded with equipment of every kind, but much of it was obsolete or deteriorating. Provided an even flow of supply was kept up, he could effect great savings in manpower, works services, storage space and airfields – not to mention money – by cutting down reserve stocks.

A week later, he sent Portal a 'strictly personal' signal to warn him that Mountbatten had signalled London alleging that extraordinary efforts would be needed to cover the deficit in air supply. That signal, said Park, had been sent without his knowledge and did not represent the correct situation. He had already strengthened the maintenance backing by transferring to Dakotas personnel and resources from other aircraft types and had also borrowed Dakota spares from the USAAF Servicing Command and improved field maintenance. There should be 'absolutely no deficit in air supply' because any additional load caused by airborne operations would be accepted by the transport squadrons which could increase their present scale of effort for a short time. Any ill effects of this overload would be made good by the two extra Dakota squadrons promised Park for early May. Mountbatten's signal, Park concluded, had probably been intended to 'ginger up' the Air Ministry; it would not have been sent from Kandy, 'where the true facts are well known.' Park's analysis impressed Portal and also Dickson, who informed the Joint Planning Staff that it 'disposed of the criticisms levelled by Admiral Mountbatten at alleged shortcomings in air supply and backing'; consequently, Mountbatten was told by the Chiefs of Staff that ACSEA would inform him of arrangements made with the Air Ministry regarding air transport.

Park appointed a Maintenance Investigation Team in April to examine and compare methods and rates of aircraft replacement, repair, inspection and wastage in the RAF and USAAF, in order to see if the performance of the British organization could be improved. His aim, he told Leslie Hollinghurst, head of Base Air Forces, South-East Asia (BAFSEA), was to ensure that every hundred American aircraft allotted to the RAF produced as good a flying effort as an equal number of USAAF aircraft doing the same job. He knew that the Americans had more of everything:

> All right, let us shout and bullyrag the Air Ministry until our squadrons enjoy the same good facilities as our Allies. Let us raise our standards and go one better than our American cousins, but for heaven's sake don't let us sit down and accept the lower standards of the past.[5]

Park wrote to Slessor, his old sparring partner, on 21 April to say how grateful he was for his warning about 'a certain high-ranking General [Leese] who, you said, had old-fashioned ideas about the control of air forces.' Park gathered that Leese had been difficult in Italy and he knew that Garrod had found him hard to handle. Leese had set up his headquarters at Hastings Air Base, near Calcutta, alongside those of George E. Stratemeyer, who had unfortunately been given operational control of Allied air forces long before Park had reached South-East Asia. Stratemeyer, as an American airman, was used to obeying orders from the army and Leese was now dominating him. Although Park had persuaded Mountbatten to order Leese to move to Kandy, this would not happen until after the fall of Rangoon. Meanwhile, Park went on, he was educating Stratemeyer into a practice of 'getting the army to state the problem or the effect required and to leave it to the Air Force Commander to decide the method of execution.'

Within a week of writing this letter, Park seized a chance to put Leese firmly in his place. Leese had complained to him about the communication aircraft provided by RAF Burma, but when Park had last been in Calcutta, Leese had expressed satisfaction with them. Park wrote, 'Now you fire a full broadside, accusing the RAF communication units both in Italy and in this theatre of being unsatisfactory and far less efficient than their American counterparts.' Leese was upset because a few Vickers Warwicks had been used recently instead of Dakotas, which had had to be returned to transport work to meet ever-increasing demands for supplying the land forces; demands, said Park, which were 'due partly to the inability of the land supply system to carry the tonnage promised at the Calcutta conference of 23 February.' Leese had made serious allegations against the morale and ability of communication pilots and Park challenged him to produce examples. If a low accident rate was any guide, they must be reasonably competent: only one army officer had been killed in the past year while flying. How many, asked Park, had been killed in road accidents during that time?

Leese thought it essential for commanders to have their own aircraft, but Park did not and neither did Mountbatten. Leese knew perfectly well that Park had had to take emergency measures to meet 'unexpectedly swollen demands' for air supply from the army, and yet he wanted a *second* Dakota for his personal use – fitted with sound-proofing, sleeping-cabin and specially polished wings. In his April report on the command's affairs, Park was recorded as telling Leese, on the subject of Dakotas: 'After Rangoon [is captured], you can have one with gold knobs on.' That was a treat Leese would be denied, because early in May he attempted to sack Slim, but was himself sacked and replaced by Slim in July.

It was with Leese in mind that Park wrote to the Director of Air Information, Eastern Air Command, on 27 April, enclosing comments by a visiting British journalist on the lack of publicity for air force achievements in South-East Asia. Greater publicity, said Park, would not only be deserved and a boost to morale, it would prevent the army from receiving 'a disproportionate share of the credit which might serve to strengthen any move of theirs postwar to demand a separate Army Air Force.' He drew attention in his April report to Slim's Order of the Day (16 April) in which he had said: 'Nor could there have been any victory at all without the constant ungrudging support of the Allied Air Forces. It is their victory as much as ours.' Park wanted this tribute widely publicized. Otherwise, the postwar integrity of the air force would be jeopardized by a belief that the air was ancillary to the ground effort and that the direction of air warfare could therefore be undertaken by soldiers. And yet Park was by no means anti-army. On 7 May, for example, he wrote in praise of the excellent work of Air Formation Signals (AFS). They were army personnel and, as Park informed the Adjutant General in Delhi, they had 'worked splendidly to provide, under the most difficult conditions, the landline communications upon which the efficient operation of the RAF depends.'

Mountbatten told Park on 8 June that he had heard from Portal that the War Office would not agree to giving Leese the acting rank of general. Portal would accede to Mountbatten's request that Park be made an Air Chief Marshal if Mountbatten assured him that this was acceptable to the other Commanders-in-Chief. He had so assured Portal, urging him 'most strongly' to promote Park in July at the same time as the Burma awards were announced. Douglas Evill, however, prevailed upon Portal to change his mind. Linking Park's promotion to the liberation of Burma, argued Evill, would be 'unnecessarily provoking' to the War Office, since he had had so little to do with it and certainly not as much as Leese. Evill therefore proposed that Slessor set about Park's promotion as a routine affair. On 9 August Mountbatten signalled Park to tell him that his promotion, with effect from 1 August, would be announced on the 14th. Sufficient time had then elapsed, presumably, to ensure that it was not associated in the public mind with the liberation of Burma.[6]

The occupation of Rangoon on 3 May 1945 marked the end of the American commitment in Burma. Each air force would thereafter prosecute the war in neighbouring theatres. 'For the Royal Air Force,' wrote Park, 'the offensive now headed down the Malay Peninsula to Singapore. For the USAAF, however, the route lay across the Himalayas to China.' The period of integration between British and American forces in South-East Asia 'had shown a very real spirit of close cooperation,' Park thought, and he did all he could to foster it. On VE (Victory in Europe) Day, 8 May 1945, he was required to present an honorary CBE to Major-General Howard C. Davidson, head of the American Tenth Air Force and former head of the Strategic Air Force, Eastern Air Command. Park ensured an impressive turnout of senior army and navy officers, as well as RAF officers, and many other notables – Chinese, Dutch, Indian, British and American. He imported a pipe band by air from Cawnpore and found some Scottish pipers; he paraded three squadrons, arranged a guard of honour, required all personnel not on duty or parade to attend as spectators and encouraged the presence of several hundred civilians. The parade was mounted with a style and zest uncommon among senior British officers and greatly pleased the Americans, as it was intended to do.

Later in May, Stratemeyer wrote to Park about the 'disintegration' of Eastern Air Command, to take effect from 1 June. He wanted to withdraw all American personnel, except for one squadron and Park's Senior Air Staff Officer (Brigadier-General John P. McConnell) who would stay with Park until the 21st. The American headquarters would remain at Hastings to represent American air interests in India and act as a 'zone of communication' for the China theatre. Park signalled Stratemeyer on 24 May to pay tribute to the work of his command since December 1943 in helping to obtain air supremacy in Burma, without which air supply would have been impossible. He emphasized that American transport squadrons had carried the greater part of the airlift in support of British land forces in Burma. Without them, 'we could not have defeated the Japanese Army so rapidly and decisively in 1945.'[7]

Park wrote the next day to Air Marshal Alec Coryton, head of RAF Burma, to say that he had asked the Air Ministry to appoint Cecil Bouchier (his old friend from Battle of Britain days) to relieve Stanley Vincent as head of 221 Group. Park thought well of Vincent and his group, which shared with Slim's army the honour of having defended India from the Japanese in 1944, but Vincent was in need of a rest and change of scene. The army had slackened its efforts in Burma after the fall of Rangoon and was making a long business of clearing up; this had affected 221 Group adversely, in Park's opinion. He therefore wanted Coryton to mount 'a real Jap-killing competition' between squadrons and wings. They must divide the whole of Burma into search areas and comb them systematically on every day fit for flying. Too many 'little yellow devils' were being allowed to escape into Malaya. Operation Zipper, a massive combined operation intended to liberate Malaya, was planned for August and very hard fighting was expected; every Japanese who escaped from Burma would make that fighting so much harder. Outside a small circle, no one yet knew of the atom bomb, and the war against Japan was thought likely to last at least another year. Park himself did not expect to be in Singapore before Christmas and thought Japan would not surrender before May 1946.

With Operation Zipper in mind, Park expressed alarm at the priority being given in London to the formation of Tiger Force, a British contribution to the bombing of Japan. The Americans had told him that because of a lack of airfields it would be impossible to redeploy part of the US Eighth Air Force in the Pacific; he was therefore certain that Tiger Force would not be deployed there either. On 6 June he reminded Portal of the many disappointments experienced by Mountbatten in the past owing to SEAC taking second place to other theatres. He was surprised to learn that the Air Ministry preferred Tiger Force to SEAC even though the invasion of Malaya had been approved by the Chiefs of Staff for execution before Tiger Force began to operate. Mountbatten believed that Tiger Force jeopardized Zipper and Park supported him, but the Air Ministry was unmoved. Agitation continued until early August, when the atomic bombs on Hiroshima and Nagasaki brought the war to an abrupt end.[8]

On 2 July Park wrote to Anthony Eden, the British Foreign Secretary. Eden's son, Sergeant Simon Eden, had been navigator of a Dakota engaged on a routine air supply flight calling at various destinations in Burma. It had landed according to schedule at Myingyan and had left there for Akyab, but had not been heard from since 23 June. Park told Eden that it would be in friendly territory if it had made a forced landing. Communications in Burma were so bad that the crew might take a couple of weeks to reach a military or air base. There had been such cases and Park promised to send Eden a most immediate signal if he heard anything. Simon had just been recommended for a commission and Park would see that the recommendation was forwarded to the Air Ministry without delay if he turned up safely. But John Grandy, Simon's CO, informed Park on 4 July that there was now little hope of finding the Dakota crew alive, and on the 17th Park informed Eden that the wreckage had been found with the remains of four bodies. 'I can only ask you both to remember that your son died doing his duty manfully,' Park wrote, 'on an operational flight of vital importance to our land forces in Central Burma.'

Eden, meanwhile, had replied to Park's first letter. It was a comfort, he said, to know how much had been done to try and find the boy and also to know the details of the flight. Park must have written another letter which has not survived because Eden continued: 'I was so much interested in your account of your talk with Simon. You are right about the sense of humour and I do think that he has a full share of common sense. . . . Sometime I will tell you what he wrote to me after you had been to see him. He was very impressed.'

Almost thirty years later, Eden – then Lord Avon – wrote to Park's son Ian to say how sorry he was to learn of his father's death. Avon was on holiday with Grandy – 'a close friend and admirer of your father's' – when he heard the news, and said he shared Grandy's admiration. 'I have, however, another and more personal reason for wishing to write to you. . . . I have on my dressing-table at the present time a snapshot of your father with another officer and my son. Simon always wrote very warmly about your father, and I am convinced that in his judgment your father held a very special place.'[9]

On 25 July Park submitted to the Air Ministry a report on morale and discipline in his command. Personnel were 'supremely confident' he said, of their ability to finish the war quickly. 'There is, however, a strong and widespread feeling that the Home effort is not being maintained.' South-East Asia had previously been the forgotten front, but now it was the unwanted front. Park had expected that after VE Day he would get the manpower needed to fill long-standing vacancies and relieve those who were 'tour expired'; he had also expected that there would be shipping available to bring the equipment necessary to improve living conditions. It should be realized, he added, that British rates of pay did not compare with American or Dominion scales. Prices in Ceylon and the larger Indian cities were high, demand exceeded supply and value for money was hard to find. Better amenities, entertainment, films, wireless sets and 'good cigarettes' were all needed. He emphasized that there was great sympathy in the RAF for the hardships endured by men of the Fourteenth Army. Their efforts against the Japanese – very tough fighters, met under the most trying conditions – were regarded as second to none and it was widely believed that people at home had never appreciated them.

Neither had they appreciated the efforts of airmen, in Park's opinion. On 7 August he wrote to Air Marshal Sir Richard Peck at the Air Ministry to ask for his help in getting a really first-class writer of international reputation to come out and write the story of air power. The chance to emphasize as clearly as possible the fact that no navy or army could fight a major battle successfully until the air battle had been fought and won should not be missed.

The next day, he got from Mountbatten himself some of the recognition he sought for the achievements of air power. 'No Army in history,' said Mountbatten in a radio broadcast from London, 'has even contemplated fighting its way through Burma from the north until now, not even in Staff College studies. The Japs came in the easy way and we pushed them out the hard way.' To keep the troops supplied, Mountbatten had asked the air forces to fly at double the authorized rates per month. It has been by far the biggest lift of the war, 'though heaven knows most other theatres had many more transport aircraft and they didn't have the monsoon and the jungle to fight.' At a press conference on 9 August, Mountbatten paid generous tribute to Park, 'who has brought with him the fighting spirit which he showed in the Battle of Britain and the Battle of Malta.' The campaign certainly turned round the Mountbatten–Slim axis. Men with little in common save 'the power of commanding affection while communicating energy', they harnessed and drove the Allied forces to victory. However, the contribution of air power to the defeat of the Japanese in that theatre was crucial and Park's part in directing it in the final stages was proficient and enthusiastic.

Japan's unconditional surrender was announced at midnight on 14 August and Park, in a message to all ranks, stressed the tasks remaining. Tens of thousands of prisoners awaited release and needed food, clothing and medical attention. The RAF must also take part in the occupation of enemy-held territory and help to restore civilian law and order. The forward movement, he warned, would absorb shipping that might otherwise have been available to carry men home. At that time, the regions for which SEAC was responsible contained 128 million people, whose pent-up nationalist feelings were swiftly aroused; there were some 250 prison camps, containing 125,000 prisoners and, not least, there were 750,000 Japanese soldiers at large.

Hugh Saunders, a South African whom Park had known since Bertangles days, had by then arrived to command RAF Burma. Park wrote to him at the end of August to say that he hoped Saunders would be able to join him for the surrender ceremony at Singapore in September. This was the war's last great occasion, marking the formal end of fighting against the Japanese in South-East Asia. Sadly, it did not mark the end of fighting there, even during the few remaining months of Park's command. This fighting, together with the problems of winding down a vast military machine and creating its peacetime successor, tested Park as severely as any other task in his long career.[10]

CHAPTER SEVENTEEN

South-East Asia Command: Troubled Days of Peace

1945 - 1946

The Allied Air Forces under your command . . . made an outstanding contribution to our final victory in this theatre; and the good work has been continued in these troubled days of peace.
Mountbatten to Park, 1 May 1946

At 10.20 a.m. on 12 September 1945, the Allied Commanders-in-Chief for land, air and sea, Slim, Park and Admiral Power, arrived together at the Municipal Buildings in Singapore. Ten minutes later, Mountbatten and his deputy, Lieutenant-General R.A. Wheeler of the US Army, arrived and were greeted by the Cs-in-C. They and other Allied officers then went into the Council Chamber, where the Japanese delegation awaited them. 'I have come here today,' said Mountbatten, 'to receive the formal surrender of all Japanese forces within the South-East Asia Command. I wish to make this plain: the surrender today is no negotiated surrender. The Japanese are submitting to superior forces, now massed here.'

In his September report, Park emphasized the fact that the invasion of Malaya had begun on the 9th and would have begun that day whether the Japanese had resisted or not. There was for Park a grim satisfaction in the spectacle of humbled Japanese commanders because he was already aware of their atrocious conduct in Burma. As prison camps were discovered and opened during the next few weeks, the horrifying evidence of inhumanity everywhere became almost unbearable. From the moment of the surrender, the liberation and transport of about 125,000 surviving prisoners, civilian and military, women and children, became Park's principal concern. All were sick and starved and the transport of medical personnel and supplies was an immediate need. Park spoke of 'the greatest mercy mission of the war' in a message to his tireless air and ground crews – tireless because the joy of those released made up for everything. There was, however, the agonizing fact that

213

aircraft could move ex-prisoners more quickly than the system could handle them: if the uplift from Bangkok and Saigon, for example, was not strictly controlled, accommodation in Rangoon would be crowded out before shipping was available to take them home.

There was also, as Group Captain Charles Ryley (CO of Kallang, Singapore) told Park early in October, the 'ticklish matter' of which ex-prisoners should be rescued first. An Australian detachment had been sent to Kallang primarily to evacuate Australian prisoners, but when the crews had made their first flights to Sumatra, they had been so overwhelmed by the pitiful condition of the sick cases among the British and other nationals there that they had all requested permission to evacuate these before the relatively fit Australians in Bangkok. Hundreds of lives were saved, but some members of the Air Board in Melbourne believed the extra time and effort spent were more excuses to spin out a comfortable stay in Singapore. Ryley suggested that Park write to the Chief of the Air Staff in Melbourne to make the facts clear to him. Park did so, promptly and firmly.[1]

Meanwhile, Japanese conquests were reoccupied. On 12 September Park issued a directive appointing Air Commodore W.A.D. Brook as AOC Hong Kong. He would command all RAF units there, other than those of Transport Command, and be responsible to Rear-Admiral C.H.J. Harcourt for the conduct of air operations and to Park for the development of an air route to Japan east of French Indo-China which British Commonwealth Air Forces of Occupation in Japan could use. Brook reported to Park on 8 October about events in Hong Kong during the past month. Nine vessels had arrived there on 4 September, carrying 3,400 officers and men of Tiger Force and an airfield construction wing. Some 18,000 Japanese had been rounded up and put in a former prison camp on the mainland. The nucleus of AHQ Hong Kong had arrived on the 12th, Brook himself had arrived a week later. The men had done everything asked of them, Brook said, in jobs for which they had no training whatever: prison supervision, police duties and the resumption and maintenance of power and transport services. They had also made full use of Japanese labour in cleaning up Hong Kong.

Park visited the island late in October, en route to an American base at Kunming in China, and wrote to Harcourt while flying from there home to Kandy. He would try to open regular air services to Hong Kong from Calcutta and Singapore, he said, and also to stage flying-boats through Shanghai. He was next in Hong Kong on New Year's Day 1946, visiting airfield construction workers. Hong Kong, said Park, would once again become a major centre of commerce and a naval base; as such, it needed the protection which only an air base could provide. In February he advised the Air Ministry that in the short term there was some danger of Chinese warlords attempting to seize the port, but he could handle them. In the long term, however, Hong Kong was indefensible against a power controlling

214

mainland China. The RAF should not therefore maintain any day- or night-fighter defences there, nor even man a radar system other than that needed for air traffic control.

The Air Ministry raised no objection to Park's choice of Brook for the Hong Kong post, but Slessor resisted his choice of Bouchier as senior RAF officer in Japan. Park knew that Slessor objected to Bouchier because he had rejected him as AOC Aden in 1944 even though the Air Ministry had supported Park's recommendation. Both Saunders and the army commander in Burma assured Park that Bouchier had done well as AOC 221 Group, but since the group had been absorbed into AHQ Burma Bouchier was spare. Park brought him to Kandy to work on the planning for the occupation forces in Japan and invited Slessor to specify his objections. Slessor merely answered that 'none of us much care for him'; however, in view of Park's opinion and the good reports he quoted, he magnanimously agreed not to press the point and Park therefore ordered Bouchier to supervise preparations for the despatch of air forces to Japan and the Netherlands East Indies. Although the Australians would have liked an RAAF officer to command the British Commonwealth Air Forces of Occupation in Japan, Bouchier's appointment was confirmed.

Bouchier fully justified the determined effort Park had made to land him the job. He spent the rest of his career in Japan, closely associated with MacArthur both before and after 1949, when he first retired. In August 1950 he was recalled to active service as MacArthur's senior British military liaison officer and did not finally retire for good until March 1953.

As for the Netherlands force which Bouchier helped to get ready, Park gave the command to Air Commodore C.A. Stevens. During the current 'unsettled period', he told Stevens on 19 October, Mountbatten had ordered all forces – British and Dutch – to be placed under army control, though they remained under Stevens's command. He was responsible to Park for advising the army on the conduct of air operations, his role being to help the army to succour and evacuate ex-prisoners, to preserve law and order, to disarm Japanese forces and to 'avoid clashes with' Dutch armed forces and the peoples of the Netherlands East Indies.

On Park's orders, Stevens used Japanese aircraft and aircrews to assist in the withdrawal of former prisoners from the interior of Java and Sumatra. At first, he restricted the use of Japanese aircraft to freight work in case lives should be lost through the use of uncertain equipment, but during a visit to Java in December, Park found that unless he authorized the use of Japanese aircraft to carry passengers, evacuation would be delayed and suffering prolonged among the thousands still to be rescued. He would also be placing a still heavier burden upon his own hard-worked men and machines. Consequently, he recommended that the risk of using Japanese aircraft and crews, under Stevens's control, be accepted. The Air Ministry and the Chiefs of Staff agreed.

Relations with the French in Indo-China were as delicate as those with the Dutch in the East Indies. At the beginning of October, Mountbatten told Lieutenant-General Leclerc, Commander-in-Chief of the French forces in the Far East, that he was responsible to himself (Mountbatten), through his Cs-in-C, for the action of all French forces within the boundaries of SEAC until it was agreed that he was able to re-establish an independent, self-supporting French command. Slim, Power and Park would continue to command all Allied land, sea and air forces within SEAC. Park appointed Air Commodore W.G. Cheshire as AOC French Indo-China on terms similar to those governing Brook and Stevens.

Cheshire signalled Park from Saigon on 13 November about a machine-gun attack by a French aircraft on a concentration of Annamite guerrillas; there had been no leaflet warning. The French claimed that they misunderstood Park's restrictions on the use of force without prior notification, which was 'manifestly untrue'. Leclerc and Lieutenant-General Gracey (the British C-in-C) wanted the French Air Force released from those restrictions and the loan of six Spitfires to be flown by French pilots. At Park's request, Saunders (head of RAF Burma) discussed the situation with Gracey and Cheshire. French ground forces, Saunders reported, were meeting stiff opposition from Annamite 'rebels' (as they called them) and Leclerc believed he should be able to use French aircraft against them. Saunders agreed with him, but did not recommend placing Spitfires under his control, with or without British pilots and ground crews. Gracey accepted this and said he only made the proposal as a diplomatic gesture, not wishing to fall out with Leclerc. But Park's signal to Leclerc, reminding him clearly and firmly of his subordination to Gracey, Mountbatten's representative in Indo-China, greatly relieved Saunders and he hoped that neither Gracey nor Cheshire would have further difficulties with the French.

Mountbatten informed Park on 23 November that Gracey had sent an officer to Delhi to discuss with him the problem of air support for French troops in Indo-China. Leclerc claimed that he was handicapped by not being allowed British air support, because he had no suitable aircraft of his own. He asked that a squadron of Spitfires be turned over to him, to be flown by French pilots. 'This seems to me to be the obvious solution,' wrote Mountbatten, and he would like Park's advice on whether the aircraft should be lent or sold. Park pointed out that he had no authority to agree to the transfer of RAF equipment to another nation without first putting the proposal to the Air Ministry. He thought the use of British Spitfires backed by RAF ground crews and flown by French pilots was to be avoided. But the Air Ministry did not share his doubts and he was ordered to meet Leclerc's requests.

Relations with the Americans were no more comfortable, once the war had ended. Mountbatten had agreed, on Park's advice, to permit no more than one C-47 a day to use Bangkok, but in mid-October the Americans were flying in as often as they liked, despite the obvious congestion and the poor condition of the landing surface. Permission had never been requested to extend their transport service to Saigon (part of Mountbatten's territory), but they had gone ahead anyway, as they had to Java and Singapore.

On 13 October, Park sent Rodcrick Carr (AOC India) 'a very confidential note' regarding discussions he had had that day with Mountbatten and General Terry, US Army (Commanding General, India-Burma Theater). Park had found Terry friendly, he wrote, and had explained to him that he was eager to help the American air trooping service, especially in the return of ex-prisoners to their homes. However the Americans had been starting up scheduled services using RAF airfields without permission or in disregard of refusal. Park had also told Terry of a report he had received about US air forces in South-East Asia destroying equipment and had asked to be given a chance to ask the British government to buy anything that was spare. Finally, Park had explained to him – in front of Mountbatten – that a shortage of spare parts caused by the sudden and unexpected cancellation of Lend-Lease was making it difficult to maintain American aircraft. Terry was cooperative in all these matters, Park reported, and he looked forward to better relations with the Americans in future.[2]

In addition to setting up subordinate formations far from Kandy and seeking a new basis for relations with old allies, Park was also deeply concerned with the problems of flying home enormous numbers of soldiers and airmen. This task attracted the closest scrutiny from both the politicians and the services because the government had promised that releases at home would keep in step with those from abroad; in effect, every man returned enabled about five to be released in Britain. Responsibility for air trooping was divided between Transport Command and ACSEA and relations between two such far-flung empires, one centred in London, the other in Kandy (and later in Singapore) were unavoidably uneasy.

Relations with Mountbatten, his large personal staff and the huge army establishment in SEAC were also uneasy, especially in matters of accommodation and command. On 1 October, for example, Park investigated and rejected Mountbatten's complaint that the RAF in Singapore had seized accommodation allotted to ex-prisoners. His challenge to Mountbatten to substantiate the complaint was not taken up. The RAF had been treated 'unfairly and unjustly', he claimed, in comparison with the army and the navy in the allocation of office and living space: 'it shows a rather sad lack of the close cooperation that won us the recent war.' The appointment of a military governor in Penang was one example of the command problem. Mountbatten offered the post to the RAF and the appointment of Air Commodore P.D. Cracroft, wrote Park, 'was acclaimed by the Air Force, approved by the Navy and Civil Affairs but accepted more in pain than anger by the Generals,' of whom there were some *eighteen* on Mountbatten's staff. They persuaded him

217

to abolish the post. For all practical purposes, Park told Portal miserably on 18 October, Mountbatten commanded 'a super Army headquarters'.

The film *Burma Victory* arrived in South East Asia at this time. Made by an army film unit, it reflected in the crudest terms the army's view of that campaign. Park's Historical Officer, Squadron Leader T.L. Muir, reported that when shown to RAF personnel it would 'create such bitter feeling, disappointment and disillusion at no proper recognition being accorded to their own service' that morale would suffer. It was an insult to the airmen who served and to their families and friends at home. The commentator, said Muir, borrowed Park's phrase 'The Army of the jungle advanced on the wings of the Air Force' and that was the sole reference to the RAF's efforts in Burma. Park found that attitude particularly distressing because Slim himself had written of the South-East Asia theatre: 'Never has an Army been better, more unselfishly, or more gallantly served by an Air Force.'[3]

The release scheme, however, was of more immediate concern to Park. Carr signalled him from India on 13 October to say that a great deal of dissatisfaction had been caused by ministerial statements and press articles which showed the RAF's release rate to be well behind that of the other services. The Air Ministry must explain why, said Carr, or there would be serious unrest in India. Park agreed and so informed Slessor, who drew his attention to a statement made in the House of Commons by the Under-Secretary of State for Air, John Strachey, on the 12th. According to Strachey, an immense transport task faced Britain over the next nine months in getting men and women home. Between now and 30 June 1946, he said, one million service personnel had to be moved. A larger proportion of airmen than of other servicemen must therefore be retained to move those people. The RAF faced a difficult time, Strachey admitted, but these were not tasks that recruits could perform.

Park told Slessor later that month that during recent tours he had addressed large gatherings of airmen in Bangkok, Saigon, Hong Kong, Kunming, Calcutta and Madras and had found general acceptance of Strachey's explanation. The fact remained, however, that when airmen *were* released, they would find army and navy men in the civilian jobs which they had hoped to get. The government should therefore either guarantee jobs to airmen on release or permit them to stay on in the RAF until work was available.

Wherever he went, especially in India, he explained to airmen why the RAF and the army had been unable to make big reductions in the overseas tour as soon as hostilities had ceased, adding that the Air Ministry had, however, accepted his recommendation to reduce the tour of single men by six months. He also said that he had recommended a further reduction – to three years, the time served by married men – and that the Air Ministry had agreed in principle. But the need to speed up the release scheme, the manpower shortage and the world-wide shipping shortage meant that no date could yet be given for the implementation of that recommendation. Slessor thought Park had gone too far. There was no prospect, he emphasized on 20 November, of the tour being reduced to three years in the near future and denied that he had ever mentioned a reduction in 1946 to three years; in his view, no reduction was likely. Park retorted that on 2 August Slessor had agreed to his recommendation, to take effect from 1 April 1946. As it happened, Park was right and Slessor wrong. A scheme to reduce the tour for single men to three years did begin to operate on 1 April 1946.

Another aspect of Park's preoccupation with India was the growing awareness of the need to separate the responsibilities of the air forces there from those farther east. Park signalled Portal from Delhi several times in November to warn him that Auchinleck (C-in-C India) wanted aircraft placed under his control because he was worried by increasingly violent rivalry between the Hindu-dominated Indian Congress and the Moslem League, which was pressing for the creation of a separate state. Portal replied that the prospect of a crisis in India did not make it necessary to rush through a reorganisation, provided that operational plans were concerted between Mountbatten and Auchinleck. Park, in short, remained the theatre commander, under Mountbatten; India remained his concern, through Carr; and Auchinleck was not to get control of air forces in India. Park, in turn, summarized the position for Carr on 30 November, ending: 'you will wear a silk hat when dealing with the Indian Government and a bowler when dealing with me.'[4]

The ACSEA HQ in Kandy closed on 24 November, opening the next day in Singapore. In December Park held a meeting at his new headquarters with his senior commanders: thirty officers, only five of whom were below Group Captain rank. Twenty-one were from ACSEA HQ and nine from elsewhere: Burma, Malaya, the Netherlands East Indies, Hong Kong, French Indo-China and Ceylon. He spoke to them about Singapore's future, revealing that Admiral Sir Bruce Fraser (C-in-C, British Pacific Fleet) agreed with him that the island's future would be as an air base, not as a naval base. Heavy bomber airfields must therefore be built and it was essential that ACSEA become self-reliant and not be at the mercy of events in India. He looked forward to a time when his headquarters would be at Changi airfield. The civilian authorities naturally wanted the RAF out of offices in the city and Park, who knew that his AOCs were being similarly pressed in their own provinces, urged them to be sympathetic in dealing with civilian authorities.

On 31 December Reverend A.W. Hopkins, the Assistant Principal Chaplain in ACSEA, submitted to Park a summary of his annual report on Presbyterian, Methodist and United Board chaplaincy services in the command. Morale, he wrote, progressively improved from west to east, as one got closer to operational conditions. It was low in Karachi and Cawnpore, high in Java and Sumatra. Park would know from his own tours how much had changed so quickly since the defeat of the Japanese and how many men were worried about repatriation and release. Hopkins had been everywhere in the command, he continued, and had often been permitted to talk to men without officers present. He assured Park that his informal talks were much appreciated: 'the personal method of your approach has been more successful than you know.' This unsolicited tribute would be much in Park's mind during the unrest of the coming weeks.

On 23 January Air Marshal Arthur Barratt, Inspector General of the RAF, reported an incident at Mauripur which, Slessor thought, 'seems definitely to amount to mutiny.' On the same day, Edward Chilton, AOC Ceylon, reported to Park on an incident at Negombo where men of a Transport Command staging-post had refused to service aircraft on hearing of the strike at Mauripur. What, he asked, was going on there? Park was in Borneo at the time, so George Pirie, his deputy, replied. Stimulated by reports on US radio of mass parades by GIs in Germany to demand speedier release, a similar demonstration had taken place at Mauripur. Pirie advised Chilton to contact Harold Davies, a Member of Parliament who was to arrive in Ceylon that day from Singapore, where he had addressed many meeting to explain the government's demob policy. Park himself signalled Chilton on the 26th. He hoped he had invited Davies to address the men because their main grievances were 'entirely political' and he could report them to his colleagues. Park then added, most unusually for him, a chirpy postscript: 'Horsey keep your tail up.'

Park received no more bad news from Ceylon, but similar outbreaks much closer to home, at Seletar and Kallang in Singapore, had serious repercussions. On 26 January servicemen at Seletar declared that they would follow the example of men in the Middle East and Karachi in staging a sit-down strike unless their grievances were immediately investigated. Park ordered the CO to address them and hear their grievances, but they expressed dissatisfaction with his answers and asked to be addressed by Park. He spoke to them briefly, listened to them at length and reported to Slessor next day. Their first complaint, he said, concerned the slow rate of release and inequalities in the rate for different trades. Secondly, they complained about repatriation. Many were unable or unwilling to understand why the RAF could not at once reduce the overseas tour to three years. Thirdly, they complained about living conditions and poor food.

On the evening of 27 January, after Park had spoken at Kallang to twenty-seven representatives of the men, six men were arrested – including three of the representatives – while calling for a forty-eight-hour strike. Later that evening, some officers at Kallang attended a meeting organized by an airman named Cymbalist. They were given a fair hearing, but Cymbalist made frequent interruptions until at length he was arrested. He called upon the men to prevent his being taken away and for a while some sixty men adopted a threatening attitude. The CO, Group Captain Ryley, interviewed Cymbalist about midnight. His manner was still aggressive and he threatened violence if he was not released. Ryley therefore confirmed his close arrest and went to speak to the men, shortly before 1 a.m. They had been given a chance to air their grievances, he said, and by striking now would alienate Park, who was 'most appreciative of their restraint in the face of the example set by Seletar.' The men accepted this, but resented the arrest of the seven men. Ryley explained that incitement to mutiny was a very serious offence, but he agreed to release all except Cymbalist. He refused to give an assurance that no disciplinary action would be taken in return for the men calling off their strike, but the meeting nevertheless broke up in an 'encouraging atmosphere'.

In the early evening of the 28th Park informed Tedder (now Chief of the Air Staff) and Slessor that the men at Seletar and Kallang were now back at work. With Mountbatten's approval, he was holding a press conference that evening at which he would make an official statement and give an 'off the record' talk on the background to the incidents. The strike in Singapore, he said, had damaged the RAF's reputation. Privately, however, he was not too distressed: 'Better than 1919 by 90 per cent', he wrote in the margin of one letter. Even so, he treated the unrest seriously. The questions asked him at Kallang were recorded, together with his answers, and arrangements made to check that the grievances they revealed were remedied.

Park received an unusually encouraging signal on 7 February from Slessor, who had had a long talk with Harold Davies, the MP. He had confirmed what was already evident, said Slessor: that the situation was being well handled by all senior commanders. Park had Slessor's fullest confidence and would not be given orders. He was the best judge of what to do. Slessor's role was to give advice, information, statements in the House and to try to keep the press in order. This signal, he ended, had the full support of the Air Council.

Park signalled his senior commanders the same day, repeating points which had long been fixed principles with him. Every officer, he said, was responsible for the living and working conditions of his men. He must train and work closely with his NCOs and was not merely to pass on grievances or problems to higher authority, but to seek his own remedies. If he was a staff officer, he must write less and get round the units more. He must realize that many unit commanders, keen and capable though they might be, were inexperienced and needed training. Those who lacked the character, energy or tact required for command must be sacked. An officer, in short, must look after his men. Park believed that Group Captain Francis, CO at Seletar, had failed to do this. He told Victor Goddard, Air Officer in charge of Administration, that when the Court of Inquiry arrived in Singapore it must have before it Francis's allegation that his group headquarters was responsible for the bad living conditions at Seletar. Had Francis raised that matter with his group commander, he continued? What action had he taken

221

to employ any of his great number of surplus airmen to improve living conditions by planting vegetables, raising poultry, keeping pigs on the swill from 4,000 men, making playing fields and building extra canteens and field kitchens?[5]

Park wrote to Slessor on 20 February 1946 to say that he had recommended to Tedder that Pirie be appointed to succeed him in April. If that was approved, Pirie should go home on leave at the end of March and be permitted to bring his wife back with him; there would be plenty for her to do. If Tedder agreed to Park accepting an official invitation to visit New Zealand at the end of April, he should like to spend three weeks there before flying to Bombay to pick up his baggage and complete the journey to England by sea. 'Of course, if I am wanted home urgently for my next job I can return all the way from the Far East by air and have my baggage follow later.'

No sooner had he written these words than he received a shattering reply to his earlier letter to Tedder. By all means accept the New Zealand invitation, Tedder wrote. 'Not only have you now fully deserved some recognition from your home country, but also such a visit would I am sure be a good thing from the Commonwealth and RAF point of view.' The rest of the letter, Tedder continued, was very much more difficult to write.

> I must tell you frankly that I see no prospect of there being any further appointment open for you in the RAF after ACSEA splits up. I rather gathered from your letter that you had not visualized this and it is indeed the irony of fate that the duty of telling you this unwelcome news should fall to me – after all our association together and in face of my very deep admiration for the magnificent jobs you have done for the service and for the country. But there it is. *Youth* must be served. . . . I only hope that some way will be found by which the country can still have the benefit of your services.

As soon as he received this letter, Park wrote to Mountbatten to ask him, supposing he had been thinking of it, not to recommend him for another honour in the next Birthday List, but for confirmation in his present acting rank. He had, he said, just had a 'very great disappointment and a shock' to hear from Tedder that he would be retired on returning to England. He was quite prepared to make way for younger men,

> but I shall protest in the highest quarter if I am asked to retire in a rank lower than Peirse or Garrod and a number of recently promoted Air Chief Marshals. None of these Air Marshals has ever held a job carrying the rank of Air Chief Marshal or ever been Allied Air C-in-C in any theatre. As I have had the good fortune to be associated throughout the six years of war with only successful campaigns – Battle of Britain, Malta, Egypt

and South East Asia – I do feel that the treatment suggested by the Air Ministry is most unjust. I hope I can count on your friendly support.

Park then flew to Ceylon to visit units and talk with navy and army officers there about air defence. On 5 March he was back in Singapore and wrote at once to thank Mountbatten for having written to Tedder recommending that the Air Ministry confirm his present rank before retirement. He also replied to Tedder's letter. He appreciated Tedder's wish to make room for younger men, but he could not see why AMP (crossed out and 'Kingsway' written in: Slessor was Air Member for Personnel and his department had its offices in Kingsway) should have picked on him first. There were older men of his rank in the service and he believed it would surprise the vast majority of men who had served in South-East Asia 'to see their late Chief relegated to Half Pay' and given less favourable treatment, in fact, than Peirse, 'who was known generally to have been a failure'.

> I cannot hide from you my disappointment and deep concern at the treatment proposed by AMP's Department [again, crossed out and 'Kingsway' written in]. I still hope, however, to leave the Service without a feeling of injustice and to continue to support the RAF in every possible way in the difficult years ahead. It has got to be better, if not bigger than in 1939.

Early in April, while Park was acting as Supreme Allied Commander during Mountbatten's absence in Australia, thus filling the highest position of his career, he received Tedder's reply. He hated the thought of Park feeling bitter, he wrote, but he was not an isolated victim: a number of the best were stepping aside. It was not a Kingsway business, it was his own responsibility. If Park still felt there was injustice, he should 'put the blame squarely where it belongs – on *my* shoulders – not on the Service.' Park replied on 13 April, apologizing for the delay and saying that with Pirie in Britain, Mountbatten in Australia and new governors to install, he had had no spare time. 'I would like to assure you,' he said, 'that I feel absolutely no bitterness towards you at being shelved . . . though I realize that you are personally responsible for accepting the suggestions from AMP's Department as to retirement.' Was there any chance, he asked, of one of the smaller governorships going to the RAF instead of to the army or navy as in the past? He asked the question tentatively because he was not certain that he and Dol could afford such a job, for their private means were slender and they had several relations to look after. 'For your very private ear,' replied Tedder on 2 May, 'we fought hard to get the Governorship of Malta offered to you'; the fight had, however, been lost on the government's decision to make it a civil appointment because the immediate problems in Malta were economic and political.[6]

Park had quickly realized that the only airfield on Singapore capable of being enlarged and strengthened to handle heavy aircraft was at Changi and work had been going ahead since December. It followed that the RAF should be grouped as much as possible around Changi and this helped Park to persuade the army to hand over its very fine cantonment there in exchange for the less commodious – and less comfortable – Tanglin Barracks in the city. Changi, built by the army before the war, was widely considered to be one of the best service quarters anywhere overseas. On 16 April he informed Tedder that the new airfield was now operating heavy aircraft and he would shortly hand over Kallang to the civil authorities. On Saturday afternoon, the 13th, he had been working in Union Buildings and on Monday morning his headquarters was functioning at Changi. It was already more efficient than it had been 'down town' and he would make Changi the finest RAF station in the Far East.

These brave words, characteristic of Park's ambition for every station where he served or commanded, were almost the last written during his active career. Resolution kept him on his feet until the move to Changi was accomplished, but he then gave in to an attack of amoebic dysentery which he had picked up in Malaya in February. After a month under treatment, he was well enough to be sent on fourteen days' sick leave to the Cameron Highlands in northern Malaya before departing on his tour of New Zealand and Australia on 26 May.

Mountbatten sent him an official farewell signal on 1 May, drawing attention not only to the air's contribution to victory in Burma but also to the good work done 'in these troubled days of peace'. He sent Park a personal letter the same day:

> You came here with a reputation for not being easy to get on with as far as the other Services were concerned . . . and I need not assure you that if ever I hear anyone say that again I shall clout him very hard over the head, for no one could have gone more out of their way than you have to be not only cooperative and helpful but loyal in every way and in the highest sense of the word. I made this very clear to Peter Portal and I shall certainly tell Arthur Tedder as well when I see him. I shall also return to the attack over the question of your substantive rank which I feel you should get, regardless of whether my recommendation for a 'G' [GCB: Grand Cross of the Bath] is accepted or not.

His recommendation was, however, accepted and on 24 May he wrote again to congratulate Park. It might interest him to know, Mountbatten said, that the only two GCBs so far given in South-East Asia had gone to Giffard and Somerville, 'both of them without my knowledge or concurrence'. He had tried and failed to get them for Peirse and Slim, so Park was the first and only recipient recommended by Mountbatten: 'this is the finest award that the Services have to offer. In your case it is so particularly well merited that I am doubly delighted.'

Well merited it might be, but it carried no income and at that stage of his career Park was thinking more of the money he needed to earn in the future than of tributes, however glowing, to the deeds he had done in the past. He wrote to Lord Winster, Minister of Civil Aviation. He expected to be free from September to 'return my energies from the destruction to the construction of things.' It had always been his ambition, he said, to return to his first choice of career – commerce – on finishing his task in the RAF, but he had insufficient capital to go into shipping where he had begun life, nor did he think that shipping would regain its world dominance for the Empire. With his early business training and his long experience of men in all walks of life, he felt he should be valuable to civil aviation in an executive or advisory capacity. At fifty-three, he reckoned on twenty years of constructive work before retiring, 'but even then I shall run my small farm on business lines instead of at a loss.' During his tour of Australia and New Zealand, he would meet all the government officials and businessmen prominent in civil aviation, 'as these contacts may be of value to me later.'

By the end of the year, Park had indeed begun a new career in civil aviation. He had also enjoyed a triumphant tour of his native land that went far to ease the pain of his departure from the service.[7]

CHAPTER EIGHTEEN

South-East Asia Command: Paper Battles

1945 - 1951

In 1945 and 1946 Park was required to submit two despatches on air operations in South-East Asia during his time in command. He was also required to comment on the despatches written by or for Mountbatten and the army commanders and to accept or reject their comments on his own despatches. Although it made sense to have the commanders commit their stories to paper while they were still fresh in their minds and could be subjected to the scrutiny of their peers and those who were directly involved, old wounds were inevitably opened and some bitter inter-service exchanges provoked before mutually acceptable texts were produced. Park entered vigorously into these exchanges, despite his uncertain health and many personal or family worries in the immediate postwar years.

Park's first despatch was requested by Air Commodore T.N. McEvoy, Director of Staff Duties at the Air Ministry, 'to counter-balance the one by General Giffard [C-in-C, 11th Army Group] which was unsatisfactory from the air standpoint.' Assisted by his historical officer, Wing Commander K.H.R. Collard, Park had by August 1945 drafted a despatch on air operations in South-East Asia from 1 June 1944 to the occupation of Rangoon on 2 May 1945. He had not arrived in South-East Asia until the end of February, but no suggestion is recorded that either Peirse or Garrod, the officers who had preceded him, were to be asked for their views on the early period. Three copies were sent to the Air Ministry in November and on 1 December a 'brief review' (fourteen pages) was circulated to thirty-eight addresses within the Air Ministry and to five commands.

The ejection of the Japanese from Burma had been made possible, in Park's view, by air power – both air supply and direct support of land forces. Air supply depended on good ground organization. Unfortunately, this had not been appreciated by the army authorities, whose attitude had been consistently parsimonious and compared poorly with that of the Americans. They had understood more clearly than British commanders that once air superiority had been achieved, the availability of airfields and transport aircraft governed the maintenance and supply of forces in the fields. The Japanese had failed to appreciate the importance of the air supply organization and had used their fighters only against forward troops. As for direct support, the Hurricane proved very effective. Visual control posts had lent extra flexibility and accuracy to air operations planned with ground forces, but the 'cab rank' (standing patrols) system had been wasteful. Given the meagre ground intelligence, regular and detailed photo-reconnaissance had been essential and the effort devoted to the support of guerrillas and clandestine operations had been justified.

On 29 March 1946, the War Office, having obtained a comment on Park's despatch from Giffard and Leese, submitted a critique to the Air Ministry. Throughout the despatch, it said, there was a tendency to attribute the basic success of the Burma campaign to air superiority. However, in the army's view the turning-point had been the defeat of the Japanese at Imphal by the Fourteenth Army. In order to conduct operations after Imphal, Leese had been convinced that he had to remain at Barrackpore (Calcutta), in close touch with Stratemeyer of Eastern Air Command. Both Leese and Giffard believed that Mountbatten had been wrong to take Park to Kandy instead of coming to Calcutta with Leese.

The value of air supply was appreciated, continued the War Office, and it therefore regretted that Park should set out for posterity 'a series of small faults on the Army side of air supply.' There was much to learn in dealing with a problem never previously visualized, let alone tackled. The comparison with the Americans was unfair because they worked from bases established months before and lavishly equipped; the British had had to make do from hastily built bases stocked as best as possible. Numerous changes to Park's text were suggested, four of which had particular substance. One, that the prime cause of Japan's defeat in Burma had been the victory of the British infantry; air supply and support had not been, in the army's opinion, the prime cause. Eventually and reluctantly, Park accepted this. Two, although Park had said, justly, that without air supply the campaign could not have been successful, it was equally true that without 'horrific efforts' by the army to provide airfields, fuel and bomb dumps, air supply could never have been exploited. Park accepted that point more willingly. Three, he had given the impression that the construction of the Ledo Road (the line of communication for Stilwell's Chinese-American forces) had been an army decision. The War Office insisted that it had been a political decision, made before the value of air supply had been proved. Although the road had been begun by the British, American engineers had continued and completed it and it had been entirely under American control. Park accepted that correction without reserve. And four, although 'cab rank' may have been uneconomical from the RAF's viewpoint, it had been quicker and more effective from the army's. Park recognized the argument, though he disagreed with it.

The War Office critique was sent to Park who replied to McEvoy from his sickbed in Singapore on 23 April: 'for the sake of pleasing the War Office I have agreed to eleven of the twenty-one suggested amendments,' he wrote; he would not agree to the others because 'they concern matters of principle which I am not altogether surprised that General Leese does not agree with.' The air had been subjected to more interference from the higher army command in Burma than elsewhere, he continued, even though it had played a more vital part there than in any other campaign of the entire war. That had been Leese's doing. Leese had insisted on keeping his headquarters at Calcutta against the express wish of Mountbatten and the other Cs-in-C; he had not been satisfied to state what he needed from air support but had interfered frequently in the method of executing air operations; he had tried to lay down a rate of effort for squadrons even though he was ignorant of the practicalities involved; he had once issued a strategic bombing directive without reference to Park despite the existence of an inter-service bombing target committee; he had ordered the withdrawal of a tactical group from Burma to India on his own initiative; and he had complained direct to the War Office that his operations were being hampered by shortage of air supply – a view not shared by other army commanders. After the capture of Rangoon, Park reminded McEvoy, Leese had been dismissed because of his failure to cooperate with the air, the navy or GHQ India.

By judicious rewording, McEvoy gradually whittled down the points on which Park refused to budge until he reached a stage where he suggested that Tedder himself might press Park to compromise. On reflection, however, he admitted that Park was concerned to protect the RAF from unfair blame and there was no good reason why his differences with Leese should not be officially recorded. He minuted G.S. Whittuck, a senior Air Ministry official, in November 1946 to say that the RAF was not bound to accept all proposed amendments to its despatches. 'I think Park has gone far enough in the emasculation of his despatch to cover up General Leese's many offences against the Royal Air Force . . . and I think we ought to inform the War Office that we cannot ask him to go further.' But Whittuck (a civil servant who had to deal frequently with his opposite numbers in the War Office) persuaded McEvoy to ask Park to give way yet again and Park – by now weary of the whole affair and preparing for an important mission in Argentina – did so.[1]

Park's second despatch, on air operations in South-East Asia from 3 May to 12 September 1945, suffered similar emasculation. He completed it in August 1946 and copies were circulated early in November. As in his first despatch, Park stressed the importance of air supply, not only during hostilities but after the Japanese surrender, when enemy-held territories had to be reoccupied and the relief and liberation of ex-prisoners begun. He dealt in detail with casualty evacuation, operations with clandestine forces, the excellent work of the RAF Regiment in guarding airfields, the need for greater squadron mobility, differences of opinion with the army and – not least – the effect of Tiger Force, Britain's proposed contribution to the Pacific War, on ACSEA.

The War Office submitted its critique to the Air Ministry in March 1947, noting 'with some surprise the paucity of references in this despatch to the part played by the ground forces and the fact that many of such references are of a disparaging kind.' It asked for the deletion of a comment that army demands were considered excessive by Mountbatten and his naval and air commanders: the comment was 'unnecessary in an Air Despatch whether true or not.' Similarly, Park's reference to 'the strong disinclination of the Army to accept responsibility for breakdowns in air supply' should be cut. 'Whether true or not, this statement is thought to be unnecessary.' The War Office also wanted Park to cut: 'Army for army, the Japanese could no doubt have held their own' and 'Our army advanced on the wings of our air force in Burma.' The despatch was written in 'a rather journalistic style' it complained, and verbatim extracts from signals sent 'in the heat of battle' ought to be omitted – those which mentioned 'little swine', 'dead bodies' and 'stink'. Despatches, so the War Office believed, should be tastefully composed and non-controversial.

Slim defended the army's insistence on an amphibious landing in southern Burma to support the advance on Rangoon from the north. The operation had necessarily been planned weeks before, he said, when it had been thought that the Japanese might make a suicide stand in the city. Slim had also wanted to split the defending forces and it would have been wrong, in his view, to risk a failure merely because subsequent operations might have had to be delayed. It was true, as Park complained, that airfields had not been prepared quickly by army engineers, but Slim had simply not had enough engineers for all the tasks required of them. Roads, railways and bridges competed with airfields for labour. Park's claim that air forces had isolated the Japanese Army in Burma was also true, but only in regard to sea transport from the end of 1943; the Siam Railway had continued to move Japanese troops throughout 1944 and while Allied air action had made troop movements into and about Burma difficult, it had never stopped them altogether.

McEvoy sent Park copies of the comments made on his despatch, emphasizing his belief that although the Air Ministry should do its best to meet objections, for the sake of inter-service harmony, it should stand firm on matters of principle and that the original despatch must be kept whatever changes were made in the version to be published. Park replied that he had, in fact, paid high tribute to the army in this despatch and therefore took the strongest exception to the War Office's reference to 'disparaging' remarks. When dealing with air supply, he had mentioned only *one or two* of the numerous difficulties he had experienced in dealing with the supply branch at Leese's headquarters. As for the 'paucity of references' to the ground forces, he was dealing with the period after the fall of Rangoon when there had been no major land operations in Burma.

In answer to Slim, Park pointed out that the army had not given airfield construction nearly as high a priority as was customary between 1942 and 1944 in the Mediterranean theatre. The air forces had proved effective in isolating Burma from *adequate* supplies and reinforcements from Siam and Japan. In his efforts not to overstress the part played by the air forces, Slim had publicly thanked his Quartermaster Major-General in June 1945 for the success of the air supply and transport system in Burma. That incident, said Park, was typical of the deprecatory attitude of the army's high command in SEAC. On the other hand, from corps headquarters down, the army had been outspoken in its praise of air force efforts in Burma. As for the distasteful remarks, they all came from *army* signals, but Park agreed to cut them if it would please the War Office.

More seriously, he emphasized the fact that great quantities of stores and supplies stockpiled in many places in Burma had either simply been left behind or again airlifted forward as a direct result of inflexible army planning. Park had written that the unexpected collapse of Japan had led to a most confused military situation in several countries. The War Office bridled at the word 'confused', but such was the situation, Park repeated, and no reflection whatever on the army, 'which seems to be super-sensitive to any remarks except of open praise.' The War Office wanted to cut his comment that the award of the humble Defence Medal (intended for those who completed at least three years' wartime service in the United Kingdom) was both inappropriate and inadequate for those who had served in India and Ceylon. It was true, Park said, that most of them had been far from the firing line, but they had endured prolonged separation from families and friends in conditions of acute physical discomfort. The War Office admitted that his reference was accurate – but it was also 'controversial'. Park replied that his words recorded the disappointment of a majority of RAF personnel in those countries, a disappointment that had contributed to the subsequent unrest. Finally, the War Office objected to Park's description of narrow roads choked for miles with slow-moving army transport. As usual, the accuracy of his point was not disputed; it was the fact of 'unnecessary general criticism' to which the War Office objected. But he regarded his criticisms as containing lessons for the future and refused to withdraw them.

McEvoy was much exercised during June 1947 in discussions with a host of Air Ministry officials as to how far Park could, or should, be pressed to accept War Office amendments. Mountbatten's opinion would have to prevail in some cases; in other cases, rewriting might disguise the differences. Whittuck replied to the War Office's critique, summarizing Park's arguments and pointing out that he had accepted as many as fifty-four of the suggested amendments and seven more with only slight changes; he was unable to accept the remaining fourteen. The War Office replied on 15 August, expressing appreciation of Park's willingness to permit so many changes to his text.[2]

The War Office sent a despatch by Leese to the Air Ministry for comment in February 1947. Park was among those invited to read it and in May sent McEvoy nine pages of comment. He was by then retired and had no need to concern himself this closely with Leese's despatch. Neither Vincent nor Bandon, still serving and both longer in the East than Park, took it so seriously when it was referred to them. Moreover, Park had been deeply involved in Argentina during recent months in work that was important, taxing and unfamiliar.

Like other commentators, Park noticed that although Leese praised the air supply squadrons he rarely mentioned the work of close support squadrons in his many long accounts of land battles. Even air supply was relegated to the administrative section of his despatch. He actually placed air transport second to *mule* transport as a means of obtaining mobility for his troops in Burma, even though he admitted that about ninety per cent of all the army's supplies were carried by air into Burma.

Leese's claim that a joint decision had been made to carry out a seaborne assault on Rangoon was not true, wrote Park: the decision had been made by Leese alone, without consulting the air, the navy or even Mountbatten. That high-handed action was the more surprising because Leese had shortly before declared that he did not consider such an assault necessary and so Park and the navy commander had made their plans accordingly. Leese had expected that supplies brought in by sea would adequately supplement those airlifted, and that was why more than half the transport squadrons had been withdrawn in June and sent to rest and refit prior to moving to China. No one expected it to take so long to restore Rangoon port to full working order, nor had Mountbatten and Park expected that the army would retain such large forces there. Those were the reasons, said Park, why the air had been unable to meet army demands in June 1945.

Park had provided the Air Ministry with a great deal of ammunition wrote McEvoy, though his comments had been 'slightly toned down for the sake of inter-service harmony.' There was general agreement with Park's view that Mountbatten should not have permitted Leese to establish his headquarters in Calcutta, leaving only a liaison staff in Kandy, because thereafter the whole chain of command in SEAC was distorted. That was the root cause of most troubles. Whittuck sent to the War Office in August 1947 a list of forty points for amendment in Leese's despatch. Six months passed before a reply came but, when it did, Leese had agreed 'to the most important' of the amendments suggested.[3]

Mountbatten's despatch was made to run a fierce gauntlet. The buffeting began in February 1946 when Mr J.C. Nerney, of the Air Ministry's historical branch, arrived in Singapore for a conference with ACSEA's historical officers. He told Park how keen he was to see adequate recognition given to the air forces' work in the East and Park agreed to support him. Nerney later met Mountbatten, who said he felt strongly that, in the first draft of his despatch, 'the air action is not accorded the prominence which the campaign justified.' Nerney had therefore arranged for the officer preparing the despatch to establish and maintain liaison with Park's historical section.

In June 1946 Stanley Vincent, formerly head of 221 Group, commented that little credit was given in Mountbatten's draft to the work of his old group. The Japanese left Imphal, he said, not because they were beaten by a superior army but because they were short of ammunition, medical supplies and food as a result of ceaseless air attacks. From Imphal to Rangoon, scarcely a single Japanese position had been captured by the army before it was flattened by aircraft. The field commanders knew this and were suitably grateful; they also appreciated regular reconnaissance and rapid casualty evacuation. The Earl of Bandon made the same points in respect of his old group (224) and its relations with 15 Corps: they had been with them all the way, but their efforts were barely mentioned. Other senior commanders confirmed by their detailed criticism the misgivings which Mountbatten himself had expressed.

George Pirie, Park's former deputy and his successor in Singapore, was appalled at the lack of appreciation shown for the RAF's work after VJ Day. In Hong Kong, the RAF had played a major part in restoring public services. Air operations in the Netherlands East Indies and elsewhere should also be considered. Not least, Mountbatten's despatch should appreciate the grave situation caused by the abrupt end of Lend-Lease. Many American aircraft had been grounded through lack of spares and this had seriously affected airlift operations. The failure to discuss the operations which had been mounted to find, release, succour and transport ex-prisoners particularly distressed Pirie because those operations, in Park's words, were among 'the greatest mercy missions of the war'. The difficulties resulting from the enormous distances between India and the liberated territories were ignored; by March 1946, equipment shortages and delays in moving supplies forward from India were so acute that morale as well as efficiency suffered.

Almost a year later, in September 1947, Mountbatten sent Vincent a copy of the second version of his despatch, rewritten from start to finish 'in conformity with my own personal ideas and wishes'. The result did not impress Vincent, who thought it lacked the breadth and balanced view which one expected from a Supreme Commander. The Air Ministry agreed. There was no summary of the overall effects of air superiority, wrote Group Captain F.G. Brockman, and since Mountbatten had been offered ample information on that subject, it must be taken that the omission was deliberate. The omission of tributes to forces or their commanders, remarked Brockman, contrasted sharply with Mount-batten's frequent references to himself.

Despite Air Ministry protests, Mountbatten refused to accept amendments, but in April 1949 he personally composed a tribute to the RAF, one that was as brief as possible. Throughout 1945, he wrote, it was 'under the bold leadership of ACM Park'. Some other names were also mentioned – again, as briefly as possible. He insisted that his despatch be published before all others, but it was not ready for publication until February 1951. Only then, in the following April, could six other despatches appear, all of which had been gathering dust for years: two by Giffard, the two by Park and one each by Peirse and Leese.[4]

PART FOUR

1946 - 1975

CHAPTER NINETEEN

End of a Career

1946

On 24 February 1946, Douglas Evill, Vice-Chief of the Air Staff, asked Park to spend some time during his official visit to New Zealand in informal talks with the Royal New Zealand Air Force about its postwar plans. What were New Zealand's views, for example, on taking part in air garrisoning in the Far East? Would training be standardized with that of the RAF and other Dominions? What was planned in the way of air defence organization?

In March Park wrote to Sir Leonard Isitt, Chief of the Air Staff, RNZAF, to name the places that he wished to visit and the subjects he could talk about, ending on a characteristic note:

> . . . having had many Dominion and American squadrons serving with me, I am accustomed to informal meetings and gatherings of flying personnel so please don't turn on any ceremonial for normal visits to any of your units unless you particularly want to have a parade to tee up the boys' turnout.

He and Dol landed at Ohakea, near Palmerston North, at 5.20 p.m. on 29 May 1946. Dol had never been to New Zealand and it was more than thirty-one years since Park had left.

The next day, at a luncheon in Wellington, he made the first of numerous speeches. He spoke about a subject always close to his heart: the need to maintain the 'Empire Spirit' in the RAF. British navigation, armament and other training schools would continue, he hoped, to attract men from the Dominions and this would help to ensure a vital standardization in equipment. One of an air force's greatest assets was flexibility, but this would be lost without standardization. His ideal, he said, would be to transfer a New Zealand squadron to Canada at a moment's notice and to operate it there as efficiently as at home. He looked back with great pleasure on his days in Malta, Egypt and the Far East when men from Canada, South Africa and Australia as well as New Zealand had served under him in British uniforms.

237

They had worked together like a good Rugby XV, regardless of shoulder flashes, and this was the spirit which Park hoped to see live on and strengthen.

It was during this first weekend in Wellington that nurse Betty Neill met her famous uncle and his English wife. Betty was instructed by her mother (Park's sister Lily) to be on her best behaviour because Aunt Dol, being English, would certainly be prim and proper. Betty was overwhelmed by Dol: her blue-tinted hair, elegance and boundless sense of fun. Dol asked them what they would like to drink and Lily, very properly, asked for lemonade, but Betty – who had had a long day – asked for whisky. In later years, when Park, Dol and Betty had become firm friends, he would often refer in mock despair to the problems he was having with his hard-drinking niece.

The Parks left Wellington on 1 June and flew to Oamaru, in the South Island, to see James Park. Now eighty-nine and very frail (he had only a few more weeks to live), James was in a nearby hospital. It was there that he saw his youngest son for the first time since he had achieved an international reputation. The Park family enjoyed a long overdue reunion and then, on the 7th, Keith and Dol drove down to Dunedin. He had always taken an interest in his old school – Otago Boys' High – and spoke to the boys during the afternoon. He received a vociferous welcome, partly because of the glamour then surrounding one of the leaders of the Few, partly because it was known that his school record was, in his own assessment, 'undistinguished', and partly because the headmaster gave him a detention card for an offence then thirty-five years old – carving his name on a desk.

That evening, the Parks were accorded a rousing welcome at a civic reception in the Dunedin Town Hall. The notes for Sir Keith's speech on that occasion survive: sixteen main headings and many sub-headings, all typed on a single sheet of paper. He praised Dunedin and spoke of his father, who had taught in the university there for many years; he recalled his own early years and later triumphs, spiced with anecdotes about the great, and ended with a tribute to New Zealand's war effort – providing food and safe bases as well as brave soldiers and airmen. Only his opening words were not rehearsed. For thirty years, he said, when the cheering died down, 'I have been looking forward to coming back to my native land, but never in my wildest dreams did I expect such a regal reception.'

After an exhilarating weekend in Dunedin, reviving memories of people and places often talked about, the Parks returned to Christchurch and then flew to Auckland. In both cities there were civic receptions, guided tours and interviews with the press. On 14 June they visited Thames, Sir Keith's birthplace. He confessed that he was overwhelmed by his welcome; everywhere he went, he said, he felt like a travelling circus. The Parks were certainly travelling. From Thames they returned to Auckland, a five-hour drive, and the next day (15 June) celebrated Sir Keith's first birthday in New

Zealand for thirty-two years by driving to Tangiteroria, near Dargaville, to meet a boyhood friend and talk about ancient fishing trips until it was time to press on to Whangarei and another reception.

On the 19th, almost at the end of his tour, he made his most revealing speech. Appropriately, it was delivered at a meeting of the Royal Empire Society.

> War [he said] is a dirty, rough game, but people will fight if there is within their hearts revenge, fear or jealousy. I am not a particularly religious person, but I have seen so many thousands of fine young men wiped out that I believe we must have a great religious revival to prevent another war. It is no use banishing war from our thoughts. War will not be prevented if we do. It is more likely to be stopped by open discussion. When economic, political and ideological theories and ways of living clash and diplomats get into a mess, they throw the burden to the sailors, soldiers and airmen, who settle the dispute in the cruellest and crudest way.

Park may not have considered himself 'a particularly religious person', but no one who knew him well would have agreed. He made no display of his beliefs and only rarely mentioned them in private, let alone in public, but he remained throughout his life a convinced and practising member of the Church of England.

Park's official report on his tour revealed that political and service leaders in New Zealand were ready to fall in with the Air Ministry's wishes in regard to standardization of methods and equipment. The morale and discipline of the RNZAF appeared good: it 'is not politically conscious and is quite popular with the people and the press', but it suffered from a shortage of skilled, experienced ground staff as a result of rapid demobilization. Ex-servicemen were highly organized and therefore the government appeared to be doing more for them than was the case in Britain or Australia. Although several secondary industries had developed during the war, New Zealand remained primarily agricultural and unless the government imported more labour, these industries would expand at the expense of agriculture, 'which may not accord with Empire Economic Planning'. There was abundant food, but many people would reduce their consumption: one, if only they were asked by the Government and, two, if they were assured that food so saved would go to the population of Great Britain and not to ex-enemy countries in Europe'.[1]

On 21 June Park left for Sydney and spent ten days in Australia before returning to Singapore. As in New Zealand, he had discussions with political and service leaders about air force plans. Morale and discipline in the RAAF were poor, he thought. Although there were many fine junior officers, lack of confidence in the service's future was widespread and there was little of the camaraderie seen and felt in the RAF and the RNZAF. The press was unfriendly to the fighting services and not interested in his comments on the vital part played by air power during the war; it was not even interested in Australia's contribution to victory.

He wrote to Dan Sullivan, Minister of Supply in New Zealand, from the Cameron Highlands in northern Malaya on 8 July. 'The folks in Australia,' he said, 'were most hospitable but not in the same charming way as in my own native land. . . . Perhaps a bit ostentatious after the nice informality of many of our engagements in dear old NZ.' He had worked his way so high, Park continued, that there were no jobs for him in the RAF. Out of sight had meant out of mind, and the air chiefs in Europe had soon picked up any jobs that were going while he was busy 'mucking about' with Java, Sumatra and Japan. He planned to remain in England for a few months to write his memoirs and then sell up and return to 'dear old NZ'. His wife had loved 'our country', he ended, and Park wanted to invest his energies, time and small capital there rather than in some strange land.[2]

From Singapore the Parks embarked for England on 16 July and during the voyage Sir Keith wrote to Mountbatten. He felt confident that Tedder would have agreed to his substantive promotion, but the recommendation must have been blocked by Slessor: 'He caused so much anger to be vented against me, you will recollect, over your rejecting his nominee, Master THORNTON.' (Nothing is now known about this incident.) Park still felt unfairly treated over his rank, in comparison with other officers whose records were inferior. 'If the Air Ministry persist in not acting upon your recommendation, would you advise me to mention the matter to His Majesty when I report on return to England from foreign service?' The Parks landed in England on 3 August and Sir Keith wrote again to Mountbatten on the 9th to say that he had taken his advice and spoken to Tedder, who was prepared to tackle the Treasury. It would help, Tedder had said, if Mountbatten confirmed his earlier recommendation. He did so at once: 'I must say once again that I feel that as Richard Peirse was retired with the rank and pension of an Air Chief Marshal, it would surely be an injustice to give Keith Park less favourable treatment, especially in the light of their respective service.'

Early in September, Park received formal notification of his retirement. He would get fifty-six days' terminal leave plus fifty-four days in recognition of his overseas service since the outbreak of war. In effect, his retirement began on 20 December 1946. The Air Council granted him permission to retain the rank of Air Chief Marshal and expressed 'warm appreciation of the distinguished services which you have rendered throughout your career in the RAF and more particularly during the recent war.' A kindly note from Trenchard helped soften the blow: 'I am more than sorry to hear that you are finished,' he wrote, 'but the young must have their turn, though it is hard for men of your age to start afresh. Come to lunch with me when you are next in London.'

He was medically examined in London on 16 September. The doctors noted that he had undertaken a strenuous tour of New Zealand and Australia before he had fully recovered from amoebic dysentery and although he had put on a little weight during that tour and returned to Singapore feeling rather better, he still lacked energy. The voyage home had not helped him and since his arrival in England he had been working at the Air Ministry and was exhausted by 6 p.m. He was sleeping poorly and losing weight: 136 pounds, in trousers and shoes, was much too light for a man of six foot three inches. His loss of flesh was so severe that he found sitting or lying on any unpadded surface very uncomfortable. In his right lung the doctors observed (without further comment) that there was a metallic object. They concluded that he was suffering from general debility as a result of arduous duty overseas and should be granted sick leave as from 1 September and re-examined on 9 October.

Here the doctors erred. An officer whose retirement had been decided was only entitled to sick leave if there was a reasonable chance of his return to duty. Park thought that because his illness had been contracted months before he was officially informed that he was to retire, his retirement leave should not begin until he was passed fit for duty, presumably on 9 October. The Air Ministry found, however, that the decision to retire him had been made before he fell ill and thereby saved itself at least five weeks' sick pay.

Praise, unlike money, was never in short supply. Viscount Stansgate, who had succeeded Sinclair as Secretary of State for Air in August, wrote to Park on 30 September to convey to him the thanks of His Majesty on his long and distinguished service. During the grim days of the Battle of Britain, Stansgate added, 'and later in command of Malta, you played a great and active part in the organization of victory against odds which were at times overwhelming. No one did more to deserve to be raised to the position of C-in-C, as you eventually were, and in the final stages of the war to be the only airman to hold a major command against an active enemy.'

Unfortunately, he had not done enough to earn the full pension of an Air Chief Marshal. He retained the *rank*, but received only the pension of an Air Marshal plus one-third of the increment for an Air Chief Marshal. Not all the efforts of Tedder, Mountbatten and even Slessor were sufficient to extract from the Treasury the other two-thirds. The part he played in helping to rescue the world from German, Italian and Japanese tyrannies may be debated endlessly, but there can be no doubt that he was entitled (by qualifying service) to the full pension of an Air Chief Marshal and he never got it.[3]

Some shocking news about Park's son Colin became public property on 8 October 1946. *The Times* reported that at a Court Martial in Iserlohn in Germany on the 7th two British army officers had pleaded guilty to charges of gross negligence leading to manslaughter in fatally wounding a ten-year-old

German boy by using the guns of an armoured car. Captain Colin Park, aged twenty-one, of the Black Watch, and Lieutenant John Armstrong (twenty-two) of the 11th Hussars, had offered no defence except that on the night in question, 3 August, they had been drinking and were unaware that anyone had been hit when they fired the guns during a drive from Mohne See club towards Neheim. Mr Basil Nield, King's Counsel, pleaded in mitigation the men's excellent war and character records up until that night. Captain Park, he said had been a member of the War Crimes Investigation Branch of the Rhine Army and had suffered a head wound in Burma. Nield raised the question of why he had been on duty and not undergoing treatment. In Berlin, on 11 November, the findings were confirmed and both men were dismissed the service.

On the day following the report of Colin's Court Martial, Sir Keith underwent his last service medical examination. The doctor reported that he had definitely improved and put on five pounds. He was working and sleeping better and considered fit for ground duty in the United Kingdom. Next day, 10 October, he took his place at a press conference with Mountbatten, Slim and Power to discuss the Burma campaign and a forthcoming account of it by Frank Owen of the *Daily Mail*. Park began his speech lightly with a tribute to Fleet Street and a small joke. He then emphasized the value of a free press. It has played a far bigger part in the Second World War than in the First and if commanders had had to face press conferences and explain their aims in the first war, some muddles might have been avoided. He thought the correspondents in SEAC had done well, except the one who had written 'as I flew over Burma' while downing a burra peg in Calcutta. He congratulated Owen, thanked the Press Club for a good lunch and sat down. Owen told him two days later that his speech 'exactly hit the nail on the head. It was what this band of cynical ruffians needed to hear. I am assured that with this team of speakers we could win any by-election, even as Liberals. In fact, the current summing-up is "What a hell of a Front Bench!"'

Churchill wrote to Park on the 16th, enclosing an account he had written of his visit to Uxbridge on 15 September 1940. He would be obliged, he wrote, if Park would look through it and 'correct me on the technical detail, because of course I paid only three or four visits and I may not have depicted the organization of the Control Centre in proper terms. This was a heart-shaking moment in our struggle for life.' So it was that on the 18th, with memories of his – and Churchill's – finest hour freshly revived, Park was received by the King at Buckingham Palace to mark his relinquishing of his last command and to be invested with the insignia of a Knight Grand Cross of the Most Honourable Order of the Bath (GCB).

He wrote to Tedder on 7 November to thank him for giving his name to Shenton Thomas for the post of Director-General of the Royal Overseas League (founded to promote, maintain and expand friendship and cooperation among Commonwealth countries) but he had just heard that the council had decided not to give the appointment to an officer of such high rank. Life was full of surprises, said Park. This was not the first time recently that the high rank given him during the war had been more of a hindrance than a help in landing a good job outside the service. Though disappointed, he was not downhearted or idle for an hour, despite living 'in the wilds of Sussex'; his mail was heavy and there was always his book.

'Even my agent said my chapter on the Sicily Campaign is good,' Park told Group Captain L.V. Dodds (formerly his public relations officer in ACSEA) the same day, 'and I know the one on Malta is better. The chapters on Dunkirk and the Battle of Britain will be better still as I wrote good despatches on both and have lots of good material.' Would Dodds go ahead and tell the world that Park was leaving the RAF and intending to go into business? For the next couple of months, however, he was going to stick to his writing, 'as I feel sure that I must write the book now, this winter, or I shall get absorbed in some new activity. Then the desire, the urge and the opportunity may pass never to return. That would be a pity as I now find I have a good story to tell.'

Within ten days, 'the desire, the urge and the opportunity' had passed – to his immense relief – because he was asked to represent the Hawker Siddeley Group 'in connection with commercial negotiations in the Argentine'. It was a wonderful opportunity not only to start a new career in aviation, but also to revive his hard-earned linguistic skills and his military, diplomatic and social contacts in South America. It was then just ten years since he had left Argentina. Not too long to pick up old threads, given his rise to eminence during the earth-shaking events of that decade.[4]

CHAPTER TWENTY

Argentina Revisited

1947

Many of the notes sounded ten years earlier by Park in his reports from Argentina were echoed in October 1946 by Air Commodore W.K. Beisiegel, Air Attaché in Buenos Aires, in a letter to the Air Ministry. The importance of sending top men to Argentina, he wrote, was realized in the fields of commerce, banking or railways, but not in aviation. It was impossible to compete with the United States in the production of glossy brochures, but famous people could be sent out whose presence would have an 'important and far-spreading effect . . . on the easily flattered Latin American temperament.' Britain was trying to sell aviation equipment in a very large potential market 'on a shoestring which is now fraying badly under American pressure'. Beisiegel's letter was widely circulated by the Air Ministry. Whether or not Hawker Siddeley was directly influenced by it in deciding to employ Park, his appointment certainly filled the bill as far as Beisiegel was concerned.

On the afternoon of 4 December, Park called on Sir Orme Sargent, the Permanent Under-Secretary of State for Foreign Affairs. Sargent had been forewarned by J.V.T. Perowne, head of the South American Department of the Foreign Office, that he would ask about the sale of arms to Latin America. Sargent should therefore be advised that Britain regarded herself as 'uninhibited in principle' from supplying arms to any Latin American state except Argentina and Santo Domingo. As for these two, a 'gentleman's agreement' had been made with the United States, which was holding Britain to it despite the embarrassment it caused. Its existence was widely suspected, but had never been publicly admitted. The terms were interpreted as literally as possible to permit Britain to sell articles 'generally civilian in character, although they may be capable of military uses'. Perowne informed Sir Rex Leeper, the ambassador in Argentina, on 7 December that Park's Spanish was fairly fluent and that he had been acquainted with Perón when he was no more than an instructor at the Buenos Aires military school. On the 20th, the first day of his new life as a civilian, the Parks happily embarked for Buenos Aires.[1]

On 8 January 1947 Park had a successful interview with the Argentinian Minister of Aviation. The questions of supplying aircraft and building a factory were raised and Park, who was shortly to meet Perón, was clearly regarded as empowered by Hawker Siddeley to sign a contract. A few days later, Park wrote to Max Aitken at the *Sunday Express* office in Fleet Street from his hotel in Buenos Aires. He and Dol, he wrote, had had a grand reception, 'much better than we got when we returned to England after five years' successful campaigning in the Mediterranean and in the Far East.' On that occasion Slessor's department had said that the Prime Minister was too busy to see him, but the President of Argentina, 'who is just as busy as Mr Attlee', had given Park a forty-five minute interview. They had discussed politics and economics – without an interpreter – and Perón had invited Park to dinner. He expected his mission to be completed by May and looked forward to seeing Aitken then. He hoped to take up one or two directorships in England, but that depended on what prospects they offered 'of useful and interesting work, that will take me abroad occasionally.'

On 24 January he wrote to Roy Dobson, Managing Director of Avro, part of the Hawker Siddeley Group, who had asked if the Argentinians were really serious about a deal. Park thought they were and sent him confidential information to use when dealing with the British Ministry of Supply. Evans, Thornton, the group's agents in Buenos Aires, also wrote to Dobson that day. Matters had reached deadlock, they reported, due to their inability to promise supply of any combat aircraft within a guaranteed period. Several private talks had taken place in an attempt to find a way to resume negotiations, but nothing had come of them. A meeting, intended to be final, had been held on the 22nd. Park had recommended that the request for an export licence be lifted from the commercial to the diplomatic level and that had been done. Evans, Thornton had also agreed to draw up and sign an *ad referendum* contract, valid for three months, as a means of opening detailed negotiations. They realized that the contract was no more than 'a bold statement', since they had acted without the group's technical or financial advice, but that advice could follow because the contract would be 'as flexible as we are allowed to make it, and will be subject to your approval.'

A Foreign Office memorandum on 'Combat Aircraft for Argentina' appeared on 28 January. In view of the expected end of the gentleman's agreement with the United States regarding the supply of military material to Argentina, British firms were authorized to tender for ships and aircraft. Hawker Siddeley had been approached by the Argentine Air Ministry for large quantities of civil and military aircraft. Negotiations were proceeding and Park was in Buenos Aires for that purpose. He and the Argentinians, thought the Foreign Office, had in mind 200 Sea Fury fighters, 30 Lincoln bombers, 200 Meteors and 50 Meteor trainers. All told, the deal should be worth £10–£12 million. In fact, Park and two representatives of Evans Thornton signed a secret *ad referendum* contract that day worth £18.5 million to supply 380 Meteors, 20 Meteor trainers and 30 Lincolns. Some aircraft were to be imported complete, some assembled locally and the balance totally manufactured in Argentina; spares to a value of one-fifth of the contract were to be supplied. The contract gave Hawker Siddeley ninety days' priority over its competitors. 'This must be the work of Sir Keith Park,' commented N. H.C. Bruce of the Foreign Office. 'It is enterprising but it forces our hand rather unnecessarily.' A minute on the whole question, he said, was under consideration by the Secretary of State for Foreign Affairs and action must await his decision.[2]

The contract had been signed for two reasons, Park told Dobson on 3 February: the imminent lifting of the embargo and Argentine aversion to being trapped into standardization on American equipment. Having persuaded the Argentinians to buy British aircraft, his next task was to advise them how to organize and expand their air force to make proper use of those aircraft. The air force had been a separate arm for only two years and a British mission was badly needed to offset growing American influence. The embassy, however, opposed a mission, ostensibly in case it infringed the Monroe Doctrine, but actually, thought Park, because it would cause more work.

The United States was informed that as from 6 February Britain would no longer consider herself bound by the gentleman's agreement. Perowne thought news of the contract secured by Park should not be suppressed. It was worth a great deal and the Foreign Office would cut a poor figure if it became known that it was impeding acceptance of such a valuable order. But what of the danger of an arms race in Latin America? Britain needed hard currency from Argentina even though she was not her most favoured Latin American state; Britain also needed to import food from Argentina and her neutrality in the war had led the United States to deprive Argentina of the modern aircraft supplied to her neighbours. Perowne therefore offered these conclusions: Britain's hand should not be forced by Park's contract – but neither should Britain yield to the Americans or spurn customers, and the Foreign Office should authorize Hawker Siddeley to go ahead – on the understanding that no export licence could be granted.

E.W.G. Haynes of the Ministry of Supply wrote to the Air Ministry on 14 February. His ministry, he said, attached enormous importance to the Argentine market. It offered great scope for British industry and Britain could get in on the ground floor. If a factory were once established to assemble and manufacture British aircraft, there was every hope that Argentine aviation, civil and well as military, would be closely linked to Britain for many years to come. Haynes therefore wanted to enlist the Air

Ministry's support in his pressure on the Foreign Office to approve both sale and factory. The latter, thought Haynes, would be a definite strategic advantage in any future war. 'A source of supply in Argentina could, I suggest, prove to be of the very greatest value in the defence of Africa and the Middle East.'

Haynes reminded the Foreign Office that in August 1946 he had wanted to invite the Argentinian Minister of Aviation, Brigadier de la Colina, to visit the air show at Radlett, but the Foreign Office had put him off in case this upset the Americans. Park had now reported that Colina expected to visit Europe in spring 1947 and would welcome an official invitation to England. Much agitated debate followed on Foreign Office minute sheets about the implications of such an invitation until at length it was agreed that all might be well because *civil* aircraft were displayed at Radlett. Even so, American opinion should be sounded.

Beisiegel informed the Air Ministry on 26 February that he and Park had recently entertained Colina to lunch. Colina wanted to model the Argentine Air Force on RAF lines and if the Hawker Siddeley deal went through it was clearly in British interests to see that Argentinian pilots were properly trained by British instructors. The best way to do that would be to send out a training mission. If Colina were invited to England, he could help to arrange this. The embassy in Buenos Aires sent a copy of this letter to the Foreign Office, urging an invitation. 'The interests at stake are very large and we just cannot afford to be backward in taking every opportunity of securing the largest possible share of the immensely valuable Argentinian aircraft market.'[3]

Park had agreed to stay in Argentina for up to six months if necessary to obtain a contract. At the end of February, however, he wrote to Dobson wondering whether there was any point in his staying on after a final contract had been signed, within the next two months. As soon as the provisional contract had been signed, he had given up the suite of rooms arranged by Dobson's agents, but even living quietly 'in two rooms looking into the back side of a block of flats' expenses were heavy. He would like to return to England by sea because the recent hot weather had brought on a mild attack of the dysentery which had led to his being ordered home from Singapore the previous summer. By giving lectures in Spanish and writing articles for the daily papers he was doing all he could to encourage the build-up of the tiny Argentine Air Force, but this was work for an RAF mission. He had asked Tedder to appoint such a mission because it should lead to orders for British aircraft. At present, there was an American mission in Argentina which had no competition.

Dobson asked Park to stay on, if his health permitted, but said it would be wonderful if he was returning to see Tedder about going back as head of an RAF mission. Park, however, had already considered and rejected that possibility. 'Although I would be happy to take over and command the

Argentine Air Force for a few years, to put it on its feet, I would not be attracted with the idea of being Head of a Mission having only advisory functions.' He had arranged to leave Buenos Aires by sea early in May and should be home by the end of the month. After a week in London, he would return to his cottage in Sussex to get on with his book. When it was finished, he would sell up and go out to South Africa, 'where there are better business openings than in poor old England.'

Early in March the Foreign Office signalled the ambassadors in Washington and Buenos Aires to make clear to them its position on the sale of aircraft and other weapons in Latin America generally and Argentina in particular. Britain needed to earn hard currency, especially by the sale of aircraft while the present sellers' market lasted. These sales would keep Britain's own industry going and thereby contribute to her defence. They would also give Britain influence over the states she supplied. Britain should be candid with the Americans about her financial needs and defence interests, about her needs for food which Argentina could supply and, not least, about Latin American reluctance to be tied to United States suppliers. Park was pressing for a decision and it must be recognized that he was himself under pressure, that the Americans would step in if Britain failed, and that the provisional contract expired on 28 April.[4]

By 17 April Park had completed a memorandum entitled 'The Battle of Buenos Aires' to help two representatives of Hawker Siddeley sent to conclude a real contract. The Minister of War, he wrote, had told him the day before that he had practically no close-support aircraft and the week before the Minister of Marine had told him that he was desperately short of aircraft for the British carriers he intended to buy this year. Argentina had been buying American aircraft for its civil airlines, but Park hoped to sell forty-five Ansons and was meeting the Director of Civil Aviation that morning to see if there were any other openings.

Under 'Factors in Our Favour', he wrote that Perón had told him in January that his five-year plan included the establishment of heavy industry, including an aircraft industry, to make Argentina less dependent on foreign products. Perón wanted the British to help set up aircraft factories because he thought their airframes and engines the best in the world. His Air and War Ministers thought the same. The American embargo on arms exports to Argentina had not yet been lifted and that was greatly to Britain's advantage. Finally, since Britain had not yet found the money to cover her purchase of Argentine meat for the winter of 1947–8, aircraft sales were in the interest of both countries.

'Factors Not in Our Favour' included the opposition of the Finance Minister to the build-up of armed forces and the great influence of the American ambassador, who had persuaded Perón to accept the help of American engineers and business experts to implement his five-year plan.

The Americans had already supplied surplus air equipment cheaply and would build a factory at their own expense if the government agreed to buy all its output. Not least, the Air Minister objected to certain clauses in Hawker Siddeley's contract – prices subject to variation, for example, and the absence of penalty clauses should Hawker Siddeley fail to deliver as agreed.

The following day, Colina told Park that a firm order depended on twelve Meteors being available to fly to Argentina on National Day (9 July). Park explained that it would be impossible for the Gloster Aircraft Company (part of Hawker Siddeley) to deliver in time. Colina then asked if the Air Ministry would divert to Argentina Meteors intended for the RAF. Park agreed to enquire. Various Foreign Office officials exchanged waspish remarks about Latin arrogance and love of vain display and agreed that Colina was hustling Park. On 1 May he was informed that the Air Ministry would release twelve Meteors at once. The British Trade Delegation then in Moscow used that decision as a lesson for the Russians: Argentina had provided food and would now get aircraft, the Russians had not provided timber and would therefore not get the aircraft they wanted.

The Ministry of Supply, meanwhile, had formally advised Hawker Siddeley that if a firm order for the aircraft mentioned in Park's contract was obtained, an export licence would be granted. As Park told Dobson, by starting at the top, with Perón, he automatically got the authorities seriously interested in British aircraft. An agreement was signed on 5 May to supply 100 Meteors and thirty Lincolns, plus spares to a value of up to thirty per cent of the contract. Twelve Meteors were to be delivered by the end of May, the rest were to be delivered in five batches by September 1948 and an option to purchase a further 300 was agreed.

Park remained in Buenos Aires until the contract was signed and then caught a ship at Montevideo which reached London on 29 May. He was glad of the sea voyage to recover from the shock and pain of having all his top teeth extracted in hospital because the doctors had decided that bad teeth were responsible for his 'tummy troubles' in Buenos Aires. An undated typescript survives in which he reflected briefly on 'Argentina Revisited'. He commended the ambassador, Leeper, for his efforts on Hawker Siddeley's behalf. In the old days, he wrote, he well remembered the horror one ambassador had shown at the mere suggestion that he personally should assist his commercial secretary in a trade matter. Before Park had returned to Argentina, his impression was that the Perón whom he first met in 1936 had become an American Mussolini. Actually, he seemed charming and friendly, but Park was well aware of the violence and corruption endemic under his rule.

American reaction to news of the aircraft deal was mild and on 10 May the Foreign Office asked Leeper to invite Colina to visit England. However, Evita Perón wanted Colina out of office (as Beisiegel informed Park) and he was therefore reluctant to go abroad. Bruce, of the Foreign Office, was keeping a wary eye open for signs of trouble. On 29 May he remarked that so far there had been less press comment than he expected. It was still 'explosive material', he added hopefully, and 'there may well be fireworks'. As it happened, there were none. Lights did not burn in embassy windows far into the night. At least, not on this issue, nor to any more purpose than usual.[5]

CHAPTER TWENTY-ONE

His First, Best Country

1948 - 1975

Such is the patriot's boast, where'er we roam,
His first, best country ever is at home.
Oliver Goldsmith, *The Traveller*

At the end of May 1947, soon after his return to Chichester from Buenos Aires, Park accepted an appointment as Pacific Representative of the Hawker Siddeley Group, to be based in Auckland. His duties would be similar to those he had had in South America as an air attaché in 1934–6: to meet influential people in military, political and commercial circles and gather information to send home. He would also act as a conduit for complaints or requests to the group's head office from customers in his region. During his last months in England he still claimed to be working on a book while in reality planning his return to New Zealand, writing newspaper articles on Argentina and Commonwealth Defence, enjoying the sailing season and, not least, relishing two exceptional public tributes to his past achievements.

The first of these came on 25 June, when he was awarded the honorary degree of Doctor of Civil Laws by Oxford University. This award was made all the sweeter by the company he kept that day: Field Marshal Lord Wavell, General Sir William Slim and Admiral Lord Fraser of North Cape, as well as Lords Oaksey and Goddard, received the same degree. Remembering Park's two years with the university air squadron in 1932–4, the Orator warmly welcomed back 'the bold innovator who first dared take a Vice-Chancellor for a flight, with you, Mr Registrar, flying in attendance!' Indeed, he continued, he had himself been taken up and Park twice looped the loop, 'then skimmed the elm-tops at hair-raising speed while shouting through some stentorian instrument into both my ears at once: "How do you like flying? Isn't it grand?"' His one object had been to make 'us older people' still better disposed towards his young airmen, an heroic generation. 'How keenly, too, his own vision pierced the future, and how single-hearted was his patriotism!'

The second tribute was the work of Sir Eustace Missenden, General Manager of the Southern Railway, who arranged for one of the newly built Light Pacific 'Battle of Britain' class locomotives to bear his name. The *Sir Keith Park* was named by Park at Brighton in September 1947. The first three engines in the class came into service in December 1946, the *Lord Dowding* and the *Sir Keith Park* were next (in January 1947) and the *Lord Beaverbrook* was sixth. As in 1940, Park had Dowding and Beaverbrook at either hand. Of the forty-three engines in the class, only seven bore the names of individuals. The others were the *Winston Churchill*, the *Sir Frederick Pile* (named after the head of Anti-Aircraft Command), the *Sir Archibald Sinclair* and, last but one in the class, the *Sir Trafford Leigh-Mallory*. Sir Quintin Brand, unfortunately, was not commemorated.

Park was in touch with J.D. Heaton Armstrong, Chester Herald, at this time about the design of his arms. He wanted them to allude particularly to the Battle of Britain and Malta and for his motto chose the words 'Look Skywards'. No comment by or to Park on this choice survives and so his biographer may reflect on the significance of looking skywards in his life. As a professional airman and lifelong amateur seaman, he was acutely conscious of the need to seek guidance from the stars, clouds and winds. As a most loyal officer, the words echo the motto of the RAF, *Per Ardua ad Astra*. They invoke aspiration, to reach as high as possible, and they invoke also the heaven beyond the stars, for Park was a devout Christian. On the morning of 4 December, having placed his knightly and personal affairs in order, he was received by the King for the last time at Buckingham Palace to bid him farewell.[1]

A few days later he and Dol, accompanied by their son Ian, his wife Marie and their daughter Keithia (aged five months), sailed from Southampton for New Zealand in the *Akaroa*. They arrived in Auckland on 13 February 1948 and were at once besieged by reporters. Both Parks gave the press the bright, breezy quotes and anecdotes it wanted. Dol was wearing one of Keithia's nappies disguised as a turban – a bizarre fact which she announced with characteristic delight in discountenancing interviewers. Park said that he thought airlines made a fetish of speed at the expense of comfort; mail and freight should travel as fast as possible, but not passengers. He had returned to New Zealand, he said, 'to enter trade': to help New Zealand and Australia to modernize their air forces. They needed modern aircraft to defend themselves and protect Pacific bases. However much they cost, it would be less than the cost of surface vessels and a more effective use of money.

In April he commented on the overall defence policy of New Zealand. The only *new* equipment promised was six frigates for the navy, but the RNZAF needed jet aircraft to replace the obsolete Mosquito. He was more than ever convinced of New Zealand's need to look to its security through high quality equipment compatible with that of its allies because the United Nations had already shown itself to be 'one of our more brilliant failures'. It provided no machinery for the control of atomic weapons and had not even approached the problem of disarmament. If New Zealand still believed the Empire worthwhile, she would have to pull her weight in its support. Britain must be helped to win her economic war because until that was won, fighting services could not be provided with the latest weapons. He urged the dispersal of manpower and industrial resources from Britain to other parts of the Empire. Britain was much more vulnerable to sudden, devastating attack than she had been in 1939 and such a dispersal would enable the Dominions to become self-supporting more quickly, thus reducing the strain on British resources.[2]

Park also spoke in April 1948 of New Zealand's need for a modern well organized and efficiently managed air service, handling both internal and external flights. He advocated a two-part system: fast aircraft to handle mail, perishable freight and a few passengers travelling on urgent business; slower aircraft would suffice for normal passenger traffic, providing a service that was safe, reliable, comfortable and convenient. The National Airways Corporation was, he thought, doing a good job. Its crews were to be commended because they flew without modern navigational aids. Their aircraft must soon be replaced and their airfields greatly improved and moved closer to city centres: Park had visited Wellington recently, he said, and someone had asked him how he had travelled from Auckland. By bus most of the way, he had replied, though the early part had been by air. Wellington airport was then at Paraparaumu, some thirty miles from the city centre.

During the rest of 1948, Park often spoke about New Zealand's aviation problems, military and civil, and in February 1949 he made some notes of a meeting he had had with Sholto Douglas, now Lord Douglas of Kirtleside and a director of the British Overseas Airways Corporation. Douglas told Park, who passed the information on to his employers and to the New Zealand government, that the Australian air force was reasonably efficient, but in need of new aircraft, that both Australia and New Zealand should encourage a greater rate of immigration of Britons and displaced Europeans, and that New Zealand's airfields were the worst in any dominion that Douglas had visited.

Later that month Park addressed the Auckland Chamber of Commerce on the needs of civil aviation. When Pan American Airways introduced their giant Stratocruiser on South Pacific routes, Auckland would be bypassed unless it was provided with an airport of international standard; and if Auckland (the largest city) was bypassed, New Zealand would be bypassed. As early as July 1945 the Civil Aviation Department had declared that Mangere was the best site for such an airport in the Auckland area, but Whenuapai (an RNZAF base) had been made available by the government at no cost to the local authorities. Although Whenuapai was obviously unsuitable for prolonged and increasing civilian use, it was not until

253

February 1951 that the Auckland city council combined with the chamber of commerce to form an International Airport Committee. Park, unable to attend the first meeting, was elected chairman at the second. He was active and persuasive, seeking support from airline operators, technical information from the government, engineers' reports on particular sites, reports on the new airport under construction at Los Angeles, and ways of obtaining support from local bodies.

In the midst of all this activity the Parks learned the shattering news that their younger son, Colin, had been murdered in Malaya. He had been one of three European officers of the Perak Aboriginal Areas Constabulary who were killed on 3 September 1951 when bandits ambushed their raft on the Sungei Plus, a tributary of the Perak river. They had been on a tour of inspection with a native guide when a volley of shots swept the raft. One officer had been killed immediately, the other two had fallen into the river, wounded; the guide, unhurt, swam ashore. On 4 September 1952 Dol wrote to her niece, Betty Neill, 'A year ago today Colin and I died. I include myself as all the best of me died with him. What rubbish people talk about Time healing, it just isn't true, Betty dear.' As for Park, he did what he had always done in the face of disaster, public or personal. He squared his shoulders and got on with his work.

He had talks with various ministers who made it clear to him that the government believed it had exhausted its resources for the present. He was, however, aware of the need to determine a site and secure it against the day when work could begin. By May 1952 a site at Mangere was under investigation, and Park asked the Minister of Works for a survey in July and corresponded with the landowner. In April 1953 he outlined progress over the past year and it was agreed that a new approach – direct to the Prime Minister, S.G. Holland – was needed. Park led a delegation that met Holland in May and in October asked for his confirmation that Mangere was the favoured site. At length, the Auckland city council 'paid the ransom demanded by the Holland Government (assent to a 50/50 government/local bodies share in the cost of building and maintaining the airport) before it would commence a complete engineering survey (August 1954).' Mangere was chosen in August 1955 and Park resigned from the committee, because of the demands of other business, before the end of the year.

Work actually began at Mangere in October 1960. Following his election to the Auckland city council two years later, Park was appointed first chairman of a committee formed to oversee the construction of suitable facilities there. The first passengers used the new international airport in January 1966, almost fifteen years after the original committee had been set up. Air Marshal Sir Rochford Hughes, who had served under Park in the Middle East and later lived in Auckland, campaigned for years to have the airport named after Park, because 'he was the man largely responsible for it being built.' The gesture would cost practically nothing, said Hughes, 'but it would ensure that in a hundred years the name of Keith Park, which will be in world history, is clearly identified as a New Zealander.' The government, however, took the view that it was only when a city was served by more than one airport that the name survived; otherwise, as with the official name of Sydney airport, Kingsford Smith, it did not.

Park's most obvious memorial in Auckland is to be found at the Museum of Transport and Technology. He had often visited that museum and taken an interest in the exhibits and expansion plans. A representation of a wartime airfield, named in his memory, is now under development and the exhibits are dominated by a fibreglass replica of the Hurricane (OK1) which he flew in 1940.[3]

In 1949 Park found himself involved in an attempt to sell a jet fighter to the Australians. It was reported in October that a proposal to construct jet fighters in Australia had been discussed by Park with the Prime Minister, J. B. Chifley. In January 1950 Sir Frank Spriggs, Hawker Siddeley's Managing Director, said that he was prepared to begin production almost at once. The Australian government decided in February to build, under licence, seventy-two Hawker P.1081 single-jet fighters, to be fitted with Rolls-Royce Nene engines, already in Australian production. Park announced in Canberra in March that the first Australian-built fighter would probably be completed and tested by mid-1951; it was, he later wrote, 'more modern than anything possessed by the RAF.' Late in 1950, however, it was learned in Australia that the P.1081 would not be going into British production and the Australian order was therefore cancelled. Park had been placed in an impossible position by the joint failure of the Australian government and Hawker Siddeley to ensure that the fighter was ready for production before it was bought and sold. The collapse of the deal was not his fault, but it impaired his standing in Australia and undermined his confidence in his employers.

From that time on, Park was increasingly aware of the growth of American influence in Australian aviation and more wary than ever of the Australian press. He offered a 'kindly warning' in September 1951 about its strange ways to his old Battle of Britain colleague, Harcourt-Smith, newly appointed to the United Kingdom Services Liaison Staff in Melbourne. Only those phrases from his comments on Australian aviation that could appear critical would be published. Nevertheless, Park continued to travel regularly to Australia on Hawker Siddeley's behalf, keeping up his contacts with civil and military authorities, and necessarily, the press. In June 1952 his announcement that the British government had placed an order worth £70 million with the group was widely reported in Australia. He went on to say that two factories would be established in South Australia for the construction of long-range weapons and the repair and maintenance of airframes and engines. Inevitably, as Park turned sixty and the group's interest in Australia became larger, it made sense to appoint a younger representative based in that country. That was done in May 1953, but Park continued to represent the group in New Zealand and Fiji.[4]

Despite his personal prestige and best efforts, Park had little success in selling Hawker Siddeley's products in New Zealand. However, he did what he could. In April 1950, for example, he told Sir Arthur Nevill (Chief of the Air Staff, RNZAF) that he was shortly to spend a week in Canada and a month in England visiting aircraft factories. On his return, he promised to brief Nevill on the latest developments overseas 'before going round my Australian parish'. He also told Nevill that there was a definite need for a specialized aerial top dressing aircraft in New Zealand and Australia. He believed he might be able to persuade one of the group's British or Canadian factories to produce an aircraft more suitable than the Tiger Moth for such important work. In the years 1950–1, the RNZAF placed orders for new aircraft from De Havilland, Handley Page and Bristol, but none from the Hawker Siddeley Group. Park was reduced to attempting to sell Nevill prefabricated aluminium houses (made by one of the group's subsidiaries) for use as married quarters.

A later Managing Director of Avro, J.A.R. Kay, went to New Zealand in 1954 to try to sell Shackletons to the RNZAF. He found Park charming and helpful on 'the grand strategy of the New Zealand Government as far as aircraft procurement was concerned', but because Park disliked Avro's representative in Wellington, said Kay, he declined to join Kay in the battle to persuade the RNZAF to buy Shackletons:

> . . . had Park put his important voice behind our efforts we would have sold Shackletons. I never forgave him for it as I felt he allowed silly prejudices to influence his judgment. I suppose it rather typified what I always regarded as his rather conceited, possibly arrogant attitude. God knows he had enough reason to be conceited but it spoilt what was otherwise, in my opinion, a very fine gentleman. To me he was always charming and helpful but that was not always his attitude to others.

Park usually received copies of the same secret brochures on the latest military aircraft that were sent from London to the Air Department in Wellington and discussed them with the Chief of the Air Staff and senior government officials. Sometimes he wearied of working behind the scenes and spoke to the press. In September 1955 he said it was a shame that RNZAF pilots, who were as good as the best, should still be flying Mustangs and Vampires when even Peru had ordered the superb Hawker Hunter. His advocacy was not restricted to aircraft built by his own group: the English Electric Canberra was, he said, 'another British answer to the Americans' and he also praised the Bristol Britannia and the Vickers Viscount.

That same advocacy brought a Spitfire to New Zealand, though not for

256

flying purposes. In 1955 he asked his old friend, Sir James Barnes (Permanent Under-Secretary for Air) if a Spitfire could be made available to the Auckland War Memorial Museum. Barnes replied that one could be presented as a gift, provided that New Zealand met packing and transport charges. A choice of two was offered and Park, who visited London in September, chose a Mark XVI (TE 456) which flew in the 1955 film about Douglas Bader, *Reach for the Sky*. With the help of the Conference Shipping Lines, the RNZAF, friends of the museum and a grant from the government, the Spitfire was transported to Auckland, placed on display in November 1956, and dedicated as a memorial to the Battle of Britain. Park gave an 'inspiring address', according to the museum's director, and in the first weekend afterwards attendance jumped from the normal 1,500 to over 6,000.

His reputation and the cogency with which he expressed his views ensured that they were fully reported at home and overseas. Naturally, the licence which he gave himself to comment on aviation matters was not to the liking of all official quarters in New Zealand. As well as speaking out for modern military aircraft for the RNZAF, he was always critical of the government's monopoly over New Zealand aviation, internal as well as external. His outspokenness – and his advancing age – led at last to his retirement. In March 1960 Dol told Betty Neill that the group would no longer need his services after next June: 'so goodbye to our main source of income . . . keep this under your kilt as Keith is not broadcasting the news, he's a bit sensitive about it.' But he himself announced it to Beaverbrook. The group had sacked him, he wrote, because he had criticized the New Zealand government for ordering American Electras instead of British Comets, as recommended by the airline's management.

Although his relations with his employers were sometimes uneasy, most of the senior executives remembered him with respect and affection. If his public criticism of aviation policies in Australia and New Zealand at times embarrassed them, it was always obvious that he had the interests of British aviation very much at heart. They also recognized that his distinguished record and personal authority opened doors in Australia and New Zealand, no less than in Argentina, for men with other skills – commercial, legal and technical. In the opinion of Frank Murphy, a test pilot with Hawker Siddeley, 'it is not a good think for a salesman to be as senior and authoritative as Sir Keith was in relation to the company's potential customers'. But Hugh Burroughes, Deputy Managing Director of the group, concluded that Park was 'an outstanding man of charm and integrity and a first-class 'ambassador', reliable and well-informed.'[5]

'Maybe, when I reach seventy, in a couple of years, I shall go into semi-retirement from business,' Park wrote in September 1960 to an old friend from his days in Flying Training Command, 'but I have not yet fully

257

unwound my main spring after the excitement of the last war. I find it difficult to take more than a few days off work in this young country, where there is so much to be done in development.'

A year later, he was invited by an Auckland journalist to reflect upon his long-standing interest in business. In 1919, he said, he had invested his war gratuity (£500, all the money he had in the world) in British government stock; making that money multiply had been his hobby. His methods were orthodox, 'except that I have never borrowed money and to this day have never had an overdraft.' He studied the market carefully and read widely on investment, accountancy, management and company law. When he retired from the RAF, having always ploughed back profits and lived plainly, his investments were worth more than £10,000. That excellent result had been achieved in spite of losing half his capital overnight in the Wall Street crash of 1929. But he emphasized the fact that his financial interests had been a sideline in his life, never an obsession. After his wife and family, his first interest had always been his career and he had worked hard for promotion, but when his friends had gone on leave skiing in Switzerland or sunning themselves in the south of France, he had been just as happy to stay at home and play the London stock market.

A few days before his seventieth birthday, in June 1962, the *Auckland Star*, named Park one of New Zealand's ten greatest men, and later that year, at a time when many men and women believe their useful lives to be over, he embarked on a new career as an Auckland city councillor. He stood for the Citizens and Ratepayers Association and served three terms of three years. In October 1962 he came fourth of the twenty-one candidates elected from a field of fifty-six; in 1965 he came second in a field of fifty-nine, and in 1968 he was third of forty-six candidates.

Sir Dove-Myer Robinson, then mayor of Auckland, had persuaded Park to stand for the council because he shared Robinson's opposition to a Drainage Board decision to release untreated sewage into the Waitemata harbour. As a keen yachtsman, Park was vehemently opposed to such procedure, but Robinson never quite forgave him for joining the Citizens and Ratepayers instead of his own party, the United Ratepayers. He twice refused to stand for the mayoralty in 1965, on the grounds that it was a job for a younger man. Those were years of bitter personal conflict in Auckland politics and relations between the mayor and many of his councillors were often tense, but Park was never involved in any of the squabbling.

Although Robinson thought Park knew 'as much about politics as I do about aeroplanes . . . sweet bugger all', he also thought him calm and logical in debate, and, in a word, a gentleman. His fellow councillors respected him for his past achievements, but did not regard him highly as a councillor. Certainly, he was gentle, courteous and dignified; he was also, in their view, without much political sense. As a businessman, he consistently supported the interest of shoppers and commuters in the central city and helped to make

Auckland more beautiful and better signposted. He also looked after his own neighbourhood, helping to preserve a magnificent gum tree in Lucerne Road (where he lived) and public access to Orakei Basin (which his home overlooked) against the wishes of a water-ski club.[6]

Park devoted much of his later years to his charitable interests. He was chairman of the Board of Trustees of the New Zealand Foundation for the Blind in 1956 and 1957. He toured the branches in the same spirit that had taken him to so many RAF units and his reports were characteristically crisp and clear, laying out the essential facts and naming the important names. In April 1958 he spoke up boldly in defence of the government's decision to raise the amount that blind workers were able to earn without loss of social security benefits. As a result of ill-informed press comment, he said, some people supposed that blind persons were now able to support themselves, but this was emphatically not the case: the increases affected only a few and all the others needed at least as much help as in the past.

A hostel for epileptics in the Auckland suburb of Mount Eden was named Park Lodge in 1961 in appreciation of the part played by both Parks in raising money to buy and furnish it. By September 1969, the Epilepsy Association, in which Park served in several capacities, was ten years old and had ten New Zealand branches. He and his wife were part of a small group of devoted, hard-working people ready to tackle an illness that was often neither understood nor 'acceptable' to many, including employers, insurers and motel owners. For over seventeen years Park worked for the welfare of epileptics and was still chairman of the hostel committee at the time of his death: 'one of our most respected and greatly loved members', as the secretary wrote to his son.

Park was also chairman of a committee that raised enough money to save the church of St Matthew-in-the-City, Auckland. When Maurice Russell became vicar in 1967, the crypt was under water, the roof leaked and many windows were cracked or broken. The bishop feared that the church might have to be demolished, even though it was an important building, one of the few New Zealand churches with a stone vault over the choir, chancel and sanctuary. It was Russell who had the idea of seeking Park's aid because he was a member of the small regular congregation and a man well known and admired in the community at large. His business interests brought him regularly into the city and he soon proved himself an active, no-nonsense leader of the appeal committee, assigning specific tasks to the members and expecting frequent progress reports. When St Matthew's became a centre for single-parent functions, however, Park moved away. He did not criticize new customs and tolerances, but he did not share them.

He became the city council representative on the committee of the Pakuranga Children's Health Camp in February 1966. Until 1974 he rarely missed a monthly meeting and even in that year was present more often than not. Opened in 1949, the camp (one of six in New Zealand) was originally intended for children who were physically ill or disabled. Increasingly, however, it came to cater for children who were mentally or emotionally disturbed. Each child spent six weeks at the camp and six courses were run each year. The director, Ernest Edwards, remembered Park well. He would often stay on after meetings to talk to the children. As a rule, he turned away questions about his military exploits and spoke instead about the thrills of flying and sailing. Edwards thought him calm and soft-spoken, but practical and even blunt when it came to acquiring equipment for the children: he never hesitated to telephone those who had what he wanted, whether he knew them or not, and would ask for donations.

Dol died on 10 August 1971. After more than fifty years together, it was a heavy blow to Park even though she had been very ill in her last years. Betty Neill thought she was his opposite in many ways, not only in size. Her sense of fun, her lack of seriousness (about either him or herself), made a valuable contrast in his life. He took great delight in her ability to make important people laugh and relax, and Betty believed that her private influence on his career had been important: he had few other close friends with whom he could discuss the options facing him. When she chose, Dol could match her husband's famous efficiency. In 1942, for instance, she had organized a week-long 'Wings for Victory' campaign in Itchenor that raised more money per head of population than any other community in Britain that year. Her ability to raise money for good causes was put to regular use in New Zealand, and when she died the *Auckland Star* in just three words gave her a fine memorial: 'helper of many'.[7]

In his last years Park corresponded frequently with Betty Neill, who lived in Wellington. His letters were affectionate and usually signed 'Skipper', a name by which he was often known to his immediate family. He still flew regularly to Sydney on business and there he would see his 'kid sister', Dorothy. 'I miss Dol greatly,' he admitted to Betty in December 1971, 'but so far I have kept busy from early morning and Ian has been a great help.' From time to time, he and Ian went fishing and in April 1972 they enjoyed a cruise round the Hauraki Gulf in boisterous weather. A week in bed with influenza (insisting, as a good sailor should, that this was by no means the result of the cruise) made him realize how lucky he was to have good health as a rule, '*and* little spare time on hand.' On 16 June 1972, the day after his eightieth birthday, he wrote to Betty in high humour: 'Never have I had so many telegrams, cards and gifts on a birthday.'

Early in 1973 he was involved in two traffic accidents. In the second, his car was rammed from the right and he was badly hurt: a broken arm, broken ribs and several bruises. Although he spent six weeks in hospital, Betty only learned this later. Typically, he made light of his injuries and stressed his grief for the damage done to his 'lovely Triumph'. In June he took his annual over-seventy test for a driving licence. He admitted to a reporter that he had felt 'terribly nervous' beforehand, but he passed. 'I'm very proud to have this little thing here,' he said, holding a battered old licence.

On 8 May 1974 he wrote to tell Betty about the sudden death of his niece and much-loved housekeeper, Grace Stevens. A week before, said Park, Ian, Grace and he had been having tea when suddenly she had got up and gone through to the kitchen. She had called for Ian and he rushed after her, just preventing her from falling. He and Park had done what they could, but she was dead by the time the doctor arrived. The passing of 'dear Grace' was a great shock and Park missed her very much in the last months of his own life.

According to Marjorie Jones (nominally his secretary but in fact more of a companion at this time), he suffered several heart attacks in the 1970s. He did not like it known that his heart was faulty and very much disliked doctors. Arthur Parrish, a contemporary who had flown with the RFC in Palestine, came to know Park well in his last years and he too has said that Park was reluctant to admit he had an uncertain heart. When attending Battle of Britain parades in the 1970s, he liked to have Parrish near him, 'in case he felt wobbly', though Parrish was himself frail. Whatever his unease about his heart, Park carried himself as erect as a guardsman to the end. Late in 1974, he made his last public appearance when David Frost, the British television broadcaster, visited New Zealand to make a series of programmes, one of which concerned itself with the suggestion that life begins at seventy. Park, at eighty-two, was one of a number of men and women invited to testify to the truth or otherwise of this suggestion. He spoke so convincingly on a favourite theme – life begins afresh at every age – that many viewers later expressed regret that the whole programme had not focused on him.

He was over eighty when he last handled the controls of an aeroplane, with a young pilot at his side, and was as happy as a boy on his first flight, Betty recalled, when he landed. In earlier days, he had been a first-class amateur seaman and navigator and remained a willing, efficient crew member until the end. He also loved a circus and came close to actually wasting time whenever one was in his vicinity, going to watch the setting up and pulling down, and angling for invitations to go 'back stage'. Never a man to sit still for long, unless to some purpose – such as preparing for or attending a meeting – he much preferred to be up and doing: driving to town, flying to Sydney or Wellington, sailing a yacht, digging the garden or playing bowls. Dol would gossip half the night, but Park was off to bed at 9 p.m. sharp whenever he was at home. He was very much a morning man, bright and breezy at dawn. 'What shall we do today?' he would say. 'Let's get organized!' This phrase became a standing joke in his home, but he always lived by it. All his days, at work or play, were planned from start to finish. Near his end he told Betty: 'I want you to know in case I don't see you again that I have had a most wonderful life and enjoyed almost all of it.'[8]

On 2 February 1975 Park was admitted to an Auckland hospital and died peacefully in his sleep on New Zealand Day, 6 February. Among the many death notices appearing in Auckland newspapers was one from veterans of the Battle of Britain, who described him as 'a father to us in those dark days'. He received a military funeral at Holy Trinity Cathedral, Parnell. Hundreds of people packed inside and many more stood on the lawn outside. The service was conducted by the Dean of Auckland, the Very Reverend J.O. Rymer, who spoke of his charitable work, Christian faith, 'integrity of character, simplicity and graciousness in life', but very properly emphasized his 'steel-like sense of duty, which had to be exercised at whatever personal cost.' The final hymn was 'Now Thank We All Our God', striking a cheerful, confident note, appropriate for Park's farewell to this life. The Queen sent a message of condolence and the British government declared that he was a man 'whose name will stand in the roll of honour of defenders of freedom for all time.' On 20 February, at Ian's request, an Auckland Aero Club aircraft scattered his father's ashes from the air, the element in which he earned his fame, into the Waitemata harbour, the water which he loved all his life.

Numerous tributes were paid to his memory. Alan Light wrote to say 'I have always felt that I owe my long and happy life to his skill and daring when I was his Observer in France in 1917.' The CO of 48 Squadron told Ian that 'the squadron has long been proud of its association with such a distinguished officer. We therefore share your deep loss.' Stuart David, who had met Park in Egypt in the 1920s, remembered him as 'a man I have liked and admired more than any man I have met in my life.' Air Commodore A. R.D. MacDonell wrote on behalf of the Battle of Britain Fighter Association, of which Park had been Life President since Dowding's death. MacDonell had served under Park in 1940 and 'he occupied a special place in my heart and admiration.' Group Captain J. A. Kent, who had 'the very great honour to serve under him throughout the Battle of Britain', offered his condolences. 'He was an outstanding leader in the field,' wrote Sir Rochford Hughes, 'and never displayed the slightest physical fear. Yet he was a humble and kindly person, just as friendly to the lowest-ranked man as he was to his senior staff – and just as ruthless when they were inefficient.' In Malta, Hughes recalled, Park could often be seen waiting for pilots as they taxied in after a patrol. With bombs exploding nearby and guns firing away, he would put an arm over a pilot's shoulder and stroll calmly to the office, while the pilot's one wish was to dive into the nearest slit-trench. Walking with Park during an air raid was for some a greater strain than fighting.

By no means all the tributes came from former servicemen. Many came from men and women who had known Park only in one or other of his civilian capacities, as a businessman, city councillor, charity worker, churchman or yachtsman. According to an *Auckland Star* editorial, 'Few men who win history-book fame choose to turn to community activities in their retirement. Nor do many famous New Zealanders return home to take up such activities.' But Park, never a man to bask in old triumphs, had done both.

A memorial service in his honour was organized by the Battle of Britain Fighter Association and timed to coincide with the celebration of the thirty-fifth anniversary of the battle. It was held on 12 September 1975 in St Clement Dane's Church in the Strand and Group Captain Sir Douglas Bader was among those present. Although it may have seemed appropriate to invite an old friend of Park's to give the address on such an occasion, or to ask one of the pilots whom he so much admired (Alan Deere, perhaps, his fellow-countryman), the association wisely invited Bader to perform that task. He agreed when MacDonnell assured him that such was the unanimous wish of the association; everyone, he said, wanted Bader to do it. The present author, who met Bader in 1981, can testify that he was anxious that his words should be worthy of the subject and put an end to whatever bitter feelings remained about events in 1940. Bader, in fact, did Park proud. 'He spoke for every one of us,' said an old pilot later. The Battle of Britain, said Bader,

> . . . was controlled, directed and brought to a successful conclusion by the man whose memory we honour today. The awesome responsibility for this country's survival rested squarely on Keith Park's shoulders. Had he failed, Stuffy Dowding's foresight, determination and achievement would have counted for nought. . . . This is no sad occasion. Rather is it a time during which we can let our memories drift back to those halcyon days of 1940 when we fought together in English skies under the determined leadership of that great New Zealander we are remembering now. . . . Keith Park was one of us. We all shared the great experience. That is what we remember today. British military history of this century has been enriched with the names of great fighting men from New Zealand, of all ranks and in every one of our services. Keith Park's name is carved into that history alongside those of his peers.[9]

Straight and True

Keith Park left New Zealand in 1915 as a Lance-Bombardier and returned in 1946 as an Air Chief Marshal, the highest rank attained at that date by a New Zealander in British service. Among his many achievements during those thirty-one years, he had conducted a successful defence in a prolonged campaign, the Battle of Britain, which will hold a place in world history for the foreseeable future. He was personally brave and in his day had been an exceptional fighter pilot. Unlike many other senior officers, he remained a first-class pilot throughout his service career. He had the personality required to command men, in the air and on the ground, in small numbers under his eye and in thousands far away. Time and time again, men who served with him have emphasized the endless trouble he took to see that everyone under his command felt personally involved in and aware of what was going on. During his years in the Mediterranean and in South East Asia, between 1942 and 1945, he showed a positive liking for Americans and their methods that was not common among British commanders. In peace as well as war, Park was an outstanding officer.

And yet he did not quite make it to the top. He did not reach the highest rank in his service, he was not elevated to the peerage and took no part in the higher direction of the war. No place was found for him after the war in the British public service, despite Tedder's recommendation, nor in British aviation, despite his triumph in Argentina. He played no direct part even in New Zealand's tiny aviation world; he held no public appointment there nor was he made Governor General of that country. No biography of him has hitherto appeared and he abandoned work on his own account of his life. Of course, precious few of his contemporaries in any service climbed higher, but Park was an ambitious man and there were times in his career when he must have thought himself a match for men such as Newall, Douglas and Slessor, to say nothing of Portal and Tedder, leaders of unusual distinction. Did anything more than 'time and chance' separate him from them?

He never held an Air Ministry position, nor did he serve on the directing staff at the RAF Staff College at Andover; he never held an inter-service appointment at the Army Staff College at Camberley nor at the Imperial Defence College. Although the absence of such experience did him no harm as a man and an officer, it may well have hindered his career. There is no evidence, incidentally, that his colonial origins were held against him. He himself made no such claim, though it has often enough been voiced on his behalf in New Zealand, where such slights are keenly looked for. It may be, however, that his personality was considered, at the highest level, a handicap. He was a solitary man with few close friends. Unfailingly courteous, he yet remained apart, if not aloof, and was thought by some to be vain and humourless. He had little taste for music, theatre or literature, none at all for the social round, and preferred to relax privately with his family, reading the *Financial Times*. When opportunity offered, he would go flying or riding or sailing – alone, if possible. Brought up in New Zealand, he had in England none of the family, school, university, social or political contacts which assisted Douglas and Slessor, for example, to fashion their careers. His ambition, though strong, was perhaps insufficiently focused. He merely wished to get on – and get on he did – but at the highest level a particular aim is needed. Specifically, in the service with which he grew up experience with bombers would have been an advantage, because until 1940 the bomber force was the RAF's élite arm, but Park was never closer to that arm than to the Air Ministry.

He suffered four major setbacks during his career. The first came in 1919 when administrative bungling cost him the rank of Major/Squadron Leader at a critical moment and committed him to a longer haul than he expected to achieve senior rank: he was already in his forty-third year before he made Group Captain, a significant year or two older than some other very high flyers. His second setback was his dismissal from Fighter Command, a rebuff from which, in career terms, he never fully recovered. Had he remained in that command, his spiritual home, he might have had the place Leigh-Mallory filled in the invasion of Europe. Park's relations with the Americans would certainly have been better, and his handling of operations more skilful. Almost as critical was the setback he suffered late in 1943 when Tedder resisted Portal's proposal to make him head of the Second Tactical Air Force, an appointment that would have kept him in the front line after the conquest of Sicily. His final setback was the decision to retire him, prematurely as he believed, and thus deprive him of an opportunity to help in the shaping of the postwar air force in Britain and Germany.

On the other hand, time and chance could well have cut him off long before then. As a man who had survived Gallipoli, the Somme and air fighting on the Western Front, Park was acutely aware that he was lucky to have any kind of career ahead of him at the end of 1918 – and ill-health almost ended that career within the next six months. His arrival at Bentley Priory, the move which gave him the opportunity to make his name, was as second choice to Harris. In December 1941 he was nearly sent to Iraq. Two years later he nearly went to Delhi. In 1944 he might have been packed off to Melbourne before Leigh-Mallory's accident made it possible for him to reach the pinnacle of his career. Had the war against Japan lasted another year, as many expected, he might have established his reputation more broadly – if his eagerness to fly into operational areas had not killed him.

Overall, he gained as much on the swings as he lost on the roundabouts. When the music stopped, however, he was left awkwardly placed: very high indeed, but not quite at the top. He had met everyone who mattered on the Anglo-American side. Many of them spoke of him with respect and, at times, he shared in their most serious deliberations, but he was never one of them. No one can say how he would have handled responsibilities that never came his way. All one can say is that he did not fail at any task he was given throughout his service career nor, indeed, in the many years that followed. He had the capacity and energy to handle both continuous pressure and sudden emergency. He had also the will to persist. All his life, in fact, he gave all he had to whatever he did.

Despite his natural reserve, Park had a compelling personality and great charm of manner (when he cared to exert it) and men responded to his obvious concern to see a job sensibly done. He was a practical, active man, shrewd and forthright, not given to brooding on the past. He always looked ahead, looked skywards in fact, even in the last days of his life. His resilience was phenomenal, tested not only by wounds and ill-health and the abnormal strains of two wars but also by such crushing personal blows as the murder of his younger son and the long painful illness of his beloved wife. His resilience, founded on a no-nonsense Scottish/New Zealand upbringing of a kind now unfashionable, was developed by his Christian faith and gave him the strength for years of community service during his 'retirement' in New Zealand. His manner of living remained plain and simple until the end. He was a man of integrity, straight and true.

NOTES and BIBLIOGRAPHY

Notes

The references in the notes are abbreviated versions of titles which can be found in full in the Bibliography following. PP (IP) and PP (NZI) stand for the Park papers held by his son Ian Park and for those held by the New Zealand Insurance Company, respectively.

PROLOGUE

1. James Park's unpublished autobiography is in the Hocken Library, Dunedin. Information on Keith Park's early years is from correspondence and conversation with members of his family and with T.J. Lovell-Smith, Group Archivist, Union Shipping Group Ltd, Wellington. See also P., 'Statement of Service'; *Oamaru Mail*, 5 June 1946; *Dunedin Evening Star*, 7 June 1946; *Otago Daily Times*, Dunedin, 8 June 1946; *Truth*, Wellington, 12 June 1946; *Thames Star*, 17 June 1946; *Weekly News*, Auckland, 31 July 1963; *Auckland Star*, 18 Sept, 1965 (interviews with P.).

CHAPTER ONE

1. Taylor, *English History*, 24–6 (Gallipoli); P., 'Statement of Service', 'Gallipoli Memories', Army Book 439, PP (NZI) Item 2 (transcript from War Diary of 10 Battery, RFA 1915–16); WO 95/4308, WO 95/4351 (War Diaries), AIR 10/973 P.'s essay), FO 132/407 (his early service); Byrne, *History of the New Zealand Artillery*, Waite, *New Zealanders at Gallipoli*; Liddle's Archive (Jenning's letter); *Otago Daily Times*, 8 & 10 June 1946, *Weekly News*, 21 Apr. 1965 (interviews with P.); Raleigh and Jones, *War in the Air*, ii, 75.

2. WO 95/2292, 4306, 4308, 4349–51 (War Diaries); P., 'Gallipoli Memories', PP (NZI) Item 2, AIR 10/973; AIR 23/2320 (P.–Beaverbrook, 21 Apr. 1945 re evacuation from France in 1916); memoirs of Dudley Meneaud-Lissenburg and Hiram Sturdy.

CHAPTER TWO

1. AIR 10/973; AIR 1/131/15/40/218, AIR 1/136/15/40/271, AIR 1/682/21/13/2215, AIR 1/683/21/13/2234 (all flying training); AIR 1/971/204/5/1111 (Trenchard-Brig. Gens.);

P., Army Book 439; PP (NZI) Item 1 (brief notes by P. on WWI career); *Cross & Cockade GB*, vol. 3 no. 2 (1972) p. 45 (on Reading); Harvey, 'The Bristol Fighter'; Jefford and Morgan, 'British Airfields on the Continent'; Winter, *The First of the Few*, passim; correspondence/conversation with Betty Neill (P.'s niece), Light and A. Parrish; *Auckland Star*, 18 Sept. 1965, *NZ Herald*, Auckland, 17 June 1972 (interviews with P.).

2. AIR 1/1185/204/5/2595, AIR 1/1566/204/80/52, AIR 1/1567/204/80/53, AIR 1/1572/204/80/61, AIR 1/2247/209/43/7-8, AIR 1/2389/228/11/96 (all patrols/combats, July–Sept. 1917); AIR 1/1032/204/5/1434 (P.'s MCs); AIR 1/822/204/5/33 (Noss's death); Puglisi, 'Jacobs of Jasta 7' (Hartmann); Skelton, 'Jasta Boelcke' (Pernet); Wills, 'The Eagle of Lens' (von Chelius); correspondence/conversation with Light.

3. AIR 10/973; AIR 1/1567/204/80/53, AIR 1/1574/204/80/70, AIR 1/1602/204/83/99, AIR 1/1809/204/162/2, AIR 1/2222/209/40/17, AIR 1/2247/209/43/10 (all patrols/combats, Sept. 1917–Apr. 1918); AIR 1/1582/204/82/1 (winter training); AIR 1/1560/204/80/21 (P.'s Croix de Guerre); his Army Book 439; Liddle's Archive (F.C. Ransley, 48 Squadron, tape 595, Apr. 1980, and typescript); correspondence/conversation with Betty Neill and Ian Park (Sir Keith's son);

CHAPTER THREE

1. AIR 10/973; AIR 1/686/21/13/2251, AIR 1/692/21/20/48 (48 Squadron); AIR 1/1809/204/162/2 (P.'s return to 48 Squadron); AIR 1/2389/228/11/102 (Steele on retreat); AIR 1/2222/209/40/17, AIR 1/1811/204/162/9 (patrols/combats); AIR 1/1602/204/83/99 (restriction on squadron commanders); Liddle's Archive (Ransley tape); conversation with Parrish on P. and Richthofen.

2. AIR 10/973; AIR 1/533/16/12/117 (48 Squadron's establishment); AIR 1/2223/209/40/18–20, AIR 1/1567/204/80/53 (patrols/combats); AIR 1/1592/204/83/15 (Ransley recommendation); Liddle's Archive (Ransley tape); Voss, *Flying Minnows;* Liddle's Archive (J. Pugh, tape 611, Nov. 1980); Pugh, 'War Memories'; correspondence/conversation with Pugh.

3. AIR 10/973; AIR 1/1030/204/5/1433, AIR 1/1580/204/81/53, AIR 1/1825/204/202/5 (Palmer, Paterson, Ridler); AIR 1/2389/228/11/102 (Steele's essay); AIR 1/858/204/5/417 (air raid report); *Cross & Cockade GB* tapes (E.N. Griffith, tape LN21, Sept. 1977); Liddle's Archive (Pugh tape); Rycroft, *Memoirs of Life in Three Worlds*, 19–31; correspondence/conversation with Griffith, Pugh, Rycroft; Whipple, 'War Memories'; Whetton, 'Flying with 84', (Boudwin); Voss, *Flying Minnows;* Douglas and Wright, *Years of Combat*, 299–301, *Years of Command*, 180; Slessor, *Air Power and Armies*.

4. AIR 10/973; AIR 1/1825/204/202/5 (a 'new' squadron); AIR 1/2232/209/41/21–2, AIR 1/1580/204/81/52, AIR 1/972/204/5/1114 (patrols/combats); AIR 1/865/204/5/513 (P.'s forced landing); correspondence/conversation with Griffith, Pugh, Rycroft – see also their memoirs cited above.

5. AIR 10/973; AIR 1/162/15/124/5 (Air Ministry list), III M/19/P.21/1 (P.'s personal file); correspondence with Christopher Shores, aviation historian, on P.'s combat record; AIR 1/2386–9 (Staff College essays: see especially Baker, Beaulah, Godfrey, Wadham, Warburton); correspondence with Walters, Liddle's Archive (P. tape 240, June 1974, after his Gallipoli memories); *NZ Herald*, 17 June 1972 (interview with P.).

CHAPTER FOUR

1. III M/19/P.21/1–3; FO 132/407 (P.'s early service); James Park's letter to Sir James Allen; Wigram's Aviation Papers, Item 400, Box 4 (Diary); *Southland Times,* Invercargill, 25 July 1919 (Dickson), 31 July 1919 (Bettington); Alfred de Bathe Brandon, DSO, MC, made his mame attacking Zeppelins in 1916: unpublished research on NZ airmen made available by E.W. Martyn of Invercargill; *NZ Herald,* 26 Nov. 1968 (interview with P.).

2. Lee, *Open Cockpit,* 173–4, *Flypast,* 35–7; AIR 2/129/Box (Andover flights); Lewis, *British Racing and Record-Breaking Aircraft,* pp. 30, 43, 61, 70–1 and 89–97; Barnes, *Handley Page Aircraft,* 107, and correspondence with Barnes; *Aeronautics* (15 May 1919), 520, *Flight* (15 May 1919), 633, *The Aeroplane* (11 June 1919), 2380 (P.'s flight).

3. III M/19/P.21/1–5 (P.'s rank, health); Lee, *Flypast,* 46 (P. at Hawkinge); Douglas and Wright, *Years of Command,* 14–15, *The Aeroplane* (7 July 1920), 5 (tournament); AIR 2/4427 (Trenchard on second tournament).

4. AIR 2/251 (Brooke-Popham on Andover); AIR 5/881 (Trenchard's opening address); AIR 29/527 (photograph of first course); Sylvester, 'The RAF Staff College'; Beauman, 'Some Recollections of the First Course'.

5. AIR 5/166 (value of Egypt); AIR 10/962 (notes for officers); AIR 1/2387, part II (Musgrave–Whitham on Egypt); AIR 5/341 & 352 (RAF in Egypt); AIR 1/2388 (Henderson on Egypt); AIR 5/1220 (Swann's report); III M/19/P.21/4–5 (Swann on P.); correspondence/conversation with Betty Neill, Ian Park and Neill Park (Sir Keith's nephew).

CHAPTER FIVE

1. AIR 5/1209 (P.'s move to ADGB); PP (NZI) Item 301 (P. on ADGB); Ashmore, *Air Defence* pp. 131–43.

2. AIR 27/865, AIR 5/1209–10 (111 Squadron); III M/19/P.21/5 (Siskin accident); *Flight* (31 May 1928), 411 (Sassoon Cup); *Flight* (5 July 1928), 521, 526 (Italians); *Flight* (12 July 1928), 593 (Hendon); *Aeroplane* (11 July 1928), 122–34 (Hendon); P.'s third log book.

3. AIR 5/1210 (Fighting Area); *Flight* (11 July 1929), 561; III M/19/P.21/5 (P.'s illness); his third log book; Clouston, *Dangerous Skies,* 21–2 and correspondence with him.

4. AIR 28/601 (Northolt); *Flight* (12 June 1931), 540–1; P.'s third log book.

5. AIR 10/1786 (University Air Squadrons); *Flight* (3 & 10 Nov. 1932), 1037 & 1047 (Abingdon move); *Flight* (26 July 1934) 764, *The Times,* 15 July 1934 (P.'s MA); his third log book; correspondence/conversation with Hope and Gleave.

CHAPTER SIX

1. AIR 2/4103 (Peirse–Salmond); FO 371/17449 (Maycock on assistant); FO 132/407 (Maycock on P.); *Burke's Landed Gentry* (Woodbine Parish family); *The Times,* 26 May 1930 and 10 July 1935 (Woodbine Parish and Argentina); *The Times,* 12 and 16 May 1938 (Woodbine Parish's death); correspondence/conversation with Betty Neill; AIR 2/4102 (Wood, touting).

2. FO 371/18639 (Argentina); FO 371/19763 (Annual Report on Argentina); FO 371/20459 (neglect of Latin-American market); Batten, *Alone in the Sky,* 117–20.

3. FO 371/18653 (Brazil).

4. FO 132/422 (Chile, 1935), FO 132/436 (Chile, 1936).

5. FO 371/18781 (Uruguay); FO 371/18717 (Paraguay); Rauch, 'The Green Hell Air War' (Chaco War); FO 371/19847 (Venezuela).

6. FO 132/422 (Chile, 1935); P.'s third log book (Air Ministry letter enclosed forbidding him to pilot himself); conversation with Ian Park on P.'s inspections.

CHAPTER SEVEN

1. AIR 2/9495, AIR 30/122 (P.'s appointment as ADC); Gray, *Imperial Defence College;* Register of Courses, 1937 (Longmore's report, 16 Dec. 1937); correspondence with Balfour, Hope-Gill; AIR 28/815 (P. at Tangmere); III M/19/P.21/5 (his illness); AIR 2/9495 (his posting to Palestine); Harris, *Bomber Offensive,* 29; AIR 2/875 (P.'s promotion).

2. Wykeham, *Fighter Command,* 54–5: in P.'s opinion, this was 'quite the best and most comprehensive account of the making and working of Fighter Command that has been written'. (PP [NZI] Item 221: P.–Wykeham, 4 May 1960); AIR 2/2964, AIR 16/833 (Defiant); AIR 16/94 (P. on Fighter Command, Oct. 1938); AIR 5/1126 (Air Fighting Committee meetings, Nov., Dec. 1938); AIR 16/98 (P. on fighter attacks, Dec. 1938); AIR 2/3295 (P. on tactics, Jan. 1939); AIR 2/3601 (P. on fighter attacks, Feb. 1939); AIR 16/217 (Gossage–Dowding exchange); AIR 16/131 (Lawson on wings); AIR 2/4438 (head-on attacks); AIR 16/280 (Bomber Command report); AIR 2/1651 (Harcourt).

3. AIR 16/111 (P.–Ludlow-Hewitt, P.–bomber group commanders); AIR 16/109 (conference, Apr./May 1939, Dowding–P., P.–Rowe); AIR 16/118 (May exercise, P.–Bottomley); AIR 2/3492 (July exercise); AIR 16/110 (Dowding's broadcast); AIR 16/132 (Leigh-Mallory's report, reactions).

4. AIR 2/2993 (Woodley's report); Bushby, *Air Defence of Great Britain,* 115–16 (P. and Hart); Wykeham, *Fighter Command,* 52 (filtered plot); AIR 16/14 (improved interception procedures); AIR 2/2599 (WAAFS).

5. AIR 2/3034 (P. on Rowe); *Origins and Development of Operational Research* (Air Ministry publication) 7–8; AIR 16/110 (Larnder–P., July 1939); AIR 16/186, AIR 16/19 (P. on RDF).

6. AIR 16/34 (sector organization); AIR 16/122 (P. on Duxford); AIR 16/78 (Leigh-Mallory's special group orders); AIR 16/25 (Leigh-Mallory's disposition of squadrons).

7. AIR 16/92, AIR 16/97, AIR 16/115 (aerodrome and coastal defence); AIR 16/26 (Instruction No. 1, Oct. warning); AIR 16/27–28 (protection of merchant shipping); AIR 16/145 (Thames estuary).

8. AIR 2/3198 (employment of squadrons abroad), AIR 16/146 (coordination of British and French cover over Channel convoys); AIR 16/116 (P.'s monthly statements); AIR 16/359 (Dowding–Air Ministry).

9. AIR 2/2108 (bomber liaison section).

10. III M/19/P.21/5 (P.'s illness); AIR 2/10213 (postings of senior officers); correspondence with Dr Gavin Scholefield, who attended P. at the Royal Masonic Hospital; conversation with Ian Park.

CHAPTER EIGHT

1. Dowding's despatch on the Battle of Britain, paras. 15–29, 30–41; Wykeham, *Fighter Command,* 103–5, 107; AIR 16/359 (Dowding–P. exchange); Richards, *Royal Air Force,* i, 130–44, Collier, *Defence of the United Kingdom,* 111–17; AIR 20/2759

(Douglas–Newall); AIR 20/2765 (naval fire); AIR 16/216 (P.'s system); Divine, *The Broken Wing*, 220–1; Collier, *Sands of Dunkirk*, 253–5; AIR 20/2061 (Newall–Dowding); AIR 20/2778 (Peirse–Dowding).

2. Horne, *To Lose a Battle*, 597–620; Cooper, *German Air Force*, 112–19; Bond, 'Dunkirk: Myths and Lessons'; Ramsay's despatch, para. 8; AIR 2/7934 (Admiralty–Air Ministry exchanges on Dunkirk, 1946–7).

3. AIR 2/3198 (Barratt–Air Ministry, Churchill's reactions); Gilbert, *Winston S. Churchill*, vi, 471, 484 (Churchill Renaud); AIR 35/199 (Douglas–Barratt); AIR 16/216 (P. on offensive operations); PP (NZI) Item 7 (P.–Brooke-Popham); AIR 2/7281, AIR 16/352 (P.'s report).

CHAPTER NINE

1. AIR 16/36, AIR 16/122 (Debden, Tangmere); Ramsey, *Battle of Britain*, 14–28 (operations rooms); P., 'In Charge of 11 Group', ICARE article, 57–9, copy in PP (IP) Item 385; Hinsley, *British Intelligence*, i, 178; many items in P.'s papers are concerned with the battle and he also made several radio broadcasts on it, listed in *Sounds Historical*, ii, see especially D.1199 (1948) and T.285–85 (1961).

2. PP (NZI) Item 6 (Northolt conference); AIR 16/214 (P.–sector commanders); AIR 5/1139, AIR 16/281 (fighter tactics); AIR 16/901 (head-on attacks); AIR 16/186 (night operations); AIR 16/362 (Vasse–P., P. on sector control, night-fighters); AIR 16/136 (P.–Nicholl on Beaufighter).

3. AIR 20/214 (air-sea rescue); AIR 16/341 (Evill on Douglas's plan).

4. AIR 16/635 (Evill–P.); AIR 2/7355 (P.'s report; comments by Dowding, Douglas); AIR 2/7199, AIR 6/60 (night interception); Ramsey, *Battle of Britain*, 706–7 (casualties); Johnson, *Full Circle*, 189; Mason, *Battle over Britain*, 230–6 (12 Aug.); AIR 16/216 (instructions to controllers, 19 Aug.; fighter tactics, Hornchurch signal); AIR 16/735 (fighter tactics).

5. AIR 2/7355 (P.'s report); AIR 16/216 (P.–controllers, P.–Dowding); Dowding's despatch, paras. 175 (pilot combing), 144 (aerodrome damage); AIR 20/2759–60 (P.'s need of experienced pilots), AIR 25/197 (sector commanders' conference, 30 Aug.), P.'s ICARE essay, p. 59; Ramsey, *Battle of Britain*, 706–7 (casualties); AIR 16/842 (P.'s instruction, 7 Sept.; many of his instructions are found here and in AIR 41/16).

6. AIR 16/330 (conference, 7 Sept.; Evill–Douglas exchange; Nicholl's letter, 8 Sept.); AIR 20/2759, AIR 16/374 (Douglas and Evill on pilot position); Dowding's despatch, paras. 106–7 (squadron strength); PP (NZI) Box (P.'s annotation of 'The Air Battles for Britain', an abridgement of the Air Ministry's pamphlet in *Journal of the Royal United Services Institution*, lxxxvi [May 1941], 213–30).

7. Townsend, *Duel of Eagles*, 436 (de Broke); PP (IP) Item 20 (P. on 7 Sept.); P., 'Background to the Blitz', (sight of London); PP (IP) Item 68 (interview, Sept. 1943); AIR 23/2320 (broadcast, Sept. 1945); PP (NZI) Item 158 (interview in *Auckland Star*, 15 Sept. 1949).

8. AIR 2/5246 (P.'s report); AIR 16/217 (P.–sector controllers, 10 Sept.); AIR 16/842, AIR 41/16 (instruction, 11 Sept.); AIR 16/668 (emergency/alternative operations rooms); PP (NZI) Item 300 (P. on 15 Sept.); Churchill, *Second World War*, ii, 273–6 (on 15 Sept.); Collier, *Eagle Day*, 254; Mason, *Battle over Britain*, 386–95 (15 Sept.); Collier, *Defence of the United Kingdom*, 429 (the decisive factor); Churchill, *op. cit.*, 366 (P. and weather); Gilbert, *Winston S. Churchill*, vi, 848, 852, 878–9 (on invasion danger); AIR 16/212 (P.'s invasion orders).

9. AIR 2/5246 (P.'s report, Dowding's comments); AIR 25/198 (Maidstone Line patrols).

10. AIR 16/341 (Blenheim–Anson affair).

11. AIR 2/5246 (P.'s report; appendix on communications); AIR 16/635, AIR 16/281, AIR 25/198 (Evill and P. on 'Reports on Battles'); AIR 2/7281, AIR 16/901, AIR 16/185, (HF/VHF problems); PP (NZI) Item 8 (McKean–P.); AIR 16/901, AIR 16/373 (offensive intentions).

12. AIR 2/5246 (P.'s report; appendix on night-fighting); AIR 16/901 (night-fighting wings).

13. PP (NZI) Items 22 (P.–Aitken exchange, 7–10 Nov.), 31 (P.–Aitken, 14 Nov.), 24 (Evill–P.), 26 (P.–Greig, 11 Nov.), 43 (P.–Greig, 27 Nov.), 42 (Gossage–P.), 45 (P.–Gossage), 54 (P.–staff officers).

14. AIR 16/903 (conference, 29 Nov.); AIR 16/635 (Lawson–Evill on P.'s Nov. report); battle statistics from Ramsey, *Battle of Britain*, Mason, *Battle over Britain* Wood and Dempster, *Narrow Margin* Collier, *Defence of the United Kingdom*, Collier, *Eagle Day*, German Air Ministry, *Rise and Fall of the Air Force*, and Cooper, *German Air Force;* P.'s third log book; PP (NZI) Item 251 (L. Hunt on 'mahogany bomber'); *Daily Telegraph*, 7 Feb. 1975 (Donaldson's obituary notice; cutting in PP (NZI) Item 285).

CHAPTER TEN

1. *Auckland Star*, 4 July 1968 (Leigh-Mallory on Dowding; cutting in PP (NZI) Item 262); PP (NZI) Item 180 (P.–Robert Wright, 24 Feb. 1958); Items 264, 267 (Dowding–P. exchange, 8–22 July 1968); PP (IP) Item 332 (P.–Dowding, 3 Sept. 1968); Wright, *Dowding*, 200.

2. Wright, *Dowding*, Lucas, *Flying Colours*, Brickhill, *Reach for the Sky;* AIR 2/3034 (Douglas-Stevenson); AIR 16/367 (Douglas on fighter tactics, 16 Dec. 1940); Douglas and Wright, *Years of Command*, 90; P. castigated big wings on numerous occasions in his surviving papers and on radio.

3. AIR 16/330 (P.–Evill, Evill–controllers); Mason, *Battle over Britain*, 296, 306, 321 (bombing of North Weald, Debden, Biggin Hill); Wright, *Dowding*, 178–80 (Biggin Hill), 189–90 (de Broke); Lucas, *Flying Colours*, 119–21 (Bader, 30 Aug.); AIR 2/7281 (Leigh-Mallory's report; comments by Evill, Crowe, Saundby, Douglas); AIR 16/281 (Dowding on Leigh-Mallory's report); AIR 16/735 (P. on Leigh-Mallory's report); Wright, *Dowding*, 192 (Bader, 7 Sept.), 206 (Leigh-Mallory, 15 Sept.).

4. AIR 16/330 (P., Dowding, Evill, Leigh-Mallory, Lawson: exchanges and comments; P.–Dowding, 10 Oct.); AIR 16/1136 (Duke–Woolley); AIR 16/901 (P.–sectors, 1 Oct.).

5. AIR 2/7281 (Stevenson's notes; minutes of meeting and reactions); AIR 16/735 (P.'s copy of notes; Brand–P., 6 Nov.); Winterbotham, *Ultra Secret*, 15 (Slessor on meeting); Gilbert, *Winston S. Churchill*, vi, 1060–1 (Churchill on Air Ministry); AIR 16/330 (Lawson–Evill on Duxford wing); Ramsey, *Battle of Britain*, 707 (fighter losses).

6. AIR 16/330 (P., Leigh-Mallory, Evill, Lawson exchanges; Evill's comments).

7. AIR 16/375 (Douglas, Dowding, Balfour, Evill, Portal exchanges).

8. AIR 2/5246 (P.'s report, Dowding's comments); AIR 16/635 (Leigh-Mallory–Dowding, 17 Nov.); Wright, *Dowding*, 201–2 (Kent, Lacey), 237–9 (Deere); Douglas Papers, Box 2, p. 30 (Douglas-Basil Collier).

9. PP (IP) Item 386 (Saul–P.); PP (NZI) Item 44 (P.–Saul); Lucas (ed.), *Wings of War*,

pp. 92–9 (post-mortem on Battle); Gilbert, *Winston S. Churchill*, vi, 605–6 (on Air Ministry); Haslam, 'How Lord Dowding came to leave Fighter Command'; G. Lyall on Dowding in Carver, *War Lords*, 212; Deighton, *Battle of Britain*, 216 (P.'s 'base intrigue'); Wright, *Dowding*, 247 (P.'s handling over); PP (NZI) Items 57 (Evill–P.), 68 (P.–Evill), 65 (P.–Lawson), 82 (P.–Bouchier), 69 (P.–Ramsay), 30 (Hyland–P.), 71 (P.–Saul); PP (IP) Item 386 (Gossage, McNeill, Wiseman, Beamish, Bouchier, Ramsay to P.); Richards, *Royal Air Force*, i, 195.

10. AIR 16/367 (Leigh-Mallory–Douglas); PP (IP) Item 2 (paper exercise); Wright, *Dowding*, 248–50 (paper exercise); Deere, *Nine Lives*, 184–5; Johnson, *Wing Leader*, 79–81, 86–90; AIR 16/373, AIR 16/635, AIR 16/368 (operations in 1941); AIR 2/9904, AIR 16/846 (Douglas's despatch); AIR 16/406 (Robb's despatch).

CHAPTER ELEVEN

1. AIR 19/258, Gilbert, *Winston S. Churchill*, vi, 1060–1 (comment on 1941 pamphlet); AIR 20/3534–5 (comment on 1943 pamphlet); PP (NZI) Items 85 (Beaverbrook–P., 2 Apr.), 86 (Duke of Kent–P.); PP (IP) Items 386 (Beaverbrook–P., 12 Apr.; Harcourt-Smith, Douglas-Jones, Lang to P.), 1 (P.–Churchill), 4 (Morton–P.).

2. PP (IP) Items 8, 10, 11, 13 (P.–Portal exchanges); *Sunday Chronicle*, 26 Oct. 1941 (Dowding's articles; cutting in PP (IP) Item 12); PP (IP) Item 7 (Dowding–P., 29 July); PP (NZI) Items 88, 88b, (Dowding–P., exchange, Oct.); PP (IP) Item 20 (draft of radio talk printed in *Times of Malta*, 15 Sept. 1942); AIR 40/1497 (appraisals of P., Leigh-Mallory); *Dominion*, Wellington, 11 Feb. 1947 (Tedder on P.); PP (NZI) Items 160, 162, 167 (P.–Watson-Watt exchange).

3. *Otago Daily Times*, 9 Sept. 1952 (P.'s answer to Joubert; cutting in PP [NZI] Item 168; PP (IP) Items 274 (Rich on P.), 284 (P.–Rich), 276 (Beaverbrook–P.), 282 (P.–Beaverbrook), 384 (P.'s reply to Joubert), 277 (O'Connell–P.), 283 (P.–O'Connell); *News Chronicle*, 20 Sept. 1956 (review of *Wing Leader;* cutting in PP [IP] Item 290); PP (IP) Items 291–2 (Hunt–P. exchange).

4. *Listener*, 19 Sept. 1957 (Slessor's article; cutting in PP [IP] Item 306), PP (NZI) Items 172, 175 (Salmond–P. exchange); PP (IP) Items 310 (Air Cdre. Lionel Stubbs–P. quoting Hollinghurst), 305, 312 (P. on Slessor).

5. PP (NZI) Items 170, 192, 205, 228–30, 232, 235–6; PP (IP) Item 321 (P.–Lee exchanges).

6. PP (IP) Item 323, PP (NZI) Item 186 (Dowding–P. exchange); PP (NZI) Items 184 (Lyons on P.), 183, 185 (de Broke–P. exchange).

7. PP (NZI) Items 255 (P.–Saltzman), 256 (Fisz–P.), 257, 261, 265 (Wallace–P.), 264 (Dowding–P.). 266 (Howard–P.), 279, 283 (Lang–P.), 278, 281 (*NZ Herald*–P. exchange), 282, 303 and *NZ Herald*, 21 Oct. 1969 (P. on film); *NZ Herald*, 4 July 1968 (P,'s outburst; cutting in PP (NZI) Item 262; Mosley, *Battle of Britain*, 170–1 (scene in Dowding's office); Dowding, *Wright*, 281 (Dowding–Howard on P.); Dol Park–Betty Neill, 15 Oct. 1969.

8. PP (NZI) Items 263, 270, 271 (Townsend–P. exchange); Deere, 'Tactics in Dispute'; Slessor's letter made available by Deere; correspondence/conversation with Porter and Gleave.

9. Correspondence/conversation with Dowding, Wiseman, Johnstone, Crossley, Westlake; Scott, *Typhoon Pilot*, 129.

CHAPTER TWELVE

1. AIR 24/654 (P.'s succession); AIR 41/4 (RAF monograph, *Flying Training, 1934–43*, 294–306); PP (IP) Item 332 (P. on peacetime routines); P. radio broadcasts, *Sounds Historical*, T.285–85 (1961) (P. on flying training on NZ radio); AIR 2/4516 (composition of 23 Group); Clouston, *Dangerous Skies*, 26; P.'s third log book; Balfour, 'The Battle of Training', 276–7: undated typescript in Balfour Papers.

2. AIR 25/525 (weekly conferences); AIR 2/8062 (P.–Command HQ, 12 Jan.); AIR 41/4 (309–32).

3. Rothenstein, *Men of the RAF*, plate 17, p. 57; AIR 19/220 (Pattinson on flying training); AIR 24/662 (conferences, 2 Apr., 8 May); AIR 41/4, AIR 24/654, AIR 24/662 (Air Ministry enquiry, Little Rissington experiment); AIR 2/8101 (report on experiment, P.'s comments).

4. AIR 24/654 (Welsh's succession); AIR 24/662 (Welsh–group commanders; conferences, Welsh at Brize Norton; Welsh–P., 12 Sept.); this copy of Austin's book now belongs to Ian Park

5. AIR 41/4 (importance of overseas schools); AIR 20/2769 (Garrod on P., 22 Nov.); AIR 24/654, AIR 25/521 (P.'s postings).

CHAPTER THIRTEEN

1. Correspondence with John and Lloyd Mason; AIR 2/7545 (air defence of Egypt); AIR 20/5469, AIR 2/7546, AIR 23/6556 (Evill's mission); AIR 24/1139, AIR 23/6200, AIR 20/5532 (P.'s forces in Egypt); AIR 24/476, AIR 41/19 (raids/reconnaissances, visits to units); PP (IP) Items 38, 39 (P. on Egypt, 1942); *Evening Standard*, 28 May 1942 (tribute to P. cutting in PP [IP] Item 15); AIR 41/50 (RAF narrative, first draft, *Middle East Campaigns*, vol. iv, p. xxiii: Rommel, Hercules); AIR 41/26 (RAF narrative, second draft, *Middle East Campaigns*, vol. iii, p. 106: Hercules); Churchill, *Second World War*, iv, 330.

2. AIR 24/476 (P.'s succession); PP (IP) Item 298 (P.'s arrival in Malta); P. radio broadcasts, *Sounds Historical*, T.285–85 (1961) (Park on Malta on NZ radio); PP (IP) Item 16 (Beaverbrook–P.); DoI Park's scrapbook (praise of P.); correspondence/ conversation with Lucas, Whitley, Johnstone and Philip Vella (secretary of National War Museum Association, Malta).

3. AIR 23/1201 (P.'s immediate needs); AIR 16/626 (Bottomley–P. exchange); AIR 20/5322, AIR 23/5644, PP (IP) Items 18, 19, AIR 41/26 (vol. iii, app. xxiii), AIR 20/5532 (Sqn. Ldr. J. N. White, draft despatch for Tedder, p. 59) (all P.'s conduct of operations); AIR 8/687, AIR 23/6034 (relations with Gort); Winterbotham, *Ultra Secret*, 99, 104–5; Hinsley, *British Intelligence*, ii, 418–19.

4. AIR 41/50 (v, 143 *et seq.*: Tedder, Harwood, Pedestal, Weichold); AIR 23/6034 (fuel shortage pre-Pedestal); AIR 23/5755 (P.'s report on Pedestal); AIR 23/5746 (Sinclair's congratulations); *Times of Malta*, 6 Sept. 1942 (P.'s dinner); Shankland and Hunter, *Malta Convoy*, Smith, *Pedestal*.

5. AIR 23/6035 (post-Pedestal offensive, Gort's resistance); Tedder, *With Prejudice*, 345 (Gort's fear); AIR 2/2705 (P.–Gibbs exchange); AIR 2/7754, AIR 23/6035, AIR 41/50 (vii, 239 *et seq.*) (fuel and other shortages); WO 216/129 (Scobie–Nye); PP (IP) Items 22, 24, 28 (Portal–P. exchanges).

6. AIR 23/6036, AIR 41/50 (vii, 239 *et seq.*) (Oct. offensive); AIR 23/5746; PP (IP) Items 23, 26, 30 (congratulations to P.); DoI Park's scrapbook (Bishop of Gozo–P.; Malta and P.); *Daily Mail*, 19 Oct. 1942 (praise of P.; cutting in PP [IP] Item 29); *Picture*

Post, 31 Oct. 1942 (front-page picture; cutting in PP [IP] Item 32); PP (IP) Items 390 (P.–Beaverbrook), 31 (Beaverbrook–P.); *News Review*, 5 Nov. 1942 (praise of P.; cutting in PP [IP] Item 33); AIR 28/433, *Times of Malta*, 11 Nov. 1942, *The Times*, 11 Nov. 1942, Dol Park's scrapbook (all Qrendi),

7. AIR 41/33 (RAF narrative, first draft, *North African Campaign*, app. vi; Malta and Torch); Dol Park's scrapbook (Trenchard, Portal–P.); *The Times*, 24 Nov. 1942 (P.'s KBE); AIR 41/50 (ix, 364 *et seq.*, x, 417 *et seq.*, Stoneage); Power Diary; AIR 23/6036 (Tedder and Americans in Malta); PP (IP) Item 34 (P.–Beaverbrook).

8. AIR 23/1202, AIR 2/8068 (Wood in Malta); PP (IP) Item 37 (photocopy of paper-knife); WO 216/129, (Nye–Scobie); Playfair, *The Mediterranean and Middle East*, iv, 526 (Eisenhower–Churchill); Power Diary; AIR 23/6037, AIR 23/5682, AIR 23/5667, AIR 2/7829 (Mosquitos, air power build-up); PP (IP) Item 36 (Eisenhower–P.).

CHAPTER FOURTEEN

1. *Daily Telegraph* (cutting in PP [IP] Item 43); AIR 19/391 (Eisenhower, Sinclair–Portal); Gibbs, *Survivor's Story*, 88–95; AIR 23/5654 (Gibbs on Malta); Power Diary; conversation with Wykeham; AIR 23/5756, AIR 1202 (Malta's soldiers); AIR 23/5649 (air defence control); PP (IP) Items 42, 157, SEAC South East Asia Command newspaper, 23 June 1945, *Press*, Christchurch, 10 June 1946 (all Beaufighter incident); conversation with Piper.

2. AIR 23/5655 (aerodrome works); PP (IP) Item 46 (Coningham's address); AIR 20/5292 (Mediterranean Air Command); Tedder, *With Prejudice*, 430–4; Power Diary; AIR 23/6039, PP (IP) Item 53 (spring offensive).

3. Power Diary; AIR 23/5756 (rebuke to squadron commanders); Tedder, *With Prejudice*, 430; Joubert, *Third Service*, 213; 'Malta, 1943', *The Tablet* (14 Aug. 1943), 78–9 (log-rolling); correspondence with Duncan Smith.

4. AIR 23/5726, AIR 23/5754, AIR 19/384 (visitors to Malta); *The Times*, 22 and 23 June 1943 (King's visit); PP (IP) Item 58 (Portal–P.).

5. Cunningham, *Sailor's Odyssey*, 550; Parkinson, *A Day's March Nearer Home*, pp. 136–68; AIR 23/5655 (P. and Husky); PP (IP) Items 59 (P. on Malta as springboard), 75 (losses from friendly fire), 61, 62 (Eisenhower–P. exchange); *Sunday Times of Malta*, 17 Apr. 1955 (jeep Husky); *Times of Malta*, 23 Aug. 1943 (work of Malta aircraft, Eisenhower–P.); correspondence with Walston; AIR 23/5754, *Times of Malta*, 3 and 4 Sept. 1943, Thomas, 'Faith, Hope and Charity', 74 (Gladiator presentation and legend).

6. AIR 23/7585 (P.–Freeman); AIR 23/7773 (Portal–Tedder exchanges); AIR 23/7439, AIR 23/14440 (Robb–Coningham exchanges); AIR 19/379, AIR 20/2662, AIR 23/7536, PP (IP) Items 71, 72 (Portal, Sinclair, Tedder on P.'s next posting); Douglas and Wright, *Years of Command*, 238–44 (Douglas's posting); AIR 23/7774, AIR 24/916, AIR 23/5754 (P.'s succession); *Times of Malta*, 4 Jan. 1944 (P.'s departure; cutting in PP [IP] Item 84).

CHAPTER FIFTEEN

1. AIR 23/1534, AIR 23/7314, AIR 23/7535 (Douglas on Middle East); AIR 23/895 (Slessor's directive); AIR 23/869 (Slessor on P.); correspondence with Walston; AIR 24/1058, PP (IP) Item 83 (P.'s succession); correspondence/conversation with Coralie Pincott, née Hyam; AIR 23/1304 (personal aircraft).

2. AIR 23/1304 (conference with staff officers); PP (IP) Item 87 (Smuts message); AIR

23/1377 (P.–Rawlings); Beaverbrook Papers, file D/142 (P.–Beaverbrook); conversation with Grandy; AIR 19/334 (P.–Sinclair); AIR 2/8635 (Wives overseas); AIR 23/870 (Slessor on wives overseas); Beaverbrook Papers, file D/142 (Dol Park, Beaverbrook, Balfour exchange); AIR 24/1059 (Dol in Cairo).

3. AIR 40/1837 (training of Yugoslavs); AIR 23/888, AIR 23/1448, AIR 23/6019, AIR 23/6028, Cruickshank, *Deception in World War II*, 146–55 (guerrilla support, Zeppelin); AIR 23/889 (P.–Slessor); AIR 23/888 (silence on partisans); *Egyptian Mail*, 4 Apr. 1944 (P.'s tour; cutting in PP (IP) Item 89.

4. AIR 23/889 (P. in East Africa); AIR 23/6201 Evans (ed.) Killearn Diaries, pp. 290–305 (Egyptian crisis); FO 371/41313–5, AIR 23/889, AIR 23/6024 (P. on REAF).

5. Eaker Papers, Box 7 (P.–Eaker exchanges); AIR 23/889 (transfers to front line); PP (IP) Item 91 (Slessor's thanks to P.).

6. FO 371/41314–5 (parachute needs); McCarthy, *Air Power and Australian Defence*, 252–3; Odgers, *Air War Against Japan*, 436–7; AIR 23/889 (South African visit, disputes with Slessor); AIR 24/1059, AIR 2/8429, Documentation Services, Defence HQ, Pretoria (P. in South Africa); *Rand Daily Mail*, 8 Nov. 1944 (P. on Brand, etc., cutting in PP [IP] Item 94).

7. AIR 23/895 (P.–Slessor exchanges).

8. Beaverbrook Papers, file D/142 (Beaverbrook–P.); AIR 2/4994, FO 371/41413 (Farouk's Anson); PP (IP) Items 99, 101 (Giles–P.); PP (NZI) Item 290 (Legion of Merit citation).

CHAPTER SIXTEEN

1. AIR 20/2663 (Leigh-Mallory's appointment); AIR 2/10593 (Leigh-Mallory's death, Court of Inquiry); AIR 23/2305 (P.'s appointment); AIR 20/813 (briefing pre-departure).

2. P.'s despatch on air operations, 1944–45; AIR 41/37 (RAF narrative, first draft, *Campaigns in the Far East*, v, 29–51); SEAC 6 Feb. 1945 (appreciation of P.; cutting in PP [IP] Item 100); *Aeroplane*, 9 Feb. 1945 (appreciation of P., cutting in PP [IP] Item 102); AIR 23/2318 (Mountbatten–P., 21 Feb.); AIR 23/2310 (P.–Slessor, 25 Feb.); AIR 20/2663 (P.–Evill, Sutton, 25 Feb.); AIR 23/2319 (meetings with Courtney); AIR 8/1280 (Courtney–Portal).

3. AIR 23/2320 (speech to staff, P.'s tour); AIR 23/4970, AIR 23/2682 (P.'s tours); AIR 20/2152 (poor conditions in SEAC); *Statesman*, Calcutta, 15 Mar. 1945 (P.'s tour; cutting in PP [IP] Item 103); AIR 24/1338 (P. on good food); correspondence/conversation with Ewing; AIR 23/4970 (plans for operations in Malaya).

4. AIR 23/2320, AIR 8/760, Beaverbrook Papers, file D/142 (P.'s broadcast and associated correspondence).

5. AIR 8/1431 (Dickson, P., Portal exchanges); AIR 23/2682 P.'s report to Portal); AIR 8/1270 (P.–Portal on air supply and consequences); AIR 23/2682 (maintenance investigation, P.–Hollinghurst).

6. AIR 23/2321 (P.–Slessor); AIR 23/2682 (P.–Leese); Lewin, *Slim*, 237–45 (Leese/Slim affair); AIR 23/2682 (publicity); AIR 23/2306 (Air Formation Signals); PP (IP) Item 105, AIR 19/379 (Mountbatten–P. on promotions); AIR 20/2663 (Evill on P.'s promotion); PP (IP) Items 109, 110, 112 (P.'s promotion).

7. P.'s despatch on air operations, May–Sept. 1945, paras. 50–3; AIR 23/2306 (Davidson's award); *Ceylon Daily News*, 12 May 1945 (Davidson's award); PP (IP) 182 (disintegration of EAC).

8. AIR 23/2334 (P.–Coryton); AIR 23/2320 (P. on duration of war, Apr. 1945); AIR 8/1278, AIR 24/1339 (Tiger Force).

9. AIR 23/2358 (Simon Eden's death), PP (IP) Item 352 (Lord Avon–Ian Park).

10. AIR 23/2310 (morale); AIR 24/1339 (P.–Peck); AIR 8/760, AIR 8/763 (Mountbatten's broadcast); Lewin, *Slim*, 1, 128 (Slim, Mountbatten); PP (IP) Item 123 (P.'s VJ Day message); Smith, *Battle for Burma*, 159–60 (releases); Lewin, *Slim*, 248 (SEAC responsibilities); AIR 23/2364–5 (P.–Saunders).

CHAPTER SEVENTEEN

1. Kirby, *War Against Japan*, v, 272 (Mountbatten); AIR 23/4970 (P.'s report); AIR 23/2349 (Rangoon crowding; Ryley, P., Jones exchange).

2. AIR 23/2374 (P. and Hong Kong); AIR 23/2320 (P. in Hong Kong); AIR 20/2664 (Slessor, P. on Bouchier); AIR 23/2331, AIR 23/2379, *Aeroplane* (4 Aug. 1950), 123 (all Bouchier); AIR 23/2331, AIR 23/2354 (Netherlands East Indies); AIR 23/2349 (use of Japanese aircraft); AIR 23/2376 (Mountbatten–Leclerc, Cheshire–P.); AIR 23/2377 (P. on Leclerc, Saunders–P.); AIR 23/2327 (Saunders on Leclerc); AIR 23/2376 (P.–Saunders on Americans); AIR 23/2326 (P.–Carr on Terry).

3. AIR 23/2340–1, AIR 23/2315, AIR 23/2336 (all air trooping problems); AIR 23/2382 (P.–Mountbatten exchange); AIR 23/2372, AIR 20/2664 (Penang affair); AIR 8/768 (Dickson on SEAC HQ); AIR 23/2699 (*Burma Victory*); AIR 8/1361, PP (IP) Items 116–17 (Slim's tribute).

4. AIR 23/2321 (Carr–P.; Strachey); AIR 8/1099 (tour reduction, P.–Slessor exchange); AIR 23/2354–5, AIR 19/379 (P., Auchinleck, Portal exchanges on Indian air forces).

5. AIR 23/2382 (Kandy–Singapore move); AIR 23/2315 (meeting with AOCS); AIR 23/2335 (Hopkins–P.); AIR 23/2312 (unrest at Mauripur, Negombo; P.–Chilton exchange); AIR 23/2314 (P.–Slessor on Seletar, Kallang; Kallang affair); AIR 23/2315 (reports to Heard); AIR 23/2312 (Slessor–P., 7 Feb.); AIR 23/2311 (P.–senior commanders); AIR 23/2315 (P.–Goddard on Francis; P.'s evidence); AIR 23/2311 (P.'s evidence).

6. AIR 23/2356 (P.–Slessor); PP (NZI) Items 89–91, 93, 97, 287, PP (IP) Item 126 (Tedder, P., Mountbatten exchanges on P.'s retirement); AIR 20/2658, PP (IP) Items 127–8 (P. as SAC).

7. AIR 23/2347 (accommodation problems); AIR 8/1453 (P. on Changi); III M/19/P.21/5 (P.'s illness); PP (NZI) Items 103–4, 107 (Mountbatten–P.), 110 (P.–Winster).

CHAPTER EIGHTEEN

1. AIR 23/2699 (P.–Collard); AIR 2/7908, AIR 20/6688, AIR 23/4970 (debate on P.'s first despatch); PP (IP) Items 130–1, PP (NZI) Item 108 (Brockman, P., McEvoy exchanges).

2. AIR 2/7938, FO 371/54024 (debate on P.'s second despatch), PP (NZI) Items 139, 141 (Mountbatten–P. exchange on despatch); *Statesman*, Calcutta, 20 June 1945 (cutting in PP [IP] Item 106) (Slim's thanks to Q Maj. Gen.); Beaverbrook Papers, file D/142 (P.–Beaverbrook, 20 June 1945) (Slim's silence on air raid).

3. AIR 2/9883 (debate on Leese's despatch).

4. AIR 20/6688 (Nerney–P.); AIR 2/7926 (debate on Mountbatten's despatch), Vincent Papers, Box AC. 76/32.

CHAPTER NINETEEN

1. AIR 2/5943 (Evill–P. exchange, P.'s report on RNZAF); file 1A1, 152/535 (National Archives, Wellington) on P.'s tour, correspondence and press cuttings; *The Times*, 31 May 1946 (P.'s first speech), 22 June 1946 (Empire standardization); PP (IP) Items 158 (P. in Dunedin), 175 (P. in Thames); Unit History, RNZAF Ohakea (P.'s arrival); correspondence/conversation with Betty Neill and Dr. Keith L. Park (P.'s nephew).

2. AIR 2/5943 (P.'s report on RAAF and Australian press); PP (NZI) Item 111 (P.–Sullivan).

3. PP (NZI) Items 115, 117 (P.–Mountbatten, 1 and 9 Aug.), 118 (Mountbatten–Tedder), 120 (P.–Tedder), 126 (Air Council–P.), 127 (Trenchard–P.); III M/19/P.21/5/ (P.'s health); III M/19/P.21/6 (Stansgate–P); PP (NZI) Items 128, 130 (Mountbatten, Tedder on P.'s promotion), 131 (P.–Mountbatten).

4. *The Times*, 8 Oct. and 12 Nov. 1946 (Colin Park); PP (IP) Items 139 (press conference), 367 (P.'s speech); PP (NZI) Items 133–5 (Churchill–P. exchanges); *The Times*, 19 Oct. 1946 (P. at Buckingham Palace), PP (NZI) Items 295, 296 (P.–Tedder, Dodds); PP (IP) Item 155 (new job).

CHAPTER TWENTY

1. FO 371/51770 (Beisiegel–Air Ministry; Perowne–Sargent, Leeper).

2. FO 371/61138–9 (Foreign Office comments, correspondence on negotiations); PP (NZI) Item 137 (P.–Aitken); PP (IP) Items 185 (P.–Dobson), 186, 188 (Evans Thornton–Dobson, 24 and 31 Jan. 1947).

3. PP (IP) Item 189 (P.–Dobson); FO 371/61139–40; AIR 2/10449 (Haynes–Air Ministry).

4. PP (IP) Items 193, 198, 201, 205, 208 (P.–Dobson exchanges), 207 (P.'s articles); FO 371/61139–40; AIR 2/10449 (British currency needs).

5. PP (IP) Items 221 (P.'s memo), 222 (P.–Colina), 227 (P.–Dobson), 232 (P.'s illness); PP (NZI) Item 299 (Argentina Revisited); FO 371/61140–1; AIR 2/10449 (contract signed, aircraft deliveries, training mission in Argentina).

CHAPTER TWENTY-ONE

1. *The Times*, 26 June 1947, PP (NZI) Item 291 (Oxford degree); PP (IP) Items 236, 238, 241, Winkworth, *Bulleid's Pacifics* (locomotives); PP (NZI) Items 146–8 (arms); *The Times*, 5 Dec. 1947 (P. at Buckingham Palace).

2. *NZ Free Lance*, 25 Feb. 1948, *White's Aviation* (Mar. 1948), 17, PP (IP) Item 257 (all P.'s arrival in New Zealand); *Press*, Christchurch, 14 Feb. 1948 (P. on aviation); *Dominion*, Wellington, 9 Mar. 1948, *Press*, 10 Mar. 1948 (P. on air defence); *Press*, 8 Apr. 1948 (defence policy).

3.*Press*, 15 Apr. 1948 (P. on air service); PP (IP) Item 263 (Douglas notes); *Press*, 18 Feb. and 13 May 1949 (Auckland airport); Bush, *Decently and in Order*, 412–15; minutes of International Airport Committee, Auckland Chamber of Commerce; *The Times*, 5 Sept. 1951, Dol Park–Betty Neill (Colin Park's death); *Press*, 26 Nov. 1958 (airports v seaports); *Auckland Star*, 8 June 1978 (Hughes on airport name); *NZ Herald*, 14 Jan. and 1 Mar. 1976 (MOTAT).

4. Correspondence with Trevor W. Boughton, Australian aviation historian, who provided many of the following references: Wackett, *Aircraft Pioneer*, 183–92, Miles, *Testing Time*, 48–50, *Sydney Morning Herald*, 15 Oct. 1949, 10 Feb., 30 Mar. and 11 Aug. 1950, *Brisbane Courier–Mail*, 4, 5 and 12 Jan. 1950, *Brisbane Sunday Mail*, 3

Sept. 1950, *Melbourne Herald*, 14 Dec. 1950 (all P.1081 affair); PP (NZI) Items 164, 166 (P.–Harcourt-Smith exchange), 165 (P.–Courtney); *Aircraft* (Oct. 1951), 40 (P.'s letter to the editor); *Border Morning Mail* (Albury, NSW), 13 and 27 June 1952 (Hawker Siddeley expansion); *Aircraft* (May and July 1953), 44, 74 (P.'s replacement).

5. AIR 100/16–17 (National Archives, Wellington) (P.–Nevill exchanges); AIR 1/39/1/3, part 50 (National Archives, Wellington) (RNZAF orders); correspondence with Kay; file 213/5/25 (Air Department, Wellington) (secret brochure); *Press*, 9 and 15 Sept. 1955 (P. on RNZAF, British aircraft); Spitfire correspondence (Auckland Institute and Museum); *Press*, 7 and 8 Sept. 1956 (aircraft needs); DoI Park–Betty Neill (P.'s retirement); Beaverbrook Papers, file D/512 (P.–Beaverbrook); PP (NZI) Items 187–92 (exchanges with A.S.G. Lee and Sir John Cordingley on proffered resignation, June/July 1958); correspondence/conversation with E.G. Rubython, H.P. Wills, J.A.R. Kay, H. Burroughes, A. Hicks, F. Murphy. British Aerospace took over the aviation interests of the Hawker Siddeley Group in 1977. Mr Rubython, Deputy Chief Executive, British Aerospace, told me on 29 June 1981 that 'we hold no documents relating to his [Park's] period of employment with Hawker Siddeley.'

6. PP (NZI) Item 239 (P.–Air Cdre. A.T. Whitelock); *NZ Herald*, 12 Sept. 1961 (Robert Gilmore interview); *Auckland Star*, 9 June 1962 (NZ's greatest men); Bush, *Decently and in Order*, 429, 531, 604, *NZ Herald*, 31 Mar. 1965, *Auckland Star*, 11 Aug. 1965, correspondence/conversation with Robinson and with councillors G. Barnaby, M.L. Tronson, J. Firth, I.W. McKinnon, W.J.H. Clark and Mr J Edgar (research student, History Department, University of Waikato) (all on P.'s council career).

7. *NZFB Chronicle*, vol. 1, nos. 11, 12 and 14 (Auckland, 1957–8), *Press*, 10 Apr. 1958 (P. and blind); *NZ Herald*, 28 Oct. 1961, *Auckland Star*, 18 Sept. 1965, *NZ Epilepsy Association Journal, vol. iv, no. 1 (1969), Central and Southern Leader*, 23 Sept. 1969 and 4 Aug. 1970, PP (IP) Item 351 (P. and epileptics); conversation with B. Reid (vestryman), Russell (P. and St. Matthews); correspondence/conversation with Edwards, Mr A.C. Morcom-Green (Chairman, NZ Health Camp Federation), *Auckland Star*, 6 Sept. 1972 and 7 Feb. 1975, *NZ Herald*, 25 Oct. 1980 (all Pakuranga); *Auckland Star*, 11 Aug. 1971 (Lady Park's death); correspondence/conversation with Betty Neill, Mrs Noel Wells (P.'s niece).

8. Correspondence/conversation with Betty Neill, P.–Neill letters; conversation with Mrs Jones, Parrish; *Press*, 12 June 1973 (driving test); *Auckland Star*, 1 Oct. 1974 (television programme).

9. *The Times*, 7 Feb. 1975 (P.'s obituary); *Auckland Star*, 11 and 12 Feb. 1975, *NZ Herald*, 13 and 21 Feb. 1975 (P.'s funeral); PP (IP) Items 340 (Rymer's address), 354 (Light), 342 (CO of 48 Squadron), 350 (David), 344 (McDonell), 343 (Kent); *Auckland Star*, 6 Feb. 1975 (Hughes); *Auckland Star*, 7 Feb. 1975 (editorial); *The Times*, 13 Sept. 1975 (memorial service); Lucas, *Flying Colours*, 161–2, text of Bader's address, 289–91.

Bibliography

Unpublished sources

DOCUMENTS AND RECORDINGS RELATING DIRECTLY TO SIR KEITH PARK:

Park Papers, held by Mr I.K.W. Park, Sir Keith's son, at his home in Lucerne Road, Auckland

Park Papers, held by New Zealand Insurance Co., Queen Street, Auckland

'Statement of Service' of Park in NZ Territorial & Expeditionary Forces: D.26/560/6/A, National Archives, Wellington

'Gallipoli Memories': tape no. 240, made in Auckland, 14 June 1974, by P.H. Liddle for his 1914–18 Archive (*q.v.*)

Army Book 439 (Officers' Record of Services), Museum of Transport & Technology, Auckland

'Experiences in the War, 1914–1918': essay written at Staff College, Andover, 1922–3 (file AIR 10/973, Public Record Office, London)

Personal file, III M/19/P.21/1, Air Ministry Historical Branch, London

Third log book (3 July 1930–10 July 1941 plus summary of previous flying)

Radio broadcasts, *Sounds Historical* (Catalogue of the Sound History Recordings in the Sound Archives of Radio New Zealand, 1982), vol. ii (M–Z) (RNZSA, Timaru, NZ)

Obituary, Ministry of Defence Library, Wellington

AIR, numbered Air Ministry records, Public Record Office, London

AUCKLAND, Spitfire Mk 16 (TE456) correspondence, Auckland Institute & Museum

BALFOUR PAPERS, House of Lords Record Office, London

BEAVERBROOK PAPERS, House of Lords Record Office, London

DOUGLAS PAPERS, Imperial War Museum, London

EAKER PAPERS, Manuscript Division, Library of Congress, Washington, DC

FO, numbered Foreign Office records, Public Record Office, London

LIDDLE'S ARCHIVE, P.H. Liddle, 1914–18 Archive, Sunderland Polytechnic

Meneaud-Lissenburg, Capt. Dudley, MS. in Imperial War Museum, London: gunner with 29th Division, Gallipoli and Somme

Park, James, letter to Sir James Allen, Minister of Defence, Wellington (Dunedin, 14 Feb. 1919): D.26/560/6, National Archives, Wellington

POWER PAPERS, British Museum, London, Add. MSS. 56097 (Diary)

PRETORIA, Documentation Services, Defence HQ, Pretoria

Sturdy, Hiram, MS. in Imperial War Museum, London: gunner with 29th Division, Somme

VINCENT PAPERS, RAF Museum, Hendon

WIGRAM PAPERS, Canterbury Museum, Christchurch: Item 400, Box 4 is his diary of the Canterbury Aviation Company

WO, numbered War Office records, Public Record Office, London

Published sources

Air Ministry, *The Battle of Britain: An Air Ministry Account of the Great Days from 8 August to 31 October 1940* (HMSO, 1941)

——, *The Battle of Britain: Air Ministry Pamphlet 156* (Dept. of the Air Member for Training, Aug. 1943)

——, *The Origins and Development of Operational Research in the Royal Air Force: Air Publication 3368* (HMSO, 1963)

——, *The Rise and Fall of the German Air Force, 1933–1945* (Arms & Armour Press, London, 1983)

Ashmore, E.B., *Air Defence* (Longmans, London, 1929)

Balfour, H. (Lord Balfour of Inchrye), *Wings over Westminster* (Hutchinson, London, 1973)

Barnes, C.H., *Handley Page Aircraft Since 1907* (Putnam, London, 1976)

Batten, J., *Alone in the Sky* (Airlife, Shrewsbury, 1979)

Beauman, E.B., 'Some Recollections of the First Course', *The Hawk* (Independent Journal of the RAF Staff College), no. 34 (Feb. 1973), pp. 27–9

Bond, B., 'Dunkirk: Myths and Lessons', *Journal of the Royal United Services Institution,* vol. 127, no. 3 (September 1982), pp. 3–7

Brickhill, P., *Reach for the Sky: The Story of Douglas Bader* (Collins, London, 1954)

BURMA, *Wings of the Phoenix: The Official Story of the Air War in Burma* (HMSO, 1949)

Bush, E.W., *Gallipoli* (Allen & Unwin, London, 1975)

Bush, G.W.A., *Decently and in Order: The Centennial History of the Auckland City Council* (Collins, Auckland, 1971)

Bushby, J.R., *The Air Defence of Great Britain* (Allan, London, 1974)

Byrne, J.R. *The History of the New Zealand Artillery in the Field, 1914–1918* (Christchurch, 1922)

Churchill, W.S., *The Second World War* (6 vols, Cassell, London, 1948–54;

Clouston, A.E., *Dangerous Skies* (Cassell, London, 1954)

Collier, B., *The Defence of the United Kingdom* (HMSO, 1957)

Collier, R., *Eagle Day: The Battle of Britain* (Pan, London, 1968)

——, *The Sands of Dunkirk* (Fontana, London, 1963)

Colville, J.R., *Man of Valour: The Life of Field Marshal the Viscount Gort* (Collins, London, 1972)

Cooper, M., *The German Air Force, 1933–45: An Anatomy of Failure* (Jane's, London, 1981)

Notes and Bibliography

Cruickshank, C.G., *Deception in World War II* (Oxford, 1977)

Cunningham, Viscount, *A Sailor's Odyssey* (Hutchinson, London, 1951)

Deere, A.C., *Nine Lives* (Hodder & Stoughton, London, 1959)

——, 'Tactics in Dispute', *RAF Souvenir Book, 1970* (J.P. Milford Reid, London, 1970)

Deighton, L., *Battle of Britain* (Cape, London, 1980)

Divine, D., *The Broken Wing* (Hutchinson, London 1966)

Douglas, Sholto (MRAF Lord Douglas of Kirtleside) with R. Wright *Years of Combat* (Collins, London, 1963)

——, *Years of Command* (Collins, London, 1966)

Douglas-Hamilton, Lord James, *The Air Battle for Malta: The Diaries of a Fighter Pilot* (Mainstream Publishing, Edinburgh, 1981)

Dowding, H.C.T., *The Battle of Britain, Supplement to the* London Gazette (HMSO, 11 Sept. 1946)

Dowling, C., 'Battle of Britain' in N. Frankland and C. Dowling (eds.), *Decisive Battles of the Twentieth Century: Land-Sea-Air* (Sidgwick & Jackson, London, 1976), pp. 115–26

Evans, T.E. (ed.), *The Killearn Diaries, 1934–1946* (Sidgwick & Jackson, London, 1972)

Gibbs, G.E., *Survivor's Story* (Hutchinson, London, 1956)

Gilbert, M., *Winston S. Churchill*, vol. vi, 'Finest Hour, 1939–1941' (Heinemann, London, 1983)

Gray, T.I.G. (ed.), *The Imperial Defence College and the Royal College of Defence Studies, 1927–1977* (HMSO, 1977)

Harris, A.T., *Bomber Offensive* (Collins, London, 1947)

Harvey, W.F.J., 'The Bristol Fighter', *Cross & Cockade GB*, vol. 1 no. 1 (1970), pp. 3–7

Haslam, E.B., 'How Lord Dowding came to leave Fighter Command', *Journal of Strategic Studies*, vol. 4, no. 2 (June 1981), pp. 175–86

Hinsley, F.H. (with others), *British Intelligence in the Second World War*, vols 1 and 2 (HMSO, 1979 and 1981)

Horne, A., *To Lose a Battle: France 1940* (Penguin, London, 1979)

Howard, M., *The Mediterranean Strategy in the Second World War* (Weidenfeld & Nicolson, London, 1968)

ICARE, 'The Battle of Britain': essays published by ICARE, the French Airline Pilots' Association, in French and English to mark the 25th Anniversary of the Battle, Paris, 1966

James, R.R., *Gallipoli* (Batsford, London, 1965)

Jefford, C.G. and W.E. Morgan, 'British Airfields on the Continent', *Cross & Cockade GB*, vol. 10 no. 4 (1979), pp. 168–9

Johnson, J.E., *Wing Leader* (Chatto & Windus, London, 1956)

——, *Full Circle: The Story of Air Fighting* (Chatto & Windus, London, 1964)

Joubert, P., *The Fated Sky* (Hutchinson, London, 1952)

——, *The Third Service: The Story Behind the Royal Air Force* (Thames & Hudson, London, 1955)

Kent, J.A., *One of the Few* (Corgi, London, 1975)

Kirby, S.W. (with others), *The War Against Japan*, vols iv and v (HMSO, 1965 and 1969)

Lee, A.S.G., *Open Cockpit: A Pilot of the Royal Flying Corps* (Jarrolds, London, 1969)

——, *Flypast: Highlights from a Flyer's Life* (Jarrolds, London, 1974)

Leese, O., *Operations in Burma, from 12 November 1944 to 15 August 1945, Supplement to the* London Gazette (HMSO, 12 Apr. 1951)

Lewin, R., *Slim: The Standardbearer* (Pan, London, 1978)

Lewis, P., *British Racing and Record-Breaking Aircraft* (Putnam, London, 1971)

Liddle, P.H., *Men of Gallipoli: The Dardanelles and Gallipoli Experience, August 1914 to January 1916* (Allen Lane, London, 1976)

Lucas, L., *Flying Colours: The Epic Story of Douglas Bader* (Hutchinson, London, 1981)

Lucas, L. (ed.), *Wings of War: Airmen of all nations tell their stories, 1939–1945* (Hutchinson, London, 1983)

Lyall, G., 'Dowding' in M. Carver (ed.), *The War Lords: Military Commanders of the Twentieth Century* (Little, Brown & Co , Boston, 1976), pp. 202–12

Mason, F.K., *Battle over Britain: A History of the German Air Assaults on Great Britain, 1917–18 and July–December 1940, and of the Development of Britain's Air Defences between the World Wars* (McWhirter Twins, London, 1969)

McCarthy, J.M., *Air Power and Australian Defence: A Study in Imperial Relations, 1923–1954* (PhD thesis, ANU, Canberra, 1971)

McKee, A., *Strike from the Sky: The Story of the Battle of Britain* (Souvenir Press, London, 1960)

Miles, J., *Testing Time* (Neptune Press, Melbourne, 1979)

Mitchell, A.W., *New Zealanders in the Air War* (Harrap, London, 1945)

Mosley, L., *The Battle of Britain: The Making of a Film* (Pan, London, 1969)

Mountbatten, Earl, *Report to the Combined Chiefs of Staff by the Supreme Allied Commander, South-East Asia, 1943–1945* (HMSO, 1951)

Odgers, G., *Air War Against Japan, 1943–1945* (Canberra, 1957)

Park, K.R., 'In Charge of 11 Group': see ICARE (above), pp. 57–9

——, 'Background to the Blitz', *Hawker Siddeley Review* (Dec. 1951), pp. 100–2

——, *Air Operations in South-East Asia from 1 June 1944 to the Occupation of Rangoon, 2 May 1945, Supplement to the* London Gazette (HMSO, 12 Apr. 1951)

——, *Air Operations in South-East Asia from 3 May 1945 to 12 September 1945, Supplement to the* London Gazette (HMSO, 19 Apr. 1951)

Parkinson, R., *A Day's March Nearer Home: The War History from Alamein to VE Day based on the War Cabinet Papers of 1942 to 1945* (Hart-Davis, MacGibbon, London, 1974)

Playfair, I.S.O. (with others), *The Mediterranean and Middle East*, vols iii and iv (HMSO, 1960 and 1966)

Price, A., *Battle of Britain: The Hardest Day, 18 August 1940* (Granada, London, 1980)

Pugh, J., 'War Memories', *The Ludlovian* (Ludlow Grammar School magazine), vol. xviii (1919), pp. 122–4

Puglisi, W.R. 'Jacobs of Jasta 7', *Cross & Cockade US*, vol. 6 no. 4 (1965), pp. 307–34

Raleigh, W. and H.A. Jones, *The War in the Air* (6 vols, Oxford, 1922–37)

Ramsay, B.H., *The Evacuation of the Allied Armies from Dunkirk and Neighbouring Beaches, Supplement to the* London Gazette (HMSO, 17 July 1947)

Ramsey, W.G. (ed.), *The Battle of Britain: Then and Now* (Battle of Britain Prints International, London, rev. edn, 1982)

Rauch, G. von, 'The Green Hell Air War', *Air Enthusiast Quarterly*, no. 2 (no date), pp. 207–13

Richards, D. and H. St G. Saunders, *Royal Air Force, 1939–45* (3 vols, HMSO, 1974–5)

Rothenstein, W., *Men of the RAF* (Oxford, 1942)

Rycroft, W.S., *Memoirs of Life in Three Worlds* (New Jersey, 1976)

Scott, D., *Typhoon Pilot* (Secker & Warburg, London, 1982)

Shankland, P. and A. Hunter, *Malta Convoy* (Fontana, London, 1963)

Skelton, M.L., 'Jasta Boelcke: A Crisis in Command', *Cross & Cockade US*, vol. 22 no. 2 (1981), pp. 122–37

Slessor, J.C., *Air Power and Armies* (Oxford, 1936)

——, 'Looking Back on the Battle of Britain', *The Listener* (BBC, London), 19 Sept. 1957, pp. 417–20

Smith, E.D., *Battle for Burma* (Batsford, London, 1979)

Smith, P. *Pedestal: The Malta Convoy of August 1942* (William Kimber, London, 1970)

Sylvester, A.E., 'The RAF Staff College', *RAF Souvenir Book, 1972* (J.P. Milford Reid, London, 1972), pp. 66–70

Taylor, A.J.P., *English History, 1914–1945* (Oxford, 1965)

Tedder, Lord, *With Prejudice* (Cassell, London, 1966)

Thomas, D.B., 'Faith, Hope and Charity', *RAF Souvenir Book, 1972* (J.P. Milford Reid, London, 1972), p. 74

Thompson, H.L., *New Zealanders with the Royal Air Force* (3 vols, War History Branch, Dept of Internal Affairs, Wellington, 1953–9)

Townsend, P., *Duel of Eagles* (Corgi, London, 1972)

Voss, V., *Flying Minnows: Memoirs of a World War One Fighter Pilot from Training in Canada to the Front Line, 1917–1918* (Arms & Armour Press, London, 1977)

Wackett, L.J., *Aircraft Pioneer* (Angus & Robertson, Sydney, 1972)

Waite, F., *The New Zealanders at Gallipoli* (Christchurch, 1921)

Whelan, J.A., *Malta Airmen* (War History Branch, Dept of Internal Affairs, Wellington, 1951)

Whetton, D., 'Flying with 84', *Cross & Cockade GB*, vol. 3 no. 1 (1972), pp. 25–7

Whipple, S., 'War Memories', *Hartford Daily Courant*, Connecticut, 8 June 1919

Wills, K., 'The Eagle of Lens – Hans Waldhausen', *Cross & Cockade US*, vol. 8 no. 2 (1967), p. 108

Winkworth, D.W., *Bulleid's Pacifics* (Allan, London, 1974)

Winter, D., *The First of the Few: Fighter Pilots of the First World War* (Allen Lane, London, 1982)

Winterbotham, F.W., *The Ultra Secret* (Futura, London, 1975)

Wood, D., *Attack Warning Red: The Royal Observer Corps and the Defence of Britain, 1925–1975* (Macdonald & Jane's, London, 1976)

Wood, D. with D. Dempster, *The Narrow Margin: The Battle of Britain and the Rise of Air Power, 1930–1940* (Arrow Books, London, rev. edn, 1969)

Wright, R., *Dowding and the Battle of Britain* (Corgi, London, 1970)

Wykeham, P., *Fighter Command* (Putnam, London, 1960)

Index